The Politics
of Timor-Leste

T0349768

 Cornell University

Michael Leach and Damien Kingsbury, editors

The Politics
of Timor-Leste

Democratic Consolidation
after Intervention

SOUTHEAST ASIA PROGRAM PUBLICATIONS
Southeast Asia Program
Cornell University
Ithaca, New York
2013

Cornell Southeast Asia Program Publications
640 Stewart Avenue, Ithaca, NY 14850-3857

Studies on Southeast Asia No. 59

Printed in the United States of America

ISBN: hc 978-0-87727-789-7
ISBN: pb 978-0-87727-759-0

Cover: designed by Kat Dalton
Cover image: Photograph by Pamela Martin, reproduced with permission.

TABLE OF CONTENTS

ACKNOWLEDGMENTS

The editors would like to express their appreciation to the contributors for their essays, with special thanks to our colleagues at Timor-Leste's Anti-Corruption Commission and the National University of Timor Lorosa'e. Thanks also go to Alex Gusmao and Alarico da Costa Ximenes for research assistance and collaboration in recent years. We are also grateful to Pamela Martin for the cover photo, and especially to Deborah Homsher and Fred Conner at Cornell for their close and patient editing of the manuscript, which improved it immeasurably. Michael would like to thank his partner Janis, whose support makes the research possible. Damien acknowledges his wife, Rae, whose commitment to the people of East Timor has inspired so many.

Introduction: East Timorese Politics in Transition

Michael Leach and Damien Kingsbury

This edited collection examines key issues in the contemporary politics of Timor-Leste. In particular, it focuses on democratic consolidation and the ongoing development of political institutions during an especially critical period for the young nation: the transition from more than a decade of international state-building assistance. It assesses challenges that have burdened the young state since formal independence in 2002 and considers its future prospects. Issues of particular focus include constitutional debates, political party formation, the operation of the government, decentralization, foreign policy, development, gender discrimination, combating corruption, security sector reform, the politics of justice, relations with traditional authorities, and the challenges of nation-building. In examining these themes, the contributors highlight the fledgling state's successes and failures as well as matters that remain unresolved as international state-building forces prepare to depart. While each theme addressed in the collection focuses on Timor-Leste's specific experience, these issues also pertain to many post-colonial and developing countries, particularly those of the southwest Pacific and sub-Saharan Africa. As the object of five consecutive UN missions with varying mandates, Timor-Leste is a critical case study of international state-building projects. In these respects, the Timor-Leste experience offers a model for comparative consideration across a much wider field.

Colonialism, Independence, and International State-Building

Timor-Leste was a late arrival on the post-colonial scene, gaining its independence at the tail end of the post–World War II decolonization process. First colonized by Portuguese Dominican priests, along with Portuguese traders and their descendants from nearby islands in the sixteenth century, Portuguese Timor remained a colonial backwater until its invasion and occupation by Japan in 1942. Following Japan's defeat, Portuguese Timor slipped back into colonial obscurity, notable mostly for the presence of occasional political prisoners who were banished to the then-Portuguese Timor by Portugal's Salazar regime. Following the "Carnation Revolution" in Portugal in 1974, and the related and rushed process of decolonization, Timor-Leste began to develop its first local political parties. In 1975, neighboring Indonesia began to foment discord between Timor-Leste's nascent political parties, leading in August 1975 to a brief but bloody war between the two largest parties, the Revolutionary Front for an Independent Timor-Leste (Frente Revolucionária de Timor-Leste Independente, FRETILIN) and the Timorese Democratic Union (União Democrática Timorense, UDT). Indonesia soon after engaged in cross-border raids. In December 1975, just days after Timor-Leste declared independence, its giant neighbor launched a full-scale invasion of Portuguese Timor, followed by progressive occupation and forced integration of the province in 1976. The restoration of Timor-Leste's independence was to be put off for another quarter of a century.

Resistance to Indonesia's invasion and twenty-four-year occupation led to the deaths of as many as 180,000 people,[1] the establishment of a disciplined underground resistance, and an extensive international support network. Timor-Leste was never recognized under international law as part of Indonesia and remained a major diplomatic, military, and financial problem for the occupying state. When Indonesia came under increasing external pressure following the financial crisis of 1997–98, its then recently appointed president, B. J. Habibie, announced that Timor-Leste could vote on whether it wished to remain a part of Indonesia. On August 30, 1999, the East Timorese people voted overwhelmingly for independence in a referendum conducted by the United Nations Mission in East Timor (UNAMET). Violence and destruction, which had accompanied the lead up to the referendum, broke in a storm after the announcement of the ballot results, leaving more than three-quarters of the population of Timor-Leste displaced and more than 70 percent of its buildings and infrastructure destroyed. Australian-led INTERFET (International Force for East Timor) military forces, under the auspices of the United Nations, intervened, Indonesian forces departed, and the process of rebuilding the shattered territory and people as an independent state was begun under the United Nations Transitional Administration in East Timor (UNTAET).

As the site of one of the United Nations' first experiments in direct governance of a territory, and of ongoing international state-building assistance, Timor-Leste remains a unique case study of a double transition to independence and democracy through a period of direct international governance. Under its Security Council mandate, UNTAET exercised full legislative and executive authority from 1999–2002, running both the security forces and an international peacekeeping mission in Timor-Leste while seeking to build new governmental institutions for the emerging state and overseeing the formation of a constitutional assembly in 2001. The scope of the UNTAET mission was unprecedented in the region. While the United Nations had briefly administered West New Guinea from September 1962 until May 1, 1963, this "seat-warming" interregnum did not develop and execute policy decisions as it did in Timor-Leste between 1999 and 2002. The United Nations' role in Cambodia in

---

[1] See CAVR (Comissão de Acolhimento, Verdade e Reconciliação), *Chega!: The Report of the Commission for Reception, Truth and Reconciliation in Timor-Leste* (Dili: CAVR, 2005). CAVR's estimate of the minimum total number of conflict-related deaths is 102,800. This figure includes both killings and deaths due to privation. The often-cited figure of 180,000 is CAVR's upper estimate of total conflict-related mortality.

1991–92, while substantial, is best described as co-administration,[2] as the UN operated alongside a sovereign government, wielding decision-making powers in certain areas and primarily focused on peacekeeping.[3] The year 1999 was to prove an important year in the practice of UN-led international state-building, as the Security Council endorsed three separate missions mandating the direct international administration of a territory.[4] Of these missions, the United Nations Interim Administration Mission in Kosovo (UNMIK), in conjunction with the European Union, most closely paralleled the United Nation's state-building experience in Timor-Leste. But perhaps even more so than in Kosovo, the United Nations' role in Timor-Leste was notable because it had to construct the institutions of a new state from what was, in effect, a tabula rasa.

Timor-Leste therefore stands as a critical exemplar of contemporary international state-building. Distinct from other forms of development assistance in the level of intervention in national sovereignty,[5] state-building is concerned with "constructing or reconstructing institutions of governance capable of providing citizens with physical and economic security.'"[6] As Mark T. Berger notes, the policy rationale for contemporary international state-building missions reflects the perceived connection between international security and development, with a clear emphasis on the pathologies "failed states" present for regional or world orders. State-building missions are seen as an effort to maintain a stable world, or regional order, in the face of a range of assessed risks, from humanitarian concerns to systemic concerns over the spread of international crime syndicates or terrorist networks. Reflecting the diversity of these concerns, state-building can encompass "formal military occupation, counterinsurgency, peacekeeping, national reconstruction, foreign aid, and the use of stabilization forces under the auspices of the USA, Britain, France, NATO [North Atlantic Treaty Organization], the UN, or another international or regional organization."[7]

Timor-Leste has also experienced two major periods of state-building assistance since independence. The United Nations Mission of Support in East Timor (UNMISET), in operation from May 2002 to May 2005, was mandated by the Security Council to provide peacekeeping forces and state-building assistance in the devolution of security functions to East Timorese authorities. This operation wound down in May 2005, with policing handed to East Timorese authorities and a smaller political mission, the United Nations Office in Timor-Leste (UNOTIL), in place until August 2006. By early 2006, Timor-Leste was widely seen as a UN success story.[8]

---

[2] Erika de Wet, "The Direct Administration of Territories by the United Nations and Its Member States in the Post Cold-War Era: Legal Bases and Implications for National Law," *Max Planck Yearbook of United Nations Law* 8,1 (2004): 297.

[3] Ibid. The 1993 United Nations Operation in Somalia (UNOSOM) and the UN High Representative in Bosnia-Herzegovina in 1995 are likewise best characterized as co-administrations.

[4] United Nations Transitional Administration in Eastern Slavonia (UNTAES), established in 1999, was limited to two years before sovereign functions were handed over to Croatia.

[5] Julien Barbara, "Rethinking Neo-Liberal State Building: Building Post-Conflict Development States," *Development in Practice* 18,3 (2008): 308.

[6] David Chandler, *Empire in Denial: The Politics of State-Building* (London: Pluto Press, 2006), p. 1.

[7] Mark T. Berger, "From Nation-Building to State-Building: The Geopolitics of Development, the Nation-State System and the Changing Global Order," *Third World Quarterly* 27,1 (2006): 6.

[8] Ibid., p. 20.

Despite what appeared to be a sound beginning after independence in 2002, the political-military crisis of April–May 2006 shook erstwhile confidence in the success of the UN's first comprehensive state-building mission, highlighting unresolved social divisions left from the occupation era, which were compounded by competition for scarce resources and the weight of unmet popular expectations.

Timor-Leste entered its second major period of international state-building assistance following independence with its key security institutions in disarray. Having downscaled the UNMISET mission in 2005, with the strong support of Australia, the United Nations returned after the crisis in 2006 with a new peacekeeping mission: the United Nations Integrated Mission in Timor-Leste (UNMIT). Authorized by the Security Council to reestablish a UN police force until the PNTL (Policia Nacional de Timor-Leste, the National Police of Timor-Leste) could be retrained and reformed, UNMIT has also played a major role in institutional capacity building in the formal justice sector and in electoral administration. Alongside UNMIT in 2006 was a new Australian-led military force, the International Stabilisation Force (ISF). This represented a newer strand of thinking in regional state-building, as Australia and New Zealand chose not to "blue helmet" their military forces as they had in the previous UNTAET and UNMISET eras. Operating outside the structure of the UN mission under a bilateral agreement with the government of Timor-Leste, the ISF subsequently concluded a mutual cooperation agreement with UNMIT, though without an overarching coordinating body between the two missions. This decision was formally justified as providing "greater operational and logistical flexibility; proven command and control arrangements; and alleviation of UN budgetary pressure,"[9] and allowing the UN to focus its contribution on state-building rather than security.[10] However, the decision was also determined, in part, by Australian government dissatisfaction with UN command structures in the earlier missions. According to an Australian Senate report, the ISF mission and the Regional Assistance Mission to the Solomon Islands (RAMSI) instance a growing commitment to direct roles in regional peacekeeping where Australian "security interests" were seen to be at stake.[11]

Timor-Leste's importance in comparative studies extends to its significance in illustrating the distinct challenges of nation-building: the processes of forming a cohesive "national" political community based on a unifying sense of national identity. The history of post-colonial state-building has often been one of attempts to build functional state institutions while overlooking the critical issues of national cohesion essential to political stability. In Timor-Leste, as in many other post-colonial societies, many of the forms of national unity developed during the Indonesian occupation fractured in the wake of independence. Especially in contexts of weak economic development, latent ethnic, regional, or social divisions may be

---

[9] Australian Embassy and Permanent Mission to the United Nations (press release), "East Timor: Recent Unrest and UN Security Council Agreement on International Security Force," November 3, 2006.

[10] Australian Senate Standing Committee on Foreign Affairs, Defence, and Trade, *Australia's Involvement in Peacekeeping Operations*, Commonwealth of Australia (2008), p. 52, http://www.aph.gov.au/binaries/senate/committee/fadt_ctte/peacekeeping/report/report.pdf, accessed August 7, 2012.

[11] Ibid., p. 44. Former prime minister John Howard justified the ISF commitment as "the problems of weak and fragile states, especially ones on our doorstep, can very quickly become our problems."

compounded by—and sometimes recruited in—competition for scarce resources, producing forms of national politics characterized by intergroup contests for control of the state, to benefit regional or clan-based patronage networks. Timor-Leste also serves as an exemplar of the particular nation-building challenges in subsistence societies, where the integration of rural communities into "modern" economic and political systems regulated by the state may be minimal. Such environments are normally characterized by the ongoing presence of "local administrative mechanisms capable of operating independently from the state in accordance with the principles of 'traditional authority,'"[12] and some degree of popular perception that the modern-state model has been "imposed" on the citizenry. Reflecting these issues, Timor-Leste has also become a site in which debates over new "hybrid" institutions are played out publicly. Despite the avowedly forward-looking attitudes of its current leaders, Timor-Leste remains strongly tied to its past, both through the persistence of custom and the memory of conflict. In the evolving process of liberal democratization, there have been calls for and against greater incorporation of traditional authority and dispute resolution,[13] especially at the local government level.

Internationally, as a small and relatively dependent state, Timor-Leste has also been the focus of discussion over the growing role of China's "soft power" and global resource diplomacy, and over how Timor-Leste balances its two major neighbors, Australia and Indonesia, as well as its involvement with the global Lusophone community. Most notably, perhaps, Timor-Leste is a site in which the difficult issues of post-conflict justice and reconciliation remain a source of social discord, set against a recent history of systematic and widespread human-rights abuses. These are each critical issues that continue to inform and inflame the politics of Timor-Leste, as in many other post-conflict societies around the world.

EAST TIMORESE POLITICS SINCE 2007

While Timor-Leste has, to date, avoided the mantle of a "failed state," unresolved divisions within East Timorese society, together with bitter intra-elite political maneuvering contributed to the complete breakdown of security forces in 2006, with open conflict between army factions and between the army and police. This institutional breakdown was followed by widespread youth gang violence and arson in Dili, primarily (though not exclusively) directed against people from the eastern districts living in Dili, and the resignation of Prime Minister Mari Alkatiri, who had led the FRETILIN government since independence in 2002. Though ultimately short-lived, the politicization of regional identity saw *Loromonu* (western) and *Lorosa'e* (eastern) gangs in open conflict in the streets of Dili and led to the crisis being widely referred to in media coverage as the "east-west" crisis.[14] However,

---

[12] Rod Nixon, "The Crisis of Governance in New Subsistence States," *Journal of Contemporary Asia* 36,1 (2006): 75.

[13] Jose Trindade and Bryant Castro, *Rethinking Timorese Identity as a Peacebuilding Strategy: The Lorosa'e–Loromonu Conflict from a Traditional Perspective* (Dili: European Union's Rapid Reaction Mechanism Programme, 2007).

[14] While the terms *"Loromonu"* and *"Lorosa'e"* (literally, "sunset" and "sunrise" in Tetum) gained currency in the 2006 crisis, there is a deeper popular tradition dating to colonial times of collectively referring to East Timorese from the western districts as *Kaladi*, and easterners as *Firaku*. See Dionisio Babo-Soares, "Branching from the Trunk: East Timorese Perceptions of Nationalism in Transition" (doctoral dissertation, Australian National University, 2003).

those studying the conflict's origins in unresolved legacies of the Indonesian occupation, in the politicization of the security sector, and in unmet popular expectations for both economic progress and justice came to accept the term "political-military" crisis as the most appropriate.[15] In conjunction with international state-builders, the East Timorese state since 2006 has attempted to address the social, economic, and institutional deficits that have consigned many post-colonial states to a cycle of internal repression and resistance.

A key initial mandate of the UNMIT mission was to oversee the 2007 presidential and parliamentary elections, which took place in the still-tense wake of the crisis, with more than 160,000 internally displaced persons (IDPs) in and around Dili, an international presence of 1,600 UN police, and an ISF military presence of 1,000 troops. The first round of the presidential election was held on April 9, 2007. FRETILIN's Francisco "Lu Olo" Guterres (27.89 percent) and Jose Ramos-Horta (21.81 percent) emerged as the leading candidates, with a second-round runoff election held on May 9. The weight of the eliminated-candidates' support fell behind Jose Ramos-Horta (69.18 percent), who was inaugurated as the second president of Timor-Leste on May 20, 2007. Fourteen political parties, including two formal coalitions, then contested the June 30 parliamentary elections. The entry of several new parties was significant, especially that of National Congress of the Timorese Reconstruction (CNRT), led by former President Xanana Gusmão. Echoing the historically significant acronym of the National Council of Timorese Resistance, formed by Gusmão in 1998 to unite all East Timorese pro-independence factions (the council had previously been titled the National Council of Maubere Resistance, formed in 1988), the original CNRT led the independence campaign in the 1999 referendum, then dissolved to allow for a multiparty system. The new party acronym CNRT thus resurrected a well-known symbol from the latter period of the independence struggle. With his long-term political ally Ramos-Horta winning the presidency, Gusmão sought to challenge FRETILIN's domination of post-independence politics and secure the more powerful post of prime minister. The dissident *Mudança* (Change) group within FRETILIN supported the CNRT campaign.

In line with the presidential poll, FRETILIN's vote fell significantly to 29 percent, representing just over half its 2001 performance. In second place, CNRT secured 24 percent of the national vote, polling especially strongly vote in Dili. The rise of CNRT clearly affected the more established opposition parties, preventing major gains on their 2001 performance. Seven parties or coalitions exceeded the 3 percent threshold to be eligible for seats in the new, smaller parliament (reduced to 65 from 88 seats in 2001). While the former governing party, FRETILIN, emerged as the single largest party with 21 seats, no single party secured a governing majority of 33 seats in its own right. Gusmão's CNRT won 18 seats and quickly commenced alliance negotiations with the Democratic Party (PD, Partido Democrático; 8 seats) and the social democratic coalition (ASDT-PSD; 11 seats).[16]

---

[15] For a detailed examination of developments in East Timorese politics from 2002 until late 2006, including the political-military crisis, see Damien Kingsbury and Michael Leach, "Introduction," in *East Timor: Beyond Independence,* ed. Damien Kingsbury and Michael Leach (Clayton: Monash Asia Institute Press, 2007), pp. 1–16.

[16] The Timorese Association of Social Democrats (ASDT, Associaçao Social-Democrata de Timor) and the Social Democrat Party of Timor-Leste (PSD, Partido Social Democrata).

One notable trend from the presidential elections was the emergence of three geographic voting blocs. The eastern districts of Baucau, Lautem, and Viqueque returned majorities for FRETILIN's presidential candidate, Lu Olo, while the districts around the capital (Dili, Manatuto, and Liquica) were Ramos-Horta's stronghold, and the western districts recorded their strongest votes for other opposition party leaders, such as Fernando "Lasama" de Araujo of PD, or Xavier do Amaral of ASDT. With minor exceptions,[17] the pattern was repeated in the parliamentary election in regionalized voting for FRETILIN, CNRT, and ASDT-PSD or PD. These outcomes demonstrated that while political divisions in Timor-Leste were more complex than the claimed "east-west divide" of 2006, there was a substantial risk that FRETILIN would be seen to primarily represent the three eastern districts, while the parties in negotiation for an alliance would effectively be seen to represent the rest of the country.[18]

With no clear mandate for any one party, and with highly regionalized party affiliations suggesting wider problems of national unity, President Jose Ramos-Horta had initially raised the prospect of a government of "grand inclusion" comprising all major parties. Despite initial support from PD leader Fernando "Lasama" de Araujo, FRETILIN and CNRT ruled out working together, the former stating its members would prefer to act as a strong opposition if they could not form a government. On July 6, notwithstanding some well-publicized criticisms of CNRT by PSD leader Mario Carrascalão, a post-election coalition between CNRT, ASDT-PSD, and PD was formally confirmed, with the announcement of the AMP (Parliamentary Majority Alliance) controlling 37 seats.[19]

FRETILIN argued that, as the largest party, it should be presented the first opportunity to form a government by testing its program on the floor of the parliament. As the new parliament was sworn in, the election of PD leader Lasama as president (speaker) of parliament over the FRETILIN candidate, by 42 votes to 21, strongly suggested that a FRETILIN minority government presenting its program to the legislature would face insuperable difficulties. This result, and the clear AMP coalition majority it demonstrated, determined Ramos-Horta's subsequent decision. On August 6, President Ramos-Horta invited Xanana Gusmão to form a government. Gusmão was sworn-in as prime minister on August 8, with *Mudança* leader Jose Luis Guterres as deputy. PSD's veteran leader and former governor during the Indonesian interregnum, Mario Carrascalão, was later sworn in as a second deputy prime minister. FRETILIN claimed the president's decision was unconstitutional but dropped the threat of a legal challenge in favor of working toward a "political solution." FRETILIN members returned to parliament in late August and soon commenced work as a parliamentary opposition.

---

[17] The exceptions were the western district of Cova Lima, which returned a slightly stronger FRETILIN vote and small CNRT leads in the western districts of Bobonaro and Oecussi. See Michael Leach, "The 2007 Presidential and Parliamentary Elections in Timor-Leste," *Australian Journal of Politics and History* 55,2 (2009): 219–32.

[18] International Crisis Group, "Timor-Leste's Parliamentary Elections," *Asia Briefing* 65 (June 12, 2007), p. 4.

[19] The smaller party, UNDERTIM, later joined the AMP coalition, giving the alliance thirty-nine seats.

The AMP in Government

The AMP government came to office in August 2007 promising to boost broad-based development in the areas of food sufficiency, health care, education, and infrastructure. On taking office, the AMP parties had anti-FRETILIN sentiment in common, shared the Catholic Church's endorsement, and had broadly concurred on the need to encourage greater levels of foreign investment. As an executive, the AMP government also comprised a wide range of actors with starkly different histories and agendas, combining national heroes of the resistance era with a host of younger upcoming leaders and, more controversially, some erstwhile supporters of "autonomy" within Indonesia occupying ministerial positions. The AMP coalition nonetheless itself proved durable, despite major eruptions of disunity.

The development policies pursued by the AMP were broadly similar to those that had been pursued by the previous FRETILIN government, both being focused on the allocation of state resources to alleviate illiteracy, malnutrition, and simple illnesses. Aside from the far larger budgets available to the AMP administration—itself an enduring legacy of difficult oil revenue negotiations with Australia conducted by the former FRETILIN government—the principle policy differences were the AMP government's slightly more pro-business, pro–foreign-investment orientation, its desire to spend more of Timor-Leste's growing petroleum revenues for development needs, and its inclination to countenance the idea of borrowing. In 2007, the overriding political demands facing the incoming government remained those of improving the basic government services, infrastructure, and employment opportunities destroyed by departing Indonesian troops and their militia proxies in 1999. Both the interim UN administration and the first post-independence government were perceived as having underperformed on these fronts, though both were operating within severe infrastructure and human-resource constraints, and the latter, at least, remained highly constrained by limited annual budgets.

The AMP government's performance in implementing its program was mixed, and continually hampered by low levels of government capacity, which slowed the rollout of major infrastructure programs, including programs to increase the supply of potable water, provide badly needed road maintenance, and begin electrification of the country. Thanks to high global demand for oil, which boosted prices and hence government revenue, and the fact that government spending was driving almost all other economic activity, Timor-Leste rode out the Global Financial Crisis of 2009-12 unaffected. Timor-Leste's economic situation had begun to improve, with an economic growth rate of around 10 percent a year for the three years to the end of 2011, though from a low GDP base and almost entirely driven by government spending. However, the government was consistently unable fully to disburse its available funds. This lack of "absorptive capacity," particularly beyond Dili, meant that government spending, as the main driver of economic growth, continued to run at lower than optimal levels. Even in the capital, economic growth was unable to spark employment growth, and drove considerable inflation in the prices of both essential and consumer goods[20]. Electrification proceeded with two heavy oil generators to be replaced by gas-powered generators around 2015, though the contract process proved highly controversial, with extended delays in contract

---

[20] See Ministry of Finance, "Consumer Price Index—Dili Region," Issue 21, October 2011. The CPI for the Dili region was estimated at 14.4 percent from October 2010 to October 2011.

establishment and major contract renegotiations. Notably, beyond Dili, there were often very few signs of any government spending, with most of the country remaining in a state of poverty and often decrepitude.

Several headline development indicators were promising, including a decline in the overall poverty rate from 50 percent to 41 percent of the population from 2007 to 2011. The widespread provision of subsidized rice, cash transfers, and the spread of health clinics supported by Cuban doctors and their medical training programs led to improvement in key health indicators. Infant mortality rates fell by half between 2004 and 2011, maternal mortality rates more than halved, and average life expectancy increased from 58 years to more than 62 years. The country's fertility rates, for several years the highest in the world at just below eight live births per woman, moderated to just under six. Some of these gains reflected improved access to health care, greater food security and better crops due to the end of a debilitating drought, and the powerful Catholic Church quietly acknowledging that the country could not sustain the growth rate it had been experiencing. Literacy, however, remained problematic, at about 50 percent. In part, this low literacy rate reflected a disconnect between official and actual teaching practices and the clash of languages at different levels of education—Tetum or another local language at early primary school, Portuguese at higher levels of primary school and high school, and the continuing, though no longer exclusive, importance of Indonesian at university. One bright spot was that the literacy rate in the youth demographic was at 77 percent, considerably better than that of the overall population.

Particularly in rural areas, however, many East Timorese saw only modest improvement in their lives. The UN special rapporteur on extreme poverty estimated that a majority of the 75 percent of East Timorese living in rural areas were "entrenched in inter-generational cycles of poverty,"[21] and that some 58 percent of East Timorese children suffered from chronic malnutrition, with almost half of all children under five underweight for their age (a problem that had historically afflicted Timorese children). The same report claimed that income inequality had "risen significantly," with particularly stark gaps between Dili—where 71 percent of the highest income quintile resided—and rural areas. Despite large and growing annual budgets, just over 10 percent of the funds was dedicated to social spending in the key areas of education, health, and agriculture (areas heavily supported by international aid programs), with the majority of the budget focused on infrastructure funding.

A petroleum fund worth some US$11 billion by the middle of 2012 made Timor-Leste the envy of other smaller emerging states in the region. However, the reliance of annual budgets on petroleum revenues (more than 93 percent of government revenue in the 2012 budget) demonstrated the longer-term potential for Timor-Leste to suffer the "resource curse" pathologies of other oil-dependent, developing states. In particular, Timor-Leste's high-cost and low-skills-based economy precluded development of alternative export sectors. In August 2010, the AMP government outlined a National Strategic Development Plan for 2011–30 that, once again, highlighted the goals of economic diversification for the future. Other controversies have attended the petroleum fund, including the decision of the AMP to withdraw

---

[21] UN News Centre, "Not All Timorese Benefiting from Economic Gains, UN Human Rights Expert Says," November 18, 2011, http://www.un.org/apps/news/story.asp?NewsID=40437&Cr=timor&Cr1=, accessed August 7, 2012.

annual amounts above the Estimated Sustainable Income threshold, broadly calculated at around 3 percent, to prompt more rapid development, and the decision to relax some of the investment rules governing the fund that mandate lower risk investments.

If the broad economic and development indicators highlighted the deep challenges facing the post-independence state, the AMP government's performance on entrenched social conflicts demonstrated its capacity to solve problems. The oil-price spike of 2008 gave the government windfall gains, which it was able to use in the form of cash grants to buy off disenfranchised groups, including disaffected former soldiers, internally displaced persons, and veterans, as well as providing small pensions for the relatively small number of people over sixty-five. The provision of heavily subsidized rice also helped avert the perennial problems of seasonal starvation, making life easier for many Timorese. The tension that had pervaded Dili into 2008 disappeared with the closure of the IDP camps and the payment to family heads of US$5,000 to rebuild their homes. Less successful, perhaps, was the government's attempt to deal with entrenched and complex land disputes, which had led to occupations of contested land and forced evictions.[22] Following the violence that began in 2006, continued beyond the elections, and finally ebbed in 2008, Timor-Leste has since experienced relative stability and calm, and the streets of the main towns, particularly Dili, have an air of normalcy, with people promenading and cooking along the foreshore in the evenings and markets filled with produce. While the various programs aimed at displaced and disaffected groups brought about a sense of peace and security, criticisms that the government had "bought" peace, in ways which may prove unsustainable, will be tested after international forces withdraw.

Despite the AMP government's relatively good performance in some areas, it has also attracted considerable criticism, in particular for alleged corruption, with persistent, though in many cases unproven, charges of large government contracts being awarded to AMP party officials and relatives of key ministers without full transparency with regard to tender processes.[23] In response, the government established an anti-corruption commission and launched a visible anti-corruption campaign, including signing up to the global Extractive Industries Transparency Initiative. Despite these moves, the increasing range of budget funds not subject to detailed parliamentary oversight presented a further source of concern over transparency, with key East Timorese civil society groups arguing that the limited information provided on special development funds in the 2011 state budget law created a "dangerous precedent" that stood to "erode parliamentary authority" over time.[24] In September 2010, in a dramatic development, Deputy Prime Minister

---

[22] International Crisis Group, "Managing Land Conflict in Timor-Leste," *Asia Briefing* 110 (September 9, 2010), pp. 1–19.

[23] Mark Dodd, "Gusmao's $15m Rice Deal Alarms UN," *The Australian*, July 7, 2008, http://www.theaustralian.com.au/news/gusmaos-15m-rice-deal-alarms-un/story-e6frg6t6-1 111116839519, accessed August 7, 2012. In 2012, the former Justice Minister Lucia Lobato was found guilty of unlawful economic participation in a tender process and sentenced to five years jail.

[24] "La'o Hamutuk Submission to National Parliament Committee C (Economy, Finances and Anti-corruption) regarding the General State Budget for 2011," December 15, 2010, updated January 10, 2011, http://www.laohamutuk.org/econ/OGE11/LHsubComCOGE11Dec10En.htm, accessed August 14, 2012.

Carrascalão resigned after a clash with Prime Minister Gusmão, citing issues of transparency and accountability and claiming that personal attacks had been made against him as a result of his anti-corruption work.

Of all the dramatic developments that have wracked East Timorese politics, the greatest unfolded early on the morning of February 11, 2008, when President Ramos-Horta was shot and gravely wounded by a member of Alfredo Reinado's rebel group during an armed invasion by the group of the president's residence. Demanding to see the president, Reinado and one of his men were shot and killed by F-FDTL (Falintil-Forças de Defesa de Timor Leste) presidential guards. Returning from his morning walk shortly thereafter, Ramos-Horta was shot and critically wounded by one of Reinado's group. This incident was immediately followed by an ambush on Prime Minister Gusmão's residence at Balibar in the hills above Dili. The surviving members of the group involved in these incidents, including the petitioners' leader Lieutenant Gastão Salsinha, who later claimed the episode was part of a "negotiation strategy" that had gone wrong, were sentenced in March 2010 to lengthy jail terms, then pardoned by presidential decree in August 2010.[25]

The release of the Salsinha group, which followed the release of Martenus Bere, a former pro-Indonesian militia leader indicted by the UN's Timor-Leste-based Serious Crimes Unit over the Suai massacre in 1999, and the pardon of Joni Marques, one of the few militia members to be convicted and jailed after the violence, reinforced increasing concern over what has been widely described as a "culture of impunity" in Timor-Leste. The Bere case, in particular, raised concerns over the operation of the separation of powers, as Bere, after being arrested, was released by executive order without judicial oversight of the process. This, in turn, had implications for the popular understanding of and faith in the legal process.

Despite representing a key area of UNMITs mandate, security-sector reform remained an area of critical concern. After extensive rebuilding and retraining, the PNTL progressively reassumed responsibility for policing from their UN counterparts, albeit with mixed reception by the public. Many of the complaints that had dogged the PNTL up until 2006, including corruption and brutality, resurfaced as the PNTL took control of policing operations.[26] Though the full handover was completed in early 2011, the security-sector reform agenda, so long a focus of international state-building assistance, was widely considered to have failed in several of its core goals, at least partly as a result of limited cooperation from the East Timorese government.[27] While recommending the reduction of UN policing forces and noting major improvements in the security situation since 2008, the International Crisis Group acknowledged that latent security threats remained, most the product of failures to prosecute those involved in the violence of 2006 and 2008, including the failure to pursue United Nations Commission of Inquiry–recommended prosecutions for the events of 2006.

---

[25] In early 2011, Salsinha launched a claim on behalf of the members of his group who missed out on petitioner compensation payments as a result of their participation in these events.

[26] Matt Crook, "Ramos-Horta Says East Timor Finds Peace," *Sydney Morning Herald*, May 20, 2010, http://news.smh.com.au/breaking-news-world/ramoshorta-says-east-timor-finds-peace-20100520-vman.html, accessed August 7, 2012.

[27] International Crisis Group, "Timor-Leste: Time for the UN to Step Back," *Asia Briefing* 116 (December 15, 2010), pp. 1–14.

One of the areas of PNTL responsibility—the border—had become again a site of dispute between Timor-Leste and Indonesia, particularly in the enclave of Oecusse where there had been Indonesian military incursions into some border villages (in one case when Prime Minister Gusmão was about to visit the area). Other incidents included Indonesian naval patrols in Timor-Leste waters, allegedly to forestall "piracy." These incidents, in turn, put a halt to the finalization of the border between Timor-Leste and Indonesia. In addition, regional tension flared over Australian proposals to create a regional asylum-seeker processing center in Timor-Leste. The proposal was rebuffed quickly by the East Timorese parliament, though the executive government was less direct in its opposition, referring the matter to the regional "Bali process" forum, where the proposal was subsequently rejected. Tensions between the AMP government and major hydrocarbon development partner Woodside Petroleum over the location of a natural gas processing plant also continued to cause friction in the bilateral relationship, as the East Timorese leadership rejected Woodside's preference for a floating offshore plant, and the government doggedly pursued its ambition to have the plant built on the south coast of Timor. Prime Minister Gusmão declared he would rather see Timor-Leste go without the benefits of this project than to accept the offshore plant proposal. Though the location of the plant was a commercial decision by Woodside, Timor-Leste's stance could result in the lapse of its contract by February 2013, meaning Timor-Leste would need to find a new development partner more agreeable to its plans. There were some preliminary signs, however, that the parties to this $20-billion discussion would find a mutually constructive way forward, with Woodside offering the possibility of establishing a smaller onshore processing center at Beaco, on the south coast.

In early 2011, the UNDP came under sustained attack from the Timorese government for its draft report, which was critical of the government's performance on urban youth unemployment, rising rural poverty, and expenditures of oil and gas revenues.[28] Highlighting the ongoing challenges of energy supply, food security, and education and health-service provision, the report raised the ire of the Timorese government by also questioning its opposition to war crimes and its efforts to prosecute those guilty of past violence. The government considered these issues beyond the UNDPs brief. A short-lived furor highlighted the impatience of domestic political elites for the end of the long decade of state-building, after several missions. The UNMIT mission and its associated international policing forces were scheduled to be withdrawn by the end of December 2012. The stated position of the ISF was that it would also withdraw at that time if the situation proved stable, leaving Australia's separate Defence Cooperation Program (DCP) with the Timor-Leste Defence Force in place.

The 2012 Elections

In 2012, President Jose Ramos-Horta was voted out of office, to be replaced by the then-recently retired head of the armed forces, Taur Matan Ruak. Without the support of a major party, Horta received 18 percent in the election's first round in

---

[28] See, for example, Lindsay Murdoch, "East Timor Leaders Scathing about Crucial UN Report," *Sydney Morning Herald*, January 3, 2011, http://www.smh.com.au/world/east-timor-leaders-scathing-about-crucial-un-report-20110102-19d22.html, accessed August 7, 2012.

March, finishing behind Ruak and Fretilin's Lu Olo. Running as an independent, but with the open support of CNRT, Ruak defeated Lu Olo in the second-round runoff in April, by an overwhelming margin of 61 percent to 39 percent. The one feature that Ramos-Horta and Ruak had in common was, at the time of their political ascendancy, they were both strongly supported by Xanana Gusmao.

The parliamentary elections held on July 7 saw just four of the twenty-one parties competing win seats. Prime Minister Xanana Gusmao's CNRT performed strongly and finished in first position, with 36.66 percent of the national vote, followed by FRETILIN, with just under 30 percent. With the collapse of the former ASDT-PSD vote, the Democratic Party (PD) emerged clearly as the new third party, with 10.3 percent of the vote, and Frenti-Mudança, a small breakaway party from FRETILIN, received 3.11 percent. These parliamentary election results gave CNRT thirty seats; Fretilin, twenty-five; PD, eight; and Frenti-Mudança, two seats in the new parliament.

As in 2007, no single party gained an absolute majority of thirty-three seats in its own right. However, a large number of small parties failed to clear the 3 percent threshold in 2012. This meant that 20 percent of the national vote—the total received by eliminated parties—was excluded for the purpose of seat distribution. As such, CNRT's 37 percent vote share brought them closer to 45 percent of the seats, putting them in a strong position to lead a new alliance. A week after results were known, the CNRT party conference announced its intention to form a governing alliance with PD and Frenti-Mudança, suggesting continuity with the 2007 result, albeit with a smaller number of parties in alliance. This alliance, later to be known as the Bloku Governu Koligasaun (BGK, Government Coalition Bloc) would control forty seats in the sixty-five seat parliament. The CNRT's decision, which was televised live,[29] saw a brief outbreak of violence by disgruntled FRETILIN party members in Dili, with some sixty-five cars reportedly burned or otherwise destroyed, and, more seriously, eight people wounded, including at least four police officers. Other incidents, including arson, were reported in Lautem and Viqueque. In the most serious incident, a young FRETILIN member was killed by police in Hera, just outside Dili. Though the latter episode raised ongoing questions over police violence, the post-election environment calmed considerably within days. More broadly, international observers declared that the elections substantially met the international criteria for being free and fair, which was a notable achievement for Timor-Leste's two electoral bodies, running national elections without major external support for the first time. Notwithstanding these positives, which marked Timor-Leste as a frontrunner in a region noted for poor electoral administration, there were a number of minor, mostly technical problems with the election process, including inconsistency of ink for marking fingers in the first presidential round, concerns over the print quality of some parliamentary ballot papers, and rare occasions of party agent interference in the administration of the vote. Some observer reports also called for greater scrutiny of corporate donations to CNRT's electoral campaign, and for clearer guidelines and sanctions relating to political party and campaign financing.

CNRT finished first in all but four districts: the three eastern districts where FRETILIN once again dominated the poll, and the neighboring western district of Manufahi, where FRETILIN narrowly led the count. In general, CNRT's success

---

[29] FRETILIN leaders attributed the violence to what they claimed were provocative comments broadcast from the CNRT conference that day.

came overwhelmingly at the expense of small, western-based parties such as ASDT, PSD, and PUN, which received no seats. Overall, while the association between region and party affiliation remained noticeable in 2012, it had moderated since 2007, with FRETILIN's vote staging a minor recovery (3.7 percent) in the western districts, and CNRT and PD increasing their vote shares in the eastern districts, such that the FRETILIN vote declined 5.6 percent in its heartland. This trend, already evident in the presidential elections, represented a welcome—if modest—sign that regionalized vote affiliations were trending away from their 2007 peak.

TIMOR-LESTE'S POLITICAL SYSTEM

Timor-Leste is a unitary democratic republic with multitiered governance. The constitution is closely based on the Portuguese model, with a directly elected president as head of state, a parliament having all legislative authority, and a prime minister as head of the executive government and cabinet. Parliamentary representatives are elected under a party-list proportional representation system to serve five-year terms.

More broadly, it is important to appreciate the procedural separation of executive and legislature in the East Timorese political system. A minister does not need to be a member of parliament (MP), although most are, and any MP subsequently appointed to the executive government is replaced in the legislature per party lists.[30] Thus, while the prime minister requires the confidence of the parliament, and the executive frequently attends sittings in the legislature (and parliamentary committee meetings in order to be questioned), the executive does not have a legislative vote, as in a Westminster parliamentary system. This feature is made possible by Timor-Leste's party-list proportional representation electoral system. When a member is appointed to the executive government, a member of the same political party from the original list replaces that member in the legislature. This shift may also happen "in reverse," as evidenced by Mario Carrascalão's return to the legislature as a PSD member of parliament after his resignation as deputy prime minister in September 2010.

Under changes to the electoral law passed in December 2006, the thirteen district-representative positions were abolished and the size of the National Parliament decreased overall from eighty-eight members to sixty-five.[31] Each party was required to submit a list of sixty-five candidates and twenty-five *suplentes* (reserves).[32] Under the changes to the electoral system, parties or coalitions must reach a 3 percent threshold to be eligible for seats. This new hurdle requirement would rule out half the parties running in 2007, and all but four parties in 2012. Parliamentary seats are then distributed proportionally among qualifying parties— based on a single national constituency—to ensure "broad representation in the parliamentary composition."[33]

The constitution also mandates that the government enact legislation to achieve greater decentralization, to establish a full judicial system and other matters of conventional state function. As of mid-2012, Timor-Leste did not yet have a supreme

---

[30] Government of Timor-Leste, Law on the Election of the National Parliament, Law No. 6/2006, 28 December, Article 15.5.

[31] Ibid., Article 10.

[32] Ibid., Article 12.1.

[33] Ibid., Preamble.

court, so constitutional questions were in theory being addressed by the appeals court. The judiciary is generally regarded as a weak state institution, plagued by inadequate training, staffing problems, and judicial shortages, all complicated by a language policy which—unlike parliamentary deliberation—requires processes to be conducted in Portuguese, making the court system heavily reliant on cumbersome translation processes and, frequently, resulting in the effective disenfranchisement of citizens involved with the courts. The National Parliament is expected to pass legislation to progressively replace laws that were inherited from Indonesia and then adopted as interim law by UNTAET. The backlog of legislation before the National Parliament is, in part, a result of parliament or its committees regularly failing to achieve a quorum, and is also due to the lack of adequate research and staffing support for MPs. Issues of translation of legislation from the official Portuguese into languages better understood by many parliamentarians (usually Tetum) have also slowed the legislative process.

Decree laws passed by the executive (sitting as the Council of Ministers) are issued in a wide range of standard regulatory areas and in some key policy areas, including the penal code and the establishment of the National Petroleum Authority.[34] This has the effect of limiting public debate over key legislation and limiting parliamentary scrutiny of the executive government. More broadly, government capacity is limited, falling away quickly beyond the ministerial and bureaucratic-director levels, and constrained by the central government's limited reach outside the major towns. Decision making is slow, and efficiency often depends on personal relationships. A decision by the prime minister or another senior minister will ensure quick action, often across departments. Implementing state policy through conventional bureaucratic processes is frustratingly slow and often unsuccessful.

Elected district councils are intended to replace national-government-appointed district administrators by 2014, although some parts of the enabling legislation had not been passed at the time of writing. Certain local councils and authorities have already been established and are functioning. There are the locally elected, nominally non-party hamlet and village chiefs (*chefe de aldeia, chefe de suco*) and elected *suco* councils. *Suco* elections have been held twice since independence, and party political competition at that level has been formally proscribed since 2009. Decentralized funding is intended to be allocated by the central government on a pro rata basis. This plan to implement limited decentralization and establish district assemblies recognizes Timor-Leste's diverse ethnic makeup and largely rural demography. High turnout rates in the 2009 *suco* elections again reflected the strong popular commitment to participating in the electoral process.

National elections have been held every five years since 2001. It is too early in the life of independent Timor-Leste to determine whether elections will be held more frequently in the future, although representatives are legally required to serve a maximum of five years per term. Voting is voluntary. Considering that voter rolls are not being adequately updated to take into account deaths, double registrations (a result of re-registrations that do not imply double voting), and the presence of nonresident East Timorese on the voter roll, the participation rate of just under 82

---

[34] Dennis Shoesmith, "Remaking the State in Timor-Leste: The Case for Constitutional Reform," *Proceedings of the 17th Biennial Conference of the Asian Studies Association of Australia* (2008), pp. 1–19.

percent in the 2007 elections, as officially reported, was likely closer to 90 percent. Despite a slight downturn in 2012 to 75 percent (with a similar level of under-reporting likely), enthusiasm for voting remains very high across the country.

THE CHAPTERS

Among the problems facing post-colonial states is that of establishing a durable balance between the national government and the various centrifugal forces that might threaten state sovereignty. The relative strengths of national and local loyalties represent a key polarity of this balance, which may impede long-term aspirations for national integration. Long-time observer of Timorese cultural life David Hicks examines this issue through his study of rural Timorese communities, whose members frequently identify more strongly as residents of those local communities than as citizens of the state. Hicks's central argument is that the failure to transform villagers into citizens indicates the existence of two political cultures of such disparate character that they militate against the ambitions of Timor-Leste's government to foster an integrated national identity. His chapter argues that a synthesis is necessary if the mass of the Timorese population is to be transformed from villagers into citizens. Hicks concludes by arguing that although each political culture possesses distinctive traits that might at first sight appear irreconcilable, it is yet possible to synthesize an integrated national political culture that draws on the strengths of both sources of political identity.

Because Timor-Leste has a directly elected president and a prime minister accountable to the parliament, the political system is commonly described as a semi-presidential system. However, Maurice Duverger's classic definition of a semi-presidential system also requires that that president possess "quite considerable powers."[35] The relative weakness of presidential powers in Timor-Leste's system of government—compared with the governments of some other Lusophone states—has led other commentators to describe this system as a parliamentary republic, lacking the substantive division of executive power that typifies semi-presidential political systems. This debate over the character of Timor-Leste's government is examined in close detail in this collection, with contributions from Rui Feijo and Damien Kingsbury, respectively, outlining the claims in favor of interpreting the Timor-Leste political system as semi-presidential or as parliamentary republican.

Rui Feijo argues for classifying the system as semi-presidential, seeing Timor-Leste as an example of the "premier-presidential" sub-type. He argues that the East Timorese president retains significant powers that mark the office as more than symbolic, including certain constitutional powers yet to be facilitated by legislation. Feijo makes the case that semi-presidentialism has also allowed the creation of a "common house" for competing poles of power and remains preferable, in the East Timorese context, to the alternatives of a presidential or parliamentary political system.

By contrast, Damien Kingsbury proposes that Timor-Leste's constitution defines its political system as a parliamentary republic, taking into account the limited powers of the Presidency, the exclusive responsibility of executive government to the legislature, and, above all, the undivided capacity of the Prime Minister to appoint

---

[35] Maurice Duverger, "A New Political System Model: Semi-Presidential Government," *European Journal of Political Research* 8 (1980): 166.

the executive government. Since Timor-Leste's Head of State lacks executive authority in all but a small and circumscribed area of affairs of state, Kingsbury argues that overstating presidential powers can potentially undermine the stability of the state.

One of the major challenges facing Timor-Leste is that of corruption, which Aderito Soares tackles in his chapter. Although there have been few major prosecutions for grand-scale corruption to date, Soares notes that the public has been highly critical of a perceived rise in corruption in the period following independence. Soares contends that these public perceptions are justified, and that forms of corruption exist at various levels of government and in the public sphere. There is, therefore, general agreement that it is timely to address the issue of corruption with a comprehensive anticorruption strategy, including the establishment of Timor's Anti-Corruption Commission (CAC), of which he is head. Soares's chapter goes on to examine some constraints and opportunities in tackling corruption in Timor-Leste. The chapter highlights the rationale behind the fight against corruption, and also identifies the different entities that play a role in the area. Soares's key argument is a warning against forms of "institutional ritualism" in the fight against corruption, which he sees as the inclination of governments to "form new agencies rather than address the actual problems."

Andrew Marriott's chapter develops a parallel analysis to that of David Hicks, but from a legal rather than an anthropological perspective. Marriott argues that as a still-young state, Timor-Leste has not yet been able to put its turbulent history fully behind it. While the state and its citizens require new institutions and social dynamics, historical crimes remain as much a concern as contemporary injustices. Though the democratic architecture of the East Timorese state guarantees some commendable protections, he says, the ability of formal institutions to respond directly to the range of everyday legal needs remains limited. Some of these shortcomings are simply a reflection of Timor-Leste's emergence from a period of violence and turmoil. Other shortcomings, according to Marriott, represent developmental oversights or missteps, which he suggests require attention and correction. As comparisons between various post-colonial countries demonstrate, actors in the legal sphere can play an important role in the nation-building endeavor.

In Timor-Leste, as elsewhere, a competitive multiparty system remains a fundamental cornerstone of democratic consolidation. In his contribution, Dennis Shoesmith examines political parties in Timor-Leste, analyzing the strengths and weaknesses of the party system and the degree of institutionalization of contemporary political parties. Commencing with an examination of the historical development of the party system in Timor-Leste, Shoesmith assesses the contemporary health of the party system, reviewing its basis in constitutional and electoral law, and some key constraints on the role of parties in the context of Timor's political system. Shoesmith argues that Timor-Leste has performed creditably compared with many post-conflict states, exhibiting a degree of political stability in interparty competition. Nonetheless, his chapter identifies warning signs that some persistent maladies characteristic of weak party systems are emerging, including patron-client politics, low levels of accountability to the public, and the use of political parties as vehicles to extract state resources for the benefit of political elites.

In his chapter, Pedro Seabra argues that Timor-Leste has become increasingly vocal and assertive on a range of foreign policy topics since overcoming some of the internal strife that scarred the nation-building process from 2006 to 2008. For Seabra, this assertiveness indicates the new nation's political will to enhance or diversify its role in the region. The potential ripple effects across the region—given the level of international focus on Timor-Leste, the country's strategic geographic location, and its significant natural wealth—are as yet unpredictable. Accordingly, Seabra starts by examining the current context of Timor-Leste's foreign policy, identifying the main external partners and foreign policy goals it has established since joining the international community, with a detailed focus on relationships with four key actors: Australia, China, Indonesia, and Portugal. Seabra then examines some instructive episodes in Timor's foreign-policy development that have raised concerns among its traditional partners, who are now confronted with an increasingly assertive and independent actor.

Deborah Cummins's and Michael Leach's chapter returns to the theme of the evolving relationship between traditional and modern forms of political authority, examining the case of local government in Timor-Leste, and the ways elected *chefes* interact with traditional authorities at the *suco* level. Cummins and Leach identify three distinct models of hybrid authority in local government: two "co-incumbency" models and an "authorization" model, emphasizing a separation of powers between traditional and modern authority. As Cummins and Leach note, the "clash of paradigms" between traditional and modern democratic ideas of legitimacy in Timor-Leste is widely considered to be an important issue for the stability of the young state. The balance of this relationship is likewise considered integral to engaging local communities in the project of nation-building, peace-building, and democratization. There are also critical and ongoing issues for government to consider in the continuing decentralization process, and in regulating aspects of customary law, particularly at the local level.

Bu Wilson's chapter evaluates the security-sector reform agenda in Timor-Leste during the period between 2006 and 2012, including the specific process of reforming the national police. The political and security crisis of 2006, with its origins rooted in conflicts within and between the uniformed forces, highlighted the necessity of reforming Timor-Leste's police and military, and their respective oversight ministries. Yet, as Wilson notes, the reform project, which was premised on cooperation between international and national actors, has stumbled, faltered, and perhaps even failed in key respects. Wilson examines how an ill-defined project, contests over sovereignty, shortcomings in capacity, and incompatible international and national agendas have worked to produce poor long-term prospects for the security sector in Timor-Leste.

In his chapter on informal security groups, James Scambary builds upon this theme, examining the origin and impacts of martial arts and ex-veterans' groups in the post-independence political landscape. Charting the historical progression of these groups as they evolved from resistance movements to protest vehicles, and their interactions with formal political actors, Scambary highlights the ongoing strength of these groups beyond the intense conflicts of 2006–07. Scambary argues that the combination of a poorly functioning justice system with an inefficient policing force continues to encourage a default situation in which communities look to informal security groups for protection, as evidenced by further outbreaks of urban violence in Dili between 2009 and 2012.

Since independence, economic development has remained a major challenge for national policy makers and, at times, a keystone of popular dissatisfaction. Tim

Anderson's chapter identifies key contemporary approaches to development strategy and assesses their application in the case of Timor-Leste since independence. He contrasts the influence of market-economy approaches with those of developmental-state models and an alternative "human development" approach, which focuses on developing core capabilities in areas such as education, health, gender equality, and participation. Anderson reviews the history of development strategy in Timor Leste's National Development Plan and analyzes the approaches of the two major post-independence governments in relation to key issues of economic stimulus, infrastructure development, tax policy, and petroleum revenues. In particular, Anderson analyzes recent debates over the management and expenditure of the Petroleum Fund, arguing that while diversification from low-return US bonds may be prudent, Timor-Leste currently lacks the financial expertise required to manage the funds in more volatile, higher-risk financial and equity markets. Overall, Anderson makes the case that the critical importance of the informal sector, and particularly staple-food production, has not been matched by comparable state investment.

Sara Niner examines the critical theme of the contemporary politics of gender in Timor-Leste. Arguing from the starting point that traditional concepts of gender remain extremely influential in the country, Niner examines the ways these conceptions have been reinforced or modified by the legacies of Portuguese and Indonesian colonialism. She also examines the influence of militarized conceptions of masculine identity that emerged in the resistance era, which were echoed by recent popular figures such as the rebel military leader Alfredo Reinado. Noting the especially poor development outcomes for women in Timor-Leste, along with disturbing levels of domestic violence and the little acknowledged, but central, role of women in the resistance, Niner makes the case that gender relations remain a key priority in Timor-Leste's development, calling for a "national dialogue on masculinities and the legacy of the war."

In his second contribution, Damien Kingsbury examines the evolving politics of political and financial decentralization in Timor-Leste. Using the wider regional history of centralization in post-colonial developing states as context, Kingsbury assesses the potential strengths and weaknesses of this agenda for both development and democratic consolidation in Timor-Leste. Principally concerned with creating greater responsiveness between the state and its citizens by devolving a degree of political and economic authority to the district level, decentralization will also allow for greater recognition of the diversity of Timor-Leste's society. As Kingsbury notes, the process of decentralization in Timor-Leste began in 2003, but with progress on a final model delayed at least until 2014, this agenda remains a work in progress.

Beyond UNMIT: Challenges to Political Stability

As a recently decolonized state, Timor-Leste has faced the fundamental challenge that frequently besets developing-post-independence states: seeking to balance popular aspirations against limited state capacity. Having stumbled in 2006, Timor-Leste now appears to be charting a steadier course. In the short period since its independence referendum of 1999, Timor-Leste now stands as a state that embodies many of the important contemporary challenges of post-colonial democratization, development, and international state-building. More than any other country, Timor-Leste has been the product of international support. There is little doubt, for example, that Timor-Leste's political institutions reflect, with degrees of embeddedness, the liberal character of the international community in general, and the United Nations in particular.

The withdrawal of UN peacekeeping forces from Timor-Leste in 2005 soon proved to have been precipitous, necessitating an unplanned and hasty return of international peacekeepers in 2006. Both domestic and international state-builders will have this experience in mind as external forces withdraw in late 2012, along with the knowledge that the Security Council is unlikely to approve another support mission at the scale of UNMISET or UNMIT. The period of transitioning toward full responsibility therefore places the focus squarely on Timor-Leste's ability to run its own affairs without succumbing to the type of internal conflict witnessed in 2006–7. Considering the turmoil of the crisis, the period since 2008 has been characterized by a remarkable degree of stability and real, if modest, improvements in Timor-Leste's human development indicators. This has facilitated the staged transition to local policing, completed in early 2011, and the accompanying drawdown of international forces, to the point in 2012 at which the UNPOL contingent had declined from 1,600 to 1,300 and ISF numbers represented less than half their 2006 peak force of 1,100 soldiers.

Several major tests will confront the East Timorese state beyond the UN withdrawal. The most important of these will be the challenge of stimulating economic growth, a task constrained by the passing of the state-developmental era and the rise of neoliberal free-market approaches to state-building.[36] As Barbara notes, the era of neoliberal state-building has been characterized by an aversion to promoting specific industry policies. Constrained in this manner, neoliberal efforts have generally proven ineffectual in stimulating economic development in post-conflict states, thus undermining prospects for state consolidation.[37] In his review of state-building missions of the 1990s and 2000s, Fukuyama identifies three distinct phases, suggesting that while the United Nations has a respectable track record in the initial stabilization of post-conflict societies, and in the development of local institutions for governance, it has a far weaker track record in strengthening those institutions to the point that enables sustained economic growth and social development to occur.[38]

Central to this challenge will be the task of effectively managing Timor-Leste's oil and gas reserves. There has been considerable debate about the wisdom of accessing increased shares of Petroleum Fund capital to more rapidly develop local projects. On one hand, the injection of cash-accelerated projects has increased their number and reach, which has had positive social benefits. A number of observers, however, have expressed concern that this influx of revenue may lead to a "resource curse," whereby funds are squandered, corruption increases, and the funds are ultimately depleted without the development of alternative industries. In conjunction with a weak party system, the proliferation of oil and gas revenues also has the potential to foster the growth of patron-client politics, and the type of intergroup contests over control of state resources likely to exacerbate the risks

---

[36] Mark T. Berger and Heloise Weber, "Beyond State-Building: Global Governance and the Crisis of the Nation-State System in the 21st Century," *Third World Quarterly* 27,1 (2006): 201.

[37] Barbara, "Rethinking Neo-Liberal State Building," p. 316.

[38] See Francis Fukuyama, *State-Building: Governance and World Order in the Twenty-First Century* (Ithaca, NY: Cornell University Press, 2004), pp. 99–104.

associated with regionalized political affiliations. In particular, local NGOs warned that if government spending was not made more sustainable, Timor-Leste's current oil wealth could be depleted within ten years, just as a massive demographic explosion of young adults is due to enter the labor market.[39]

Another challenge likely to confront Timor-Leste will be the transition to a new generation of political leaders. Much of the bitter conflict within Timor-Leste's small political elite was intimately linked with longstanding personal alliances and feuds among the senior leadership of the country. While the series of "historical leaders" meetings[40] held by members of this group have been a welcome development for political stability, a transition to a younger generation is inevitable and perhaps overdue. Aside from PD, the major political parties are still led by the older generation, though there is now more open discussion among members of the "generation of '75" about the inevitability of a hand-over of power, probably in the wake of the 2012 elections, with FRETILIN's 2011 congress formalizing a decision to transition to a younger generation of political leaders in 2017. Along with high youth unemployment, the "disconnect" between the political elite and younger East Timorese remained a background factor in latent political tensions and gang violence. A youth parliament launched in January 2010 and the greater (though still inadequate) recognition of the contribution youth resistance leaders made during the Indonesian occupation are welcome signs of a renewed political engagement with younger East Timorese. The fact that the former chief of the armed forces, Taur Matan Ruak, was elected president in 2012 signaled a transition beyond the oldest members of the generation of '75, though a transition to those raised in the Indonesian era would wait until at least 2017.

A significant challenge, as noted above, lies in ongoing concerns over justice and the rule of law in Timor-Leste and, in particular, in reconciling popular desires for post-conflict justice with the government's political support for a reconciliation agenda. There are grave concerns that a culture of impunity for past crimes in Timor-Leste continues to undermine social harmony. Indicative of these concerns, in late 2009, the parliament finally discussed the Commission for Reception, Truth, and Reconciliation (Comissão de Acolhimento, Verdade e Reconciliação de Timor Leste, CAVR) report on deaths and human-rights abuses between 1974 and 1999, a full four years after formally receiving the final report in November 2005. Throughout 2010 and 2011, the parliament repeatedly delayed consideration of two proposed laws on victim reparations and the establishment of a National Institute of Memory, designed to "promote, facilitate, and monitor the implementation of the Recommendations" made by the CAVR and the bilateral Indonesia–Timor-Leste Truth and Friendship Commission. No progress had been made on related legislation as of mid-2012. In light of wider concerns over Timor-Leste's poorly functioning judicial system, in many, and perhaps most cases, local people in the districts had reverted to traditional justice systems, which allowed for greater accessibility, speed, and local acceptance in resolving local disputes. However, there were also concerns over the use of traditional justice, which remains vulnerable to abuses of power, often

---

[39] La'o Hamutuk, "Timor-Leste Is Going for Broke," March 19, 2012, http://laohamutuk.blogspot.com.au/2012/03/timor-leste-is-going-for-broke.html, accessed August 14, 2012.

[40] "Breaking News: Timorese Historical Leaders Hold Closed Meeting in Maubisse," *Tempo Semanal*, August, 22, 2010, http://temposemanaltimor.blogspot.com.au/2010/08/breaking-news-timorese-historical.html, accessed August 7, 2012.

reinforces traditional hierarchies, may be subject to inconsistent application, and threatens to reduce state legitimacy. How Timor-Leste reconciles the benefits and strengths of tradition with the requirements of a modern liberal citizenship-based polity will remain a key focus in the areas of local government and dispute resolution.

The multifaceted issues involved in democratic consolidation will also remain a key focus beyond the international state-building era. Timor-Leste fulfills many of the conventional criteria for fulfilling democracy's procedural requirements, such as free and fair regular elections, free association (including forming political parties and the right to protest), a relatively free media, and a moderately active civil society. Key state institutions, including the judiciary, police and defense forces, and other government departments, have all been set in place. The relatively peaceful conduct of the three polls in 2007 and 2012 and the degree of institutional capacity demonstrated by the National Electoral Commission (CNE), along with the goodwill of the international community, augured well for the future of East Timorese democracy.

However, the extent to which Timor-Leste conformed to substantive interpretations of democracy was debatable. While representatives were freely elected, the process for selecting candidates was relatively closed, and political leaders frequently appealed to voters on the basis of primordial loyalties rather than policy preferences. State institutions existed, but the notion of the separation of powers, for example, was compromised by occasional executive interference in judicial processes, a practical (as opposed to constitutional) confusion of roles between the president and the prime minister, the army's adoption of civil policing functions, an inadequate and poorly performing judiciary, a police force still known for its corruption and brutality, and low levels of institutional performance in the public service.

This state of affairs was perhaps not surprising, given the very low level of state development and capacity at the outset, and the observation that democratic institutions tend to function best, particularly in multiethnic societies, where accountability and rule of law are already established.[41] As such, while most of the procedural criteria for democratic process could be identified, as indeed they had been by the international community, each of these criteria required an often serious qualification, which, in the period leading up to the peacekeepers' withdrawal, much of the international community seemed willing to gloss over.

The party system, and its ongoing development and maturation, will also pose challenges. With the clear exception of FRETILIN, and the possible exception of CNRT, political parties in Timor-Leste are overly reliant on key personalities; many lack wide-ranging policy platforms, sufficient depth in their districts' organizations, coherent internal rules, and organizational discipline. In 2006, the return of "resistance era" tactics of political opposition, including the systematic use of unemployed youth and martial arts gangs as a political resource for warring factions of the elite, signaled a clear warning sign for the future of East Timorese democracy. With the assistance of the international community, and the wise restraint shown by senior East Timorese leaders, the 2007 national elections in Timor-Leste marked a turning point, with the emergence of a genuinely competitive multiparty system in

---

[41] P. Collier. *Wars, Guns, and Votes: Democracy in Dangerous Places* (New York, NY: Harper-Collins, 2009), pp. 173–76, 186.

Timor-Leste and, importantly, a viable and substantial parliamentary opposition party. Across the term of the 2007–12 parliament, the AMP government could be credited with resolving many of the entrenched grievances that had beset Timorese politics after the 2006 crisis. Conversely, FRETILIN received too little credit for its key role in fostering a culture of democratic parliamentary opposition in that period—even if its continuing rhetoric about "de facto" governments had been less than helpful in this regard. Rather than the heavily monitored 2012 election period itself, the months following the polls, and the subsequent withdrawal of state-building forces, would prove the most rigorous test of this newfound political stability, and Timor-Leste's capacity to function as a fully independent and sovereign state. The brief but disturbing outburst of violence that followed the announcement of a new governing coalition in July 2012 highlighted these concerns.

In the years leading up to the 2012 elections, East Timorese political leaders expressed increasingly pointed observations that Timor-Leste was a sovereign state that no longer needed or desired a high level of external involvement in its affairs. Public attacks on the UNDP, for example, reflected growing impatience within government circles for the departure of international state-building forces. But while the decade-long international presence generated some discontent in 2011 and 2012, Timor-Leste's experience as an emerging state was, in fact, far from unique in the context of the region, with the Solomon Islands approaching the ten-year anniversary of the regional state-building mission, RAMSI (Regional Assistance Mission to the Solomon Islands). In different contexts, the emerging states of New Caledonia and Bougainville were both in negotiated long-term transitions to potential independence, involving the progressive transfer of government powers, and referenda on full independence expected between 2014 and 2020. The southwest Pacific region was, in many respects, a hothouse of new experiments in international state-building, staged decolonization, regional autonomy, and transitions to full independence. Frequently judged in comparison with well-established Southeast Asian states and found wanting, Timor-Leste's performance, relative to more suitable comparisons with emerging Melanesian states, was favorable. Buttressed by its oil and gas revenues, and with a formidable history of determined struggle for independence, Timor-Leste has grounds for cautious optimism about its future.

ADAT AND THE NATION-STATE: OPPOSITION AND SYNTHESIS IN TWO POLITICAL CULTURES

David Hicks

This notice, which appeared in *Embassy News*, was issued from the Embassy of the United States in Timor-Leste, dated April 23, 2010, accompanied by a photograph of United States Ambassador Ambassador Hans Klemm helping with the preparation of a presumably related ritual:

> Sacred House Inaugurated in Hatobuilico
>
> ... *Uma luliks* in Oecussi, Bobonaro, and Lautem are part of the same cultural preservation project. The total cost is $32,000.
>
> *Uma luliks* are the spiritual center of communities throughout Timor-Leste. Each village uses its *uma lulik* as a gathering place for traditional rituals and as a spiritual resting place for the village ancestors. The United States provides financial support for *uma lulik* preservation out of respect for the roots of Timorese national and cultural identity. [1]

Among the problems facing post-colonial states is that of establishing and maintaining coherence between the central government and centrifugal forces that might threaten their sovereignty. The latter commonly involves the issue of national loyalty versus local loyalties and central government versus local governments, a polarity that may impede the country attaining an effective measure of national coherence. A case in point is that of the post-colonial Democratic Republic of Timor-Leste where, even after eight years of independence, the majority of Timorese (especially the less educated) in the *sukus* (small communities made up of a varying

---

[1] "Sacred House Inaugurated in Hatobuilico," *Embassy News*, April 23, 2010, available at http://timor-leste.usembassy.gov/news-events/press-releases-2010/sacred-house-inaugurated-in-hatobuilico-april-23-2010.html, accessed June 5, 2012.

numbers of villages) identify themselves more as residents of those local communities than as citizens of the state. The central argument in this paper is that this failure to transform villagers into citizens indicates the existence of two political cultures of such disparate character that they militate against the ambitions of Timor-Leste's government and the United Nations to create an integrated national identity. One model, based on Western values of governance and jurisprudence, is that of the nation-state. The other is that of the *adat* and comprises indigenous values. Having identified the existence of these two polities and shown their disjunctive relationship, I will argue in this paper that a synthesis is necessary if the mass of the Timorese population is to be transformed from villagers into citizens. I conclude by arguing that although each model possesses distinctive politico-cultural traits that might, at first, appear irreconcilable, should the government and United Nations modify this Western model by accommodating local *adat,* thus creating a syncretic single political culture, Timor-Leste would be given more opportunity than it presently has to evolve into a unified nation-state.[2]

Before describing Timor-Leste's two political cultures some consideration of certain definitions—more particularly, an explanation of such categories as "nation," "state," "nation-state," "civil society," and "citizen"—is appropriate. The terms "nation," "state," and "nation-state" are, of course, open to interminable semantic refinements, but the definitions proposed by Kingsbury reduce the possibility of ambiguity, and I shall adopt them in the discussion that follows. The term "nation," therefore will be understood to refer to "a group of people who regard themselves as possessing an aggregate political identity, most often based on a shared language (means of conceptualization) and other fundamental cultural signifiers."[3] A "state," on the other hand, is "the organizational territory under a political authority and which can (or can attempt to) claim or compel the compliance of its citizens to its laws." Finally, the combinatory category of nation-state implies "a nation of people who claim the state as their collective territorial and institutional expression (or, less plausibly, as an administrative territory that claims a unity of the people within its boundaries)."[4]

---

[2] The contemporary importance of this theme is attested to by the collection edited by David Mearns, which is full of pertinent insights relevant to the present article; see: David Mearns, ed., *Democratic Governance: Reconciling the Local and the National* (Darwin: Charles Darwin University Press, 2008). Outside of the particular region of Timor-Leste, the "Third World" abounds with examples of post-colonial nation-states, derived from the Western post-treaty of Westphalia (1848) concept of "nation-state," that find themselves vitiated by the kind of political strains inherent in relations between "tradition" and "the modern." In the case of Africa, for example, Basil Davidson, in his *The Black Man's Burden: Africa and the Curse of the Nation-State* (New York, NY: Times Books/Random House, 1992), argues that the willingness of African governments to embrace the Western notion of the nation-state has been a prime factor in impoverishing the lives of citizens. Another scholar, among others who have sounded skeptical notes, is Eric Hobsbawm, whose *Nations and Nationalism since 1780: Programme, Myth, Reality* (Cambridge: Press Syndicate of the University of Cambridge, 1990) casts a similarly skeptical eye. And, of course, in Benedict Anderson's definition, a "nation" was merely an imaginary political community. Benedict Anderson, *Imagined Communities: Reflections on the Origin and Spread of Nationalism*, revised and extended edition (London: Verso, 1991).

[3] Included among these cultural signifiers are common values, history, institutions, and myths. Damien Kingsbury, *The Politics of Indonesia*, 3rd ed. (Oxford: Oxford University Press, 2005), p. 88.

[4] Ibid., p. vi.

THE POLITICAL CULTURE OF THE *ADAT*

Despite the lapse of thirty-six years during which the Timorese people have been subjected to relentless pressures to change their values, villagers with whom I talked, during the course of several periods of research since 2002,[5] appear to have only a shallow understanding of the verbal currency of the so-called "international community" ("democracy," "equality," "civil society," "citizenship," and so forth), and only a vague notion of what citizenship in a nation-state might mean.[6] On the other hand, they are thoroughly cognizant of what Émile Durkheim called the *"réprésentations collectives"* (collective representations)[7] that comprise their indigenous culture—the Timorese refer to it as their *adat*, or *lisan*, of which each *suku* possesses its own.[8] The former is a Malay term and the latter is its counterpart in the Tetum language. *Adat* is usually glossed as "customary law" but is actually considerably wider in its connotations: it includes rules that govern the inheritance of property, spouse eligibility, ritual etiquette, taboo observance (*tara bandu*), land-ownership, political authority, sanctions incurred when the *adat* is breached, interpretations of the past, oral literature, and cosmology. During my first period of research in what was then known as "Portuguese Timor," in 1966–67,[9] I cannot recall

---

[5] Specifically, in 2005, 2007, and 2009.

[6] The confusion also extends to social scientists, as we see by their different perspectives on such concepts as "citizen" and "civil society"; see, for example, Jean L. Cohen and Andrew Arato, *Civil Society and Political Theory* (Cambridge, MA: MIT Press, 1992); Jean Comaroff and John Comaroff, "Law and Disorder in the Postcolony," *Social Anthropology* 15,2 (2007): 133–52; Marlies Glasius et al., *Exploring Civil Society: Political and Cultural Contexts* (London: Routledge, 2004); John A. Hall and Frank Trentman, *Civil Society: A Reader in History, Theory, and Global Politics* (New York, NY: Palgrave, 2005); Mikael Karlström, "Civil Society and Its Presuppositions: Lessons from Uganda," in *Civil Society and the Political Imagination in Africa: Critical Perspectives,* ed. Jean Comaroff and John Comaroff (Chicago, IL: University of Chicago Press, 1999), pp. 104–23; Michael Mann, "Nation-States in Europe and Other Continents: Diversifying, Developing, Not Dying," *Daedalus* 122,2 (1993): 115–40; Adam B. Seligman, *The Idea of Civil Society* (New York, NY: The Free Press, 1992); and Gary Wilder, "Practicing Citizenship in Imperial Paris," in *Civil Society and the Political Imagination in Africa,* ed. Comaroff and Comaroff, pp. 44–71.

[7] That is, the corpus of ideas, notions, concepts, values, and institutions held or adhered to in common by members of society.

[8] One should perhaps use the word *adat* in the plural since each *suku* in Timor-Leste has its own *adat*. However, conventional usage justifies the use of the singular, and common usage is fortified by the fact that virtually all the various *adats* have a great deal in common. Something like a single, generic *adat* is very easily imagined and I do so here. There are 442 *sukus* in Timor-Leste according to the *Report of the Secretary-General on the United Nations Integrated Mission in Timor-Leste,* September 24, 2009, to January 20, 2010, p. 1. These are spread over thirteen districts and sixty-seven subdistricts. See Frédéric Durand, *Timor Lorosa'e Pays Au Carrefour de l'Asie et Du Pacifique Un Atlas Géo-Historique* (Bangkok: Press Universitaires de Marne-la-Vallée, IRASEC [Institut de Recherche sur l'Asia du Sud-Est Contemporaine], 2002): 28.

[9] The fieldwork on which this paper is based was carried out over the course of six visits I made to East Timor, my most recent occurring in 2009. My original research in 1966–67 was funded by the London Committee of the London-Cornell Project for East and South East Asian Studies, which was supported jointly by the Carnegie Corporation of New York and the Nuffield Foundation. Subsequent field research was funded by the American Philosophical Society and the J. William Fulbright Foreign Scholarship Board. I also thank the State University of New York for granting me a sabbatical (2004–05) and a research leave (2007)

ever having heard the word *adat* used, and it appears to have become widely applied only after the 1975 invasion by the army of Indonesia. Since then, however, the term has gained widespread popularity, and because it is also used throughout the Indonesian archipelago, I shall use it here instead of *lisan*. Although the *adat* may be likened to a body of "tradition," the term must be handled with some discretion since what might be understood to be "tradition" or "traditional" may actually include not only customs surviving from a more distant past but also alien mores from outside that have only recently been assimilated into the *adat*.[10] Timorese "traditional" values, therefore, cannot ipso facto be assumed to provide a window through which the past may be glimpsed, and even though village folk may insist that their customs were instituted in mythological times by their ancestors (*mate bein*), their historical source may, in reality, be external to their culture. This could hardly be otherwise, since Europeans have involved themselves in Timorese cultures since the sixteenth century. That figure known as the *liurai*, or "king," for instance, might seem to qualify as an exemplary instance of a traditional political category but is actually a synthesis of Portuguese innovation and indigenous tradition. The process whereby indigenous social and political categories assume a modified meaning is nothing new, therefore, and, as we shall see, is a phenomenon that continues today. As the epigraph for this article suggests, the traditional ritual house, the *uma lulik*, for instance, has now become engaged as part of the political dialogue and so has taken on a political character. Nor is it the only example of this phenomenon in contemporary Timor-Leste. The *barlaque*, a social institution involving marriage, has come to be looked upon by many non-governmental organizations (NGO) as implicated in the depreciation of women and, as such, has assumed the connotations of a political instrument.

Social Rank

Although the *adat*—as it has always done—is undergoing modification, one pervasive characteristic that still exerts force is the concept of inequality. In Timor-Leste inequality, which finds expression in the level of prestige an individual is accorded, is a consequence of his or her social status. Although an individual's social status can be improved by personal achievement, the basis of social status is rank, gender, and age. A person's right to membership in a particular rank descends to him or her through either the father (patrilineal descent) or the mother (matrilineal descent),[11] the most important right being eligibility for membership in a corporate group of a kind known in social anthropology as a "descent group," of which there

during which I carried out my fieldwork. I also wish to extend my gratitude to the persons who helped me in a multitude of different ways in Timor-Leste while I was collecting the information presented here: Katherine S. Hunter, Rod Nixon, Karen Polglaze, José A. Fernandes Texeira, Nicol Seibel, Maria Rosa Biddlecombe (*née* Maria Rosa da Costa Soares), José Henriques Pereira, Rosa Maria Pereira, Luís da Costa Soares, and Teresa da Luz Simões Soares.

[10] Cf. Eric Hobsbawm and Terence Ranger, eds., *The Invention of Tradition* (Cambridge and New York, NY: Cambridge University Press, 1992).

[11] Of the sixteen or so ethnic groups in Timor-Leste, all but one can be confirmed as subscribing to a regime of patrilineal descent, the Tetum-speaking peoples in Cova Lima and southern Manufahi and Manatuto, the subdistrict of Lacluta (Viqueque district), and a single *suku* (Luca) in Viqueque subdistrict. Others, however, may exist.

are several forms. The most inclusive form of descent group is the clan (or "house"), which is usually segmented into smaller units of kinship known as "sub-clans," or "lineages," consisting of extended families or nuclear families. Besides eligibility for clan membership, the bundle of rights a person inherits through either "patri-line" or "matri-line" also includes (in the case of a man) eligibility for any formal office that group controls, for example, head of clan, lineage, or sub-lineage. In a patrilineal system, the eldest son is considered the leading candidate for whatever official position his deceased father might have occupied. In a matrilineal system, he is the leading candidate for such a position upon the death of a mother's brother.[12] Such ascriptions, though, are qualified by considerations that include executive capability and moral character, and male elders (*katuas*) of the group will ignore the hereditary claims of a son they deem unsuitable in favor of a more capable man from the deceased's clan. Post-marital residence after a man marries is also a factor of fundamental importance. Residence for the husband after marriage near the father's house (patrilocal residence) accompanies patrilineal descent, while residence near that of the wife's father (uxorilocal residence) accompanies matrilineal descent. Because of the rights accruing to the patrilineal descent group (or "patri-group") as the result of the marriage of one of its male members—that is, control of children and the right of the husband to remain near his father—bridewealth (or brideprice, i.e., the prestations the bridegroom's group gives to that of the bride) must be given as compensation to the wife's patrigroup. In matrilineal descent, since the ‚children of the marriage belong to the wife's matrilineal descent group (or "matrigroup") and after marriage the husband must reside near his father-in-law, either no bridewealth is given or else the amount will be significantly smaller. However, as I describe below, marriage under the rules of the *barlaque* has entailments that far exceed the personal consequences of a union between two individuals and the giving of bridewealth.

There are three social ranks in contemporary Timor-Leste arranged in a hierarchy that, in descending order of prestige, consists of the *liurai* rank ("royalty"), *dato* rank ("aristocrats"), and *ema reino* rank ("commoners"). Membership in a rank is ascribed by descent, but social status is not inflexibly decided by rank since education, occupation, and wealth make it possible for someone of a lower rank to elevate his or her status. A *dato* or *ema reino* able to converse in Portuguese or influential in church matters would likely command greater respect than an impoverished person from the *liurai* rank of inferior education.

The most important figure in *adat* politics is the aforementioned *liurai*,[13] a category not to be confounded—though typically it is—with the category of *chefe de suku*, an administrative officer under the Portuguese and now under the government of Timor-Leste. In the case of a particular *suku*, it may be that the *chefe de suku* is, in fact, a *liurai*, but he may equally well be a *dato*. When the Portuguese established themselves in Timor in the sixteenth century, the eastern half of the island—roughly

---

[12] In a matrilineal system, a person belongs to his or her mother's clan and is bound by its precepts. But although property (tangible and intangible) descends down the female line, control over it remains in male hands, and so, in practice, a man inherits from his mother's brother and upon death property discharges to his sister's son.

[13] The term applies to the rank itself, to families within that rank, and also to this political figure. As we shall see, it also has evolved another element and, so, has become even more ambiguous. There is a hierarchy of "authentic" *liurai families* within the rank of *liurai*, such that certain *liurai* families have more prestige.

today's Timor-Leste, excluding Oe-Cussi—was covered by a patchwork of territorial units called *rai*,[14] at the head of which was a figure known as the *liurai*, a term the Portuguese translated as *rei* ("king") and whose territories they called *reinos* ("kingdoms"). These kingdoms were composed of smaller territorial units called *sukus*, which also had heads. After 1912, when the Portuguese crushed what proved to be the final rebellion of the kings, they abolished virtually every kingdom, retained the *sukus*, which they converted into administrative units for the purpose of governing the colony, and installed loyal *liurais* as the chiefs of the *sukus* (*chefes de suku*). The indigenous heads of these *sukus* were completely by-passed. They continued to function, however, in at least some *sukus*. The *suku* of Caraubalo in the subdistrict (*posto*) of Viqueque district (*concelho*) today, for instance, still retains its indigenous polity, which is that of a diarchy consisting of a figure called the *makair fukun* and another called the *dato ua'in*.[15] There were, of course, considerably more *sukus* than there had been kingdoms, and so the Portuguese recruited men who had not been *liurais*, that is, men from *dato* families. In this reorganization of the colonial system of administration, all *chefes de suku*[16]—whether of *liurai* or *dato* rank—were entitled to be known by the honorific *liurai*.[17] Thus, in Portuguese Timor, and later in Timor-Timur,[18] two categories of "*liurai*" came to exist and occupy the office of *suku* chief: men from *liurai* families and men from *dato* families. In Timor-Leste the same distinction continues.

Under the Portuguese administration, even the most powerful *liurai*/*chefe de suku* never exercised autocratic power,[19] as some observers have imagined,[20] and only with the support of the local elders (*katuas*) could a *liurai* effectively administer his *suku*. In Caraubalo *suku*, at least, the *liurai* worked closely with the *makair fukun* and *dato ua'in* both informally and in regular sessions of the indigenous *suku* council/court, though (unlike today's *suku* council) the *liurai* was not a member of it.[21] Throughout the Portuguese period, the *makair fukun* and *dato ua'in* constituted

---

[14] Frédéric Durand's map of the Timorese kingdoms at the end of the nineteenth century puts the number at forty-four for Portuguese Timor. See Durand, *Timor Lorosa'e*, p. 55.

[15] David Hicks, *Tetum Ghosts and Kin: Fertility and Gender in East Timor* (Prospect Heights, IL: Waveland Press, 2004), p. 15.

[16] The political context of Timor-Leste differs in various significant particulars from those of the post-colonial nations analysed by Africanists, but the bureaucratization of the Timorese chiefs under the successive colonial administrations of Portugal and Indonesia was similar to that described for the aforementioned Bantu of Uganda by Lloyd A. Fallers, *A Bantu Bureaucracy* (Chicago, IL: University of Chicago Press, 1956).

[17] It is unclear whether any *ema reino* was appointed under the Portuguese administration. I suspect this would have been rare.

[18] Under the Indonesian administration, the dual political personality of the *sukus* became more complicated since only governmental *apparatchiks* were eligible to occupy the office of "*liurai*" or *chefe de suku*.

[19] Unless otherwise noted, from this point on the terms "*liurai*" and "*chefe de suku*" are used interchangeably.

[20] Certain FRETILIN leaders in 1974–75, and foreign commentators, it might be noted, wrongly claimed that the powers wielded by *liurais*/*chefes de suku* were of an autocratic nature. With relatively few exceptions, writers who have discussed *liurais* and *chefes de suku* have not realized the difference between these two sociopolitical categories.

[21] Married women (*feriks*) did not usually attend the council/court meetings, which were held about once a month; they were expected to provide input to the *macair fukun*, *dato ua'in*, and *katuas* though their husbands.

the indigenous leadership of the *suku* since the chief was a full-fledged officer in the colonial bureaucracy from which the *makair fukun* and *dato ua'in* were excluded. The Viqueque administrator (*administrador*) himself probably did not know the offices existed. The chief, on the other hand, depended on the *makair fukun* and *dato ua'in* to see that the weekly orders he received from the administrator were carried out in the seven villages (*povoações*)[22] of Caraubalo *suku*. In addition to acting as enablers for the *liurai*, the *makair fukun* and *dato ua'in* functioned as the day-to-day grassroots managers of the *suku*, most visibly in heading the *suku* council/court, the *adat* institution that has today been supplanted by a Western-style council/court. There was some measure of indigenous democracy involved in the selection of a chief, in that married men elected the chief, but their choice was subject to endorsement by the colonial authorities for whom loyalty to the administration was a sine qua non, and the administration could discharge an incompetent or unpopular *chefe de suku*. The *suku* council also functioned as a court of law through which it officially administered the *adat*, the *macair fukun*, *dato ua'in*, and *katuas*, mediating between the contending parties and determining what sanctions to evoke if the *adat* were breached.

This *adat* model of mediation continues to claim the adherence of villagers,[23] and, as in Indonesian villages, reciprocity is a key element of *adat*, which means that something approaching the *status quo* that existed prior to an offense must be sought through mediation.[24] This is accomplished through compensation being made to the injured parties. The restoration of the status quo necessitates using the services, not of an unknown (to the community) individual delivering judgment inflected by notions of guilt, intent, or innocence, but of a mediator possessing personal knowledge of the individuals concerned and fully aware of the social context in which the offence was committed, and whose function it is to negotiate a mutually acceptable settlement. The foreign codes of jurisprudence offer, instead, an abstract conception of justice administered by agents who have no stake in the community nor interest in communal harmony, a drawback that, in part, helps account for the failure of criminal laws to have as much compelling authority as the government and United Nations expect.[25] This disconnect between the national government and the *sukus* is particularly striking with hot-button issues like "domestic violence," "sexual abuse," and rape, which obsess the United Nations and their fellow agencies.[26] With the backing of the world body, the government has enacted laws designed to mete out Western sanctions to men guilty of such offenses, and imprisonment is regarded as fitting punishment. While satisfying foreigners' (foreigner is *malai* in the local language) sense of justice, this sanction fails to reconcile the parties involved or deliver compensation to the injured party. Worse, from the wife's perspective, is that

---

[22] Today, villages are known as *aldeias*.

[23] Murder, sedition, and other offenses classified by the colonial authorities were dealt with by the administration.

[24] Cf. James Siegel, *Naming the Witch* (Stanford, CA: Stanford University Press, 2006), pp. 193–203.

[25] See *Report of the Secretary-General on the United Nations Integrated Mission in Timor-Leste (for the period from 24 September 2009 to 20 January 2010, S/2010/85)* (New York, NY: United Nations, 2010), 41 pp.

[26] I enclose the terms "domestic violence" and "sexual abuse" within quotation marks to signal their imprecision as verbal tools appropriate for scholarly analysis.

when a socially indifferent authority commits her husband to jail, she loses her provider. A woman in this position sees herself as doubly abused: firstly, by her husband and, secondly, by the *malai's* notion of what constitutes justice. With *adat* justice, her husband would remain working his fields, and she would receive some material compensation, in the form of money, a pig, or suchlike, in an arrangement negotiated between her husband's family and her father's family. True, the wife may receive only part of the compensation, and advocates for Western-style gender equality find plenty of fodder here for criticizing a system in which the injury to the victim is merged into a more communal offense against her family; but whether this arrangement finds favor with the *malais* or not, that is how gender operates in terms rural Timorese understand.

Gender

Some *adats* provide a prominent role in public ritual for women,[27] but women's primary role lies in the private, domestic realm rather than in the public, political sphere. Womanhood is seen as defined in terms of wife and mother, and the *barlaque* is the prime vehicle through which gender values manifest themselves in political, symbolic, economic, and ritual dimensions and reveal most clearly how the Timorese define the concept of *feto* ("womanhood"; "woman"). Just as the *uma lulik* seems to be on the way to attaining iconic status as a material symbol of a modern Timor-Leste, as explained later, so does the *barlaque* remain emblematic of traditional Timor-Leste. Paradoxically, in light of its centrality in Timorese culture, the *barlaque* is misunderstood by most *malais* and even by some educated Timorese. For both, its sole meaning lies in marriage.[28] This, however, is far from being true.

In the *barlaque's* most generic form, it involves the bridegroom's descent group, or sometimes only his family, giving bridewealth (*folin*) to his bride's descent group in exchange for a set of counter-prestations. The wife-takers give horses, buffaloes, goats, chickens, the golden pectoral plates worn by men, ancient war swords, and money. Their wife-givers counter these prestations with gifts of cloth, pigs, rice, the coral necklaces worn by women, and the all-important gift of the bride herself. Nor is the affinal relationship between wife-giver and wife-taker symbolically expressed only at the wedding itself. When the families celebrate births and deaths, each party contributes food for their communal meal consistent with the species of animal they exchanged at marriage—the wife-takers bringing buffalo and goat meat, as well as chickens, while their wife-givers bring pork. Educated Timorese and *malai* fault the *barlaque* on the grounds that it supposedly demeans the status of women, and they cast it as an institution for "buying a wife." But although the term *folin* means "price"

---

[27] Hicks, *Tetum Ghosts and Kin*.

[28] Typical is the comment by Regina Varolli who, in composing a list of undesirables in the lives of Timorese women (25 percent literacy, mothers averaging seven children each, and "only" 30 percent having access to birth control), remarks with evident disapproval, "Also in East Timor, traditional dowries, or 'bride prices,' remain common"; see Regina Varolli, "U.N. Scrutinizes Women's Rights in East Timor," *Women's eNews*, September 16, 2009: 1. She appears to assume dowries and brideprice are the same, whereas, the dowry is the money or property the bride's family gives to that of the husband. While the prestations given by Timorese wife-givers to their wife-takers might be regarded as a dowry, it would appear unlikely Varolli has "groom-price" in mind, dealing as she does with women's rights and not men's rights.

and "value," and an alternative term for marriage is *hafolin* (*halo* ["to make"] + *foli* [*n*]), "to make the price," the bridewealth is only one of a number of prestations exchanged. The *barlaque* also includes political, ritual, and economic obligations that bind the two alliance parties in an enduring relationship, which before 1912 included mutual support in war.[29] As an encompassing system of practices and values, the *barlaque* is a microcosm of Timor-Leste's most fundamental ideas about gender, reciprocity, politics, economics, myth, and ritual, and the *barlaque* joins those staple anthropological institutions, the *potlatch* of the Indians of the Northwest Pacific and the *kula* of the Trobriand Archipelago, as an exemplary instance of what the sociologist Marcel Mauss called a "total social phenomenon." Far from diminishing womanhood, therefore, the *barlaque* demonstrates the preeminent value placed on the concept of *feto* by empowering women to function as exclusive agents through which descent groups exchange economic resources, while fertility and life are transferred from their fathers' groups to their husbands' groups. The *barlaque* thereby installs womanhood at the heart of biological and social life, since only through their reproductive powers can life be transmitted to the husbands' next generation. The Kemak of Marobo (Ermera district)[30] say that life "flows" from wife-givers to wife-takers, and expand this image in the expression "the flow of life," a trope they put into action every time a *barlaque* marriage, birth, or death is celebrated.[31]

Age

Age under the *adat* assigns social status as definitively as do rank and gender, with older persons accorded greater respect. This hierarchy of age is observed to advantage within the family, in which the eldest son acts as surrogate father in the absence of the head of household and exercises executive and disciplinary authority over his siblings. While generally evoked as the repository of the highest moral values, especially as they involve respect and cooperation, the Timorese family is, in reality, a fairly volatile social unit, within which destructive forces hinging on the authority of age work themselves out. Fathers and older brothers at times unduly exploit younger members of their families, and the *adat* justifies this exploitation, since the *adat* requires adult sons to help fathers and brothers to help one another in such tasks as house-building, repairing houses, and contributing to a brother's bridewealth. When these prescriptions are disregarded, mutual recriminations provoke ill will all round. Because patrilocal residence results in adult brothers residing in close proximity after marriage, opportunities for confrontations occur frequently, and a common motif in village histories depicts a community

---

[29] This was true among the Atoni, of Indonesian Timor: "In the case of war the bride-receiving ruler could marshal the support of his bride-giver"; see H. G. Schulte Nordholt, *The Political System of the Atoni of Timor*, trans. M. J. L. van Yperen (Verhandelingen van het Koninklijk Instituut voor Taal-, Land- en Volkenkunde, 60) (The Hague: Martinus Nijhoff, 1971), p. 388.

[30] Brigitte Clamagirand, "The Social Organization of the *Ema* of Timor," in *The Flow of Life: Essays on Eastern Indonesia*, ed. James J. Fox (Cambridge, MA: Harvard University Press, 1980), p. 145.

[31] In an interview with a man from Mamulak village (Caraubalo *suku*), who learned I had not given bridewealth for my wife, I was informed—with politeness—that Timorese did not copulate like animals. Unlike *malais*, they gave bridewealth.

disintegrating following quarrels between brothers or cousins on the paternal side. In these histories, a typical cause is failure to lend assistance when demanded.

THE POLITICAL CULTURE OF THE NATION-STATE

The political culture of the nation-state has evolved from Timor-Leste's Constitution, put into effect, and the Constitution's roots are embedded, not in Timorese culture as manifested through local *adats*, but in Western political thought. Regardless of its foreign origins, this is the only form of polity the Timor-Leste government and United Nations recognize as legitimate for a nation-state and, accordingly, impose on the *sukus* in their drive to build a nation and reconstitute villagers as citizens. Understandably, therefore, not all Timorese are satisfied with the choice that has been made, and among their number are educated young people who can articulate their dissatisfactions in public forums. One of the most articulate is José "Josh" Trindade,[32] who has recently reminded those who, it might be thought, need to be reminded that "the process of nation-state formation led by a few elite from the East Timorese diaspora and the UN relied heavily on elements of foreign cultures and values and undermined the cultural identity of the East Timorese." The "elite," as Trindade terms them, have indubitably achieved a certain degree of success in interjecting their values into the cultural traditions of the population, but their achievements have created a disjunction between what the sociologist Edward Shils[33] famously distinguished as the "center" and the "periphery,"[34]—the center being the national government and the periphery being the *sukus*. It might be worth remarking that the Shils model has its limitations for Timor-Leste, not least being the fact that Timorese of the periphery by no means generally look to the center for their values.

When Timor-Leste attained independence in May 2002, the new nation-state owed its emerging polity to the United Nations, which, acting through the United Nations Transitional Administration in East Timor (UNTAET), had commenced laying the foundations of a civil society in October 1999. The United Nations based its efforts on the values of a Western notion of democracy,[35] roughly corresponding to Max Weber's "legal authority system,"[36] that is, a system of "rationality-focused" legal institutions. This system Weber contrasted with his "traditional authority system," that is, a system founded in "irrational" ancestral sanctions,[37] which, in

---

[32] José Trindade, "Reconciling Conflicting Paradigms: An East Timorese Vision of the Ideal State," in *Democratic Governance: Reconciling the Local and the National*, ed. David Mearns (Darwin: Charles Darwin University Press, 2008), p. 165.

[33] Edward Shils, *Center and Periphery: Essays in Macrosociology, Selected Papers of Edward Shils* (Chicago, IL : University of Chicago Press, 1961, 1975), pp. 3–16.

[34] David Hicks, "Community and Nation-State in East Timor: A View from the Periphery," *Anthropology Today* 23,1 (2007): 13–16. Compare the use Trindade makes of the notion of the center in his discussion of reconciling paradigms; see Trindade, "Reconciling Conflicting Paradigms," pp. 160–88.

[35] United Nations, *The United Nations and East Timor: Self-Determination through Popular Consultation* (New York, NY: UN Department of Public Information, 2000), pp. 56–60.

[36] Max Weber, *Economy and Society, Vol. 1*, ed. Guenther Roth and Claus Wittich (Berkeley, CA: University of California Press, 1978), p. 227.

[37] I owe this observation to Rod Nixon, the first scholar, to my knowledge, to see the applicability of Weber's binary model for Timor-Leste. It is one of a number of acute insights

Timor-Leste, is the *adat*. Since Weber's "traditional authority system" is typical of local polities characteristically occurring at the margins of the wider national polity, whereas his "legal authority system" occurs at the center of the national polity, his two models, in this respect, are structurally coterminous with Shils's "center/periphery" paradigm. The contrast between the two systems is nowhere more apparent than in governance and jurisprudence, where the contrast appears to advantage in the aforementioned *suku* council/court, an invention of the government and United Nations. Article 3 of the 2004 law on "the Election of *Suco* Chiefs and *Suco* Councils" sets forth the protocols under which *sukus* are to be governed and local justice administered,[38] according to the following terms:

> 1. A *suco* council shall be composed of the *suco* chief, the chiefs of all villages comprising the *suco*, and the following members:
> a. two women [*representante feto*];
> b. one young person from each gender group [*juventude feto; juventude mane*];
> c. one elder from the *suco*.
> 2. For the purposes of this law, a young person is an individual aged between 17 and 35 on the polling day, and an elder is an individual aged over 50 years on the polling day or an individual recognized by his or her community as a *lian nain*.

Under these protocols, *suku* chiefs are elected by popular vote and not, as under the *adat*, by hereditary succession, and women become eligible for election.[39] With the implementation of this system, one consequence has been the emergence of two political figures who provide villagers with alternative sources of authority. One is someone who might be called the "legal authority" (*suku* chief); the other, the "traditional authority" (*liurai*). The claims of *adat* can be so compelling that even those villagers who voted for the former may be more inclined to respect the latter and turn to him when they need advice or require assistance. In part, this results from the fruits of familiarity. Villagers know what they can expect from their *adat* leader, whereas, the workaday functions of the democratically elected incumbent are still—despite much public proselytizing by the agencies—only vaguely apprehended. Villagers profess not to understand what the new-style *suku* chief is supposed to do and how they are expected to relate to him. Chiefs (and council members, for that matter) have also been perplexed even as their job descriptions are still being fleshed out. Before the *suku* elections in Cova Lima district in 2009, there was a "public consultation" carried out in the subdistrict of Suai by the National Parliament Committee A "to explain the [latest] draft law, clarify areas of

---

into the problems associated with the operation of two systems of governance in Timor-Leste. See Rod Nixon, *Justice and Governance in East Timor: Indigenous Approaches and the "New Subsistence State"* (Abington, Oxford, and New York, NY: Routledge, 2012), pp. 12–13.

[38] Democratic Republic of Timor-Leste National Parliament (2004) Law, "… on the Election of Suco Chiefs and Suco Councils," see http://www.unmit.org/legal/RDTL-Law/RDTL-Laws/Law-2004-2.pdf, accessed July 3, 2012.

[39] At least one woman has been elected under the new order, in Taroman, in the subdistrict of Fatululik (Cova Lima district), where Luisa Guterres is currently chief. Interestingly, this is a matrilineal region.

confusion and gather public opinion."[40] This took place *seven years* after independence, but it was nevertheless considered necessary to inform the *sukus* about "the responsibilities of the village chiefs," and although the meeting was attended by the subdistrict administrator, village chiefs, political party leaders, and NGOs, it seems *suku* folk were sparse on the ground. One may reasonably assume they remain as ignorant or unconcerned about the latest government and United Nations initiative as they were of previous initiatives. Uncertainties of this sort only add to the sense of alienation experienced by people wary of national directives they see as designed to seduce them from an *adat* in which women and young men have less status in public matters and cannot attain the position of village chief, become heads of descent groups or hamlets, or lead discussions in *suku* council meetings. The new order has radicalized their status: they now take their seats at the heart of *suku* authority.[41]

Alienation between the two conceptualizations of governance is again evident in the domain of language, where the government and the United Nations have found themselves creating novel political categories when nothing comparable to suit their purpose exists in traditional *suku* polity, and redefining established categories in some cases where an accepted nomenclature already exists. As the Portuguese did with the category *liurai*, so have the government and United Nations done with the category *lia na'in*. In Timorese culture, the *lia a na'in* is a "teller of tales," a sort of bard, who besides publicly reciting myths, legends, and verses of all kinds to a *suku* audience, also possesses detailed knowledge of his *suku's* history and *adat*. As its human repository, a *lia na'in* would be consulted by the *liurai* when the latter wanted advice about some finer points of the *adat*, but today the *lia na'in* is no longer an informal storyteller/advisor but an elected officer of a newly invented council/court. The process of linguistic "massaging," undertaken in order to bring *suku* polity into line with the needs of a modern nation-state, has also resulted in the discarding of Tetum terms in favor of Portuguese. In the wording of Article 3, *juventude* (youth; young person), qualified where appropriate by the terms *mane* (male; man) and *feto* (female; woman), substitutes for the Tetum term *labarik*, because *labarik* (also qualified by *mane* and *feto*) can mean lad, boy, unmarried male, youth, girl, or unmarried female—an array of referents lacking the privileged Western connotations of the term "youth," which the author's language in Article 3 apparently wished to convey.

In this manner, *suku* categories of political thought are in the process of being undermined as part of a policy designed to substitute international values (democracy, social equality, gender equality, and age equality) for *suku* values

---

[40] United Nations Integrated Mission in Timor-Leste (UNMIT), *Baseline Study on Sexual and Gender-Based Violence in Covalima and Bobonaro Districts*, released August 13, 2009, available at http://easttimorlegal.blogspot.com/2009/08/unmit-baseline-study-on-sexual-and.html, last accessed May 29, 2012.

[41] This is also true of another United Nations/Timor-Leste national government invention, the Polícia Nacional de Timor-Leste (PNTL), which includes "male youth," of course, but also "female youth." Andrea Molnar has reported that in Atsabe subdistrict (Ermera district), "where age status matters significantly in local cultural context," the "young officers do not have much status or the confidence of the population to solve problems." She adds that "there were many unkindly comments made about the young police officers by the locals ... particularly the female officers." See Andrea K. Molnar, "An Anthropological Study of Atsabe Perceptions of Kolimau 2000: A New East Timorese Religious Cult or Internal Security Problem?" *Anthropos* 99 (2004): 377.

(heredity, patriarchy, and control by senior men).[42] Accordingly, the former *suku* council/court, formerly entrenched in its masculine, elder, exclusivity, has now been displaced in favor of an institution of national government that privileges adult women, male youth, and female youth. Up to a point, the government and United Nations have therefore succeeded in reforming the political culture, and one might claim that, since villagers voted, thereby apparently engaging in the spirit of things, these new values have really taken hold. But ethnographic evidence, as well as agency reports, attest to peoples' continuing non-compliance with governmental laws and regulations, and one might wonder, why should this be so? I suggest that people's defiance may be a product, not so much of an active antipathy toward *malai* notions, as such, or even simple resentment of having foreign ideas injected into their collective representations, but of an uncertainty about what these foreign ideas mean and what relevance they have in people's lives. Reports document how misunderstandings and ignorance of these values persist despite attempts by NGOs' people to propagate them. A typical example is that by the HAK Association,[43] which remarked in a tone of apparent puzzlement:

> Ironically [*sic*], when it commemorated the international day for "Rural Women" [October 15], the Government organized a concert in Dili and invited an Indonesia band "Tri Macam" [the commemoration named for Rural Women, but women in rural areas didn't know or have any feelings about it].

A recent United Nations Integrated Mission in Timor-Leste (UNMIT) report shows how difficult it is for the gender lobby to accept the *adat's* authority in gender matters.[44] In a fusillade of indictments, the writers denounce the values of the very people they hope to make adherents of change: "Tradition, culture of silence, domination and inequality, ignorance of rights, the lack of law, weakness of the judiciary system, as well as economic dependence, are among the key factors that make women more vulnerable to sexual and gender-based violence." This raft of misconceptions ("the lack of law," "economic dependence") and presumptive naivety ("culture of silence," "domination," "ignorance of rights," "weakness of the judiciary system") shows how poorly understood *adat* is by typical international agents. If the government and United Nations are serious about persuading the *sukus* to change, they will have to recognize the reality that local people regard their *adat* as being at least as legitimate as Western-derived jurisprudence—as, of course, it is; otherwise two political cultures will remain alternative options for the Timorese. Although some *sukus* appear more receptive to the claims made in support of

---

[42] The Procrustean term "human rights" is naturally evoked as a handy catch-all phrase when these three concepts require justification or simply propping up. As a practical matter, the notion of "human rights" is as alien to Timorese thought as it is to the thinking of most of the non-Western world.

[43] HAK Association for Law, Human Rights, and Justice, "Human Rights Situation 2008: Out of Civil Disorder towards the Challenges of Well-Being," report issued May 6, 2009 (Dili, Timor-Leste), p. 4; see http://etan.org/news/2009/05hakhr.htm; see under "4. Women's Human Rights"; accessed July 3, 2012.

[44] United Nations Integrated Mission in Timor-Leste, *Baseline Study on Sexual and Gender-Based Violence*.

international values, the sincerity of the majority of *sukus'* commitment must remain open to question,[45] since, like other Third World people when dealing with powerful foreign agencies, the Timorese have developed the capacity for outward conformity but internal resistance. One recalls that Indonesia's twenty-four years' occupation failed to erode *suku* self-identity and that the Timorese never became genuine Indonesian citizens despite apparently conforming to what was expected of them.[46]

The building of *uma luliks* today is, therefore, a particularly intriguing socio-political phenomenon since it is an overt—and therefore unexpected—expression of Timorese self-assertion and non-conformity. In constructing them, villagers are declaring their fidelity to the ancestors, creators of the old order who built the first *uma luliks*,[47] and they serve as the symbol not only of a family's oneness with its ancestors but also the unity of the family, lineage, clan, or *suku* owning it. At the same time, of course, the building also signals its owners' distinctiveness as a social group. Like the *barlaque*, though, *uma luliks* are not universally acclaimed. Educated Timorese, not to mention *malais*,[48] point out that constructing *uma luliks* wastes valuable resources that should be more rationally expended on education or on meeting other needs of a young nation-state rather than satisfying the *adat*. To be sure, the labor involves not only the muscle power of dozens of men and women for weeks on end, but also craftsmen who mastermind the building's every architectural detail and specialists, like the *lia na'in*, who ensure every detail of the *adat* code is adhered to. But it would seem that such criticism is inspired by something more than mere protests against waste; one detects, as well, resentment that villagers are affirming their self-identity as people of the *adat*. Building an *uma lulik* is a statement, if you will, of unapologetic parochialism that challenges the demands of the Other to have villagers transcend their *suku* mentality and embrace the wider, abstract, community of the nation-state. Constructing these houses, therefore, demonstrates something outsiders have not become accustomed to from rural Timor—defiant self-assertion in action. At the same time, as José Trindade has intimated,[49] *uma lulik* construction may also harbor the possibility that this phenomenon may conceivably be used as a model for some form of accommodation between *adat* and nation-state,[50] so raising the prospects that a synthesis of the national and the parochial may not, after all, be implausible.

---

[45] For a discussion of six possible factors that may incline some *sukus* to be more receptive than others to Western values, see David Hicks, "United Nations' Values and *Suku* Traditions: Appearance and Reality," in *Nation-Building across the Urban and Rural in Timor-Leste*, ed. Myra Walsh, Damian Grenville, Januario Soares, et. al. (Melbourne: RMIT University, 2010), pp. 44–45.

[46] The role the *barlaque* and *uma luliks* played in social life during the occupation is a topic deserving of a more extended discussion than is possible on these pages.

[47] *Uma* = building, house, descent group; *lulik* = sacred, set apart, prohibited. The building is also known as the *uma lisan* or *uma adat*. Much has been written in the past decade about *uma luliks*, which Henry Ogg Forbes first brought to the attention of the English-speaking public in his *A Naturalist's Wanderings in the Eastern Archipelago* (New York, NY: Harper & Brothers, 1885). A more recent account of this artifact may be found in David Hicks, "Afterword Glimpses of Alternatives: The *Uma Lulik* of East Timor," *Social Analysis* 52,1 (2008): 166–80.

[48] With apparent exceptions, such as the United States ambassador.

[49] Trindade, "Reconciling Conflicting Paradigms."

[50] The unifying nature of the *uma lulik* system, however, must not be allowed to obscure its potential for division in that it distinguishes those persons who identify themselves with an *uma lulik* from members of other descent groups who identify with other *uma luliks*.

A SYNCRETIC POLITICAL CULTURE?

I have argued that the political culture of Timor-Leste is actually, in fact, two political cultures. One, the political culture of the *adat*, gains its substance from a system of descent (predominately patrilineal) and patrilocal post-marital residence for a man, a hierarchy of social ranks, and a local governance in which authority (generally ascribed rather than achieved, and consisting more of influence to persuade than an autocratic power to compel) derives from the descent system, but is subject to democratic checks to an extent not appreciated by some commentators. In matters juridical, the *adat* requires the exchange of compensation that has been mutually agreed upon, and the mediation necessary to negotiate the exchange, for its sine qua non is a return to social harmony rather than to constitute a set of mandated abstractions that have little bearing on how people interact. *Adat* also privileges senior males in public life at the expense of women and younger men.

The other, the political culture of the nation-state, promotes values at odds with the *adat*, above all those of democracy, gender equality, and age equality. That the disparity between the two models appears so stark after eight years of independence might seem to support assertions that Timor-Leste is a "failed" nation-state,[51] and that hope of a unified nation-state is chimerical. Against this view is the history of the Timorese people who have for centuries revealed a capacity to absorb foreign ideas, a trait that suggests that an unprejudiced endeavor to reconcile these different perspectives on human experience might have a chance of success. Education would help in this attempt, since rural Timorese wish for education for their children, and, as these children and their parents grow aware of what advantages accrue from citizenship, their imaginations might gain a firmer purchase on the notions of "citizen" and "nation-state." But without concessions that mean something to the *sukus*, such attempts by the government and United Nations are likely to have limited success. No synthesis that has a chance of being sustainable is probable without whole-hearted endorsement by the people most affected, who will continue to live in their *sukus* after the latest crop of *malais* has departed. It is unrealistic to expect the rural Timorese to abandon their *adat* in toto, and so it behooves those who promote the national political culture to come to terms with the reality that *adat* plays a decisive part in peoples' lives. The United Nations' signal achievement was to make possible Timorese independence, and the Timorese are in their debt. But as others have observed, the United Nations failed to build on this success, and in no small measure this was due to the United Nations' insistence that nation-building means imposing the unique Western nation-state model—in a one-size-fits-all manner and without concessions—on countries that are unsuited to it. One complication for the United Nations is that its commission to "nation-build" in a way compatible with democracy disparages the *adat* as an alternative system for meting out justice and providing authentic governance.[52] That this prejudice does not issue

---

[51] See the titles of three such articles (albeit the contents are more positive than the titles suggest): José Ramos-Horta, "East Timor is Not a Failed State," *Wall Street Journal*, June 9, 2006, p. A14; Paulo Gorjão and André Monteiro, "Is Timor-Leste a Failed State?" *Portuguese Journal of International Affairs* 1 (Spring 2009): 12–21; and Jane Perlez, "A Nation-Building Project Comes Apart in East Timor," *New York Times*, July 14, 2006, p. A4.

[52] Interestingly, this intolerance is inconsistent with United Nations' claims to support cultural diversity.

from ignorance is seen clearly in the UN report cited earlier.[53] The document contends that "the reporting of crimes to any forum outside the family structure is still hampered by stigma associated with such crimes [i.e., violence against women and children] and socio-cultural acceptance," adding that "most domestic violence and sexual assault cases against women are *mediated* [i.e., dealt with by time-honored *adat* procedures] in traditional justice forums *instead of* being formally prosecuted, despite the fact that domestic violence is not a public crime under the new Criminal Code."[54] "Finally," it concludes, "limited access to justice [i.e., as defined by the government and United Nations] contributes to a climate of impunity, having a negative impact on respect for human rights, in particular those of women and children."[55] While the report's description of *suku* ethnography is accurate, as far as it goes, one wonders if the writer or writers had considered how many villagers have heard of the Code or, if they have, how many are willing to concede it any measure of compulsive hold over how they live their lives? In all likelihood, the most that might reasonably be expected is that any villagers aware that the Code even exists would look upon it as yet another irrelevant attempt by government to interfere in their lives. The report, with its mixture of conceit and naivety, continues: "Only a small number of [law] cases are appropriately dealt with before the courts."[56] In response to the resourcefulness the Polícia Nacional de Timor-Leste (PNTL), the national police force, has displayed when faced with problems the Code has created, the report patronizingly contends that "the lack of understanding of new laws is another serious challenge faced by PNTL, frequently leading to its officers "mediating" between perpetrator and victim on criminal offences."[57] Who, one might ask, is really displaying a lack of understanding here? Another presumptive condescension toward the values of people living in the countryside is indicated by the United Nations Development Fund for Women (UNIFEM), which responded to the National Parliament passing, on May 3, 2010, the domestic violence law, with the remark that "further steps must be taken to change [*sic*] public attitudes [i.e., to matters of gender]."[58] Would UNIFEM like its *own* attitudes changed?[59]

Bridging the divide separating the two political cultures requires amenability on the part of the United Nations, international agencies, and government in their policies toward the *sukus*, a quality—it must be said—not much evidenced thus far,[60]

[53] *Report of the Secretary-General on the United Nations Integrated Mission in Timor-Leste.*

[54] Ibid., pp. 20–21. The italics in both instances are mine, for emphasis.

[55] Ibid., p. 21.

[56] Ibid., p. 20.

[57] Ibid., p. 13.

[58] UNIFEM (United Nations Development Fund for Women), "Domestic Violence Law Passed in Timor-Leste," May 6, 2010, available at http://www.unifem.org/news_events/story_detail.php?StoryID=1087, accessed June 5, 2012. Timorese womens' organizations, like Rede Feto and Fokupers, are, of course, supportive of national laws, derived from the Western Tradition, that are intended to corrode the customary gender hierarchy and elevate the status of women.

[59] This said, it may well be that UNIFEM and customary male attitudes may converge to some extent in the future.

[60] In light of the above discussion of the lack of effective understanding between Dili and the *sukus*, advocates of decentralization may wish to consider in a cautionary vein the implications decentralization might have for national unity (cf. Hicks, "Community and Nation-State in East Timor").

except perhaps by the USAID, the Asia Foundation, and the US ambassador. Now that the United Nations shows signs of being somewhat less confident about its success in winning over *sukus'* populations, there could conceivably be prospects for an attitudinal reassessment. The same report does, after all, go on to suggest that "synergy between formal justice institutions and traditional justice mechanisms may be enhanced through the development of a draft customary law to ensure that customary practices are consistent with national and international human rights standards, particularly in relation to women and children."[61] But even with this concession, a grudging tone is discernible, and one notes that it is the *"customary practices"* (my emphasis) of the people of Timor-Leste that are to be made consistent with the national/international standards, rather than the national/international standards being brought more into alignment with "customary practices." Rarely have the *malai* permitted village people to make their own decisions, whether the former were the Portuguese, Indonesians, or—today—the United Nations, international agencies, and national NGOs who are incessantly pressuring the Timorese to do as they are told. The rousing scolding of one such organization, Amnesty International, last year by José Ramos-Horta,[62] comes as a timely warning that some Timorese may not be as accepting as they once were of gratuitous interference. "I don't need lectures from experts in human rights sitting on the 38th floor of the UN building in New York," the president declaimed. Nor are signs of attitudinal change limited to a Founding Fathers of the Republic, as the writings of one of the educated "youth," José Trindade, have shown.[63]

That the rural Timorese do not reflexively reject Western notions is demonstrated by their attitude to the Catholic Church. Referring to the findings of Tanja Hohe and Sofia Ospina,[64] Trindade has noted that, while Christianity is recognized for what it is, viz, a "foreign" institution, it is nevertheless "respected,"[65] whereas the same seems not so for the government and United Nations. "The population always says: 'First the traditional system, then the Church, and then the Government.'" Catholic dogmas that at one time were alien have now been assimilated into the *adat,* and ecclesiastical experience might serve as a workable precedent for a syncretic model of reconciliation. It requires, however, compromises by the government and United Nations. Catholic missionaries, it must be conceded, have had centuries to reconcile their dogmas to *lulik, mate bein, uma lulik,* the *barlaque,* and suchlike, but their successes demonstrate that accommodation can work. Rather than have their opinions disregarded or reflexively deflected, *suku* residents of *all*

---

[61] UNIFEM, "Domestic Violence Law Passed in Timor-Leste," p. 18.

[62] José Ramos-Horta, "E Timor Leader Rejects Criticism," British Broadcasting Company, September 29, 2009, http://news.bbc.co.uk/2/hi/8228155.stm. accessed May 29, 2012.

[63] Since Ramos-Horta has acquired the reputation of a politician with a mercurial fancy for adopting postures seemingly designed to provoke, one cannot be at all sure if he really meant what he said. As a reviewer of this paper suggested, this might be "political grandstanding" on his part. Ramos-Horta's words were, in part, a response to the criticism that he is not as open to pursuing human rights issues arising out of the Indonesian occupation in Timor-Leste as some *malais*—and also many Timorese—would like him to be. It has also be pointed out that Ramos-Horta has himself been a prominent "importer" of Western ideas.

[64] Tanja Hohe and Sophia Ospina, *Traditional Power Structures and Local Governance in East Timor: A Case Study of the Community Empowerment and Local Governance Project* (Geneva: Études Courtes 5, Graduate Institute of Development Studies, 2002).

[65] Trindade, "Reconciling Conflicting Paradigms," p. 166.

social categories need to be consulted and asked for specific details as to what *they* desire and what they are willing to accept rather than what *malai* presume to think they need. Traditional *liurais*, who often know more than other persons about *suku* matters, and village folk alike (*datos, katuas* and *feriks*)—not just the educated "youth" or social categories selectively privileged under international formulae ("spokespersons," "targeted groups," and so forth)—need to be included in this dialogue. In a letter published in the *New York Times*, Professor Amitai Etzioni offers advice to the US government regarding Afghanistan, and his advice is relevant for current UN policy in Timor-Leste.[66] Etzioni writes that, while competent local governance is important, it cannot be the sort of government Westerners immediately envision but something more akin to the sort of governance that worked for Chicago and New York City a hundred years ago. Local leaders (aldermen or tribal chiefs) resolved disputes "in line with local norms and traditions," provided a social network in return for loyalty, and, although favoring their cadres and relatives, also took care of everyone else. *Liurai* families lack the authority the Afghan leaders command, but their influence would lend incalculable weight to any attempt the government and United Nations made to gain the confidence of the *sukus*. The *suku* of Uma Ua'in Craik in Viqueque subdistrict currently illustrates the influence *liurais* still exercise. The Indonesian army forced the inhabitants of one of its villages, Uha Cae, to abandon their homes and reside in Viqueque town, which was located several hours' walking distance away. Today, any villager could return. But none has. Why? Because Viqueque is the seat of the *suku*, and, according to the *adat*, the *liurai* must be the first person to resettle. The current incumbent prefers to live in the town; and so, therefore, must his villagers.

CONCLUSION

Given the current disinclination of the government and United Nations to assimilate *suku* traditions into the national polity, any form of political adjustment between the the *adat* and the nation-state might seem unrealistic, and the evolution of a hybrid model of governance and justice, remote. But that serious rethinking of *malai* attitudes may be happening could be presaged by another initiative made by Ambassador Klemm who, two weeks after attending the *uma lulik* ceremony noted above, reconfirmed his respect for *adat* when he participated in a *tara bandu*[67] ritual in Bidau Santana, a *suku* in Dili, "to affirm local norms of traditional justice as part of a USAID-funded project on community policing being implemented by the Asia Foundation."[68] Were steps like this followed by the government and United Nations,

---

[66] Amitai Etzioni, "Afghanistan's Government," letter to *The New York Times*, May 2, 2010, p. 9.

[67] This term refers to what is considered taboo or prohibited. As such, it shares some meaning with the Tetum term *lulik*.

[68] Asia Foundation, "Tara Bandu Ceremony Cements Community-Police Cooperation in Bidau Santana, Timor-Leste," in *The Asia Foundation News Archives*, May 20, 2010, www.asiafoundation.org/news?tag=timor-leste (US Embassy, Dili, Timor-Leste), accessed May 7, 2010. Credit is also due to USAID and the Asia Foundation. As one reviewer of an earlier draft of this article noted, the US ambassador's attitude may have been mere lip service. Indeed, that may be true, but a demonstration in public of even a contrived respect for an institution so rooted in customary practices, yet slighted by the majority of *malais*, conveyed to those who attended the ceremony that their values at least merited some acknowledgment by a foreigner.

suku acceptance of change might be more enthusiastic and a hybridized political culture assimilating both national and *adat* values have a fighting chance to develop. The educated youth also have a role to play and, as we have seen, some are willing to think in terms of a hybrid model of nationhood. The revival of that most conspicuous material artifact of *adat*, the *uma lulik*, as an ostentatious index of local self-identity has not been lost on modern young Timorese, some of whom have proposed the construction of a national *uma lulik* that would symbolize the nation-state in much the manner as the *uma luliks* symbolize the *suku*.[69] Ensconced as the material embodiment of a syncretic conjunction of *adat* and nation-state, no symbol would be more expressive of, or better serve the interests of, a single and cohesive political culture in the Democratic Republic of Timor-Leste.

---

[69] Trindade, "Reconciling Conflicting Paradigms," p. 181.

SEMI-PRESIDENTIALISM AND THE CONSOLIDATION OF DEMOCRACY

Rui Graça Feijó

National Unity does not consist of politicians rubbing shoulders with each other to show our teeth to the people.
— Xanana Gusmão (June 22, 2006)

Democratization is a dynamic process that always remains incomplete and perpetually runs the risk of reversal.
— Charles Tilly

The political experience of Timor-Leste after the country became the first new independent nation of the twenty-first century has been rich and varied. The choice of a system of government is certainly a significant milestone in its journey toward a consolidated democracy. This chapter will examine the controversy over the characterization of the East Timorese system of government and offer historical and theoretical insights as to why the semi-presidential system may be considered a positive factor, contributing to political stability and democratic consolidation.

IS TIMOR-LESTE A (CONSOLIDATED) DEMOCRACY?

Discussing the democratic consolidation in Timor-Leste presupposes that a basic characterization of the current state of affairs in the country be made explicit and agreed upon. One approach to this problem consists in referring the matter to a credible international organization. Freedom House regularly publishes a list of what it calls "electoral democracies," that is, polities that abide by the following criteria: a competitive, multiparty political system; universal adult suffrage for all citizens (with exceptions for restrictions that states may legitimately place on citizens as sanctions for criminal offenses); regularly contested elections conducted in conditions of ballot secrecy and reasonable ballot security, and in the absence of massive voter fraud that yields results that are unrepresentative of the public will;

and significant public access of major political parties to the electorate through the media and through generally open political campaigning.[1]

In the judgment of Freedom House, independent Timor-Leste has consistently been regarded as an "electoral democracy." This organization then rates polities according to two other criteria—political rights and civil liberties—that converge to define a narrower "liberal democracy" as polities that combine free elections with "a substantial array of civil liberties." "Free Countries" are simultaneously "liberal" and "electoral democracies"; "Partly Free Countries" are "electoral democracies" that lack some features of "liberal" democracies. Timor-Leste has always been considered by this organization as a Partly Free Country, implying that its "democracy" exists but requires a positive and substantial evolution.

Looking elsewhere for an operative definition of democracy, José António Cheibub's "minimalist stance" may serve our purposes. He defines democracy as "a system in which government offices are filled by contested elections," and reverts to three main operational rules: First, the chief executive must be elected; second, the legislature must be elected; and third, there must be more than one party. The third rule about political parties is subject to a "consolidation rule," that is, the need to establish that the introduction of a democratic system does not lead to any of the following situations: a non-party rule; a one-party rule; or a permanent electoral domination by the winner party.[2] Timor-Leste does respond positively to all these tests, and can thus be considered a democracy as defined by objective and basic rules. This, however, must not blind us to a myriad of problems that have surfaced in this country's recent history that may qualify this assessment.

It is an undisputed fact that the ten years since independence have been marked by political instability (riots of December 2002, incidents in Lospalos in 2003, Catholic-inspired demonstrations in 2005) and even violence (culminating in the severe crisis of the second quarter of 2006 and, later on, in February 2008, in the attacks on the president and the prime minister). Several analysts have noticed the manifestation of "authoritarian temptations,"[3] or seen the country on a "path to authoritarianism"[4]—perhaps too strong a characterization of the way FRETILIN exercised executive power.[5] The editors of the present volume also expressed their concern that in 2006 Timor-Leste's political system "remain[ed] immature and potentially susceptible to single-party dominance."[6] In Portugal, Pedro Bacelar de Vasconcelos and Ricardo Sousa da Cunha expressed their critical appraisal in this manner: "In spite of undeniable merits and bold initiatives [the FRETILIN

---

[1] See www.freedomhouse.org/report/freedom-world-2012/methodology, accessed on May 21, 2012.

[2] José António Cheibub, Michael Alvarez, Fernando Limongi, and Adam Przeworski, "Classifying Political Regimes," *Studies in Comparative International Development* 31,2 (1996): 3–36.

[3] Sven Gunnar Simonsen, "The Authoritarian Temptation in East Timor: Nation Building and the Need for Inclusive Governance," *Asian Survey* 46,4 (2006): 575–96.

[4] Jacqueline Siapno, "Timor-Leste—On the Path to Authoritarianism?" *Southeast Asian Affairs* 1 (2004): 325–42.

[5] Rui Graça Feijó, "Timor-Leste: o sobressalto democratico" (Timor-Leste: The democratic upheaval), paper presented at the Fourth Congress of the Portuguese Political Science Association, Lisbon, March 6–7, 2008.

[6] Damien Kingsbury and Michael Leach, eds., *East Timor beyond Independence* (Victoria: Monash Asia Institute, 2007), p. 4.

government] did not have enough stamina to mobilize society in the construction of a plural and common project, to privilege conciliation over sectarian temptations and naked political confrontations."[7] We cannot forget that the Timorese authorities were compelled to call—in a united effort combining the representatives of all branches of power: the president, prime minister, and speaker of the House—for international military assistance to maintain a modicum of public order in the wake of the demise of the national police and the breakdown of the armed forces—surely a major setback in the consolidation of the new republic and its institutions.

My claim, however, is not that Timor-Leste has managed to consolidate its democracy—given the nature of this process aptly expressed by Charles Tilly in the epigraph to this essay[8]—but that it has so far been able to steer the boat over rough seas without resorting to unconstitutional, or otherwise deviant, solutions to the enormous problems it has faced, no matter how a number of responsible political actors may have attempted to operate outside the boundaries of the constitution or to advance unconstitutional legislation.

The constitution has remained in force throughout these eight years, never being suspended or abolished and effectively circumscribing the limits within which political life and the legitimate forms of competition for power should take place. Along with other actors, the court of appeals—acting in its interim constitutional capacity—has been a critical element in stopping the deployment of "authoritarian temptations" by ruling several bills proposed by the majority government to be unconstitutional. The 2007 round of elections was declared "free and fair."[9] Presidential elections were fought in two rounds (in April and May 2007), resulting in a clear winner (former nonpartisan minister for foreign affairs and prime minister, José Ramos Horta). Parliamentary elections brought in a replacement of the incumbent government by a coalition of opposition parties led by the former president, Xanana Gusmão, thus enacting a practical example of a competitive democracy accepting a turnover of majority and government. The transition from the old to the new government, even if coupled with tough political fighting, was mostly peaceful.

A few months into the "second cycle" of Timorese politics, all these institutions reacted in a constitutional manner to a serious challenge. President Ramos Horta was shot and seriously wounded, and forced to leave office (and the country) temporarily, and Prime Minister Xanana Gusmão was ambushed. An interim president was appointed in accordance with the constitution; he eventually returned his power to the rightful president when Ramos Horta was ready to reoccupy his post.

---

[7] Pedro Bacelar de Vasconcelos and Ricardo Sousa da Cunha, "Semipresidencialismo em Timor-Leste: um equilíbrio institucional num contexto critico" (Semi-presidentialism in Timor-Leste: An institutional equilibrium in a critical context) in *O Semipresidencialismo nos Países de Língua Portuguesa*, ed. Marina Costa Lobo and Octávio Amorim Neto (Lisbon: Imprensa de Ciências Sociais, 2009), p. 254.

[8] Charles Tilly, *Democracy* (Cambridge: Cambridge University Press, 2006), p. x.

[9] Christine Cabasset-Semedo and Frédéric Durand, *East Timor: How to Build a New Nation in Southeast Asia in the 21st Century* (Bangkok: IRASEC, 2009)<AU: pages?>; Rui Graça Feijó, "Counting Votes that Count: A Systemic Analysis of the Timorese Elections of 2007 and the Performance of the Electoral Institutions," in *State, Society and International Relations in Asia*, ed. Mehdi Pervizi Amineh (Amsterdam: Amsterdam University Press, 2010), pp. 103–17.

In brief, the constitutional rule of law has survived in times of hardship; elections have been held according to the prescriptions of the constitution and internationally accepted rules; no political office is held, formally or informally, in defiance of the expressed will of the people; and changes in the holders of executive powers have been achieved peacefully. These transfers of power have actually been limited: Timor-Leste has had three prime ministers (Alkatiri, 2002–06; Ramos Horta, 2006–07; Estanislau da Silva, May–August 2007, and Xanana Gusmão, since 2007), and two presidents of the republic (Xanana Gusmão, 2002–07, and Ramos Horta, elected in 2007) in the two electoral cycles. As such, Timor-Leste can legitimately claim the status of a democratic polity, even if the regime is far from achieving "consolidation," the term set out by Juan Linz and Alfred Stepan[10] and by Larry Diamond.[11]

IS TIMOR-LESTE A "SEMI-PRESIDENTIAL" REGIME?

Background: On the Notions of "Semi-Presidentialism"

The emergence of "semi-presidentialism" as a tercium genus of democratic, constitutional systems of government, clearly individuated and distinguished both from "parliamentarism" and "presidentialism," is a major development of twentieth-century political theory,[12] in spite of a continuing academic debate ranging from issues regarding nomenclature to the fine-tuning of its definitions. This system of government extends its roots back to the Weimar Republic (1919–33), under the influence of Max Weber,[13] but for many decades remained a nameless child with few siblings,[14] all of whom lived in Europe.

In 1970, Maurice Duverger coined the term in his attempt to single out the novelty of the French Fifth Republic, namely the regime that emerged from the 1962 amendment to the 1958 constitution, which introduced direct popular elections for the Presidency of the Republic. Duverger would expand on his proposal in his *Échec au Roi*[15]—during a time when Portugal had adopted a similar system of government—and summarized his views for the Anglo-Saxon academic world in a much acclaimed paper in 1980. These are the intellectual roots of this concept of a

[10] Juan J. Linz and Alfred Stepan, *Problems of Democratic Transition and Consolidation: Southern Europe, South America and Post-Communist Europe* (Baltimore, MD: Johns Hopkins University Press, 1996), pp. 7–15.

[11] Larry Diamond, *Developing Democracy: Towards Consolidation* (Baltimore, MD: Johns Hopkins University Press, 1999) pp. 732–77.

[12] Lobo and Neto, *O Semipresidencialismo*, p. 261.

[13] Horst Bahro, "A influência de Max Weber na Constituição de Weimar e o semipresidencialismo português como sistema de transição" (The influence of Max Weber on the Constitution of the Weimar Republic and Portuguese semi-presidentialism as a transition system), *Análise Social* 31,4 (138), pp. 777–802.

[14] As stated by Sartori, "In 1919 there was no notion of semi-presidentialism." See Giovanni Sartori, *Comparative Constitutional Engineering: An Inquiry into Structures, Incentives and Outcomes* (Basingstoke: Palgrave, 1994), p. 127.

[15] Maurice Duverger, *Échec au Roi* (Checkmate) (Paris: Albin Michel, 1978). For a Portuguese translation with an exclusive preface, see *Xeque-Mate—Análise Comparativa dos Sistemas Políticos Semi-Presidenciais* (Lisboa: Ediçõem Rolim, 1980). See also Duverger's "A New Political System Model: Semi-Presidential Government," *European Journal of Political Research* 8,2 (1980): 165–87.

particular system of government, which have been further developed in recent decades.

The onset of the "third wave of democratisation" that Samuel Huntington dates to the Portugal's Carnation Revolution of April 25, 1974,[16] constitutes a second factor explaining the explosion of interest in this system of government, both in academia and in the political arena. Whereas Spain (1975–76) and Greece (1974) made their transitions from authoritarianism to democracy through the more conventional "parliamentary" route, Portugal chose the new model—and, as democracy has expanded throughout the world since, the number of countries moving along this path has steadily increased. From an almost residual category, "semi-presidentialism" saw its popularity grow to the point that in 2002 it represented 22 percent of 114 democracies.[17] The most recent and comprehensive survey of "semi-presidentialism" carried out by Robert Elgie reveals that, in 2010, there were fifty-two countries with this type of constitutional arrangement—including countries that cannot be considered democracies.[18] More important is the fact that the popularity of this system derived from its appeal to young democracies, in central and eastern Europe, Africa, and Asia.[19] For various scholars, this is not a mere coincidence, as they acknowledge a positive impact of "semi-presidentialism" on "the consolidation and the maintenance of democracy,"[20] even if no consensual explanation of the reasons for this trend has yet emerged. To analyze this question, it is appropriate to start with Duverger's classic definition of "semi-presidentialism":

> A political regime is considered as semi-presidential if the constitution which established it combines three elements: (1) the president of the republic is elected by universal suffrage; (2) he possesses quite considerable powers; (3) he has opposite him, however, a prime minister and ministers who possess executive power and governmental power and can stay in office only if the parliament does not show its opposition to them.[21]

This definition is composed of two objective elements (the first and the last) and a quite subjective one. So then, what are to be considered "considerable powers" of a president? There seems to be no litmus test to gauge an answer to this question. Attempting to solve the problem while remaining as close as possible to the original

---

[16] Samuel P. Huntington, *The Third Wave of Democratization* (Norman, OK: Oklahoma University Press, 1991).

[17] José Antonio Cheibub, "Making Presidential and Semi-Presidential Constitutions Work," *Texas Law Review* 87,7 (2009): 1375–1407.

[18] Robert Elgie, *Semi-Presidentialism: Sub-Types and Democratic Performance* (Oxford: Oxford University Press, 2011), p. 24.

[19] Robert Elgie and Sophie Moestrup, *Semi-Presidentialism outside Europe* (Abingdon: Routledge, 2007), p. 9. I would like to stress that I shall be considering "semi-presidentialism" only as far as it is one particular form of democratic government. Systems of government that may present formal similarities but that are not framed by a constitutional regime respecting the rule of law (as was, for instance, the case in Angola prior to the recent constitutional revision), require particular analysis and should be treated separately from the context of the current discussion.

[20] Steven D. Roper, "Are All Semipresidential Regimes the Same? A Comparison of Premier-Presidential Regimes," *Comparative Politics* 34,3 (2002): 253–72.

[21] Duverger, "New Political System Model," p. 165.

definition has led subsequent writers in two alternative directions. On the one hand, Giovanni Sartori[22] has expanded on the number of conditions and proposed the following set of necessary characteristics: First, in a "semi-presidential" democracy, the head of state (president) is selected by popular vote—either directly or indirectly for a fixed term in office; second, the head of state shares the executive power with a prime minister, thus entering a dual authority structure the three defining criteria of which are: (a) the president is independent from parliament but cannot govern alone or directly and, therefore, his or her will must be conveyed and processed via his or her government; (b) conversely, the prime minister and his or her cabinet are "president-independent" in that they are "parliament-dependent," that is, they are subject to either parliamentary confidence or no-confidence (or both) and in either case need the support of a parliamentary majority.; and (c) the dual authority structure of semi-presidentialism allows for shifting balances of power within the executive, under the strict condition that the "autonomy potential" of both the president and prime minister executive remains.

On the other hand, Elgie thought it possible to operationalize the concept of "semi-presidentialism" as a "system where a popularly elected president exists alongside a prime minister and a cabinet who are responsible to the legislature"—thus eliding the question of presidential powers altogether.[23] In an attempt to provide a pragmatic solution for a great deal of cases, Jorge Novais has suggested that "the most decisive power a president may have in semi-presidential regimes is the power to dissolve parliament."[24] The existence of this power can solve the issue of "considerable powers" in a positive way (that is, where it exists, presidential powers can be deemed "considerable"). However, the absence of this power might not rule out the classification of a particular regime as "semi-presidential," as the authority to dissolve parliament could instead be replaced by another power of similar effect, as was the case in Portugal between 1976 and 1982 when the president had the power to dismiss the prime minister, but not to dissolve parliament.

Wide or narrow, each of these proposed definitions shares the idea that there is at the core of "semi-presidentialism" some form of duality of power. As Sartori puts it:

> The one characteristic that any semi-presidential regime *must* have [...] is a dual structure of authority, a two-headed configuration. Thus, any semi-presidential Constitution must establish, in some manner, a diarchy between a president who is head of the state, and a prime minister who heads the government.[25]

Alan Siarof argues that the critical feature distinguishing "semi-presidentialism" from other systems of government is the combination of parliamentary accountability (the definitional feature of "parliamentarism") with presidential

---

[22] Sartori, *Comparative Constitutional Engineering*, pp. 131–32.

[23] See Elgie, *Semi-Presidentialism: Sub-Types and Democratic Performance,* especially pp. 19–23, for a discussion of this definition.

[24] Jorge Reis Novais, *Semipresidencialismo, Volume 1: Teoria do Sistema de Governo Semipresidencial* (Semi-presidentialism, volume 1: Theory of the semi-presidential government system) (Coimbra: Almedina, 2009), p. 155.

[25] Sartori, *Comparative Constitutional Engineering*, p. 122.

powers, here taken in a generic sense,[26] a combination that incorporates the duality criterion. For Siaroff and Elgie, then, the analysis of the extent of presidential powers is not an initial, definitional issue in terms of the basic identity of the system, but becomes essential on a finer analysis of varieties of "semi-presidentialism." What are these varieties?

Progressing with the history of the debate, Matthew Shugart and John Carey,[27] although critics of the terminology in use,[28] proposed two models of regimes with directly elected presidents that, in fact, represent subtypes of a common, semi-presidential regime. These authors, struck by the fact that in the two decades before their book was published, "nearly all new democracies [...] had elected presidents with varying degrees of political authority,"[29] divided regimes having a directly elected president into three categories. First, they defined "presidentialism" as a "regime type based on the ideal of a maximum separation of powers (between the executive and the legislative branches), and full and exclusive responsibility of the cabinet to the president"—thus sustaining its classic definition. They then defined two new and distinct forms of government combining an elected president with a prime minister who owes his/her power to the confidence (or at least the acquiescence) of parliament: "premier-presidentialism" as "a type in which the president has certain significant powers, but the cabinet is responsible only to the assembly," and "president-parliamentary" whose defining trait is "shared—or confused—responsibilities over cabinets between president and assembly."[30]

These two cases may be regarded as species of "semi-presidentialism," since they share the basic elements pertinent to the definition of this system. Both radically differ from "presidentialism," even if the fact that the president has a fixed term and cannot be removed is a point in common. In semi-presidential models, however, the assembly that supports the cabinet can, as a general rule, be dissolved by the president; or, alternatively, the prime minister supported by the assembly can be likewise dismissed. As such, the principle of absolute separation between legislative and executive that characterizes "presidentialism" does not hold in these two cases.

---

[26] Alan Siaroff, "Comparative Presidencies: The Inadequacy of the Presidential, Semi-Presidential and Parliamentary Distinction," *European Journal of Political Research* 42,3 (2003): 290.

[27] Matthew Soberg Shugart and John M. Carey, *Presidents and Assemblies: Constitutional Design and Electoral Dynamics* (Cambridge: Cambridge University Press, 1992).

[28] Arguably, their criticism may be based on an erroneous assumption regarding a presumed continuum between two poles that Sartori (*Comparative Constitutional Engineering*, p. 124), Lijphart (Arend Lijphart, "Trichotomy or Dichotomy?" *European Journal of Political Research* 31,1 [1997]: 126), and Pasquino (Gianfranco Pasquino, "Semipresidentialism: A Political Model at Work," *European Journal of Political Research* 31,1 [1997]: 130) have convincingly argued to be non-extant in Duverger's notion.

[29] Shugart and Carey, *Presidents and Assemblies*, p. 2.

[30] Ibid., p. 15. Shoesmith's argument (as referred to by Kingsbury in this volume) that the centrality of the president's power resides in his or her capacity to influence the composition of government, if understood as a "public" rather than "private" power, is certainly not compatible with the "premier-presidential" type, which seldom gives the president such power, at least openly, but would certainly conform to the second. As such, it does not seem to be a pertinent benchmark to exclude particular regimes from "semi-presidential" classification. See Dennis Shoesmith, "Timor-Leste: Semi-Presidentialism and the Democratic Transition in a New, Small State," in *Semi-Presidentialism outside Europe*, pp. 219–35.

For most practical purposes, the item in the list of presidential powers that can better be singled out to represent the distinction between these two varieties of "semi-presidentialism" is the power to dismiss the prime minister. When the president has such a power, the chances that his powers overlap and in some way are confused with those of the prime minister is greater than in those cases in which the president cannot remove a prime minister but can dissolve the assembly and call fresh elections. This, of course, is the central feature distinguishing forms of "parliamentarism" (which does not, as a rule, accept dissolution of parliament by an external power). In Portugal, since 1982 (when the president lost his power to dismiss a prime minister but gained greater capacity to dissolve parliament), the presidential prerogative to dissolve parliament regardless of the majority opinion was only used twice,[31] both times by presidents confronted with parliaments in which political majorities existed. The scarcity of its use (twice in twenty-eight years) does not diminish its centrality in the balance of power.

Shugart and Carey are also to be credited with two other important developments in the understanding of the way semi-presidential regimes operate and can be analyzed. Instead of using long checklists of presidential powers like Timothy Frye's twenty-seven items,[32] they have sought to aggregate presidential powers into major areas, and then to divide these into "legislative" and "non-legislative" powers. Although in theory these different powers are independent of the variety of "semi-presidentialism," there is a clear tendency for "premier-presidential" regimes to offer their presidents substantial "non-legislative" powers (regarding the formation and the dismissal of cabinets, censure, dissolution of the assembly), whereas the "president-parliamentary" species shifts the balance in favor of extensive "legislative" powers (package veto/override, partial veto/override, decree, exclusive introduction of legislation, budgetary power, proposal of referendums, judicial review) for the president, who actually shares these powers with the prime minister.[33]

Shugart and Carey also introduced a zero-to-four scale to measure each one of the presidential powers. This method has been scrutinized by Lee Metcalf,[34] who proposed some revisions. Recent comparative works on "semi-presidentialism,"

---

[31] Some might count three cases, but the first one (General Eanes in 1982) was immediately after the Constitutional revision and used by a president elected before that major change, which affects comparability. In another case (Mário Soares in 1987), the majority in parliament was not "hostile" to the president, and proposed to form an alternative government to the minority cabinet of the single largest party, which had fielded a candidate against Soares and had been defeated in the House by a vote of censure. In the third case (Jorge Sampaio in 2004), there was a majority "hostile" to the president and in support of a government whose prime minister was not dismissed while fresh elections were called. In the cases of other parliament dissolutions (Sampaio in 2002 and Cavaco in 2011), all political parties agreed with early elections, thus, limiting the options of the presidents who were both confronted with the resignation of the prime minister (first, Guterres and, in 2011, Socrates). In the case of Portugal, where presidents require individual, personalized endorsement and officially reduce the weight of their party affiliation, the category of "hostile majority" should be read with caution. This point holds for Timor-Leste.

[32] Timothy Frye, "A Politics of Institutional Choice: Post-Communism Presidencies," *Comparative Political Studies* 30,5 (1996): 523–52.

[33] Shugart and Carey, *Presidents and Assemblies*, pp. 149–54.

[34] Lee Kendall Metcalf, "Measuring Presidential Power," *Comparative Political Studies* 33 (1999): 660–85.

namely the one carried by Marina Costa Lobo and Octávio Amorim Neto in the Lusophone world, including Timor-Leste, use the revised version of the initial scale.[35]

At this point, a new question must be addressed: What is the most appropriate source of information to define a political system in any given country? In 1980, Maurice Duverger stated plainly that "the concept of a semi-presidential form of government is defined by the content of the constitution." But when he passed from the general level to a discussion of individual country cases, he acknowledged that the paradox of "similarity of rules, diversity of games" called for four parameters to be taken into account: (1) the actual content of the constitution; (2) the combination of tradition and circumstances; (3) the composition of the parliamentary majority; and (4) the position of the president in relation to this majority.

For political scientists, therefore, a simple examination of formal constitutionalism will not suffice to ground the classification of political regimes as semi-presidential.[36] The "material constitution" encompasses established practices that offer a basis for actions not considered in the formal constitution,[37] but more often it operates in the opposite direction, erasing in practice some formal powers granted to the president. Examples here include a range of countries with presidents wh,o in practice, play largely ceremonial roles, in spite of the letter of the constitution granting them wider powers, as is the case in Austria.[38]

---

[35] Lobo and Neto, *O Semipresidencialismo*, pp. 264–65.

[36] Empirically oriented studies soon confront what Sartori calls a "material constitution" as distinct from the "formal constitution." There is also an ongoing debate on the extent of implicit powers versus those explicitly set in the printed word of a constitution. See, for instance, José Joaquim Gomes Canotilho and Vital Moreira, *Os Poderes do Presidente da República* (The powers of the president of the republic) (Coimbra: Coimbra Editora, 1991) and André Freire and António Costa Pinto, *O Poder dos Presidentes. A Republica Portuguesa em Debate* (The power of the presidents: The Portuguese Republic in debate) (Lisbon: Campo da Comunicação, 2005), thus reinforcing the argument in favor of historically defined studies of the ways power is actually exercised. "Implicit" powers are those not specifically stated in the listing of presidential competences but that can be derived—if only in special, abnormal occasions—from generic functions as "commander-in-chief of the Armed Forces" (to what extent does this imply that the president be constantly informed of all government policies in detail? Is a presidential agreement necessary prior to any major decision? Can he or she actively intervene?) or as "guarantor of the normal functioning of institutions." (Can the president dismiss a prime minister in breach of a constitutional obligation even if supported by a parliamentary majority?)

[37] Sometimes this can be pushed to the limits and actually oppose the letter of the Constitution. One such example was President De Gaulle's decision to initiate referendums in defiance of the Constitution of the Fifth Republic, which was not challenged either politically or legally by his opponents.

[38] Arguably, presidents of Timor Leste have regarded the letter of the Constitution as defining too narrow a scope of competences and powers in view of the "traditional" values of the land that they espoused. It is curious to remark that neither Xanana Gusmão nor Ramos-Horta were members of the Constituent Assembly and were, thus, mostly absent from the debate on the system of government. Their subsequent career at the very top of the Timorese political world, partly rooted in their past achievements, sheds light on the assumptions and political choices made by the international community and the UN administration under Sergio Vieira de Mello favoring formal procedures (party formation and elections) over the recognition of Timor-Leste's own political structures (such as the umbrella-like CNRT that encompassed all sectors of political opinion) and allowing a constituent process to go ahead without the direct participation of major players. This sort of option was made in a country where personalities

In brief, we might state that formal "constitutional engineering," or "constitutional design," matters greatly in the way it shapes the politicians' pursuit of their interests[39] and, therefore, is critical to the process of classifying particular political systems.[40] But this view cannot be separated from a historical analysis that identifies the "material constitution," or the entrenched political praxis, which combines both the formal and informal elements to provide a full picture of the environment in which politicians and citizens actually live, and the rules by which they abide

The Case of Timor-Leste

Most readings of the constitution of the Democratic Republic of Timor-Leste will recognize in its articles the basic tenets of a semi-presidential form of government. In Timor-Leste, the president of the republic is elected by universal, direct popular suffrage for a term of five years. Parliament is also elected by popular vote for a maximum term of five years, and the majority of members of parliament—be they members of one party or a number of parties in a pre- or post-electoral coalition[41]—have the right to appoint the prime minister, and only they can directly bring down the government. These two fundamental principles institute a dual structure of authority as a central element in the system of government, which allows for its classification as "semi-presidential."

Furthermore, among other powers, the president can dissolve the assembly—a power, however, that requires certain precedent conditions both in terms of timing and circumstances. But the president does not possess the right to dismiss the prime minister, whose mandate is dependent solely on the confidence of parliament.[42] The combination of these constitutional features permits us to conclude that Timor-Leste has adopted the premier-presidential variety of semi-presidentialism. This conclusion is consistent with the analysis of presidential powers according to Shugart and Carey's model, as revised by Metcalf, carried by the Portuguese constitutionalists Bacelar de Vasconcelos and Sousa da Cunha[43]: They rate the "legislative powers" of the Timorese president at 4.5 and the "non-legislative" at 4, making the Timorese president the one with the most limited powers in the

---

do carry enormous weight—they are certainly at least as important as formal ideology or any single other base for distinctive political parties.

[39] Shugart and Carey, *Presidents and Assemblies*, p. 13.

[40] Metcalf, "Measuring Presidential Power," p. 663.

[41] This issue, however, generated serious controversy in 2007 following the parliamentary elections due to the fact that FRETILIN won the plurality of votes but could not command enough support in the National Parliament to form a stable government, whereas several political parties that had run separately formed a post-election coalition that controlled the majority of seats. The Constitution does not specifically address this issue, thus leaving the door open both for presidential discretion and for any solution found in parliament—much like the Westminster parliament after the May 2010 elections.

[42] It is arguable that the very general Constitutional duty of the president to ensure the regular functioning of democratic institutions may empower him or her, in exceptional circumstances, to dismiss the prime minister (Article 112-2).

[43] Bacelar de Vasconcelos and Sousa da Cunha, "Semipresidencialismo em Timor-Leste," pp. 250–52.

Lusophone world.[44] However, as noted above, this constitutional analysis does not capture the whole picture. A major factor requiring attention—mainly when dealing with the term in office of President Xanana Gusmão, 2002–7—is the difference between the letter of Timor-Leste's constitution and the actual implementation of its provisions.

Consider two examples: the president is supposed to make certain decisions in consultation with two bodies—the *Conselho de Estado* (Council of State, CoS) and the *Conselho Superior de Defesa e Segurança* (Superior Council for Defense and Security, SCDS)—whose views are not binding but whose consultation is mandatory for the exercise of some of the president's powers, such as the dissolution of the assembly (CoS), the declaration of a state of emergency or state of siege (both councils), or the institutionalizing of the president's role as supreme commander of the armed forces (SCDS). The existence of those councils depended on the passing of ordinary legislation in parliament, which was supposed to expand the constitutional principles into operational organizations and establish their respective rules. The process took three full years, and the inauguration of both councils was only complete on May 20, 2005. In the meantime, the constitutional powers of the president were somewhat limited by the nonexistence of these constitutionally mandated institutions.[45]

More important is electoral legislation. While the president has the power to determine the date of elections—both presidential and legislative, including an early election following a dissolution of parliament—he or she can only do so provided there is an electoral law.[46] Thus, when the "crisis" erupted in April 2006, the president was actually empowered to dissolve parliament but not to call fresh elections—a dual solution that most established democracies would have attempted—because there was no electoral legislation to authorize the ballots. A highly problematic situation could arise out of a dissolved parliament in the absence of effective electoral legislation, as the constitution grants full powers to design and pass such legislation to parliament. In the actual case, electoral bills were passed by parliament when Ramos Horta was prime minister at the end of 2006, just in time for the president to call elections that would guarantee that the terms in office would not extend beyond their five-year constitutional limit.

These two examples reveal the extent to which there was a wide gap between the constitution's abstract provisions and the actual pace of implementation of the instruments necessary for principles to be operationalized and transformed into actual institutions and deeds. The presidency was slow in acquiring these instruments—from legal provisions to human resources or financial means—to put the president in a position to make effective use of the powers bestowed by the

---

[44] A reminder: The maximum number of points is 28 for "legislative" and 24 for "non-legislative" powers according to this scale. The existence of limited executive powers is supposedly typical of the "premier-presidential" variety of this system. Lobo and Neto, *O Semipresidencialismo*, p. 267.

[45] As a mere example: President Xanana made his first official visit to the military headquarters only after the inauguration of SCDS, and only then was an officer appointed to serve in his military supporting team (*Casa Militar*).

[46] The first president was elected on a provisional UN regulation, and the first parliament resulted from the transformation of the Constituent Assembly also elected under provisional UN regulations that were no longer valid after the new Constitution became the Law of the Land on May 22, 2002.

constitution. In this sense, the "material constitution" deviated from the formal one by limiting the actual exercise of formal presidential powers. In one respect, it continues to do so, as the legal framework for the use of referendums, for example, is yet to be produced.

Furthermore, on the other side of the equation, both Xanana Gusmão and Ramos Horta have been able to engage in areas of activity that lacked sufficient support in the constitutional letter, but were carried out in broad daylight. Take, for example, the first president's creation of a team to work on the issue of "veterans"—a sensitive issue in a country that owes much of its independence to a network of active resistance fighters, whom the guerrilla leader Xanana Gusmão led and knew personally in great numbers. Though this issue was taken up by Prime Minister Alkatiri, in his government reshuffle of June 2005, by creating a special department to lead the process, the moral capital of Xanana loomed larger and gave the president ample room to determine the final shape of this particular policy. Another example of practical initiatives of the president was Xanana´s involvement in the creation of the Museum and Archive of the Resistance—an initiative of high symbolic importance, arguably an expression of his duties in the realm of consolidating national unity and identity, but easily bordering on a demonstration of rivalry with government competences in cultural policies.

Ramos Horta has considered it his duty to offer a sort of "emergency aid" to cases of particular hardship that are brought to his attention. He created a team that provides responses to such appeals within one month, and sets plans that cannot last longer than six months—with more serious and lengthy cases channeled to the government for normal procedures. This represents a revised version of a similar initiative that was deemed to be in breach of the constitution by the Court of Appeal, which is now legitimized by mandated support from the government's own budget (but effectively managed by the staff of the presidency). Both cases reveal a systemic tolerance for some executive duties to be carried out by the president, regardless of the restrictions that the letter of the constitution imposes on the president's powers in this domain—an extension of powers justified in various ways. Ramos Horta stated in an interview that

> no Constitution, no Law can restrain or forbid a President to have opinions and to set up projects in favour of the poor ... In African or Asian countries, where poverty is still enormous, and where the President or the King are regarded as the "Father of the Nation" in a very patriarchal society, and where the Government has no capacity to be everywhere in this struggle against poverty and in the process of healing the wounds of society, and respond quickly to the most blatant needs of the people, the President of the Republic must intervene and give some help, complementing the action of the government and diffusing the political and social tension that may grow against the government.[47]

---

[47] In November 2009, I was fortunate to conduct two long interviews (about two hours each) with former President Xanana and current President Ramos-Horta, focusing on the nature and the workings of the Timorese political system. Those interviews were completed in 2011 and 2012, at a time when a third interview was conducted with former prime minister Alkatiri.

In this sense, the other face of the "material constitution" is one that includes those powers of the president that enhance the president's image as a paternal figure and, thus, tend to grant the president legitimacy to intervene beyond the scope of the constitutional text. Both the factors that enhance and those that limit the powers of the president in practice do not subvert the essential matrix of Timor-Leste's government system: the existence of a duality of powers between president and prime minister.

These points regarding the power and prerogatives of the president of the Republic would apply, *mutatis mutandis*, to the case of prime ministers. Although it is often assumed that executive powers not specifically allocated to the president fall in the realm of the prerogatives of the government, the powers of prime ministers in "semi-presidential" regimes are not unlimited. The political dividing line often results more from a balance of power between the two than from any exegesis of the constitution, be it "formal" or "material." Thus, it is also true that there are examples of the prime minister overstepping the constitutional line and behaving in a questionable manner.[48]

Finally, it is important to bear in mind that presidential powers—such as the power to dissolve parliament—need not be actually exerted to be considered in these assessments. With this in mind, the constitutional foundations of the governmental system should remain our main, though not exclusive, source justifying the classification of the Democratic Republic of Timor-Leste as a "semi-presidential" polity. Both Kay Rala Xanana Gusmão and José Ramos Horta—having both been president and prime minister at different times—have expressed their opinion on this issue, confirming their understanding that this is the best definition of the Timorese regime.[49]

SEMI-PRESIDENTIALISM: HELP OR HINDRANCE TO THE CONSOLIDATION OF TIMORESE DEMOCRACY?

The increasing number of semi-presidential experiments in democratic transition and consolidation requires particular corresponding attention from scholars. Of course, relationships between specific systems of government and the wider process of democratic consolidation are multiple and complex,[50] and certainly not determined by these constitutional choices alone. Karl Popper's notion of "propensity,"[51] or weighted probability, can be summoned to frame our discussion. This notion seems to be echoed in Lobo and Neto's concept of "suggestive associations,"[52] a possible way to frame relationships between the choice of a

---

[48] As an example, I would argue that the decision taken under Alkatiri's government to sack almost one-third of those who served in the armed forces at a time when the President of the Republic and Commander in Chief was out of the country, and without granting his acquiescence for such a dramatic action, reveals a very narrow conception of presidential powers without constitutional basis

[49] Interviews with the author, November 2009. This is not simply a question of supporting the current system, which might be expected (though neither was a member of the Constituent Assembly), but a question of how best to characterize it.

[50] Novais, *Semipresidencialismo*, p. 194.

[51] Karl Popper, *A World of Propensities*, (Bristol: Thoemmes, 1990).

[52] Lobo and Neto, *O Semipresidencialismo*, p. 271.

government system and the survival of young democracies, potential cause-and-effect relationships still open to debate.

Sophie Moestrup conducted a survey of countries involved in democratization processes in recent decades, assessing the impact of the adoption of this form of government on the breakdown of young democracies, that is, assessing whether this form of government exerted an eventual negative impact on democratic consolidation. She concluded that "semi-presidential regimes are *not* more or less likely than either presidential or parliamentary regimes to suffer democratic breakdown through coups or otherwise."[53] The results of Moestrup's empirical test are important, not so much for these associations or correlations, but because they stress how urgent it is for scholars to move beyond theoretical hypotheses and focus on the actual, historically situated political processes of particular regimes.

Of direct relevance to the case of Timor-Leste is Steven Roper's argument that in premier-presidential regimes (deemed to be more stable than president-parliamentary regimes[54]), "[t]here appears to be a relationship between presidential power and cabinet instability."[55] To the extent that Timor offers a historical example of an attempt to consolidate a democratic regime with a "premier-presidential" variety of semi-presidentialism,—and under this umbrella, one that is less generous with presidential prerogatives—Timor-Leste will remain an important case study.

Theoretical Assumptions

Examining the likely impact of semi-presidentialism upon democratic performance from a western European perspective, Gianfranco Pasquino has identified several "advantages and disadvantages of semi-presidentialism."[56] Among disadvantages, he includes two possibilities. First, there is the risk of a turn to "hyper-presidentialism," wherein the accumulation of executive and legislative power occurs via the coincidence of majorities in presidential and parliamentary elections. This risk seems to be greater in "president-parliamentary" varieties of government, in which the overlap between the president's and the prime minister's authority is more likely to occur (and the risk for confrontation is residual). Second, there is the likelihood that political and institutional clashes may erupt between the president and the prime minister when the parliamentary majority is not committed to the president, leading to a paralysis of the decision-making process or even to a constitutional crisis. Again, "premier-presidential" varieties seem less prone to fall into this trap, as the respective roles of president and prime minister are more clearly distinguished in regard to "executive" powers—those which more often potentiate the conflict. The latter disadvantage seems to carry a convincing argument inasmuch as it is widely echoed as the original sin of "semi-presidentialism."

---

[53] Sophie Moestrup, "Semi-Presidentialism in Young Democracies: Help or Hindrance?" in *Semi-presidentialism outside Europe*, p. 40.

[54] See Elgie, *Semi-Presidentialism: Sub-Types and Democratic Performance*, for a defense of this thesis, including updated references.

[55] Roper, "Are All Semipresidential Regimes the Same?" p. 254.

[56] Gianfranco Pasquino, "The Advantages and Disadvantages of Semi-Presidentialism: A West European Perspective," in *Semi-Presidentialism outside Europe*, pp. 14–29.

On the positive side of the coin, Pasquino calls our attention to the fact that "semi-presidentialism" has been credited with helping democracies to contain and dismiss undemocratic challenges by significant political actors against "the rules of the game," given the likelihood that some form of Arendt Lijphardt's "consensus democracy"[57]—a combination of decision-making effectiveness and a fair amount of agreement among the political elites—will prevail in a system that does not live by the "winner takes all" rule, thus retrieving Sartori's argument in favor of a flexible system. Pasquino's defense of the "relative advantage" of "semi-presidentialism" is corroborated by Novais, for whom "flexibility" translates into a better equilibrium and division of powers, a greater capacity to integrate different political and institutional actors, and an enhanced tendency to overcome blockages.[58]

Different Views of the Timorese Experience

The debate over Timor-Leste's choice of a system of government predates the 2002 constitution. In fact, it has its roots in the time of the resistance movement, and, in particular, after the creation of the CNRT in 1998, when a new political unity platform emerged and produced developments both before and after the referendum of 1999. Secondly, this choice bears on the evolution of thinking on this issue among the leadership of FRETILIN, as the most structured political force, during the period between 1999 and the moment when the Constituent Assembly—amply dominated by this party—was called to cast its vote. Unfortunately, no systematic work has been done so far to shed light on what remain obscure pages of political history.

Though we are not yet able to address the issue of the key political decisions on the nature of the government system from inside the Timorese political elite, an alternative way can be pursued by looking at what has been written by political commentators and analysts. Back in 2001, James Mackie suggested that the adoption of a semi-presidential system of government "may well be more suited to East Timor's needs than a purely presidential or parliamentary system," arguing that "if it can be combined with the sort of consensual type of legislature advocated by Lijphardt, it could conceivably deliver better governance than any of the other Southeast Asian political systems."[59] This line of argument had been sustained by various other authors right up to the present, a recent example being Bacelar de Vasconcelos and Sousa da Cunha, who argue that "semi-presidentialism" contains inherent virtues "in the equilibrium of the system of government and in the control of executive power [which are] decisive in the full implementation of the principle of the separation of powers."[60]

---

[57] Arendt Lijphart, *Democracies—Patterns of Majoritarian and Consensus Government in Twenty-One Countries* (New Haven, CT: Yale University Press, 1984).

[58] This argument echoes Robert Dahl's notion of "polyarchy"; see Robert A. Dahl, *Polyarchy: Participation and Opposition* (New Haven, CT: Yale University Press, 1971). See also Novais, *Semipresidencialismo*, p. 139.

[59] J. A. C. Mackie, "Future Political Structures and Institutions," in *East Timor: Development Challenges for the World's Newest Nation*, ed. Hal Hill and João M. Saldanha (Basingstoke: Palgrave, 2001), p. 205.

[60] Bacelar de Vasconcelos and Sousa da Cunha, "Semipresidencialismo em Timor-Leste," p. 237.

The extended roll of Portuguese scholars writing on this issue and assuming positive valuations is, of course, inseparable from the fact that Portugal was among the first countries in the last quarter of the twentieth century to adopt "semi-presidentialism," giving the scholars ample opportunity to participate in early debates;[61] and from the widespread belief that Portugal may have played a critical role in the expansion of semi-presidentialism in the Lusophone world. In fact, Portuguese scholars, mainly from the Law School of the University of Lisbon, were active players in the constitutional reforms of the late 1980s and early 1990s in Lusophone Africa.[62] However, Timor is a different case. The leading constitutional expert who served in the UN administration, Pedro Bacelar de Vasconcelos, raised objections to the overall process and resigned before the elections for the Constituent Assembly. The Portuguese legacy was nevertheless felt in an indirect way.[63] The argument I have presented elsewhere, and that I briefly recall here, is that the "Portuguese legacy" was convened insofar as it presented a practical solution that served the interests of, at least, the party that dominated the constituent assembly, and since this party had a clear majority, its power could be extended in parliament for the first electoral cycle, but no longer, for the party lacked the force of a allied, charismatic leader, and, in fact, the most potentially effective leader was a political competitor and had to be reckoned with. Too much power to the president could offset the parliamentary majority; too little might drive the popular leader to operate from outside the system, creating a strong external pressure. The delicate balance was best translated into a "semi-presidential" system that would both express the principles of division of powers and institutional cooperation and offer a practical way to implement checks and balances and foster consensual policies.

But consensus about the merits of "semi-presidentialism" in young democracies was not to be the key note in analyses of Timor-Leste. Soon after independence, critical voices were making themselves heard. Dennis Shoesmith is probably the most consistent advocate of this stance, arguing that "the semi-presidential system in the new state has institutionalized a political struggle between the president, Xanana Gusmão, and the prime minister, Mari Alkatir," which "has polarized political alliances and threatens the viability of the new state." He added, "The fault line established by a semi-presidential system complicates the already formidable task of establishing an effective and at the same time democratic system of government."[64] This negative view of the impact of this form of government upon the consolidation of democracy has continued to surface regularly as Timor-Leste emerges as a country

---

[61] See Maurice Duverger (sous la direccion de), *Les Régimes Semi-Presidentiels* (Paris: Presses Universitaires de France, 1986).

[62] The influence of the Portuguese Constitution on the fundamental laws of those countries "can be understood thanks to the presence of Portuguese jurisconsultants in their elaboration as well as the cultural proximity of many of those countries' jurists who had been formed in Portuguese universities." Jorge Bacelar Gouveia, *As Constituições dos Estados de Língua Portuguesa* (The constitutions of Portuguese-speaking countries), second edition (Coimbra: Almedina, 2006), p. 19.

[63] Rui Graça Feijó, "Weaving New Institutions, Translating Political Grammars: A Critical View on Timorese Political Institutions and the 'Portuguese Legacy,'" in Paulo Castro Seixas, *Translation, Society and Politics in Timor-Leste* (Porto: Universidsade Fernando Pessoa, 2010).

[64] Dennis Shoesmith, "Divided Leadership in a Semi-Presidential System, *Asian Survey* 43,2 (2003): 231, 252.

hampered by recurrent problems attributed, "in part, to the semi-presidential constitutional structures."[65]

True, Shoesmith recently seemed to move away, in part, from his early, critical stance when arguing the case to "remake the state" in Timor, although he still maintains that "the experience of the six years of independence strongly suggests that the current constitutional model is flawed and that there is a case for constitutional reform."[66] In the shorter term, his proposals were intended to clarify and strengthen the role of parliament. It seems that his concerns now impinge more on the relation between parliament and executive government than on the balance between this prime ministerial and presidential powers. In this sense, Shoesmith's proposal for a greater parliamentary role in the political life of Timor does not seriously question the fundaments of the semi-presidential system. Also, he seems to have shifted the burden of responsibility for the problems of democracy in Timor from "the political struggle at the centre of power" to the view that "the defining variable for both semi-presidentialism and political democracy is the relative incapacity of the state to adequately perform basic state functions"[67]—which is a supportable view, if one essentially independent of concerns relating to the operative system of government.

Moreover, the conclusion that "semi-presidentialism" has *generated* or *institutionalized* political confrontation at the core of the state sustained in the earlier texts by Shoesmith, can be revised in light of the chronology. By 1998, most of the movements and personalities involved in the resistance against Indonesia's occupation had come together under the umbrella of CNRT. But the history of Timor after 1974 is one marked by bitter rivalries (culminating in a brief civil war in August 1975) that permeated the core of the resistance. José Mattoso offers a moving history of the harsh years, and a background for the split between Xanana and FRETILIN, in the mid-1980s, on strategic grounds.[68] Shoesmith himself provides an account of the "historical legacy" and the depth and scope of divisions that existed *prior* to the referendum.[69] Political divisions (and, equally important, conflicts between personalities who were to survive the struggle for independence and translate these rifts in the formation of political parties and other socially relevant organizations, often with blurred ideological definitions), therefore, *predate* the adoption of the government system—they were not generated by it. While Shoesmith acknowledges that the leadership was divided prior to independence, the view that these tensions were "institutionalized" can also be challenged. An alternative view would acknowledge that these institutions were set up in such a way as to bring preexisting, deep political rivalries and in-fighting *inside the boundaries of constitutionally defined settings*—rather than ignoring their existence or attempting to repress their

---

[65] Benjamin Reilly, "Semi-presidential Democracy in East Asia," in *East Asia Forum,* www.eastasiaforum.org/2008/11/08, accessed on April 24, 2012.

[66] Dennis Shoesmith, "Remaking the State in Timor-Leste: The Case for Constitutional Reform," paper presented to the Seventeenth Biennial Conference of the Asia Studies Association, Melbourne, July 1–3, 2008, www.cdu.edu.au/creativeartshumanities/profiles/documents/conference_paper_july_2008.pdf, accessed June 28, 2012.

[67] Shoesmith, "Timor-Leste: Semi-Presidentialism," p. 234.

[68] José Mattoso, *A Dignidade: Konis Santana e a Resistência Timorense* (Dignity: Konis Santana and the Timorese resistance) (Lisboa: Temas e Debates, 2005).

[69] Shoesmith, "Divided Leadership," pp. 235–46.

manifestations. These arrangements facilitated contact between alternative power bases and imposed, to a certain degree, restraints upon the political actors, and were, therefore, a positive element in the process.

Representative systems need to deal with political rivalry *within* their walls, not by systematic exclusion. The claim that "semi-presidentialism" contributed to institutionalizing political conflict within the system, rather than allowing it to survive and challenge the regime from the outside, should, in fact, be read as a compliment rather than as a criticism. The years of Xanana's presidency illustrate this point, although a systematic analysis with objective benchmarks is still to be done. If one were to analyze the modus operandi of Xanana's presidency—including the institutional relations with the prime minister and his government (measured by vetoes, public criticism, or other indices), the mediator role he was called to perform and the ad-hoc committees he sponsored (all of which included representatives of government), or the ways in which he reached out to wider sectors of society, both in his formal institutional capacity (appointments to the Council of State) and informally—one would certainly agree with Sven Simonsen, who has noted that "it is first and foremost President Xanana Gusmão who has gone to great lengths in efforts to pacify political relations."[70]

Although one cannot deny the existence of rivalry and friction, these tensions were mostly contained within the boundaries of the constitution. Up until 2006, President Xanana had offered active support to the government, including at the time of the riots of 2002; he had vetoed no law other than with the backing of the Constitutional Court (he later "pocket vetoed" the Penal Code,[71] which would only be passed by President Ramos Horta in 2010); he mediated the conflict associated with the demonstrations led by sectors of the Catholic Church in 2005 without expressing any intention to give in to pressures of that kind; he may have publicly criticized certain ministers (such as Rogério Lobato), but he did not raise obstacles to their continuation in government even at a time of reshuffle, and so on.

Of course, the events of 2006 brought in a new conjuncture. But then Xanana's legal duty to "guarantee the regular functioning of the institutions"—shattered by the collapse of the security and armed forces, both under government direct responsibility—called for new forms of action in a situation in which hundreds of thousands of Timorese were living in a most precarious situation. The resignation of the prime minister—not associated with a dissolution of the FRETILIN-dominated National Parliament—was obtained through political rather than institutional means: Alkatiri preferred to offer his resignation when confronted with the likelihood of Xanana's resignation, as the president had lost confidence in the prime minister but was not explicitly entitled to use a dismissal power, though his prerogatives allowed him to dissolve parliament.[72]

---

[70] Simonsen, "Authoritarian Temptation," pp. 580–81.

[71] "Pocket veto" is an expression used in cases when a president stalls a piece of legislation without either approving or formally refusing to sign it for a period longer than the one prescribed in the Constitution. In this case, the purpose was to force government officials to reconsider the terms of the bill, which changes the prime minister tacitly agreed to redraft.

[72] In my view, Article 112-2 could be evoked to contemplate the dismissal of Alkatiri in June 2006 because, as I understand it, this provision contemplates two situations: the "previous cases," which are explicit (Article 112-1), *and* "when it becomes necessary to guarantee the regular functioning of democratic institutions." This reading is not universally accepted, as some argue that the copulative "and" refers to a necessary second condition to be read in

WHAT IF ... ? A COUNTERFACTUAL EXERCISE

Hidden behind the criticisms of "semi-presidentialism" lie implicit alternative theses: that either "presidentialism" or "parliamentarism" would be better suited to respond to the needs of Timor-Leste.[73] A brief counterfactual exercise may illuminate the merits or otherwise of these alternatives.[74]

The choice of a government system was made by the Constituent Assembly in 2002. Momentarily moving back in time to those days, what were the key characteristics of the Timorese political landscape that would inform the decision to be taken? I would sum these up in five points. First, Timor-Leste had never experienced genuine democratic government, as late Portuguese colonial rule (unlike British, French, or Dutch rule) coincided with one of the most durable authoritarian regimes in Europe, and the forced integration in the Indonesian Republic also represented an experience in authoritarianism. Second, the country lacked most of the ingredients identified in the literature as marking the basis for an endogenous drive toward democracy, which was, to a substantial degree, brought in from the "outside," partly by the returned elite who had lived in the diaspora and partly by the imposition of conditions imposed by the "international community" to insure the continuation of aid. Third, Xanana, as the leader of the guerrillas for two decades, was popular with the people and could easily win an election should he decide to run. He was also highly regarded among leaders within the international community. Xanana, however, never organized his supporters as a political party, and thus lacked the ability to influence some elections (like the legislative ones).

---

conjunction with, not as an alternative path to, the first element of the sentence. My argument is that the conditions set in Article 112-1 are valid per se, independent of their implication on the "regular functioning" of institutions (for instance, a prime minister's permanent state of incapacity, if declared, implies ipso facto dismissal from the job). Pedro Bacelar de Vasconcelos recently expressed a similar view in his detailed commentary of the Timorese Constitution; see Pedro Bacelar de Vasconcelos, *Constituição Anotada da República Democrática de Timor-Leste* (Braga: Direitos Humanos—Centro de Investigação Interdisciplinar, 2011), pp. 362–63, available at www.dh-cii.uminho.pt/crdtl_anotada_final.pdf, accessed June 28, 2012.

[73] For the sake of this argument, I am leaving aside a third, radical hypothesis that had already been discarded by the time the Constituent Assembly discussed the system of government, which consisted of an agreement amongst the Timorese elite, with the necessary backing from the "international community," for an extended "transitional period." This extended period might take place under the aegis of CNRT, which had anticipated a ten-year-long "transitional period" in its 1998 platform, prior to the launching of a constitutional experience. This option was based on assumptions stressing the need for consensual and inclusive policies that would delay the emergence of competitive politics. See Bacelar de Vasconcelos, "A Transição em Timor-Leste, 1999–2002" (Transition in Timor-Leste, 1999–2002), in *Timor-Leste, da Nação ao Estado,* ed. Rui Centeno and Rui Novais (Porto: Afrontamento, 2006), pp. 57–71.

[74] The methodological basis for this exercise can be found in Philip E. Tetlock and Aron Belkin, *Counterfactual Thought Experiments in World Politics: Logical, Methodological and Psychological Perspectives* (Princeton, NJ: Princeton University Press, 1996); P. E. Tetlock, Richard N. Lebow, and Geoffrey Parker, *Unmaking the West: "What If" Scenarios that Rewrite History* (Ann Arbor, MI: University of Michigan Press, 2008); and Hermínio Martins, "Tempo e Explicação: Pré-formação, Epigénese e Pseudomorfose na análise socio-politica" (Time and explanation: Preformation, epigenesis, and pseudomorphosis in social analysis) in *Portugal: Uma Democracia em Construção,* ed. Manuel Villaverde Cabral, Marina Costa Lobo, and Rui Graça Feijó (Lisbon: Imprensa de Ciências Sociais, 2009).

Fourth, provisions for the election of the Constituent Assembly allowed it to evolve into a national parliament without fresh elections, freezing the power balance for six years and allowing FRETILIN, which had emerged as a majority party claiming far more members than a group of smaller, divided, thinly structured political parties, to maintain control of parliament in the first legislature.[75] Fifth, relations between Xanana and FRETILIN were far from harmonious, reflecting high tensions among the leading politicians, tensions that were inherited from the resistance period and were fueled by the political manuevering that eventually led to the dissolution of CNRT and the emergence of open political competition under the aegis and approving eye of the United Nations.

Given the array of political forces in 2002, the following scenarios might have been possible. First, a "presidentialist" system might have been chosen, in which the president would be popularly elected and exercise sole executive responsibility, without being responsible to the legislature—and both the terms of office for the president and the parliament would be fixed and unchangeable (other than by the resignation of the president or an impeachment procedure). The election of Xanana as president would confront him with a parliament dominated by FRETILIN for the entire span of his term. Given that those two legitimacies and several key elements of public policies were not convergent, the risks of stalemate and rising political confrontation would have been higher than the tension that characterized the actual relations between Xanana as president and Alkatiri as prime minister under Timorese "semi-presidentialism."

The risk also existed that a popular president in a country with weak institutions (backed by an unstructured mass of voters and an undeveloped party system) would be tempted to apply his charismatic appeal to sidestep parliament's likely obstruction, and to step to the far margins of his constitutional competence. A systematic polarization of both camps would make it more difficult for the image of a "common house" to emerge, let alone to gain roots. It is hard to envisage how, in this context, the alleged "effectiveness" associated with presidentialism could overcome the increased danger of persistent confrontation or stalemate.

Sartori has acutely remarked that most of those who praise presidentialism based on the US experience fail to understand that "the American system works *in spite of* its Constitution, hardly *thanks* to its constitution," and it requires three conditions to keep delivering good results: absence of ideological principles, weak political parties, and locally oriented public policies.[76] All three elements are clearly absent in Timor-Leste, where FRETILIN is a strong and ideologically marked political party (all others being both weaker, if not for other reasons in terms their shorter history, and less ideologically marked), and the national level overshadows all local considerations except in the fact that locally based politicians, with more or less visible links to traditional forms of sociocultural organization, aspire to intervene in the national arena through parties with extremely unbalanced results.[77]

---

[75] Anthony L. Smith, "East Timor: Elections in the World's Newest Nation," *Journal of Democracy* 15,2 (2004), pp. 145–59; Dwight Y. King, "Timor's Founding Elections and the Emerging Party System," *Asian Survey* 43,5 (2003), pp. 745–57.

[76] Giovanni Sartori, *Comparative Constitutional Engineering*, p. 89.

[77] Rui Graça Feijó, "Elections and Social Dimensions of Democracy: Lessons from Timor-Leste," in *Timor-Leste: How to Build a New Nation*, ed. Cabasset-Semedo and Durand, pp. 123–38; and Feijó, "Counting Votes that Count."

Alternatively, the adoption by the Constituent Assembly of a model based on a parliament alone, giving the president no more than a ceremonial role (and perhaps establishing a president who was not chosen through direct, popular election), that is, a solution grounded on the principle of "winner takes all" and the condition that the "winners" would be judged by the people in the next election, would likely have led to the reinforcement of the tendency shown by FRETILIN to "go it alone." These conditions would have reduced incentives for the parliament to adopt any form of "consensus policies," and, in the extreme, would have excluded from all but the most formal political games important sectors of the opposition—in and out of parliament. The "path to authoritarianism" in various shades, sensed by Simonsen, Jacqueline Siapno,[78] or Bacelar de Vasconcelos and Sousa da Cunha, which could easily have led to the permanent domination of parliament by the winning party, would have been open; this sort of parliamentary "authoritarianism" characterized Mexico throughout most of the twentieth century or, perhaps more to the point, Mozambique's experience of FRELIMO's permanent domination after the country adopted a multiparty system. Bearing in mind the weakness of the judicial system in Timor-Leste, there could be little confidence in the theoretical model of checks and balances under parliamentary regimes. One can only wonder how the 2006 crisis would have ended without the intervention of a directly elected president.

In this case, a "mostly ceremonial" definition of the role of the president would have increased the likelihood that Xanana would have declined to run for office,[79] thus keeping his prestige and popularity—and his followers—outside the political institutions, with devastating power to criticize from the outside and to erode the government's institutional capacity to respond to popular demands. Alternatively, electing a president who could rapidly become a "prisoner in the palace" could tempt a frustrated chief executive to engage in a populist drive, by sidestepping the legal definition of his or her mandate and calling into question, rather than consolidating, the choices of the Constituent Assembly. In sum, the goal of "reducing the intensity of the expression of political conflict and restricting it to peaceful institutionalized channels," a goal and measure of democratic consolidation, according to Richard Gunther, Nikoforos Diamandouros, and Hans-Jurgen Puhle,[80] would certainly not have been facilitated by the decision to institute a parliamentary system of government. Conversely, the confusion between a critique of government and a critique of "the system" would be much easier to pass on to the masses of Timorese citizens.

---

[78] Jacqueline Siapno, "Timor-Leste—On a Path to Authoritarianism?" *Southeast Asian Affairs* 1 (2006): 325–42.

[79] Pedro Bacelar de Vasconcelos reports that on the last day of the electoral campaign for the Constituent Assembly, Xanana gave public assurances that he would seek a presidential mandate regardless of the system of government that the representatives of the Timorese people chose (Bacelar de Vasconcelos and Sousa da Cunha, "Semipresidencialismo em Timor," p. 233). Xanana later declared in an interview with me (Dili, November 2009) that his decision was made much later and under serious international pressure, which might, in fact, presume a more prominent role for the president in the political balance.

[80] Richard P. Gunther, Nikiforos Diamandouros, and Hans-Jurgen Puhle, eds., *The Politics of Democratic Consolidation: Southern Europe in Comparative Perspective* (Baltimore, MD: Johns Hopkins University Press, 1995), p. 9.

Moreover, Timor-Leste's weak party system is a key factor in our appraisal of the government system. As Sartori notes,[81] to be effective, "parliamentarism" requires that political parties be adapted to parliamentary life, that is, be socialized (through failure, long experience, and adequate incentive) to be cohesive and disciplined organisms. The real question seems to be which political attitude better suited the goals of consolidating democracy in 2002: to marginalize, outlaw, suppress or even repress historically rooted dissent that defied a majority of votes in one single election; or to try and incorporate differences of political opinion in a common "house." And which political system better suited the accomplishment of a preferable attitude?

These two scenarios suggest that the capacity to integrate different sectors of the political elite, with independent views, conflicting interests, and diverse forms of legitimacy,[82] into commonly accepted institutional arrangements with checks on the power of each player and power sharing—even with its attached danger of *institutionalized* confrontation—should be favored over the alleged "efficiency" of majority rule. "Semi-presidentialism" has, at its core, a dual structure of authority, unbound to fixed terms (as parliament may be dissolved early) and a capacity for flexible combinations and power arrangements between the holders of the two main political seats. These features allow this system of government to be more open and inclusive, and they attract to the institutional circle wider sectors of political society than any of its rivals.

CONCLUSION

Rather than reflect on the merits of a specific type of government system in abstract, this chapter has sought to examine Timor-Leste's choice of a system of government in the specific historical context of its quest for democratic consolidation.[83] It has been argued that the overwhelming requirement of a system of government in this particular historical case would rest on its *capacity to be inclusive.* Apart from its capacity to deliver "effective goods" and foster "behavioral" and "attitudinal" democracy, the system should be judged by its contribution to implement "constitutional" democracy, that is, a situation in which "governmental

---

[81] Sartori, *Comparative Constitutional Engineering*, p. 94.

[82] See Kelly Cristiane Silva, "Suffering, Dignity and Recognition: Sources of Political Legitimacy in Indepenedent Timor," in *Timor-Leste: How to Build a New Nation*, pp. 139–55.

[83] The fact that Timor-Leste had skipped a classic "transition" period, having existed for three years under a "UN Kingdom" (Jarat Chopra, "The UN's Kingdom of East Timor," *Survival* 42,3 [2000]: 27–39) marked by "benevolent despotism" (Joel C. Beauvais, "Benevolent Despotism: A Critique of UN State-Building in East Timor," *International Law and Politics* 33 (2001): 1101–78; Samantha Powell, *Chasing the Flame: Sergio Vieira de Mello and the Fight to Save the World* [London: Allen Lane, 2008]), or "benevolent autocracy" (Simon Chesterman, "Building Democracy through Benevolent Autocracy," in *The UN Role in Promoting Democracy: Between Ideals and Realities*, ed. Edward Newman and Richard Rich [New York, NY: United Nations University Press, 2004]), would suggest this process be protracted and shaken by some features of the leap-frogged stage like political confrontation, bargaining, and translating. The collapse of the CNRT in late 2000, only two and a half years after its creation as a national platform of unity, had revealed the depth and scope of divisions among different currents of opinion that would seem to constitute a stubborn feature of the political landscape. See Rui Graça Feijó, *Timor-Leste: Paisagem Tropical com Gente Dentro* (Timor-Leste: Tropical landscape with people inside) (Lisbon: Campo da Comunicação, 2006).

and nongovernmental forces alike, throughout the territory of the state, become subjected to, and habituated to, the resolution of conflict within the specific laws, procedures, and institutions sanctioned by the new democratic process."[84] The role of democratic institutions is not to *avoid* a vast array of possible problems—as sometimes seems to be assumed by those who replace analysis with long lists of a nascent government's difficulties and shortcomings—but to *confine the responses* to them within commonly defined and accepted boundaries. As Simonsen has pointed out, "exclusionary politics and win/lose outcomes in political disputes would seem to be counterproductive in relation to the goal of (re)building national unity among East Timorese."[85]

Sartori and Pasquino stress that "semi-presidentialism" is a flexible system that brings to the core of political life the expression of the notion of checks and balances—a consideration that both former President Xanana and current President Ramos Horta are keen to emphasize as the main virtue of a system they both believe is well suited to the actual needs of their country, and which, in their view, should not be questioned in its basic tenets for at least another two presidential terms.[86] It is a system that responds to different configurations of political alignment and parliamentary and presidential bases of power without ever losing its individuality among government systems.

A key element in the debate ought to be the role of political parties. It seems inconceivable that "presidentialism" or "parliamentarism" could operate democratically without relying on the hegemony of political parties over political life. Yet Timor-Leste does not fit this picture—nor, indeed, do several other young democracies, in which figures with great moral authority are politically active and use their prestige and capacity to influence public policies in ways that are not necessarily mediated by political parties.[87] The powers and prerogatives of presidents vary greatly in these situations, as do public perceptions of their role, even within the "semi-presidential" group of countries alone.

In the case of Timor-Leste, one key attribute of the designed system—which may be regarded as a practical expression of its inherent flexibility—is its *capacity to be inclusive*, that is, to create ways through which a vast array of sectors can find a place in public life. Take for instance the diverse range of presidential appointments to the Council of State.[88] These are clear illustrations that the construction of trust, and the distribution of roles across party lines—so critical to building democracy as a

---

[84] Linz and Stepan, *Democratic Transition and Consolidation*, 6.

[85] Simonsen, "Authoritarian Temptation," p. 595.

[86] Interviews with the author in November 2009.

[87] The most obvious example is the Catholic Church of Timor Leste, whose leaders and a great number of members publicly comment on and influence political debate, but refuse to take part in state organizations, even those of a consultative nature, such as the Council of State, other than in ad hoc committees.

[88] President Ramos-Horta's five appointees to the Council of State were: an independent member of the three governments supported by the FRETILIN majority between 2002 and 2007; a member of one of the political parties that could not elect a single MP, but as a group polled over 10 percent of the votes; a woman from the Oecussi district to demonstrate gender as well as regional sensitivity; the rector of the university, inherited from Xanana's previous appointments; and the president of the National Electoral Commission. Add to those five the appointment of Ana Pessoa, for many the second-in-command in Marí Alkatiri's government, to the important post of attorney general.

"common house"—has been facilitated by the choice of this specific system of government. Dual authority may lead, at one point or another, to some form of confrontation; but the fact that this system can delineate hierarchical order and specific powers to both president and prime minister, and, more importantly, can oscillate in giving one or the other a more prominent role when required, while remaining sensitive to power shifts expressed in elections, can truly be considered, as Sartori believed, to possess virtues of "institutional witchcraft," helping to create a common house for political actors of different or diverging persuasions. That is what the consolidation of democracy primarily requires.

THE CONSTITUTION:
CLARITY WITHOUT CONVENTION

Damien Kingsbury

As the state of Timor-Leste has begun to consolidate, there has been considerable debate about how to understand its constitution. This debate has been primarily over the role and powers of the president and the terms and conditions whereby political parties can form government. This debate is not merely academic or theoretical, for it has a direct impact on how Timor-Leste political society organizes itself, how decisions are made, and who wields power. This is particularly important given the state's fragility and its demonstrated capacity for internal political violence.

The unpacking and interpretation of a constitution is usually undertaken by the state's senior judicial entity, such as a constitutional or supreme court. Without such adjudication, there can be considerable disagreement or misunderstanding about how to understand what a constitution actually implies in terms of what is and is not acceptable political behavior. Constitutions also often function alongside convention, or a generally agreed set of political behavioral norms (especially in more established states) that are not specified in the constitution yet may become established and accepted practice.

This chapter argues that the constitution of Timor-Leste is clear on the role and powers of the president and on the formal requirements for being able to form government. Within this, the chapter argues that the Timor-Leste Constitution[1] does not define Timor-Leste as a "semi-presidential" political system, similar to some other Lusophone countries in which the president shares executive decision making with the prime minister and other ministers. Rather, the constitution defines Timor-Leste as a parliamentary political system, in which all executive power is held by the prime minister and his ministers but some reserve powers are held by the elected head of state. This is a critical distinction in times of political upheaval, during which the president and the prime minister might hold differing views on how to address particular situations.

While interpreting the constitution has usually been allocated to the judiciary, because the state did not yet possess a judiciary capable of offering sound—and, as importantly, final—constitutional interpretation, such debate continues. Moreover,

---

[1] *Assemblia Constituinte Timor-Leste* (Constitution of the Democratic Republic of East Timor), Democratic Republic of Timor-Leste, 2002.

where some, usually more established, states will have also adopted a set of practices as convention (e.g., "twinning," whereby if a government member is unintentionally absent from parliament one member of the opposition party will abstain from the proceedings), Timor-Leste has not established such conventions. In relation to the allocation of powers, some observers have suggested that, while the constitution may be understood in a particular way, the practice has been for it to be implemented in a manner that is different from the way it is formally articulated. In this case, while the president might not formally have executive authority, if he or she exercises such authority and it is followed, then the convention of its existence is established. This chapter argues that, while the president has (rarely) acted beyond his constitutional authority, this has not always been followed by others; the president's actions have been ignored by the government. When the president has acted beyond the constitutional scope of the presidency, it has been as a result of a lack of understanding of constitutional limitations, and it has been opposed by the prime minister and other ministers of the day. In that sense, the convention has not been established in Timor-Leste.

As this was written, a Supreme Court of Timor-Leste, which has responsibility for constitutional interpretation,[2] had not yet been established, the highest court being the Court of Appeals. As the highest available court, the Court of Appeals had technical authority over Supreme Court matters until a Supreme Court was established,[3] but despite "advising" twice on constitutional matters (whether the president should sign a law on amnesties, and pardons for war crimes), the Court of Appeals had not made binding determinations.

While there is now judicial expertise in Timor-Leste, in its early years, such judicial expertise was largely in the hands of international jurists while local jurists completed judicial training programs.[4] Such jurists were likely to interpret the Timor-Leste constitution according to their own political and judicial experiences. For example, a Portuguese jurist could be expected to understand the Timor-Leste constitution set against the experience of the similar Portuguese constitution and within the context of a European civil law tradition. A jurist from a Westminster parliamentary background would probably have a different interpretation of any particular law, given the British government's basis in common law. Given that Timor-Leste has followed the Portuguese civil law system, interpretations by Portuguese or Lusophone jurists might be thought to be more accurate. However, all interpretations of the new constitution and an evolving legal code remained subject to debate, not least because interpretations were largely undertaken by nonnationals, though one would expect the resolution of these questions by the Timorese themselves to be considered as a principle criterion for adjudication on matters of such significance to the state. Importantly, too, assumptions about the similarities of the Timor-Leste constitution to the Portuguese constitution, while broadly correct, may be incorrect in specific instances; the Timor-Leste and Portuguese constitutions are much alike, but they are not identical.

---

[2] Ibid., Section 124.2.

[3] Ibid., Section 164.2.

[4] United Nations Development Program, "Establishment of the Judicial Training Centre in Timor-Leste: Building Legal Capacity of the Newest Nation in the Asia-Pacific Region," 2009.

POLITICAL MODELS

On the question of the Timor-Leste political model, a number of observers of Timor-Leste politics have described it as a "semi-presidential" system, rather than as parliamentary (with an elected head of state, a "parliamentary republic").[5] That the president of Timor-Leste is directly elected (as opposed to being indirectly elected, such as via the parliament) has been claimed to enhance the authority of the office, allowing the president scope to act in ways not defined by the constitution. It has been further extrapolated that the direct election of the president also means that Timor-Leste has a semi-presidential political system. The direct election of the president, and the authority that the chief executive can assume from that process, have formed the basis of arguments against the direct election of the president in other proposed parliamentary republics (e.g., Australia). Critics have raised concerns that a directly elected president (one chosen to replace, for example, a monarch or his or her representative, such as a governor-general) might claim a popular mandate. Ireland, however, which has a directly elected president, retains a purely ceremonial presidency.

What is important to note here is that Timor-Leste's constitution details the powers ("competencies") of the president in a clear and internally consistent and logically coherent manner. In this respect, the powers of the president are similar to and derive from those available in constitutional monarchies (parliamentary democracies that formally have a monarch as head of state). Such powers commonly include appointing a government on the basis of a parliamentary majority, the swearing in of ministers, ratification of legislation, and, in some cases, powers of commutation of criminal sentences. In a number of cases, a constitutional monarch is also an arbiter of constitutional matters (such as the removal of a government), although this role can usually be challenged through a supreme court. Finally, a constitutional monarch is also commonly the nominal head of the armed forces. Such a position might otherwise have an arbitrating quality in cases of internal dispute (e.g., the monarchy in Thailand).

In that republics characteristically elect the head of state, as opposed to having a hereditary head of state, the position of president is, in effect, that of an "elected monarch." This is consistent with the development of modern republicanism, which followed the refusal of the United States' first president, George Washington, to be made "king" of the United States. In collaboration with Thomas Jefferson, John Adams, and Benjamin Franklin, Washington instead drafted a constitution that placed political authority, over which an elected president would preside, in the hands of the citizens.

This political model displaced hereditary monarchic sovereignty, through which the sovereignty of the state was manifested in the person of the monarch, and established, in its place, popular and changeable sovereignty. As a replacement model for a monarchy, the United States' republican system effectively established the president as an "elected king," with similar powers to that of a monarch (i.e., a late eighteenth-century style monarch, not a modern constitutional monarch), including the power to appoint nonelected ministers.

In that a republic is defined by a form of government in which state sovereignty is invested in the citizens of the state, those citizens are represented by the

---

[5] See, for example, in this volume, Rui Graça Feijó, "Semi-Presidentialism and the Consolidation of Democracy."

government on their behalf (from *res publica*, "public thing/wealth"). Through the assumption of popular sovereignty, a republic, thus, has an elected individual as the head of state. In most cases, the head of state in a republic is identified as a president, as is the case of Timor-Leste. If the president is also the head of government, the system is a "presidential republic," in which the president appoints ministers (sometimes "secretaries") and the legislature passes laws, in line with a classical "separation of powers" between the executive, the legislature, and the judiciary. This *trias politica* is referred to in the Timor-Leste constitution, Section 69, although its reference to "interdependence" between the state's "organs of sovereignty" qualifies the separation of powers in Timor-Leste's case.

The primary distinction between Timor-Leste's parliamentary republican system and presidential republicanism, though, is that Timor-Leste's head and executive of government derives from the parliament ("parlamento nacional"[6]), while the role of the presidency is circumscribed by the constitution. The status of Timor-Leste as a parliamentary republic derives from Section 92 of the constitution, which identifies Timor-Leste's parliament as "the organ of sovereignty of the Democratic Republic of East Timor that represents all Timorese citizens and is vested with legislative supervisory and political decision making powers" (original Portuguese: "*O Parlamento Nacional é o órgão de soberania da República Democrática de Timor-Leste, representativo de todos os cidadãos timorenses com poderes legislativos, de fiscalização e de decisão política*"). This explicit reference to parliamentary "sovereignty" and "legislative supervisory and political decision making powers," along with a range of other constitutional references, distinguishes this system from presidential republicanism, making it clear that Timor-Leste has a parliamentary political system.

Similarly, Section 1 of the constitution, and numerous sections thereafter, that refer to the president as the head of state, as well as to Timor-Leste by name, make clear that the state is also a republic. By definition, then, Timor-Leste is a parliamentary republic[7] (as opposed to other forms of republic, e.g., autocratic, people's, socialist, communist, Islamic). By way of characterization, parliamentary republics are organizationally close to constitutional monarchies, in which the authority of the head of state is circumscribed by the allocation of political authority to the parliament (legislature), which also appoints the executive (ministers) through the exercise of the parliamentary majority. In this system, the president has a largely ceremonial, rather than constitutionally politically active, role. Some observers have noted that because Timor-Leste's president has the (limited) power of veto over legislation, this implies that the president wields an executive or discretionary decision making function and, thus, qualifies Timor-Leste as a semi-presidential system. This logic does not, however, follow.

The president does have the power of veto over legislation, but this is ordinarily a ceremonial or "rubber stamp" function, in which the head of state approves legislation passed by the government of the day. The president can refer legislation for constitutional review, requiring it to be clarified by the senior judiciary competent to adjudicate on constitutional matters. This power is noted in the constitution and is consistent with the patterns in most other parliamentary democracies, including that of Portugal, upon which Timor-Leste's constitution is

---

[6] *Assemblia*, sections 92–101.

[7] See Arend Lijphart, *Parliamentary versus Presidential Government* (Oxford: Oxford University Press, 1992), for characterizations of government types.

based. In theory, the president can also simply veto legislation, although this is less likely to occur without constitutional review. That is, other than in highly unusual circumstances, the qualification of legislation devolves not, functionally, to the president but to the constitutional or equivalent court. Moreover, should the parliament again vote in favor of the legislation, the president is obliged to enact it within eight days.[8]

Section 85 of Timor-Leste's constitution provides for the promulgation (85A) and the right of veto (85C) of legislation within thirty days of the legislation having been passed. This power of promulgation and veto is consistent with constitutional monarchies and other parliamentary republics, in particular being closely related to the presidential powers available in the parliamentary republics of Portugal, in which the president has even more circumscribed powers, and of Ireland. Further, the constitution of Ireland (Bunreacht Na hÉireann[9]) identifies that state not as semi-presidential, but as a parliamentary republic. In particular, the Irish constitution clearly identifies the elected president's role as almost entirely ceremonial. The few claims to Portugal's status as such rest on debate over whether or not the powers of the president can be considered "extensive." Since 1983, in particular, such powers have been significantly circumscribed and are largely ceremonial.[10]

While the term "semi-presidential system" has been used by some observers to describe Timor-Leste's political system,[11] this could be characterized as referring to what some have seen as the practice or behavior of an individual president, on occasions, rather than to the president's constitutional authority. Particularly when Xanana Gusmão was president, there was a degree of overlap between his elected and constitutional position and the authority he held as the former leader of the anti-Indonesian resistance. That is, in keeping with the styles of political leadership in some other conflict and immediate post-conflict environments, Gusmão enjoyed charismatic legitimacy rather than formal or "rational-legal" legitimacy.

The term semi-presidential, however, was given currency to explain Gusmão's leadership style and given intellectual substance when the term was formally defined by the French political scientist Maurice Duverger to describe the French Fifth Republic,[12] who characterized the president in such a system as enjoying "considerable" executive powers. According to Ben Reilly, "Semi-presidentialism is an increasingly popular constitutional model that combines a directly elected president with significant powers as well as a prime minister chosen by the

---

[8] Assemblia, Article 88.3.

[9] Bunreacht Na hÉireann, Article 13.

[10] See Octavio Amorim Neto and Marina Costa Lobo, "Portugal's Semi-Presidentialism (Re)Considered: An Assessment of the President's Role in the Policy Process, 1976–2006," paper presented at the annual meeting of the American Political Science Association, Boston, MA, August 28, 2008; see also Darko Simovic, "The Definition of Semi-Presidential Regime—Reformulated," paper presented to VII World Congress of the International Association of International Law, Athens, June 11–15, 2007.

[11] See the chapter by Feijó in this volume. See also Reilly 2008, A. Smith, "East Timor: Elections in the World's Newest Nation," *Journal of Democracy* 15,2 (April 2004): 145–59; and D. Shoesmith, "Divided Leadership in a Semi-Presidential System," *Asian Survey* 43,2 (2003): 231–52.

[12] M. Duverger, *Echec au Roi* (Check the king) (Paris: A. Michel, 1977); M. Duverger," A New Political System Model: Semi-Presidential Government," *European Journal of Political Research* 8,2 (1980): 165–87.

legislature."[13] The defining element here is Duverger's use of the word "considerable" and Reilly's use of the word "significant," neither of which could be divined from the Timor-Leste constitution.

As outlined by Duverger, in particular in his seminal 1980 account, a semi-presidential system has a constitution that combines these qualities: 1) the president is elected by universal suffrage, 2) the president possesses quite considerable powers, and 3) the president has, opposite him or her, a prime minister and ministers who exercise executive and governmental power and who maintain their offices through enjoying the confidence of a majority of the parliament.[14] Timor-Leste's constitution conforms to the first of these criteria, which is also consistent with some conventional parliamentary systems. However, it does not conform to the second criterion—that the president "possesses quite considerable powers"—the most critical defining element of a semi-presidential system. Further, Timor-Leste's constitution only conforms, in part, to the third criterion. Reilly's interpretation of the meaning of semi-presidentialism is, then, correct. However, Reilly's identification of Timor-Leste's president as having "significant powers" is not.

According to Duverger's definition, semi-presidential political systems function in France, Finland, Russia, Pakistan, and some African states (including Portugal's former colony Mozambique). This system has also become popular in some transitional political societies, such as those of Eastern Europe. In that Mozambique has a semi-presidential system, it allows significantly greater powers to the president than does the Portuguese constitution.[15] In particular, the president of Mozambique has the authority to make decrees (Article 144b), to appoint and dismiss ministers and other officials,[16] and to "guide foreign policy."[17] These divisions of power and, in particular, power in relation to foreign policy, are much closer to those that typify the two classical semi-presidential systems, France and Finland. This does not find an equivalence in Timor-Leste.

The powers enjoyed by presidents in semi-presidential systems commonly include actual, as opposed to nominal, authority over the defense forces (e.g., France) and in the area of international relations (e.g., Mozambique, while in Finland executive authority is vested in the directly elected president, who must nonetheless enjoy the confidence of the parliament). Dennis Shoesmith, [18] however, has described Timor-Leste as having a semi-presidential system because the presidency, along with the government, the parliament, and the judiciary, are considered "organs of sovereignty" (Section 67), which follows Portugal's constitution, Article 113. Section 92 of the Timor-Leste Constitution states, however, that "the National Parliament is *the* [not "an"] organ of sovereignty."[19] That is to say, the parliament of Timor-Leste is the singular organ of sovereignty, not just one among others. Under the constitution, the parliament does not allocate "legislative supervisory and political decision making powers" to other "organs of sovereignty." The constitution of Timor-Leste

---

[13] B. Reilly, "Semi-Presidential Democracy in East Asia," *East Asia Forum* 8 (November 2008).

[14] Duverger, "A New Political System," p. 8.

[15] Constituição da República de Moçambique (Constitution of the Republic of Mozambique), 2004.

[16] Ibid., articles 160.1c, 160.2, 161a.

[17] Ibid., Article 162.

[18] Shoesmith, "Divided Leadership,"p. 231.

[19] Emphasis added.

also differs significantly from the Portuguese constitution in that it reverses the onus of a range of "competencies," or capacities, between the parliament and the president, such as the authority to call a referendum (which in Portugal resides with the parliament, which must propose the referendum to the president).[20]

Given that Portugal is sometimes considered to be a semi-presidential system and, further, that the Timor-Leste constitution is based on that of Portugal, this would seem to add weight to the argument that Timor-Leste's system is also a semi-presidential system. However, there is no consensus about whether the Portuguese political system is semi-presidential or parliamentary, especially after the considerable and further diminution of the Portuguese president's power in 1982 and that office's subsequent loss of executive office.[21]

It is worth noting, too, that Shoesmith later significantly modified his understanding of Timor-Leste's political system, away from the "semi-presidential" model, stating,

> Under the constitution, the presidency has limited powers. A key indicator of institutionalised Presidential power in a semi-Presidential system is the ability (or lack of it) of the President to influence the appointment of cabinet ministers. The President does not have these powers in Timor-Leste. Constitutionally, the President does not play a role in the actual government of the state.[22]

Despite identifying the constitutional limitations upon the presidency, Shoesmith continued to assert that the Timor-Leste system is semi-presidential because of the potential influence that a president can exercise beyond his or her formal powers. That is, Shoesmith agreed that the Timor-Leste political system was not semi-presidential in terms of presidential powers, but that sometimes Timor-Leste's presidents acted in a manner that exceeded these constitutional powers, a practice that, in turn, justified the use of the term.

Similar to—but not the same as—the Portuguese system, under the Timor-Leste constitution, the presidency is largely a ceremonial position, with only nominal authority over the armed forces, which formally devolves to the parliament,[23] and having the circumscribed power of veto of legislation and the power to appoint governments within circumscribed constitutional rules. These powers are similar to those enjoyed by ceremonial presidents in a number of other parliamentary republics, such as Ireland, as well as constitutional monarchies. That is to say, the president of Timor-Leste does not enjoy executive powers as such.

To illustrate this point about a president exceeding the office's constitutional authority and the extent of constitutional powers, the 2010 discussions about the

---

[20] See *Assembleia da Repubicla* (Constitution of the Republic), Republic of Portugal, 2005, articles 138, 139, 140, 141.

[21] See Neto and Lobo, "Portugal's Semi-Presidentialism (Re)Considered," who argue in favor of it being understood as a semi-presidential system. See also Simovic, "The Definition of Semi-Presidential Regime—Reformulated," who argues that it is a parliamentary republican system.

[22] D. Shoesmith, "Remaking the State in Timor-Leste: The Case for Constitutional Reform," paper presented to the Seventeenth Biennial Conference of the Asian Studies Association of Australia, Melbourne, July 1–3, 2008.

[23] *Assemblia* 2002, Section 95.1.o.

placement of a natural gas processing plant involved the government and, assuming resolution, would be voted on by the parliament. Under sections 95.2.B, 95.3.F and 96.1.H of the constitution, such discussions would not formally include the president. However, the president said that he believed he had the authority to "decide" on the matter. This reflected a tendency of President Ramos-Horta, as of his predecessor, Xanana Gusmão, to wish to have an active say in the day-to-day affairs of state, ambitions that reflected their charismatic status and not their constitutional authority as such. Gusmão's period as president, from 2002 to 2007, was similarly marked by his testing (and sometimes exceeding) the limits of constitutional authority. There is little doubt that both presidents, in what might be understood to be their long-standing and genuine concern for the people of Timor-Leste, wished to ensure that major decisions of the state accorded with their respective perceptions of the national interest. However, there was no constitutional authority granted to the President to "decide" on matters such as the Greater Sunrise issue, discussed below. By way of comparison, such authority is also not granted under the Portuguese or Mozambican constitutions. It is possible that the president, in each case noted above, misread the constitution in relation to this matter (and others), or perhaps did not remember reading the constitution, or, disconcertingly, had not read it completely or had read it and then ignored it. Specifically, Section 87 (d) of the constitution allows the president to conduct negotiations and oversee processes with regard to international agreements. However, this section specifically states that such negotiation and supervision must be undertaken in consultation with the government.

President Ramos-Horta had said that he wanted more information on the controversial Woodside Petroleum Greater Sunrise LNG agreement before "deciding" and expressed disappointment that he had not received a formal report on the issue from the Malaysian company Petronas.[24] This reference would merely reflect his own lack of understanding of his role if it did not have further implications. In this case, however, Woodside Petroleum, believing that the president correctly understood his Constitutional powers, targeted him to convince him of the appropriateness of its plan for the controversial project.[25] The Timor-Leste government, however, was both unhappy with Woodside's approach—Prime Minister Xanana Gusmão refused to meet with Woodside CEO Don Voelte—and with the president for having met Voelte and thereby having exceeded his constitutional capacity.[26]

The government was deeply unhappy with the president's unconstitutional intervention—without consultation—which hampered the process of negotiating the Greater Sunrise project, via Timor-Leste's regulator, the National Petroleum Authority. This then raised concerns about a lack of transparency and due process: the former because the agreement looked like an unconstitutional back-door deal and the latter because due process did not allow for an unplanned visit for a private

---

[24] Radio Televisaun Timor Leste, news report, May 13, 2010.

[25] Andrew Burrell, "Ramos Horta 'Premature' in Rejecting Sunrise Proposal," *The Australian*, May 1, 2010, p. 15. Woodside executives said they wanted to build a $5-billion floating processing platform in the Timor Sea, while the government of Timor-Leste said it wanted the gas from the Greater Sunrise Field to be processed on shore in Timor-Leste.

[26] *Tempo Semanal*, "Exclusive: President Jose Ramos Horta Meets Woodside and Lao Hamutuk's Charlie Scheiner on Greater Sunrise/Woodside," May 25, 2010, p. 1.

meeting. The view within the government was that it was "completely unacceptable" for both Voelte and the president to bypass the established mechanisms.[27] To overcome his lack of constitutional authority in this field, in meeting with Voelte, the president called a Council of Ministers meeting, which under Section 105 of the constitution would be convened and chaired by the prime minister; such a meeting is intended to be held only for emergencies and is not meant to include the president. The anger of the government at the president's unconstitutional intervention was reflected in the fact that no one from the government responded to the president's call to attend the Council of Ministers' meeting.[28] The government's concern with the president over-stepping his constitutional authority reflected not just its commitment to the constitutional principle, but its perception of the real problems that can arise when the president acts outside his constitutional authority and, thus, creates problems, in this case with what was potentially one of Timor-Leste's largest economic decisions.

In a similar and perhaps even more disturbing manner, in the face of political disturbances following his appointment of Gusmão's (Parliamentary Majority Alliance) government, in August 2007, Ramos-Horta overstepped the president's constitutional authority by ordering army units to Los Palos and Viqueque in response to an internal security matter. The president undertook this action—ordinarily an area of responsibility of the police—without consulting the government, though consultation is required except during a state of emergency, according to Section 85 of the constitution.[29] A private rebuke of the president by the government was, in that matter, gentler than the rebuke that followed his handling of the Greater Sunrise affair.[30]

Finally, in July 2010, the Australian prime minister, Julia Gillard, asked President Ramos-Horta if he would consider having Timor-Leste sponsor an Australian asylum-seeker detention center—a place where claimants to refugee status in Australia could be processed on other than Australian shores. The president said he supported the idea, although later qualified that by saying he did not think it was appropriate to detain asylum seekers and that perhaps they could be allowed to be free inside of Timor-Leste.

Again, however, the president misunderstood his own authority in this area, while the Australian government similarly misunderstood his authority. President Ramos-Horta had not "consulted" with his parliamentary colleagues before making his announcement, and his comments held no constitutional weight. He was rescued, however, two days later when Prime Minister Xanana Gusmão said that he was prepared to listen to Australia's request. This softening of what had, in the weeks prior to this issue's emergence, been a much tougher stance by Gusmão, was a diplomatic gesture, on the part of Gusmão, toward the then recently installed Australian prime minister. There was little doubt, however, that such a gesture

---

[27] This information is based on confidentially sourced information from the government of Timor-Leste, May 2010.

[28] *Tempo Semanal*, "Timor Leste Fight for Pipeline Horta Fight Xanana and Alfredo," May 25, 2010; *Tempo Semanal*, "Ramos Horta Meets Woodside," p. 1.

[29] ICG, "Timor-Leste: Security Sector Reform," *Asia Report* 143 (2008), International Crisis Group, Dili, p 16.

[30] This information is based on confidential information from the government of Timor-Leste, September 2007.

would have had a significant practical price attached to it if it were to have been given substance. In any case, the matter constituted another example of the president stepping beyond the bounds of his authority and into areas he felt he could comment upon but over which he had no real constitutional power.

The blurring of fields of competency of state officials (or "organs of sovereignty") is not unusual in relatively new states, as political actors seek to carve out areas of actual, as opposed to constitutional, competency, and to establish convention and precedents. Further, it happens that political leaders who have established their influence before a nation's constitution is formalized, who then take on a constitutional role, find that their prior achievements enhance their authority in practice, if not legally. This is consistent with the transition from charismatic-political authority to rational-legal political authority, and the blurring of boundaries between the two during the transition process. That was clearly the case under Gusmão's presidency and can, in part, explain Ramos-Horta's own transgressions of constitutional boundaries. As a result, the purpose of a particular political role, defined by a relatively new constitution, may become confused.

It was clear in late 2000, before Timor-Leste's draft constitution was formalized, that Gusmão preferred a political model with an executive presidency, with himself installed as president.[31] Gusmão's preference for this style of leadership was reflected in his frustration when the role of president to which he aspired was diminished to become largely ceremonial. Ramos-Horta has also since said, as president, that he would prefer to be President under the enhanced "French" model.[32]

By way of contrast, FRETILIN supported the implementation of a parliamentary-republican model, largely consistent with that of Portugal, in part because the executive-presidential model too closely resembled the government of Indonesia and was potentially subject to individual abuse. This response was dictated, in part, by the legitimate concern that the personality and style of a president who was granted so much centralized authority could tempt that president to claim increasing powers and become autocratic. In part, too, the decision to opt for a parliamentary-republic model, in which the presidential role was largely ceremonial, reflected conflict between Gusmão and FRETILIN under the leadership of Mari Alkatiri. This model was, then, intended to exclude Gusmão from the day-to-day affairs of running the state. The parliamentary-republican outcome was successful largely in politically sidelining Gusmão, a situation that created much angst for Gusmão and led him, arguably, to overstep the bounds of his constitutional competence. Indeed, his frustration with the ineffectiveness of the presidency was precisely why, at the first opportunity in 2007, he created a new political party as his personal political vehicle and campaigned to become prime minister, in effect swapping positions with his close colleague, then prime minister, Jose Ramos-Horta. Gusmão confirmed at this time that, despite the fact that he had sometimes transgressed its bounds, the role of the president was effectively ceremonial and that this had caused him considerable political frustration.[33]

For the Timor-Leste president to have a more active role in political affairs, stretching the interpretation of competencies as granted under the constitution,

---

[31] Damien Kingsbury, "The New Timor: A Xanana Republic?" *Jakarta Post*, December 16, 2000, p. 9.

[32] ICG, "Timor-Leste: Security Sector Reform," p. 16.

[33] Personal conversation, Dili, July 2007.

conventions to this effect would need to be established with the agreement of the government and the general public over a period greater than the term of one presidency. However, in 2010, Timor-Leste's Parliamentary Majority Alliance (AMP) government opposed the president's extra-constitutional activities, especially in relation to his discussions with the chief executive officer of Woodside Petroleum, Don Voelte, over the Greater Sunrise natural gas processing arrangements, as described above.[34] Moreover, the previous FRETILIN government had been critical of then President Xanana Gusmão's transgressions of his constitutional authority. In this sense, then, there appeared to be no government support, on either side of Timor-Leste's politics, for the extension of presidential powers through the establishment of a new convention.

FORMATION OF GOVERNMENT

Although the actions of both of Timor-Leste's presidents have raised eyebrows, if not serious concern, one power that the president does have, granted in the constitution, is to decide on and appoint the government. It was interesting, then, that the most controversial constitutional issue in 2007 was the appointment of the AMP government. Following Timor-Leste's near state failure in 2006, it became clear that all parties to that conflict, including the government, the president, the opposition, the armed forces, and the police, all needed to function in a lawfully consistent manner. The state institution that mattered above all others, in this respect, was Timor-Leste's constitution, as it was this document that outlined the roles, rights, and responsibilities of each of the respective parties to that conflict. In short, respect for the provisions of the constitution by all parties was inviolable, especially in ensuring a framework for a return to rule of law. After the crisis eased following the intervention of international troops and police, the constitution continued to be respected, if tested by the institutions that it is expected to define and, in many cases, restrict.

Mari Alkatiri, the former prime minister, who resigned on June 21, 2006, claimed he had been the victim of a "coup." However, his resignation and the appointment of a new cabinet during the period prior to the 2007 elections was constitutionally valid. FRETILIN party members continued to dominate the cabinet, and, as the majority party in parliament, indicated that there had not been a coup but rather a conventional political accounting for the events of 2006,[35] in which the political leader accepted responsibility for a major failing of government. Many who sympathized with the prime minister, both within Timor-Leste and internationally,[36] voiced significant criticism of Australia, and, to a lesser extent, the United States, for wanting to remove Alkatiri as prime minister. As the shambles of Timor-Leste continued to unfold throughout 2006, and foreign observers and politicians bayed increasingly loudly and frequently for the political blood of Alkatiri, they appeared

---

[34] "AMP Coalition Suspects Horta in Meeting with Woodside Delegations," *Suara Timor Lorosae,* May 10, 2010.

[35] Max Lane, "Analyzing East Timorese Politics: Tentative Starting Points," July 7, 2006, http://blogs.usyd.edu.au/maxlaneintlasia/2006/07/analysing_east_timorese_politi.html, accessed April 24, 2012.

[36] Within Timor-Leste, such criticism tended to come from FRETILIN party members. Internationally, criticism derived from individuals who were sympathetic to FRETILIN.

to forget some of Timor-Leste's constitutional facts, not to mention diplomatic niceties. Despite Alkatiri being widely condemned as "arrogant, dismissive of genuine concerns, and nepotistic," he remained at this time the democratically elected leader of the National Parliament, Timor-Leste's parliament legislature. Under the constitution, it is not possible for the prime minister to be sacked or his government removed other than through a vote of no confidence by a majority in the parliament.

At this time, it appeared that when parliament resumed there could indeed be a successful vote of no confidence in Alkatiri's leadership, in which case he would have been obliged to resign as prime minister. The view that there could be a vote against Alkatiri within FRETILIN was later given substance by the subsequent split within the party, in which anti-Alkatiri Mudanca ("change," or "reform") members voted with non-FRETILIN members. Alkatiri recognized that the rising tide against him was probably unstoppable, bowed to pressure, and resigned voluntarily. It had been a rough political tussle—deadly for some[37]—but Alkatiri had accepted that his continuation as prime minister was no longer tenable. Respect for the constitution remained intact.

The scheduled 2007 elections were held in accordance with the constitution. In this contest, FRETILIN saw support for its candidate, Francisco "Lu-Olo" Guterres, rise in the second round of polling to 31 percent of the vote,[38] but it was Jose Ramos-Horta who won the presidency. The parliamentary elections soon after reflected that trajectory, with FRETILIN again losing about half its vote, polling a consistent 29 percent, with Xanana Gusmão's CNRT receiving 24 percent of the vote, the rest being divided among minor parties. Prior to the elections, Gusmão had been in talks with other parties about a coalition government, but they failed to reach any formal agreement as each party expected to do well in the vote and thereby a number of ministerial positions.

Following the elections, Alkatiri tried to put together a coalition of parties but failed to achieve a majority. He then appealed to President Ramos-Horta to be allowed to form a minority government on the basis that FRETILIN had won a plurality of votes. Alkatiri argued that parliament should resume with FRETILIN in a position of power so that the party would be able to test itself against a vote of confidence. This request reflected convention in a number of Westminster parliamentary democracie,s in which a government failing to win a majority of seats but with no other party being representing a majority, is given the first opportunity to form a majority coalition, regardless of whether another party has a greater plurality (but no absolute majority). Timor-Leste does not, however, follow a Westminster parliamentary system, and rather than embark on what appeared to be further political instability, Ramos-Horta asked Gusmão if he could present him with a confirmed majority coalition, to which Gusmão replied that he could.

When the Majority Parliamentary Alliance government of Xanana Gusmão was sworn in by President Ramos-Horta on August 8, 2007, it was a logical outcome of the result of the parliamentary elections. Appointed as prime minister, Gusmão had formed a majority coalition and was therefore able to command a majority in

---

[37] Thirty-five people were killed in the violence at this time.

[38] FRETILIN did not contest the 2002 presidential elections, so popular support for the party's candidate is measured against its parliamentary standing, which in 2002 represented 57.4 percent of the vote. FRETILIN's first-round vote was 29 percent.

parliament. A majority in parliament remains the conventional democratic requirement. Yet FRETILIN was deeply opposed to the formation of this government and launched a campaign intended to discredit it. At one level, this could have been regarded as conventional oppositional parliamentary politics, except that FRETILIN did not accept the legal status of the AMP government, consistently referring to it as "de facto."

While there was considerable material progress in Timor-Leste, notably in Dili, under the AMP government, the country still faced many challenges. One of the biggest problems faced by the government, especially in its first year of office, was FRETILIN's continued insistence that the AMP government was not a legally constituted government, and the political instability and occasional violence that such challenges to the AMP engendered. As outlined in a public statement on September 6, 2007, FRETILIN spokespersons Sahe da Silva and Jose Teixeira, each of whom had a bachelor's degree in law from an Australian university, quoted part of Section 106.1 of the Timor-Leste constitution to support their claim that the appointment of Gusmão as prime minister was unconstitutional. They claimed he had been appointed in error as the result of an incorrect translation of the original Portuguese text into English. The pair said that the constitution, accurately translated, read that "the Prime Minister shall be designated by the most voted political party or alliance of political parties with a parliamentary majority and shall be appointed by the President of the republic." They then went on to declare that FRETILIN was declared by the National Electoral Commission (CNE) as the "most voted party," based on the fact that it had won the largest single plurality of votes. "This means that it [was] only FRETILIN that [could] appoint a prime minister as it was the most voted political party, i.e. the party with the most seats in the National Parliament," they said, even though this extrapolation did not necessarily follow and was not stated in the constitution as such. The pair went on to argue, somewhat confusingly, that the phrase "parliamentary majority," in this Section, did not refer to an absolute majority. They noted that Section 88.2 referred to an "absolute majority" in relation to promulgating laws and Section 109 used the term in relation to rejecting a government's program, but not in relation to the designation of a prime minister. As a result, they inferred that an absolute majority was not necessary for the designation of a prime minister, and that (simple) "majority" had a different meaning from "absolute majority." But this interpretation was incorrect.

Translating Section 106.1 of the Constitution, it reads in Portuguese:

> O Primeiro-Ministro é indigitado pelo partido mais votado ou pela aliança de partidos com maioria parlamentar e nomeado pelo Presidente da República, ouvidos os partidos políticos representados no Parlamento Nacional.

Although the translation required some minor adjustment between the languages, which resulted in more controversy, translated for meaning (as well as accuracy) it read in English as follows:

> The Prime-Minister is designated by the party with more votes or the alliance of parties with a parliamentary majority and nominated by the President of the Republic, listening to (or taking account of the views of) the political parties represented in the National Parliament.

This means that the prime minister represents either the party with the most votes, assuming that there is no simple majority and no "alliance" (coalition) or, explicitly, that the prime minister represents the alliance of parties with a parliamentary majority. It is possible within a parliamentary democracy for a prime minister to lead a minority government, and this is, in principle, allowed for under Section 106.1. However, the establishment of a minority government is conditional upon majority support, hence, any majority alliance automatically trumps an attempted minority government.

The draftees of the Portuguese version of the constitution neglected to mention in Section 106.1 the option of a simple single-party majority of the type that allowed FRETILIN to form the first government (although this exists in the Timor-Leste government-published–English version of the constitution). FRETILIN did not have this majority, either as a single party or in alliance with other parties. By contrast, the AMP coalition presented itself to the president as a ready-made majority, able to command the confidence of the parliament. In the absence of the convention mandating that the previous government, in a case when no one party has a majority, be allowed the first opportunity to form a government, the president was correct to refer to the "or" element of Section 106.1 of the constitution, where adopting the second part of 106.1, referring to an alliance of parties constituting a parliamentary majority, was a clearly available option.

Given that Section 106.1 referred to a "most voted party," this would imply a party with the single largest bloc of votes, which would have been FRETILIN. However, the word "or" which led into the second clause of Section 106.1 offered an alternative method of designating a prime minister, based on "an alliance of political parties with a parliamentary majority." The inference drawn by distinguishing between a "majority" and an "absolute majority" was that, somehow, a "majority" actually meant a "plurality," which could be other than an absolute minority of seats in parliament but holding a greater vote than other parties, hence referring back to the first clause of the sub-Section containing the phrase "most voted." It was, of course, possible to have a minority government, assuming no majority government was available. But this was not the case in 2007.

The alternative interpretation, and that which was accepted by President Ramos-Horta, as well as the Portuguese government on whose constitution the Timor-Leste constitution was based, was that the second clause—"*or* alliance of political parties with a parliamentary majority and shall be appointed by the President of the republic" (my emphasis)—refers to an alliance of parties forming a simple parliamentary majority. This was consistent with widespread democratic practice, and with the constitution, and was a workable political model. In contrast to FRETILIN's interpretation, the meaning of Section 106.1 would have been better understood to say that a government could be formed by a party that held a majority in its own right, although a minority government could be established if an alliance of other parties was unable to form a majority, with the second clause not being applicable.

Not only did FRETILIN object to being prevented from forming a minority government, it also objected to the fact that the AMP government alliance was formed after the election, rather than before, even though there was no constitutional requirement for AMP to have set up its coalition before the vote. There was an option, under Article 20 of the Law 6/2006 on the Election of the National

Parliament, for parties to form coalitions for the purpose of presenting a single list of candidates for election to National Parliament. But, unlike FRETILIN's supposition, this "may" option was not a requirement, nor did it preclude the formation of an alliance after an election.

"The real test of the strength of the Government," FRETILIN claimed, "is whether it can gather the support to pass its budget and program by absolute majority in the National Parliament." Yet, prima facie, FRETILIN could not have done this, as it was explicitly opposed by a majority of members in alliance. Similarly, the FRETILIN spokespersons noted that there was no specific provision in the constitution "which [said] that a post election coalition with an absolute majority in the National parliament [had] the right to form government." They were correct in this; the constitution simply said the alliance of parties was required to have a majority; the AMP government had this majority.

If a political party can claim the largest plurality (largest party, but without a majority) in Timor-Leste's parliament, but it does not control a majority of the votes in that body, this only guarantees that, under convention, the president will, first, ask the leader of that party if he or she is able to form a government, which, as noted, must establish that it can enjoy the confidence of the majority of the parliament. If the leader of that party cannot form such a government, the task of establishing a government then devolves to the next biggest party, and so on. If no party can form a government based on the confidence of the parliament, fresh elections are held.

Michael Clegg[39] made similar points in his analysis of the constitutional validity of the president's appointment of the AMP government. According to Clegg, when read within the context of the rest of the constitution, Section 106.1 "clearly means" that the president first asks the party with the most votes if it has a parliamentary majority, and, if it does not and cannot make an alliance to obtain a majority, the president consults all parties elected to parliament. As Clegg notes: "The President then asks each other party, in order of votes, if it can make an alliance that has a majority and appoints as prime minister the person nominated by the alliance of parties that has a parliamentary majority." This was the course of events followed by the president in 2007 prior to coming to a decision about the appointment of Timor-Leste's new government.

CONVENTION

As earlier noted, just ten years from independence at the time of writing, it was still too soon in Timor-Leste's independent history for the nation to have securely established its own political convention. However, following independence, there was some movement toward a degree of convention, which, if continued, would begin to implant and codify these conventions. The first area in which convention could become established was in the limitation—not the extension—of the powers of the president. In one sense, this was just compliance with the terms of the constitution. However, given the manner in which the first and, in particular, the second post-independence presidents conducted themselves, it was not always clear that such constitutional clarity would prevail. Both the first and second post-independence governments were clear about the circumscribed powers of the

---

[39] M. Clegg, "The Constitution of Timor-Leste: Appointment of a Prime Minister," IFES (International Foundation for Electoral Systems) White Paper, July 2007.

presidency, to the extent that a convention began to develop around this response, and this convention, based on precedent was likely to dictate that the president retain a largely ceremonial role and not have executive authority in the day-to-day affairs of the state. This limitation, then, reflected the status of the president as envisioned by the framers of the constitution when they set down the various "competencies" as a means of intentionally limiting presidential powers (as well as the short- to medium-term political reach of Xanana Gusmão).

In relation to the appointment of a government, in that there was the beginning of a convention, it too reflected compliance with the constitution. This was by adding to the balance of fairness by interpreting the constitution as requiring the president to approach the leader of a party with a plurality (but without a majority) to see if he or she could form a governing majority. It did not, however, establish a precedent beyond or outside of the constitution, which may have become convention, to allow a party with a plurality of votes, but without a majority in parliament the option of forming a minority government, as requested (or demanded) by FRETILIN, even where a majority coalition was available.

The convention, then, that appeared to be in the process of gaining acceptance, determined that Timor-Leste's parliament would not adopt or grant powers other than those articulated by the constitution. It could be argued that, without a supreme court able to interpret or adjudicate on constitutional issues, there has not yet been an opportunity to determine what, precisely, the constitution implies in Timor-Leste. However, most of the answers to such questions are available within the constitution in terms that are sufficiently clear. It may be possible to refer some constitutional matters to a supreme court (or the Court of Appeals prior to the establishment of a supreme court) for adjudication, such as the protocols surrounding the appointment of a government. But beyond FRETILIN (and, in particular, beyond a small clique in its central committee), there was widespread national and international agreement that President Jose Ramos-Horta's understanding of his obligations under the terms of the constitution were correct.

It remained to be seen, however, whether the president would be equally precise and reliable when assessing the competencies of his own office in relation to the constitution. But he and the people of Timor-Leste could be reasonably assured that the government of the day would ensure that a person whose office was intended to be largely ceremonial would, short of a catastrophe of the type that afflicted the state in 2006, perform as a figurehead of state and not as an active, day-to-day participant in its affairs.

Combating Corruption: Avoiding "Institutional Ritualism"

Adérito de Jesus Soares[1]

Introduction

Since Timor-Leste's independence in 2002, there has been increasing apprehension about corruption. Although substantiated cases of grand-scale corruption are still few in number, the public has been very critical about this perceived rise in corruption. Such public apprehension is understandable, given that many allegations are yet to be followed up legally, and citizens understand what damage corruption can do to a country (experiences of corruption in other countries around the world demonstrate why Timor-Leste should be alarmed). Vulnerability to corruption in Timor-Leste is high, given that almost 95 percent of its revenues come from oil and gas. Oil can be a blessing, but in many developing countries it is a curse, as many oil-rich, developing nations have experienced rampant related corruption.

In 2009, Timor-Leste was ranked 146 out of 180 countries by Transparency International in its corruption-perception index.[2] This was a worrying assessment, even though the index relies only on international experts' perceptions of corruption and is not based on hard evidence. Timor-Leste's ranking improved to 127 in 2010, much better than a year before, although it dropped again in 2011 to 143.[3] Slightly different from this assessment was a Management Systems International—United States Agency for International Development (MSD-USAID) report, published in 2009, which stated that "petty corruption [in Timor-Leste] is widespread, though perhaps is not yet systemic," and that while there were allegations of large-scale

[1] I wish to thank Chris Kearney for proofreading this chapter, and, especially, Michael Leach for his comments and the final editing of this paper. However, I am responsible for the paper.

[2] Transparency International, *Corruption Perception Index 2009*, http://www.transparency.org/policy_research/surveys_indices/cpi/2009/cpi_2009_table, accessed April 24, 2012.

[3] Transparency International, *Corruption Perception Index 2010*, http://www.transparency.org/policy_research/surveys_indices/cpi/2010/results#table, accessed April 24, 2012; and Transparency International *Corruption Perception Index 2011*, www.transparency.org/country#TLS, accessed June 27, 2012.

corruption, these remained "unsubstantiated."[4] The first corruption perception survey conducted in Timor-Leste in 2011 showed that while 57 percent of respondents considered corruption to be a serious issue, it did not rank highly when compared to many other problems facing the developing country. Corruption was ranked very low (0.7 percent) when compared with issues like unemployment (36.6 percent), poverty (20.8 percent), political instability (9.0 percent), crime (1.6 percent), and poor healthcare (1.5 percent).[5] Regardless of the different conclusions of these reports, there is no doubt that corruption exists in Timor-Leste, at various levels of government and in the public sphere in general. There is, therefore, general agreement that it is timely to address the issue of corruption with a serious and comprehensive anti-corruption strategy, one such strategy being the establishment of Timor's Anti-Corruption Commission (Comissão Anti-Corrupção, CAC).

This chapter examines some constraints and opportunities in tackling corruption in Timor-Leste. Following the introduction, I will discuss the rationale behind the fight against corruption. Then, I will delineate and describe the various entities that play a role in the area of combating corruption within the context of "institutional ritualism." Finally, I will describe the role of Timor-Leste's Anti-Corruption Commission.

THE REASON FOR COMBATING CORRUPTION WORLDWIDE

Corruption is an economic problem, and it is a crime—specifically, a white collar crime—as well as being a moral problem[6]. It is always tricky to give an exact meaning of corruption.[7] The United Nations Convention Against Corruption (UNCAC), to which Timor-Leste is a party, does not propose any standard definition of corruption. Instead, UNCAC delineates types of crimes within the context of corruption. Chapter III of UNCAC, entitled "Criminalization and Law Enforcement," describes type of crimes such as bribery of national public officials, bribery of foreign public officials and officials of public international organizations, embezzlement, trading of influence, and abuse of function.[8]

In Timor-Leste, corruption is regulated by the new penal code, which was adopted in 2009. Prior to that, Timor-Leste used the Indonesian Penal Code as well as Indonesia's anti-corruption law.[9] There are seven types of corruption that are identified in Timor-Leste's 2009 penal code. These include passive corruption for an illicit act, passive corruption for a licit act, active corruption, embezzlement,

---

[4] USAID-MSD, *Corruption Assessment: Timor-Leste* (2009), pp. 2–3, http://pdf.usaid.gov/pdf_docs/PNADQ697.pdf, accessed June 27, 2012.

[5] Corruption Perception Survey 2011, CAC, February, 2012 at http://cac.tl/wp-content/uploads/2011/11/CP-Survey-Report_TL11-12.pdf, accessed June 27, 2012.

[6] Mark Granovetter, "The Social Construction of Corruption," in *On Capitalism*, ed. Victor Nee and Richard Swedberg (Stanford, CA: Stanford University Press, 2007), p. 154.

[7] Oskar Kurer, "Corruption: An Alternative Approach to Its Definition and Measurement," *Political Studies* 53 (2005), pp. 222–39.

[8] "Criminalization and Law Enforcement" in *United Nations Convention against Corruption*, Chapter 3 (2003), www.unodc.org/documents/treaties/UNCAC/Publications/Convention/08-50026_E.pdf, accessed April 24, 2012.

[9] Undang-Undang Anti Korupsi (Anti-Corruption Law), UU No. 31/1999, later amended with UU No. 20, 2001.

embezzlement of use, abuse of power, and economic participation in business.[10] Some observers argue that it was more useful to use the Indonesian anti-corruption law than the 2009 penal code, as it encapsulates a broader definition of corruption, giving more room to law enforcement to carry out its mission in curbing corruption. By July 2010, lawmakers had presented a draft proposal of an anti-corruption law for debate in the National Parliament.

Even though there is no commonly accepted, standard definition of corruption, some international institutions have been trying to propose their own generic definitions. Transparency International defines corruption as "the abuse of entrusted power for private gain." This is similar to the World Bank's definition of corruption, "abuse of public power for private benefit."[11] A classic definition was proposed by Robert Klitgaard: "Corruption = Monopoly + Discretion − Accountability."[12] It is not the intention of this paper to deal with the definition of corruption, however, it is only if we understand corruption in a broad sense that we will be able to find a solution to it.[13]

On the adoption of UNCAC in 2003, Kofi Annan, the then secretary general of the United Nations, affirmed that "corruption hurts the poor disproportionately by diverting funds intended for development, undermining a government's ability to provide basic services, feeding inequality and injustice, and discouraging foreign investment and aid."[14] Annan's affirmation to some extent reflects the phenomenon of corruption worldwide. The importance of combating corruption has been shown clearly in the establishment of anti-corruption agencies in many developing countries over the last twenty to thirty years, as well as agreed-upon common action plans. For instance, some twenty-nine countries in the Asia-Pacific region have agreed on the common Asian Development Bank–Organization for Economic Co-operation and Development (ADB-OECD) Anti-Corruption Initiative action plan,[15] and many of these countries have created anti-corruption agencies, including Timor-Leste and Cambodia, which established theirs in 2010. It must be noted, however, that some of these agencies were established prior to the adoption of UNCAC. For instance, Hong Kong's Independent Commission for Anti-Corruption (ICAC) was established in the 1974;[16] Singapore's Corrupt Practice Investigative Bureau (CPIB) was established in 1950.

---

[10] The Penal Code of Timor-Leste (2009) defines in detail various types of corruption in articles 292–99, www.laohamutuk.org/econ/corruption/CodigoPenalEn.pdf, accessed June 27, 2012.

[11] World Bank, *Helping Countries Combat Corruption: The Role of the World Bank,* September 1997, p. 8, www1.worldbank.org/publicsector/anticorrupt/corruptn/corrptn.pdf, accessed April 24, 2012.

[12] Robert Klitgaard, *Controlling Corruption* (Berkeley, CA: University of California Press, 1988), p. 75.

[13] Laura S. Underkuffler, "Defining Corruption: Implications for Action," in *Corruption, Global Security, and World Order,* ed. Robert I. Rotberg (Cambridge, MA: World Peace Foundation and American Academy of Arts and Science, 2009), pp. 27–47.

[14] Kofi Annan, "Statement on the Adoption by the General Assembly of the United Nations Convention against Corruption," New York, NY, October 31, 2003, www.unodc.org/unodc/en/treaties/CAC/background/secretary-general-speech.html, accessed April 24, 2012.

[15] See www.oecd.org/pages/0,3417,en_34982156_34982385_1_1_1_1_1,00.html, accessed June 27, 2012.

[16] Klitgaard, *Controlling Corruption,* pp. 98–100.

It is commonly accepted that corruption in developing countries is rampant. This does not mean that developed countries are free from corruption. The difference is that in developed countries there are generally sufficient mechanisms to deal with the problem, while developing countries tend to lack credible mechanisms as well as the political will to deal with it. Experience shows that many former dictators in developing countries exploited their own people and their countries' natural resources, turning themselves into very rich leaders, while their own people were mired in poverty.[17] For instance, during his more than thirty-year rule, the late president of Indonesia, Suharto accumulated between 15 billion and 35 billion US dollars, while the late president of the Philippines, Ferdinand Marcos, accumulated between 5 billion and 10 billion US dollars.[18] In efforts to respond to this ominous reality, there have been growing numbers of initiatives at the local, national and international levels designed to curb corruption.

DAY-TO-DAY EXPRESSIONS IN TIMOR-LESTE AS "TECHNIQUES OF NEUTRALIZATION"

People in Timor-Leste perceive there to be a high level of corruption in their country. This perception has given rise to some common expressions associated with growing allegations of corruption. Among these expressions is *"kasih-uang habis perkara,"* which is a play on the acronym for KUHP (the Indonesian penal code, or *Kitab Undang-Undang Hukum Pidana*); the popular phrase means "the matter is finished once you have given the money." In Tetum, there is *"keta haluha ami nian serveiza"* ("don't forget our beer"), *"nia ita nian ema rasik sa"* ("come on, s/he is one of our own, therefore we should look after him/her"), and *"bui-hois"* and *"mau-hois"* (the words for corrupt female and male public officers). *Hois* literally means to squeeze, so *bui-/mau-hois* suggests the one who squeezes or milks the public purse. *"Keta haluha ami nia kolen"* ("our efforts should be rewarded") might be spoken by a public officer to a businessman after winning a tender. The most common excuse is *"ita sei iha prosesu aprendizagem"* ("we are still in the process of learning [so let's be tolerant about these mistakes, including corruption"]). On many occasions, some leaders use this expression to defend themselves when they have made mistakes in governance, and have failed to make any real effort to learn from and fix those mistakes.

All these expressions reflect a subtle consciousness of corruption shared by all sides, namely, by the potential contractors, the public in general, and public officers. Corruption can damage any of these citizens, but at the same time, if at all possible, they are trying to benefit from it. This characterization applies not only to a civil servant's big bosses, who may get a huge bonus from a contractor, but also to more junior staff who might be assisting the contractor at the administrative level. They might get a fancy mobile phone or a good laptop computer as a kickback from some profitable deal, or some cartons of beer for a family wedding party or traditional ceremony, where expensive alcoholic drinks are required, or perhaps some building materials. Such junior staff might say, "But I only got a mobile phone, not a big bonus like *katuas* or *ferik*," referring to his or her boss. This common response reflects an effective double-standard in people's relatively lax attitudes to petty corruption,

---

[17] Inge Amundsen, *Political Corruption* (Bergen: Chr. Michelsen Institute U4 Issue 6, 2006), p. 3, www.u4.no/publications/political-corruption/downloadasset/64, accessed June 27, 2012.
[18] Ibid.

while the public still demands that large-scale corruption be punished. Susan Rose-Ackerman notes that, in Nigeria and Ghana, "ordinary people condemn corruption at the elite level, but they themselves participate in networks that socially reproduce corruption."[19] While I do not compare the level of corruption in Nigeria and Ghana with that in Timor-Leste, the perspective expressed here is relevant to Timor-Leste.

This culture of gift-giving, as in the case of *wantoks* in Melanesia, seems to be correlated to a Timorese tradition of thanking people for their help. Offering something, even something very small, as a way of showing appreciation for any assistance given is quite common in Timor-Leste. Culturally, this is appropriate as there is no specific word or words for "thank you" in Tetun and other languages in Timor-Leste. The word *"obrigado,"* or thank you in Portuguese, is a loan word, not Tetun, although it has been used for generations now. Therefore, people traditionally did not show appreciation with words, but with some gesture or gift. The problem is that once this tradition is brought into a modern liberal democracy, it can lead to corruption. Traditionally, gift-giving is used in an open relationship as a genuine gesture, within a kinship system. However, once it occurs in the context of a huge government contract, for example, it can be very problematic, as the once genuine traditional gesture of appreciation can very easily become a corrupt practice.

Some of the Timorese public, especially members of the middle class who currently enjoy elements of development, try to justify why corruption occurs in Timor-Leste. The common justification is that Timor-Leste has inherited a legacy of both institutional and informal corruption from its former colonizer, Indonesia. It is true that, during the Indonesian era, corruption was rampant at all levels of society. *Tahu sama tahu* literally means "we know each other," implying that everyone knows that everyone else is involved in corruption. During the years when Indonesia ruled Timor-Leste, corruption involved both civilian and military authorities as well as the general public. There is another local expression that reflects how decision making in the day-to-day administration of the state can ignore legal standards and procedures, therefore potentially resulting in corruption—the *maun bo'ot* culture. *Maun bo'ot* literally means "big brother," and, according to Timorese culture, a *maun bo'ot* is a senior and respected person. A *maun bo'ot* figure usually has strong leverage because of past experience as a former resistance leader or a former clandestine leader. In post-independence Timor, the phrase *maun bo'ot* is also often used to refer to those who lead state institutions. A *maun bo'ot* could also be someone who is richer than the average Timorese. In daily administration, a *maun bo'ot* will tend to make decisions based on his personal judgment and use his discretionary power, instead of following the existing rules of procedure. Because a *maun bo'ot* wields this strong leverage, his subordinates will not question or challenge any of his decisions. This phenomenon of *maun bo'ot* conforms to Klitgaard's classic definition of corruption noted earlier:

$$\text{Corruption} = \text{Monopoly} + \text{Discretion} - \text{Accountability.}^{20}$$

---

[19] Susan Rose-Ackerman, "Corruption: Greed, Culture, and the State," Research Paper No. 409, *Yale Law Journal Online* 120 (November 9, 2010): 125–40, http://yalelawjournal.org/the-yale-law-journal-pocket-part/international-law/corruption:-greed,-culture,-and-the-state/

[20] Klitgaard, *Controlling Corruption*, pp. 98–100.

This common justification implicitly conceals its own sort of menace, as it effectively dissuades the Timorese from reflecting on their own mistakes. Timorese try to use "the techniques of neutralization"—to borrow Gresham Skyes and David Matza's terminology,[21] to say that corruption is not really a Timorese phenomenon but, rather, it is part of a legacy inherited from the Indonesians. Mark Granovetter elaborates further on the techniques of neutralization with what he calls the "principles of neutralization," which he recommended be used for analyzing corruption cases. He defines "neutralization" as "an account that acknowledges the causal connection between a payment and a service, or that items have been appropriated as a result of the position held, but implies that given the particular circumstances, no moral violation has occurred."[22] So, some Timorese try to rationalize the existence of corruption by saying that it is a foreign import, and that corruption, especially petty corruption, is not morally wrong.

Another justification for low-level public servants' involvement in corruption is the argument, "Why shouldn't we take the money, when the *katuas* and *ferik* (i.e., the big bosses) keep taking it?" This attitude is intensified by Timor's dire economic situation and the related hardships faced by its citizens; a typical junior public servant earns just US$150 a month, which makes living difficult. Lastly, there is the "*hakfodak* factor." *Hakfodak,* a Tetum word, means to feel shocked by and unaccustomed to certain conditions. In this context, the phrase relates to the shock of Timor being open to capital investment, and to the fact that many Timorese were unaccustomed to gaining and holding high public positions before independence. This is an interesting development where, all of a sudden, many former resistance leaders with no experience in the public sector become leaders of state institutions. They have credentials from the resistance era, but lack the experience and knowledge to run these liberal democratic institutions.[23] Some perform well and try to adjust their limited experience in the public sector, but some are simply *hakfodak*—or shocked and unaccustomed—by and to their new position. Those in this category behave as if they can do whatever they want, including engaging in corruption. They are staggered by their new status as public figures running state institutions. For them, this is the opportunity to get whatever they can get, to use what they can to gain political leverage, and to accumulate money while they are in power. They are smart at reading the weaknesses of the system. This has not only happened to public servants but, sadly, to some journalists and some representatives of NGOs as well, even though these are the people who should act as whistleblowers to help expose and stop corruption. Some from these sectors also suffer from the *hakfodak* factor.[24] The emergent urban elites are also quite *hakfodak*, because there is a lot more cash available, through government tenders, than ever before. The increased inflow of revenue from Timor's oil and gas production exacerbates the problem. Although

---

[21] Gresham M. Sykes and David Matza, "Techniques of Neutralization: A Theory of Delinquency," *American Sociological Review* 22,6 (1957): 664–70.

[22] Granovetter, "Social Construction of Corruption," p. 154.

[23] Peter Blunt, "The Political Economy of Accountability in Timor-Leste: Implications for Public Policy," *Public Administration and Development* 29, (2009): 94.

[24] It is commonly known that many local journalists prefer to cover those stories for which an interested party might offer them money, prepaid phone cards, or some other valuable benefit or bribe. It is also known that many local NGOs have problems of corruption such as failing properly to discharge their financial duties to their donors, or even committing corruption within their own NGO.

corruption is not yet systemic in Timor-Leste, the day-to-day practices as described above are worrisome.

Various studies have shown that strong kinship linkages in society can contribute to an increase in corruption. Research in Nigeria shows that, while corruption has become a major obstacle for development, with the public suffering as a consequence, concomitantly, the majority of the population is involved in or at least benefits from corruption in their daily lives.[25] Daniel Smith observes that the links between culture and corruption in Nigeria create an ambivalent attitude on the part of the public: "They are acutely aware of its consequences and ambivalent about their own role in its perpetuation."[26] Comparing such experiences and learning from them may help Timor-Leste in developing its own strategies for tackling this serious issue.

AVOID INSTITUTIONAL RITUALISM

Facing public and international concern, the government of Timor-Leste has taken several steps to address the issue of corruption. There are several main institutions that share the mandate of combating corruption. These can be divided into two categories, namely, independent state bodies and executive bodies. The former includes the Provedor de Direitus Humanus e da Justiça (PDHJ), an ombudsman-type body; the Office of Prosecutor General; and the recently established Anti-Corruption Commission (CAC). The latter includes the Inspectorate General, the National Police (PNTL), and some other institutions, such as the Office of Vice-Prime Minister on Administration and Good Governance, with some minor powers to deal with corruption. The Banking and Payment Authority (BPA), now the central bank, also has some role in preventing corruption, especially in relation to the issue of money laundering. An anti–money-laundering law was passed by the parliament in December 2011. It is hoped that a Financial Intelligence Unit (FIU) will be established as a consequence.

In addition, by July 2010, there were proposals from the government to establish an audit court as well as the Criminal Investigation Police (PIC). In the constitution of Timor-Leste, there has always been a mandate to establish an audit court.[27] The institution of this court was established by parliamentary vote in July 2011, with auditors completing their training in early 2012. This will be an important institution, with an auditing function to oversee state expenses in particular. This development is especially important given that Timor-Leste lacks an independent or external financial audit body.

The powers of the PIC, however, are less clear-cut. The proposed organization takes as its model Portugal's Polícia Judiciária (Judicial Police) and has the function of carrying out all investigations of criminal matters, including corruption cases. According to a draft law for a Timorese PIC, this force will be supervised by the minister of justice. Some have criticized the proposal because it appears as if the minister of justice would be "empire-building," including arming the PIC's officers

---

[25] Daniel Smith, *A Culture of Corruption: Everyday Deception and Popular Discontent in Nigeria* (Princeton, NJ: Princeton University Press, 2007).

[26] Ibid., p. xii.

[27] Article 129 of the Timor-Leste's Constitution on *Tribunal Superior Administrative, Fiscal e de Contas* (Superior Administrative Court of Tax and Audits).

with weapons and guns, in order to carry out criminal investigations. There is a view within some sectors of Timor-Leste society that this is an unnecessary step and not timely, as it would damage the continuing fragility of the PNTL. There was quite strong opposition to this law from some prominent individuals, including the PNTL's deputy commander and the prosecutor general. Many worry that establishing the PIC would create tension by hijacking all the investigative powers of the PNTL's Criminal Investigation Unit. This has been an issue in Portugal itself, as there have always been tensions between the Judicial Police and other police bodies, such as the Republican National Guard (GNR) and the Public Security Police (PSP). Therefore, in Timor-Leste, there is a strong view that energy should be directed at reinforcing the PNTL, especially the criminal investigation unit, instead of building a new institution such as the PIC.

Apart from its continuing mandates for human rights investigation and good governance, in the past, the PDHJ had the power to investigate corruption cases. However, this mandate was abolished following the enactment of the Anti-Corruption Commission law in July 2009. From the establishment of the PDHJ in 2005, there were at least thirty-eight corruption cases handed over by the PDHJ to the office of the prosecutor, but there has been only minor follow-up by the prosecutor. The prosecutor, in defending this scant record of convictions, has argued that there was not enough strong admissible evidence resulting from PDHJ's investigations. Many PDHJ investigations were, indeed, weak in terms of finding admissible evidence. According to the PDHJ, however, the authorities offered them no cooperation during their investigations, making it difficult to get proper information and evidence for submission to the courts. Representatives of PDHJ also admitted that they had limited investigative powers. Indeed, it is true that PDHJ can only conduct general investigations and that it has no specific power to conduct criminal investigations in corruption cases. The organization also lacks a staff of prosecutors with special expertise in fighting corruption.

As a result of this dilemma, in the past, the two institutions—PDHJ and the prosecutor's office—have attacked each other publicly through the media. This conflict has led to some positive developments, with several high-level corruption cases being sent to trial by the office of the prosecutor. This included the case against then Deputy Prime Minister José Luis Guterres involving charges of illicit enrichment and abuse of power. Interestingly, the Indonesian-era anti-corruption law mentioned above was used for the case against Guterres.[28] In August 2011, the Dili District Court dismissed all accusations against Guterres that had been brought by the prosecutor. This decision was later affirmed by the Court of Appeals. The Guterres case illustrates the need for enhanced professionalism with regard to investigative institutions and prosecutors. Another important case from 2011 was that of Ruben Braz, the Dili district administrator who was accused of embezzlement and abuse of power. In September 2011, Braz was sentenced to jail for three years by a Dili District Court judge.

According to the constitution, the public prosecutor's office is the central institution that possesses the power to prosecute all criminal acts, including

---

[28] Guterres's case sparked debate among those representing all political points of view. Members of parliament from the AMP government accused the prosecutor general of politicizing the case by pushing it to trial while ignoring other cases provided by the PDHJ over the last couple of years.

corruption. The sad reality is that, in the last ten years the prosecutor has faced a huge case backlog. To some extent, this problem has been resolved, since the appointment of a new public prosecutor in 2009, though mainly through the shelving of many cases. However, there are still corruption cases from the past that need to be prosecuted. One of the most high-profile cases reached a conclusion in June 2012 with the conviction of former Justice Minister Lucia Lobato on charges of unlawful participation in a tender process.[29]

This growing number of institutions established by the government, on the one hand, shows the government's seriousness in tackling corruption. On the other hand, when we analyze these initiatives and their significance, we must take care to account for what I call "institutional ritualism": an inclination by governments to form new agencies rather than address the actual problems. John Braithwaite and his coauthors have developed further the Mertonian concept of ritualism into several categories, including rule ritualism, objectivity ritualism, documentation ritualism, protocol ritualism, random sampling ritualism, scientific ritualism, legal ritualism, technological ritualism, participatory ritualism, and market ritualism.[30] These categories of ritualism have been used to analyze nursing homes practices in the United States, the United Kingdom, and Australia. Similarly, the concept of ritualism, especially rule and participatory ritualism, can be adapted to analyze state efforts to deal with post-independence corruption. For Braithwaite and his coauthors, rule ritualism happens when decision makers prefer to "write a rule instead of solving the problem," while participatory ritualism signifies feigned participation that tends to "alienate the supposed participant."[31]

Authorities have a very strong tendency to enact more laws in order to respond to social problems. To be straightforward, however, this chapter suggests the creation of another type of ritualism to characterize Timor-Leste's situation: that of "institutional ritualism." Institutional ritualism is the tendency to create a new institution while losing focus on resolving the problem. Worse still, institutional ritualism can also create confusion and overlaps among institutions that are supposed to be in charge of resolving the problem. Governments that demonstrate "institutional ritualism" sometimes ignore the reality facing the country, for example, the limited human and financial resources available to support the new institutions. Institutional ritualism has been a trademark of many developing countries in responding to the social problems they face. It also has been a very "sexy" trend encouraged, in part, by many international donors that support these developing countries. Since its independence, Timor-Leste has become a laboratory for institutional ritualism—partially sponsored by a number of external advisers and rich donor agencies.

The push for the minister of justice to establish the PIC is a good example of institutional ritualism. Instead of reinforcing the established criminal investigation unit in PNTL, the minister, apparently in a rush to initiate this new institution as

---

[29] The specific charge in Portuguese is "*Participação económico em negócio*," which is classed as an abuse-of-power offence. This was widely (and inaccurately) translated in the English-language press as a charge of "maladministration."

[30] John Braithwaite et al., *Regulating Aged Care: Ritualism and the New Pyramid* (Northampton, MA: Edward Edgar Publishing, 2007), p. 221; see also Robert K. Merton, *Social Theory and Social Structure* (New York, NY: Free Press, 1968).

[31] Braithwaite et al., *Regulating Aged Care*, p. 221.

soon as possible, introduced the law for establishing the PIC. Institutional realism has led to tensions in other cases as well, as demonstrated by the conflict between the offices of the vice prime minister and the minister of finance that occurred in 2010, regarding procurement. Procurement is a crucial issue, given that about 75 percent of Timor-Leste's state budget is executed through the procurement system. Instead of reinforcing the old procurement system under the minister of finance, the prime minister appointed a vice prime minister to oversee procurement, and also transferred procurement responsibilities to the vice prime minister's office. A Procurement Technical Secretariat (Secretariado Technico de Approvisionamento, STA) was established under the Vice Prime Minister's Office, but after seven months, it became clear that this was not working. So, in August 2010, the Council of Ministers suspended the procurement mandate of the Office of Vice Prime Minister.[32] Following this development, the vice prime minister stepped down.

Following the vice prime minister's resignation in early September 2010, there was a fundamental lack of clarity concerning the status of the government's procurement system for a number of months. Only in mid-2011 was there an effort to unify procurement laws. Following that effort, the finance ministry launched a government-wide procurement portal in August 2011, with the hope that it would enhance transparency in the procurement process.

TIMOR-LESTE'S ANTI-CORRUPTION COMMISSION

In order for the government's anti-corruption efforts to be widely effective, any new agencies nominally instituted to reduce corruption in Timor-Leste should not threaten or have overlapping mandates with those of the newly established Anti-Corruption Commission (Commissão-Anti Corrupção, CAC). This is important in order to avoid more institutional ritualism and to ensure that the government has a real opportunity to focus on the problem at hand.

Spurred by public frustration over the perceived growth of corruption, the National Parliament of Timor-Leste approved Law No. 8/2009, establishing Timor-Leste's Anti-Corruption Commission. The establishment of CAC was part of the administrative-reform agenda of the Fourth Constitutional government under Prime Minister Xanana Gusmão.[33] Apart from the establishment of CAC, this agenda included the establishment of the Public Service Commission in 2009.[34] Many public commentators supported the establishment of CAC and many others criticized it. Some argued that Timor-Leste did not need any specific institution to deal with corruption. They also argued that the PDHJ had to be strengthened, as it had some limited power to investigate corruption cases. Opponents doubted that CAC would be effective, given that its mandate only includes investigative powers and no prosecutorial power. Supporters of the new commission argued that Timor-Leste needed a specific institution to deal with corruption, citing the example of

---

[32] Secretary of State for the Council of Ministers, "Statement Regarding the Office of the Vice Prime Minister Mario Carrascalao," September 2, 2010, http://timor-leste.gov.tl/?p=3762&lang=en, accessed April 25, 2012.

[33] Xanana Gusmão, "2008: The Year of Administrative Reform," Government of Timor-Leste, Dili, transcript of speech delivered May 8, 2008, http://timor-leste.gov.tl/wp-content/uploads/2009/10/20080508_pm_reform_administracao_en.pdf, accessed June 27, 2012.

[34] See Law No. 7/2009, adopted by the National Parliament on July 15, 2009, www.unmit.org/legal/RDTL-Law/RDTL-Laws/Law%207-2009.pdf, accessed June 27, 2012.

Indonesia's Anti-Corruption Commission (KPK). They also argued that the PDHJ's twin mandates, to protect human rights and combat corruption, could be incompatible, given the possibility of human rights infringements in the process of investigating corruption cases. Most importantly, PDHJ was only granted the authority to carry out administrative investigations, not criminal investigations, so that it was important that the CAC be designated to investigate criminal cases of corruption. Supporters also argued that corruption is an extraordinary crime, so it needed an extraordinary institution to deal with it.

The law gives a very strong investigative mandate to CAC, though it has no prosecutorial power. Article 4 states that CAC has two broad mandates, namely prevention of corruption and criminal investigation of corruption. CAC's powers are categorized into two groups. Firstly, in terms of crime prevention, CAC's mandate includes the power to gather and analyze information on the causes of corruption and on the prevention of corruption; to raise public awareness; and to advise any institution or public entity on ways to prevent and combat corruption. Secondly, in terms of criminal investigation, CAC's mandate includes the power to conduct inquiries and carry out investigative inquires as delegated by the public prosecutor; to receive reports of crimes; to seek those responsible for the commission of crimes; to investigate evidence or reports of acts that may constitute a crime; to identify and arrest people; and to carry out necessary notifications directly or through another police authority.[35]

As for the debate over prosecutorial power, I would argue that, for the time being, CAC does not need a specific prosecutorial power. Indonesia's KPK operates in a very different environment, in which what might be described as the "judicial mafia" is still powerful throughout Indonesia.[36] Therefore, the KPK needs the power to prosecute in order for it to work effectively. The KPK cannot rely on Indonesia's corrupt prosecutor's office or the national police. That is not the case for Timor-Leste. Although capacity is still limited, the justice sector is not as corrupt as it is in Indonesia. There are still many clean young judges and prosecutors in the courts of Timor-Leste. So, these reliable public officials only need to be supported. CAC's presence can be complementary and can add ballast to the prosecution of corruption cases in the court.

However, the door has not been closed on the question of CAC having prosecutorial power in the future. The granting of these new powers would have to be accomplished through a constitutional amendment. It will be important to wait and see how these various institutions deal with corruption cases in the future. Their effectiveness and respective roles will no doubt be debated further in Timor-Leste, just as similar debates have been ongoing in other countries, such as Malaysia, regarding the Malaysian Anti-Corruption Commission (MACA). Just recently, MACA has proposed a constitutional amendment in order to grant it prosecutorial powers.[37] On the other hand, experience also shows that some other anti-corruption commissions in Asia have been successful without having prosecutorial powers. The Independent Commission for Anti-Corruption (ICAC) Hong Kong is a good example

---

[35] Ibid., Article 5.

[36] The Indonesian judiciary is widely acknowledged to be deeply corrupt, and in 2004 was cited as the most corrupt institution in Indonesia.

[37] "PM to Consider Proposal on Prosecution of Corruption Cases to be Determined by MACC," *Malaysian Digest*, August 29, 2010.

of this kind of success story. ICAC Hong Kong has no prosecutorial power, but it possesses a very strong investigative mandate. ICAC also conducted large-scale campaign and education programs.

For the time being, however, the CAC has to carry out its task in the context of the system that exists currently in Timor-Leste. There is no doubt that the commission will need to set up good cooperation and coordination with the office of the prosecutor general. The success of the commission will be determined by many other factors including strong political will and support from the government, adequate financing, strong public support, and, most importantly, a public commitment to the upholding of the rule of law. This last issue has been a true challenge for many developing countries, including Timor-Leste. All of these factors are critical if the country's government and citizenry wish to avoid institutional ritualism, for any new institutions may fail if they are not given sufficient power and support.

Following the election of its commissioner in February 2010, CAC finalized its first round of recruitments in November 2010. CAC's vision is to achieve "a democratic Timor-Leste with a strong culture of rejecting corruption in the interest and prosperity of the people." Its mission is "combating corruption through prevention, education, and investigation." Following recruitment of a staff that included ten investigators, the investigators were given six weeks of training. CAC then started criminal investigations in February 2011. By October 2011, CAC had investigated ten cases and submitted them to the prosecutor's office to be brought to trial, provided that the prosecutor was confident that the cases were based on strong admissible evidence.

INVESTIGATION VERSUS PREVENTION AND EDUCATION CAMPAIGNS

Many Timorese have become frustrated as they have observed the growing number of allegations of corruption, but relatively few corruption cases have been brought to justice. However, public frustration should not be the main reference point used by the CAC as it develops a strategy for combating corruption. There is no doubt that the CAC will concentrate on carrying out investigations as prescribed by the law. The CAC's mission, which is clearly set out in its founding law, comprises two important tasks: preventative action and criminal investigation. Although it is clear that the CAC must work in both these areas, the public tends to focus on the investigative aspect only. The public wanted to see some "big fish" investigated first, before focusing on other strategies of prevention and public education. This same approach was reflected in some political leaders' statements, which have contributed to the relatively poor awareness of the importance of educational and preventative strategies in dealing with corruption. This desire to see the "big fish" dramatically prosecuted and the related tendency to ignore the many "little fish" engaged in petty acts of corruption recalls the dualistic attitude shown in some of the common Timorese expressions described above.

This public tendency to focus only on grand corruption investigations and prosecutions reflects a misunderstanding of the strategies needed to combat corruption in Timor-Leste. While acknowledging the importance of carrying out investigations, we have to also look seriously at how to educate the public on this issue. CAC also has to take preventative action in every state institution in order to combat corruption. In short, these strategies should not compromise each other;

instead, they should be complementary. Given the small size of the population and the small bureaucracy that Timor has at the moment, a comprehensive preventative strategy, involving all stakeholders, would make a lot of difference to the country in the future.

It is imperative to establish, from the outset, a multipronged strategy to tackle corruption. Aside from its ongoing criminal investigation, CAC therefore embarked on a massive prevention campaign in 2011, including preventive activities carried out in collaboration with the Ministry of Finance, especially the customs department. Several workshops involving hundreds of custom officers were conducted by CAC. Several public meetings were also conducted targeting officers from the Ministry of Health and the Ministry of Tourism and Trade. These meetings with public servants were important in order to raise general awareness about corruption. These exercises were expected to result in the adoption of anti-corruption plans within each respective institution in the near future.

CONCLUSION

This chapter has described the importance of having different institutions to deal with the issue of corruption, but it has also highlighted the fact that establishing such institutions might create institutional ritualism, instead of actually resolving the problem. Timor-Leste still needs to avoid this phenomenon. This chapter also argues that Timor-Leste needs to develop a holistic approach to preventing corruption, as reflected in the CAC's mandate in the areas of prevention, campaigning and education, and criminal investigation. Education and campaigning are imperative to change people's perceptions and attitudes, as exemplified by the common expressions discussed above. It is clear that CAC and other state institutions will not be able to tackle corruption unless they do so as part of a national movement to combat corruption. We shall have to wait and see whether the new endeavor to combat post-independence corruption is successful in Timor-Leste in the years to come.

THE JUSTICE SECTOR: ACHIEVEMENTS, CHALLENGES, AND COMPARISONS

Andrew Marriott

INTRODUCTION

Although Timor-Leste, along with Cambodia, Sierra Leone, and others, has come to be viewed as something of a laboratory for international law, its domestic jurisdiction has generally drawn less attention. Many of the challenges it now faces in this regard have been seen before, broadly in the context of post-conflict development. Indeed, great benefits may now be derived from greater access to, and understanding of, innovations and best practices tested in comparable settings. This is not, however, license to import supposed solutions without consideration and adaptation to Timor-Leste's unique circumstances.

Those representing international agencies engaged in Timor-Leste, post-independence, understandably viewed crimes contravening established global norms as an urgent justice sector priority. Aid appears to have been directed accordingly. Despite curtailed, and diplomatically fraught, processes, a number of prosecutions of war crimes and crimes against humanity were completed through to sentencing and subsequent detention. While these select legal victories may reasonably be seen by some as helping to salve the wounds left by Timorese occupation and resistance, the need for justice extends further.

A mere decade into its renewed existence as a sovereign state, Timor-Leste is, unsurprisingly, yet to put the wrongs of recent history fully behind it. With the increasingly complex and industrious lives of its citizens requiring new institutions and establishing new dynamics, however, injustices perpetrated in the present day are as much of a concern. Though the democratic architecture of the Timorese state encompasses some commendable protections, the ability of formal institutions to respond directly to the range of everyday legal needs remains limited.

Some of these shortcomings are simply a reflection of Timor-Leste's emergence from a period of violence and turmoil. Others may represent developmental oversights or missteps that require attention and correction. With the public demand for access to (state-sponsored) justice growing in step with the investment in national identity, pressures on legal institutions will surely increase. Accordingly, as "no peace without justice" is as durable a maxim for post-conflict recovery as presently exists, it follows that swift and assiduous support to the justice sector will be needed in order to avoid a possible spillover of community tensions.

POLITICAL AND INSTITUTIONAL CONTEXT

In development terms, Timor-Leste is in the midst of a transition. The immediacy of aid provision under the auspices of humanitarian emergency has now largely been replaced by longer-term recovery and reconstruction goals. Practically, en masse delivery of items needed for survival has ceded the spotlight to less easily quantifiable issues of democratic governance. Especially in the context of a global financial crisis that has seen private philanthropy diminish and foreign aid budgets subjected to greater scrutiny, donor preference for the provision of readily monetized outcomes, reportable by the unit, appears further entrenched. In the justice sector, where gains are incremental and difficult to analyze discretely, conditions for attracting support are less than optimal.

The often nebulous nature of justice-sector development is here compounded by institutions the local norms and processes of which are still forming. Courts were a feature of colonial administration and subsequent occupation in Timor-Leste, but then, as now, they were predominantly a distant phenomenon, invoked only in rare instances.[1] In addition to the District Tribunal, and Court of Appeal, in Dili, courts now operate (albeit irregularly) in the regional centers of Suai, in Covalima; Pantemakassar, in the exclave of Oecusse; and Baucau, in its eponymous district. For a nation of just over a million citizens, at last estimation,[2] this may seem an adequate distribution of services. Factoring in the remarkably diffuse, rural, and remote population, however, means that many citizens remain practically outside of the court's reach and, conversely, lacking meaningful access to formal justice.

Given such a limited scope of operations, it is hardly surprising that national surveys, conducted sequentially post-independence, reveal a relatively low awareness and comprehension of formal justice mechanisms.[3] In isolated communities, there may be no functional understanding at all. Even where courts are present or in close proximity, they are still finding their place in the complex network of communitarian dynamics and bounded interactions that typify more traditional Timorese society. Where regional identities remain strong, and the dividends of the nation-building process are yet to filter comprehensively out, local ownership of state-sponsored legal institutions remains weak.

Regrettably, the performance of courts has, to date, done little to bolster confidence in the formal justice system. Aside from the logistical difficulties involved in presenting a case, district courts outside of Dili operate on notoriously flexible schedules and are often subject to substantial delays. In Oecusse, for example, the court typically hears matters only three or four days out of the month. Parties traveling—at great expense and sometimes risk—to contribute to a hearing have been known to be turned away from this supposedly permanent legal fixture rather

---

[1] Tanja Hohe and Rod Nixon, *Reconciling Justice: "Traditional" Law and State Judiciary in East Timor* (Dili: United States Institute of Peace, 2003), p. 19, available at www.gsdrc.org/docs/open/DS33.pdf, accessed April 25, 2012.

[2] World Bank, *World Development Indicators* (Washington, DC: World Bank, 2010), p. 3.

[3] The Asia Foundation (TAF), *Law and Justice in East Timor: A Survey of Citizen Awareness and Attitudes Regarding Law and Justice in East Timor* (Dili: TAF, 2008), p. 39.

than cause the court an hour's delay. Conversely, district courts may take eighteen months or more to bring a case to trial, during which time an informal solution has often been brokered.[4]

The principal cause of these shortcomings can perhaps be expressed in terms of resourcing. A centralized bureaucracy, elaborate procurement processes, and long supply chains all combine to complicate the business of running a legal institution. Although this situation is improving with the oversight and assistance of international development partners, many court offices and associated buildings are still without even basic amenities, such as regular power. Moreover, the erratic attendance of already sparse personnel continues to be a hindrance to courtroom operations. Despite regulations requiring judicial actors and other court staff to maintain a consistent presence at their assigned district base, and the construction of well-appointed residences for their benefit, many still, in effect, commute from Dili.[5] A roster of ongoing training and meetings is relied upon in such circumstances to provide a rationale for officials eager to return to the capital, leaving district court schedules to languish.

Other features of the justice system, though arguably performing well given the constraints, similarly demonstrate failings. The two presently operating prisons, in Dili's suburban area of Becora, and in Gleno, Ermera district, house just over two hundred detainees. Though conditions are not considered by international observers to be especially poor for the region, there are not separate holding facilities for juvenile offenders, nor for the vast number of those in pre-trial detention—a situation that can persist for months or even years.[6] Prison security is also in question following a series of high-profile escapes. Prosecutors and public defenders are few, and based mostly in Dili, meaning that investigation of a crime is far from expeditious, as much case preparation is delegated to (usually untrained) local police members. Likewise, communication between an accused and his or her mandated legal representation is often long delayed and thereafter infrequent.

Private lawyers are increasingly being called upon, especially in district locations, to serve in both prosecutorial and defense roles. Although their training was not meant to prepare them for such duties, these individuals have a greater rural and remote presence than do lawyers in public institutions and, due to their community ties (as distinct from their state-employed brethren, whose posts are often assigned with little regard to such heritage), they often enjoy a greater degree of community acceptance. Additionally, aid programming has increasingly led to private lawyers being employed as legal aid providers, whose job often encompasses awareness-raising as much as courtroom representation.[7] Though legislation passed in 2008 introduced a staged system of accreditation and regulation for the legal profession, there remains a great deal of variation in the quality of legal services.

With the formal system so impaired, it is hardly surprising that older, indigenous methods of dispute resolution remain in operation. These may provide a

---

[4] Laura Grenfell, "Legal Pluralism and the Rule of Law in Timor Leste," *Leiden Journal of International Law* 9 (2006): 318.

[5] Judicial System Monitoring Programme (JSMP), *Overview of Justice Sector 2006–2007* (Dili: JSMP, 2008), p. 11.

[6] Leanne Mitchell, *Who'll Save the Youth?* (Dili: International Committee of the Red Cross, 2007), p. 1.

[7] JSMP, *Overview of Justice Sector 2006–2007*, p. 12.

more immediate and socially durable solution to a range of conflicts, often deriving legitimacy from elements of local cosmology. These benefits, however, must be balanced against criticism that such custom often diverges from human rights principles in respect of its treatment of women.[8] Furthermore, loss of key personnel due to conflict, recent rural-urban migration, and the importation of foreign social norms are all alleged to be weakening the credibility of this traditional system. Some have claimed customary law to be increasingly arbitrary and subject to partisan capture.[9] For all these complaints, informal modes of justice remain far more familiar and so more liable to be chosen as a recourse by the majority of Timorese.

CURRENT LEGAL DISCOURSE

Given a comparison between formal and informal justice systems that generally reflects poorly on state-sponsored institutions and processes, the incorporation of custom in Timor-Leste's justice system has become a live political issue. During the period of United Nations administration, and intermittently thereafter, there have been attempts made to utilize local knowledge and authority in sentencing, to achieve a more enforceable and fitting community-focused outcome. While such restorative approaches are now gaining a substantial following in other jurisdictions, policy makers in Timor-Leste have, over the post-independence period, previously viewed direct integration warily.[10]

Some commentators have suggested that disappointment with the scope and service of the courts has prompted something of a return to traditional methods.[11] Despite a range of complaints, there remains a high degree of trust in local leadership and in the modes of dispute resolution locally employed. With two justice systems in operation, and the government associated with the lesser favored option, that government can be expected to recognize that it faces a potential political liability. Accordingly, the formerly disreputable realm of custom is presently undergoing a degree of civic rehabilitation, with a view to bringing it more under the aegis of the state.

While there is merit in seeking to draw on practices that are already familiar and trusted, care will need to be taken to ensure that the government is neither seen to condone outcomes at odds with its human rights obligations nor that it is coopting local networks. To replace credibility derived from a sense of place, and of belonging, with a license granted by a remote central power would very likely erode the locally understood validity of decision making based on customary practices and authority.

One draft law currently under consideration by the parliament proposes just this. Furthermore, this project appears to proceed from flawed assumptions that customary law is homogenous across the country, and that selective use may be

---

[8] Hohe and Nixon, *Reconciling Justice*, p. 67.

[9] David Mearns, *Looking Both Ways: Models for Justice in East Timor* (Sydney: Australian Legal Resources International, 2002), p. 52.

[10] Simon Butt, Natalie David, and Nathan Laws, *Looking Forward: Local Dispute Resolution Mechanisms in Timor-Leste* (Dili: Australian Legal Resources International for the Asia Foundation in Timor-Leste, 2004), p. 36; Andrew Harrington, "Institutions and the East Timorese Experience," *East Timor Law Journal* 7 (2006): 9.

[11] Ewa Wojkowska, *Doing Justice: How Informal Justice Systems Can Contribute* (Oslo: United Nations Development Programme, 2006), p. 18.

made of certain elements with the remainder discarded.[12] Requiring that local communities conform with national legislation can be a coercive policy tool. Education, although slower to produce results, may conversely meet with greater public acceptance and preserve vital routes of dispute resolution. Trials conducted by civil society actors in Oecusse, for example, show that traditional leaders are receptive to incorporating human rights norms in their determinations, and to facilitating referral to the formal system where necessary.[13]

One area in which some degree of synthesis may be useful is in respect of case backlog. This has consistently been an area of embarrassment for the formal justice system, with in excess of four thousand cases reported, by various sources, as pending. Some of these date from the period of the 2006 crisis, and some from still earlier times. This general situation is often cited by commentators, and especially political detractors, as reducing the courts' responsiveness to current community needs.[14]

Since many such cases deal with alleged nonviolent property crimes and associated crimes of opportunity, there is a chance to implement a more measured response. The notion of a diversion program is gaining support from some quarters of government. This would likely entail carefully vetted defendants voluntarily pleading guilty in order to avoid a custodial sentence and, instead, undertaking community service as imposed (under certain conditions) by local leaders and elders. As well as reducing pressure on the courts, this option would also promote awareness and ownership of the formal system and, so, deserves attention.

In a strongly communitarian society such as Timor-Leste, reintegration of offenders is a high priority. This is true at both local and national levels. Rightly or wrongly, the work of the Commission for Truth, Reconciliation, and Reception (known by its Portuguese acronym, CAVR) in facilitating the return of pre-independence–era combatants to their respective communities—a process referred to locally as *acolhimentu* (reception)—is widely viewed as a success. The report of the commission stands as an extensive testament to the hardships of occupation, the desperation of the independence struggle, and the violence that preceded Timor-Leste's reemergence as a state. The report also offers a detailed list of recommendations toward a more complete resolution of conflict.[15]

Political pragmatism, alongside practical difficulty, has long delayed consideration of these recommendations and caused them to be largely overlooked. Timor-Leste's post-independence leaders, no doubt keen to preserve the fragile peace enjoyed by their new nation, have seemingly been loath to provoke further displeasure from Indonesia. Given the shared border between Timor-Leste and Indonesian West Timor, as well as increasing trade links and a clear historical antipathy to negotiate, the relationship has evidently required compromise, and a

---

[12] United Nations Development Program, *Report of the Consultation Workshop on Customary Law* (Dili: UNDP, 2009), p. 2.

[13] Judicial System Monitoring Programme, *Justice Not Served by Truth and Friendship Commission* (Dili: JSMP, 2008), p. 2.

[14] JSMP, *Overview of Justice Sector 2006–2007*, p. 15.

[15] Dionisio Babo-Soares, "Nahe biti: The Philosophy and Process of Grassroots Reconciliation (and Justice) in East Timor," *Asia Pacific Journal of Anthropology* 5,1 (2004): 10; José Trindade and Bryant Castro, *Rethinking Timorese Identity as a Peacebuilding Strategy: The Lorosa'e— Loromonu Conflict from a Traditional Perspective* (Dili: The European Union's Rapid Reaction Mechanism Programme, 2007), p. 23.

deft diplomatic touch. This has sparked criticism that justice has become a casualty of realpolitik. Certainly, calls for international justice have lately been given little evident priority by Timorese leadership.

Despite sharing some characteristics with the earlier CAVR, the jointly Timorese and Indonesian Commission for Truth and Friendship (CTF) came under fire for supposedly embodying this spirit of political compromise. With the diplomatically fraught objective of settling on an agreed narrative of the conflict, hearings of the CTF were understandably controversial. From the Timorese perspective, some felt that victims were subject to inappropriate scrutiny whereas sentenced perpetrators were availed of an opportunity to exculpate themselves.[16] The fairness of the process aside, the CTF's report (cautiously prepared by an international team of researchers) made many of the same recommendations as the CAVR, adding to public pressure to see these inconsistencies addressed.

At the time of writing, a series of proposals built around the recommendations of the CAVR report are being considered by the parliament's Commission on Judicial and Constitutional Affairs. Besides suggestions for a nationwide series of memorials honoring participants in the independence struggle, and for improved education addressing this episode of Timorese history, the chief concern is reparations. With the memory of recent government-administered payments to internally displaced persons, and pensions to the elderly and to veterans likely lingering in the public mind, the prospect of further disbursements is eagerly awaited. Debate over the source of funds (perhaps involving international interests), and the framework for their administration is, however, likely to delay the advent of such monies.

This desire to see past crimes fade into history is evidenced elsewhere in the current political landscape. Enthusiastic—and controversial—use has been made of the constitutionally-afforded Presidential Pardon. Notably, in 2008, over eighty such pardons were announced to coincide with the May 20 national celebrations of the restoration of independence. Of those pardoned at this time, several had been serving sentences for war crimes and crimes against humanity. The release of one particular individual, Joni Marques, former leader of the Indonesian-backed Team Alpha militia whose exploits in Lospalos district were among the most brutal of the conflict, caused much disquiet. Given that the trial of Marques and nine of his fellow militiamen was the first post-independence prosecution (and one of quite few) concerned with crimes against humanity, this response is perhaps not surprising.[17] Commentators noted that eligibility criteria for the pardons appeared to have been generously interpreted, and some pointed to the possible influence of Catholic teachings on forgiveness and confession.[18]

The parliamentary power to authorize amnesties may also soon be invoked. A draft law is, at the time of writing, being circulated and would, in its current form, seem intended to close off many avenues for justice through international law. Distinct from the presidential power to grant clemency after the passage (and partial service) of a sentence, amnesties of this kind could afford certain exemptions from a person's liability to stand trial. Dispute may be expected to center on the period of

---

[16] JSMP, *Justice Not Served By Truth*, p. 1

[17] Judicial System Monitoring Programme, *The General Prosecutor V. Joni Marques and Nine Others (The Los Palos Case)—A JSMP Trial Report* (Dili: JSMP, 2002), p. 38.

[18] Judicial System Monitoring Programme, *Crimes Against Humanity Perpetrators Released* (Dili: JSMP, June 20, 2008), p. 1.

time during which activities took place for which amnesty may be granted. Input from the international community will likely skirt this issue, given the probability of embarrassment for many senior politicians who are not only veterans of the independence struggle but also of preceding, violent infighting between partisan interest groups.

There are limits to this prevailing attitude of forgiveness. President José Ramos-Horta has publicly declared his willingness to pardon (under prescribed conditions) those alleged to have been directly involved in the February 11, 2008, confrontation in which he was injured. As appeals against conviction are ongoing, this preemption of judicial outcome has drawn criticism on separation-of-powers grounds.[19]

The same forbearance has, however, not been shown to another of those accused of planning the attack. The sometime partner of rebel leader Alfredo Reinado (who was killed in the exchange of fire on February 11), Angelita Pires, was brought to trial despite claims of insufficient and contradictory evidence.[20] Pires having been acquitted, it appears the prosecutor-general's office has reportedly taken the highly unorthodox step of indicating to Pires's counsel an intention to appeal. Whereas pardon and amnesty provisions have prompted concerns about impunity, the seeming disparity of treatment perceived as occurring in this case, compared with other similar cases, has caused some to question whether prosecutions might also, in some instances, be subject to political direction.

ACHIEVEMENTS TO DATE

Discussions of the rule of law in Timor-Leste can focus overly on the shortcomings of the system. It bears remembering that in just over a decade of renewed independence, Timor-Leste has made significant progress toward establishing a modern and democratic justice sector. However qualified or tempered by imperfect practice, these tentative steps—taken in the most trying of circumstances—merit a certain acclaim. In particular, the constitution itself is worthy of positive regard. Admittedly bearing the marks of international assistance, it even so retains a distinctly Timorese character, incorporating judicious reference to custom and to the supportive role of the Catholic Church during the resistance era.

Remarkably, for a political system that has evolved in part from a guerrilla movement, Timor-Leste's constitution largely frames instruments of state to reflect inclusive and egalitarian values. Though its drafting does not preclude all ambiguity, it nonetheless provides a firm legal foundation for an emerging democracy. The popular mandates that determine the respective powers of president and prime minister have been cited as an interpretive fault line, particularly in light of historical antagonism between certain of the respective office-bearers.[21] Whatever may be inferred from political dynamics and expressions of policy, the constitution of Timor-Leste declares an intention to take its lead from the (predominantly Western) tradition of representative, and responsive, governance.

---

[19] ABC News, "Ramos-Horta Welcomes Assassination Attempt Trials, Mulls Pardon," *ABC News Online*, March 5, 2009, p. 1, available at www.abc.net.au/news/2009-03-05/ramos-horta-welcomes-assassination-attempt-trials/1608910, accessed May 16, 2012.

[20] Judicial System Monitoring Programme, *Overview of Justice Sector 2009* (Dili: JSMP, 2010), p. 47.

[21] Dennis Shoesmith, "Divided Leadership in a Semi-Presidential System," *Asian Survey* 43,2 (2003): 231–32.

Human rights are well enshrined in Timor-Leste's organic laws. An extensive suite of protections and guarantees is listed throughout the constitution and echoed in specific statutes. As with most jurisdictions, these must be considered primarily as hortatory statements. The practical effect of a right to housing, for example, is belied by the country's continued poverty. Similarly, research suggests that, where the Catholic Church has become bonded to Timor-Leste's modern creation myth, freedom of religion is not always a well understood, or even welcome, concept.[22]

Timor-Leste is also extensively subscribed to treaty law. In some instances, this merely reiterates constitutional safeguards, but in others (as in the proclaimed stance on arms use and proliferation) it practically extends the array of obligations owed by the government, not only to its citizens, but also to the rest of the world. Timor-Leste became signatory to a wide range of treaties shortly following independence, leading some to question the degree to which this may have been more out of a desire to be seen as a legitimate state power than a clear accord with the principles of international law documented within the agreements. Anecdotally, some senior government officials have expressed a view that Timor-Leste's observance of treaty law is, at least in part, an artefact of international pressure and ought to be interpreted in light of national interest—a position, of course, not unheard-of in the developed world.

Having inherited, by quirk of history, a set of laws that reflect neither local conditions nor best practice, Timor-Leste continues the difficult process of producing a domestic statute book. The first legal act of the United Nations Transitional Administration (UNTAET), post-independence, was to decree that all laws previously operating in the jurisdiction continued to be applicable except where inconsistent with the United Nations mandate—as with the death penalty. Although this reinforcement of existing laws was an interim measure intended to assist peacekeeping efforts, this perpetuated many features of a legal system that had been a means of oppression.

Some Indonesian statutes that have, in their originating jurisdiction, long since been repealed or redrafted, linger on as "legal revenants" in Timorese courtrooms. As a rule, these reflect an explicitly Islamic morality and an authoritarian bent that punishes any slight to state power or circumvention of hierarchy. While the most egregious of these laws have now been replaced by Timorese legislation, some examples persist, typically in less trafficked areas of law. Moreover, as the majority of Timorese legal practitioners were educated in this system, their interpretation and understanding is still somewhat colored by its precepts. In the main, however, Indonesian law has gradually been overtaken, such that Timorese law bears decreasing similarity to the statutes governing its neighboring jurisdiction.

Today, most civic activity is regulated under Timorese law. Immigration, commerce, traffic movement, and the terms of political office are all, inter alia, direct expressions of domestic legislation. Although some have criticized the distinctly Lusophone flavor of many new laws, and the influence over drafting maintained by certain international advisers, nonetheless parliamentary members of the Commission on Judicial and Constitutional Affairs have undertaken active legislative development and scrutiny.

---

[22] Belun, *Religious Identity and Conflict in Timor-Leste: An EWER Program Policy Brief* (Dili: Belun, 2009), p. 3.

A recent legal milestone was reached with the passage of the Timorese Criminal Code in late 2008. Drafts had been circulated since 2003, but had encountered resistance on two main points. Criminal defamation, used elsewhere in the region to discourage and punish critics of the government, was a holdover from Indonesian law and (aside from its incompatibility with freedom of speech) undeniably a powerful political tool.[23] Bowing to pressure from local civil society and the international community alike, this offense was finally removed, but not before the minister of justice had threatened its eleventh-hour use against an investigative journalist.

As well as updating the range of offenses to reflect technological advances, more modern social mores, and the increasingly transnational nature of crime, the Timorese Criminal Code does markedly improve legal remedies for women. While these provisions will, hopefully, soon be bolstered by a dedicated domestic-violence law, the legal code does recognize—for the first time in Timorese law—rape within marriage, and shifts the existence of a prior relationship between perpetrator and victim from a mitigating to an aggravating factor.[24]

Monumental legislative fixture though it is, the Criminal Code does contain—at least to an international audience—some regrettable inequities. With the Catholic Church a much-consulted stakeholder in public policy, it is hardly surprising that the decriminalization of abortion should provoke such a hard-fought battle. Whilst advocacy from local women's groups and the international community succeeded in seeing the Criminal Code pass with exceptions for abortion when necessary to save the mother's life, a swiftly passed amendment soon made even this exception a practical impossibility.[25]

While international input to the justice sector remains substantial, Timorese personnel are gradually taking on a greater responsibility in key court roles. Given that so few local legal professionals remained in Timor-Leste following the conflict, initially all but a few positions were taken on by foreign personnel, generally under the auspices of the United Nations. Claims continue to be made that there is an over-reliance on external expertise, but this trend is now reversing. Timorese judges now preside over hearings, Timorese prosecutors prepare cases, and Timorese public defenders represent clients. Though such individuals remain relatively few (weighed against the needs of the system), their presence is rightly a source of national pride.

The capacity of local court actors has been the subject of some contention. When, post-independence, individuals with legal experience were invited to undertake United Nations–sponsored training, all infamously failed the subsequent examinations. Although embarrassing for the participants, this result reveals poor planning at least as much as a steep learning curve.[26] Lessons conducted in Portuguese were reportedly not well understood by most of the Timorese students, and language classes undertaken alongside legal coursework did little to increase

---

[23] Warren Wright, "Criminal Defamation in East Timor—A Miscarriage of Justice," *East Timor Law Journal* 5 (2009): 1–2.

[24] Judicial System Monitoring Programme, *Draft Penal Code Needs Final Adjustment* (Dili: JSMP, 2008), p. 1.

[25] Judicial System Monitoring Programme, *Abortion Reform Still Needed: Article 141 of the East Timor Penal Code Must Comply with Constitution and International Law* (Dili: JSMP, 2009), p. 2.

[26] Carolyn Graydon, "Local Justice Systems in Timor-Leste: Washed Up, or Watch This Space?" *Development Bulletin* 68 (2005): 67–68.

their comprehension. Later efforts have utilized mentoring and on-the-job training, apparently to greater effect than by employing the parallel class methodology.

With the first cohort of Timorese court actors taking their place, attention is increasingly focused on introducing new local personnel into the system. Four universities now offer a law program—admittedly with varying degrees of consistency—and a process for legal accreditation has been established. Those fortunate enough to have secured a sought-after place at the Legal Training Centre undergo a two-year program (incorporating language training) that will authorize graduating students to take up roles in prosecution, in defense, and on the bench.

The Centre's heavily Portuguese-influenced curriculum has drawn some negative commentary, with opponents claiming that it further entrenches linguistic (and class) divides.[27] Certainly the character of legal education may merit attention, and greater assistance may be needed to ensure a supply of qualified personnel sufficient to meet the country's legal needs. The establishment of a national training scheme, however, with its objective of furthering Timorese ownership of, and engagement with, the formal justice system, stands as an important accomplishment.

NEXT STEPS

Despite substantial additions, such as the Criminal Code, there remain some notable absences from the Timorese statute book. With such lacunae precipitating an uncomfortable reliance on the outmoded and mistrusted Indonesian laws persisting from pre-independence times, there are both practical and political reasons to introduce overriding legislation. Especially in a post-conflict context, legislation may render the results of disputes more consistently predictable, a condition that, over time, would actually diminish the likelihood of parties entering into such disputes—this phenomenon is at the heart of rule-of-law theory.

With these imperatives in mind, it is no surprise to find the Timorese parliament with a busy legislative agenda. There are so many draft laws competing for attention, however, that there is now a risk that the fundamentals of the legal system may be neglected (or ignored as too contentious) in preference to politically favored topics. Though the criminal law has now largely been settled, civil law (that is, the body of laws regulating private disputes between citizens as opposed to those in which the State is a party) remains incomplete. Some associated civil procedure has been agreed upon, and passed into law, but without the substantive code in place, there is simply nothing to apply. For the time being, such disputes may be resolved by reference to an odd admixture of Timorese process and preceding Indonesian law, though in practice civil matters receive short shrift in the courts. As the Timorese economy grows, and a greater emphasis is placed on trade and commerce, the need for clearer governance in the private sphere will become even more apparent.

The passage into law of the Criminal Code, meanwhile, has not unequivocally raised the bar for the entire justice system. There remain, of course, some areas of particularly troubling practice. Not the least of these is in respect of juvenile justice. Having acceded, without reservation, to the Convention on the Rights of the Child, and its Optional Protocols (which allow for enforcement mechanisms), the

---

[27] Judicial System Monitoring Programme, *The Private Lawyers Statute: Overview and Analysis* (Dili: JSMP, 2008), p. 8.

government of Timor-Leste has explicit obligations in this area and so will require dedicated legislative structures to ensure their proper implementation.

Juvenile justice comes into starkest relief in detention. Though the prison population is relatively small, and the proportion of juveniles among this population smaller again, there nonetheless remains a live concern.[28] Best practice (and treaty law) mandates not only that incarceration ought to be a last resort in the sentencing of juveniles, but also that any custodial term be served separately from adult inmates. In Timor-Leste, this is regrettably not the case. Though civil society ensures a degree of support and oversight to youth in prison, this situation risks further marginalizing already vulnerable individuals, and on compassionate, as well as legal, grounds, ought not persist. Accordingly, a draft law in circulation at the time of writing merits immediate consideration.

The passage of legislation is, of course, not the end of the matter when it comes to reform of the justice system. The passage of a witness protection law in Timor-Leste, though signaling a laudable governmental intent, is yet to be noticeably translated into practice. As a result, victims and witnesses to crime are not well served by legal institutions. Survivors of sexual assault and domestic abuse are regularly kept by police together with their aggressors.[29] This phenomenon is addressed by the legislation, but without extensive training and socialization, no change in behavior can realistically be expected.

Witnesses, whether they are survivors of criminal acts or not, are typically reluctant to participate in courtroom hearings. Though technically the legal provisions are now in place to safeguard anonymity and personal security, in practice there is no such guarantee. In a close-knit society such as Timor-Leste, these measures would be difficult to deliver under the best of circumstances. Another factor diminishing the likelihood of testimonial evidence is the delay in reaching a hearing date. Since a case may take many months, or even years, to come to trial, there may be intense and sustained pressure on witnesses to accommodate a more immediate solution, however imperfect. Accordingly, it is often the case that in the course of a trial, because a determination has already been made according to custom and within the community, witnesses will be noncompliant and pretend no knowledge of facts to which they had previously sworn. Such cases are usually then dismissed for want of evidence.

Not all of the pressing issues facing Timor-Leste's justice system resolve exclusively to legislation. Many are, in fact, a question of process and of emerging professional culture. One of the principal impediments to improved public understanding and ownership of the courts is the difficulty of gaining information from them. This is, admittedly, a widely observed problem, affecting many sectors. The absence of a clear channel for engagement with legal institutions, however, and for the provision of data to inform policy and improve access, risks denying citizens an outlet for their conflicts and so upsetting the community's fragile peace.

At least part of this obstruction derives from a lack of role clarity among court staff. With the parameters of their employment, and the content of their jobs, not adequately delineated or understood, the exchange of even basic information is often curtailed from fear of inadvertent error. This hinders attempts toward greater

---

[28] Mitchell, *Who'll Save the Youth?*, p. 1.

[29] Aisling Swaine, *Traditional Justice and Gender-Based Violence* (Dili: International Rescue Committee, 2003), p. 3.

transparency and accountability and, moreover, makes for a typically frustrating and alienating experience among those attempting to navigate the system. The experience of civil society monitors suggests that, as with so much in Timor-Leste, obtaining pertinent facts often requires a personal connection, enough to counterbalance concerns over the extent of proper authorization. Training is needed on the distinctions between public documents and confidential information, certainly, but perhaps the greater need is in inculcating a working ethos in the courts that better reflects service to the community.

The present scarcity of hard data from the justice system is, of course, not solely a problem that results from tentative personnel. Inconsistent reporting and filing processes not only hinder access to specific case results, but also disallow aggregation and analysis of data. Such data might be used by government as empirical evidence in the formation of policy, but also by judicial actors as precedent in determining appropriate responses to a recurring legal problem. In both respects, more comprehensive and up-to-date information would help to make the legal system more responsive and less arbitrary.

There remains a great deal of debate over the introduction of a computer-assisted–case-tracking system. Despite a great deal of financial and practical support from the international community, elements within the justice sector appear resistant to this innovation, perhaps fearing the greater oversight and stricter enforcement of protocol that such a system would allow. Legitimately, concerns have been expressed about the importation of software packages from other jurisdictions without alterations and amendments to account for the unique features of the Timorese context. Whatever the rationale, delays in the introduction of such a measure effectively leave the justice system without a consistent frame of reference for analyzing its own successes and failures, and deny opportunities for well-founded innovation and improvement.

To make necessary changes, the justice system must also be adequately resourced. This is not only a matter of budgeting to reflect emerging and projected needs but also of ensuring efficient procurement and logistics. This is a constraint faced across the entire suite of state-sponsored service provision, with departmental budgets regularly under spent. The problem of disbursing allocated public funds has, in fact, been recognized to the extent that ministers are lately subject to a system of ranking by the political executive according to their ability to translate their portfolio budgets into measurable outputs.[30]

Though the situation is improving, courts still face shortages, especially at locations outside Dili. Despite budgeting for generators to be installed at all court buildings, as well as prosecutorial and defense offices—where these exist—many such buildings remain without backup power and other basic amenities. Requisitioning for even simple fixtures such as chairs and light globes has historically proven complex. Admittedly, Timor-Leste's geography can often impede the delivery of goods and the extension of services, but with assistance from other sectors also filtering out to the districts, some further investments and improvements might perhaps be implemented. Certainly it does not build public confidence in the courts to have them so undersupplied.

---

[30] ABC News, "Timor Advisory Body Calls For Budget Amendments," *ABC News Online,* July 22, 2008, p. 1, available at www.radioaustralia.net.au/international/radio/onairhighlights/timor-advisory-body-calls-for-budget-amendments, accessed May 16, 2012.

Resourcing shortfalls in the courts affect the levels of personnel, as well as material, resources. With a small corps of prosecutors and public defenders who are often recalled to Dili, and many on the bench being expatriates with obligations elsewhere, cases are regularly postponed for a lack of key staff. In some instances, private lawyers may be called upon to fill in, though their training does not always provide a firm grounding for these specific roles. Though membership of the fledgling legal professional body, the Asosiasaun Advogadu Timor-Leste (AATL), puts the number of local practitioners at just over one hundred, relatively few conduct work involving courtroom representation.[31] In part, this reflects a common experience of legal education in other jurisdictions and difficulty in adapting such learning to the Timorese system.

Legal education now occurring within Timor-Leste presents its own set of problems. Although four universities now claim law programs, in practice the curriculum in at least some institutions is inconsistent and lectures irregular. With there being so few established Timorese lawyers, and those individuals being consequently sought after, academic commitments are often held hostage to the scheduling dictates of other employment. The peculiarities of such education are compounded by the vagaries of an accreditation system that has certified successive cohorts of law graduates who are unprepared to function in the profession. While this may, in part, reflect fluctuating standards of teaching, it likely also reflects variance in the language of instruction—Portuguese seemingly being most well regarded.[32]

Whatever the cause of withholding accreditation from certain legal courses, the effect is to perpetuate a shortage in the number of qualified court actors and, meanwhile, a proliferation of quasi-legal brokers and facilitators. With the passage, in 2008, of a law regulating the legal profession, completion of a mandated two-year practical training course has become the sole route to official standing (though a grace period for compliance is, at the time of writing, yet to elapse). Entry into this Legal Training Centre is thus highly competitive, and annual intakes are limited to between sixteen and thirty students.[33]

With the duration of this extra level of instruction so long, and class size so small, qualified personnel will be in limited supply for some time to come. In the meantime, international advisors and functionaries will become further entrenched, risking perceptions that Timor-Leste's legal system remains under foreign control and leading to decreased Timorese investment in the courts. Regularization of the accreditation system for tertiary education in law, relaxation of some requirements for professional registration, and increased resourcing to extend participation in practical training would all assist in ensuring that public demand for justice services may be better met.

LONGER-TERM CHALLENGES

While some of the issues faced by Timor-Leste's justice system may be immediately addressed by way of legislation, as well as clarification of process and

---

[31] JSMP, *Private Lawyers Statute*, p. 5.

[32] Asian Development Bank (ADB), *Social and Economic Development Brief—Timor Leste* (Manila: ADB, 2007), p. 22.

[33] JSMP, *Private Lawyers Statute*, p. 8.

attendant campaigns of education, some will inevitably require a subtler shifting of institutional culture. One of the more insidious developments in the country's rapidly shifting legal terrain concerns the very means by which change is decided upon. Rather than staging open and extensive consultation among the public and key stakeholders, the government tends to draft legislation independently, which then precipitates reform and becomes the focus of debate.[34] This narrows debate to the terms considered within the document, and because of the somewhat exclusive nature of legal language, can also hamper involvement from the full range of invested participants.

Much consultation on proposed legal change is focused on Dili. This not only risks skewing the response to public consultation by reflecting predominantly urban concerns but also shifts the demographic of stakeholders and active participants in debate. In particular, there is likely to be a far higher representation of international interests involved in consultations centered in Dili. This may produce, in the public mind, an unfortunate perception that the machinery of government is geared to take into account foreign views to a greater extent than those of its actual constituency. Development partners such as the United Nations, who shoulder a considerable amount of the responsibility for authoring legislation, are increasingly seeking to engage with local civil society and with the community at large. Short timelines for drafting legislation and limited resources for raising public awareness, however, both appear to constrain these commendable attempts. Conversely, a lack of coordination among members of civil society can often hinder communication and slow consensus building.

The drafting of new laws post-independence all too often employs—without appropriate alteration—provisions from other jurisdictions, thus worsening perceptions that foreign powers have co-opted the shaping of Timorese law. While a degree of international comparison is necessary to insure best practice, and may result in useful innovations, the reflexive importation of external models entails some risk. Although there is a range of legal issues requiring urgent response, and recourse to already established legislative structures may seem efficient, this kind of legislative transplantation can rarely be done without careful examination of context.

In Timor-Leste, the system of checks and balances within which legislation is typically situated is yet to be fully realized. The absence in Timorese law of a statute defining legal terms and providing guidelines for the reading of other acts of parliament, for example, leaves judicial process open to inconsistencies until precedent is settled. Direct importation of legal norms and policy responses into the body of Timorese law, therefore, risks failing to constrain statutory interpretation adequately, producing unintended and potentially negative consequences. Also, mismatches between the reality described by the law and that experienced by the public may further erode confidence in legal institutions.

While there are a number of experienced international drafters employed by government and, promisingly, a cohort of Timorese drafters now being trained, caution must still be exercised to ensure that the true character of Timorese life and society is reflected in the law. Given the patchwork of legal influences that Timor-Leste has inherited, discerning the interrelation of laws requires a keen legal eye, and likely also considerable local understanding. Accordingly, as the building blocks of

---

[34] JSMP, *Overview of Justice Sector 2009*, p. 2.

the country's justice system are laid, care (and time) must be taken to avoid the need for later reconstruction.

A source of much contention in nearly every area of policy is that of language. One of two official languages, along with Tetum, Portuguese is now taught at primary and secondary levels and is therefore enjoying a resurgence. It nonetheless remains a minority language and historically associated with elites. Tetum enjoys a far wider acceptance and understanding, though other local languages remain common, especially outside urban centers. This diversity, however vital, represents a considerable challenge to the establishment of accessible modes of formal justice.

Overreliance on Portuguese poses risks for both law making and courtroom practice. Laws are commonly drafted in this language, with versions in Tetum (and often English) usually produced some time later or not at all. This has created an odd situation whereby parliamentarians have been known to abstain from voting on key legislation because it has not been provided, or explained, to them in a language they can understand. For the same reason, it can often be difficult to educate members of the public on their own legal rights and remedies, and more difficult still for (mostly Indonesian-trained, and Indonesian-speaking) lawyers to interpret, argue, and apply statute. Clearly, where the body of law is practically inaccessible to the majority of the citizenry, those citizens may raise questions about their government's democratic legitimacy.

Language difficulties diminish both the accessibility and efficiency of court hearings. Since most judicial actors are either international contractors or the product of Lusophone education, Portuguese is almost universally spoken at the bench. Court staff, including prosecutors and defenders, tend more commonly to be upwardly mobile Timorese and, so, to use Tetum. The parties, especially outside of Dili, seem mostly to communicate in their local language. Accordingly, in the Baucau district court, for example, testimony may be translated from the local Macassae into Tetum and thereafter from Tetum into Portuguese. Much is lost in translation, especially given legal requirements for precision. Translators are heavily relied upon, and have in some areas taken on an unusually participatory role. Such individuals may paraphrase or condense testimony, editorialize on its content, and even pose questions to the parties. Obviously, this process is hardly in keeping with the best conceptions of due process. Above even these concerns, however, is the fact that translation through three languages (a practice that this is, fortunately, decreasing at some courts where Tetum is now more widely used) inordinately prolongs the duration of hearings. Formal justice thus becomes not only less comprehensible but also less timely. While the gradual introduction of Timorese nationals as judicial actors will undoubtedly improve the process on these grounds, much institutional credibility stands to be lost in the interim.

The legal profession itself is subject to some division along linguistic lines. Some practitioners (often associated with elite interests and families formerly invested with authority during colonial times) undertook legal education in Lusophone jurisdictions, whether Portugal, Macau, Brazil, or Mozambique. Given the justice-sector preference for Portuguese, this minority has, reportedly, found steady and lucrative employment in government and with its development partners. Most Timorese lawyers, however, were trained in Indonesia, where a large proportion of them were simultaneously involved in pro-independence activism. This group has generally found it difficult to sustain a legal practice upon returning to Timor-Leste. This disparity, along with broadly observed differences of class and political background, has hampered efforts toward the development of a unified and well-coordinated legal profession.

Indonesian-speaking factions of practitioners complain that their Lusophone colleagues are deliberately producing an unnecessarily complex legal culture in order to protect and further entrench elite advantage. Portuguese-speaking lawyers have been known to retort that their detractors, for all their egalitarian critique, have not enjoyed the same standard of education and are simply envious of the associated status and financial benefits that accrue to those trained in Portuguese-language programs. With the truth likely somewhere in between, one indisputable fact is that the field as a whole suffers from the perception that it lacks a cohesive ethos of professionalism.

With such dissent among the ranks, it is hardly surprising that the AATL, as a bar-association prototype, has yet to mobilize the collective potential of the profession. While many lawyers are, as respected members of their communities, involved in legal awareness raising and dispute resolution, this broad project appears to be happening in an ad hoc and unrehearsed fashion. Professional guidelines and training materials might render such activities more consistent and effective.

Given such isolated practice, and the lack of collegial spirit, the purpose of professional membership in the AATL remains disputed. Continuing education has been mooted, but this responsibility has, to date, largely fallen to international actors. Advocacy is a sensitive topic, with so many reliant on government for their employment and therefore disinclined to criticize the system publicly. With regulation of lawyers soon to be enforced,[35] further internal contest can be expected before a coherent professional culture emerges.

Apart from the status that their education generally brings, part of the reason that lawyers are called upon to explain legal concepts (and often provide political commentary as well) is simply that there is often no alternative source of information. While attempts at distributing legal bulletins to local administrators have intermittently been made through the agency of the Ministry of State Administration, in general, civil society has been more consistent in its outreach functions. Notably, local radio stations have proven effective in disseminating up-to-date information about legal rights and responsibilities, and they have reached a broader audience than is typically engaged through official channels.

Continued need for such measures underscores the limited presence of the formal justice system outside of urban centers. Although a shift toward locally led community policing is gradually extending the reach of the state, police members receive little training on legal process, and so are rarely good ambassadors of the system. Misunderstandings and provisional responses may therefore coalesce into precedent. This is particularly evident in respect to gender-based violence, where widespread tolerance for elements of custom that are sometimes taken to license a degree of violence against women and children belies official positions in respect of human rights. While human rights terminology may be expressed and reproduced across Timor-Leste in more formal settings, it nonetheless contains relatively new ideas that may sometimes clash with preexisting norms. For a genuine understanding of human rights to integrate with the dynamics of Timorese society

---

[35] JSMP, *Private Lawyers Statute*, p. 7.

will take not only time but also a concerted effort at education, perhaps through the national curriculum.

Remote and rural communities suffer even more acutely from a lack of formal legal services. Though in recent times there have been some causes for optimism, these are more often a result of individuals acting responsibly than the result of any state-sponsored, coordinated program. Judicial actors in some district jurisdictions have, of their own accord, begun developing a "circuit court" schedule to facilitate attendance of parties at hearings.[36] Private lawyers too, many of whom have signed on with international sponsors as contracted legal aid providers, are espousing a commitment to greater professional mobility and coverage of more remote locations. With transport outside regional capitals often unreliable and always costly, this is a substantial concession to the practicalities of rural Timorese life. Despite these commendable first steps, however, obdurate geography and political caprice remain sizeable obstacles to a truly inclusive national justice-sector strategy.

The political executive must also do its part to bolster public confidence and safeguard the integrity of the formal justice system. High-profile cases, such as those concerned with individuals accused of involvement in the February 11, 2008, attacks on the president, focus public attention and, accordingly, may be instructive as models of due process. Unfortunately, there is also a risk that the progress of these cases and their political reception may add to perceptions that there is a dual-track legal system, wherein persons of standing may be accorded an advantage. Since the public has already shown a degree of rancor in response to the pardoning of controversial pro-Indonesia militiamen, and corruption investigations into senior government ministers yet to bear fruit, the justice system is sensitive to concerns over impunity.[37]

Equality before the law is an idea central to democratic notions of justice, and so must be reinforced in the public consciousness. Especially with a more immediate avenue of dispute resolution often available through custom (however imperfect), formal justice cannot afford to be seen to play favorites if it is to secure Timorese confidence. The independence of the judiciary, as expressed in "separation of powers" doctrine, must be accorded due respect. Regrettably, there have been some troubling exceptions in recent times that suggest less than complete adherence. The issuing by the president of "letters of passage" to rebel leader Alfredo Reinado who, at the time, had a court-issued warrant out for his arrest, indicates a degree of discord.[38] The preemption of the court's decision in the case of alleged February 11 conspirator Gastao Salsinha by the president, who indicated a willingness to offer Salsinha pardon, is another such example.[39]

Perhaps the most egregious failure to observe the integrity of the justice system can be seen in the capture and release of Martenus Bere. The former leader of the Laksaur militia, Bere is wanted in connection with a series of alleged crimes against humanity, most notoriously relating to the Suai church massacre on September 6, 1999. On that occasion, attacks by the militia on people sheltering in the Ave Maria

[36] JSMP, *Overview of Justice Sector 2006–2007*, p. 12.

[37] Amnesty International (AI), *We Cry for Justice: Impunity Persists Ten Years On in Timor-Leste* (Jakarta: AI, 2009), pp. 3–4.

[38] Donald Greenlees, "East Timor's Road Ahead Is Clouded by Uncertainty," *New York Times*, February 13, 2008, p. 2.

[39] ABC News, "Ramos-Horta Welcomes Assassination Attempt Trials, Mulls Pardon," p. 1.

church resulted in as many as two hundred deaths.[40] Despite this, Bere entered Timor-Leste in late 2009 to visit family, was recognized by local people and subsequently detained, awaiting trial. Appearing to bow to pressure from Indonesia, the prime minister gave orders through the Ministry of Justice for Bere to be released by prison officials and transferred to the Indonesian embassy for return to that country. As the United Nations, local civil society, and the families of the Suai dead were quick to point out, this not only contravenes the government's legal duties but also denies justice for those affected by Bere's alleged actions. The prime minister's response, in a speech delivered in Suai, proposing that justice needs to be a secondary concern in light of the need for development,[41] is decidedly less than heartening.

Post-Colonial Comparisons

Timor-Leste is not alone in grappling with this suite of post-conflict justice issues. The legacies of war, and of colonization, have scarred many nations, whose efforts at recovery and reconstruction are ongoing. Tragic as this situation unquestionably is, there nonetheless exists an inherent opportunity for constructive cross-pollination of ideas. Criticism that the United Nations and others have perhaps been institutionally predisposed to reproducing a uniform legal model across transitional justice contexts does, conversely, warn against minimizing the uniqueness of respective cultures of dispute resolution.[42] Though most organizations are now resiling from that former one-size-fits-all bias in post-conflict justice support,[43] this trend ought not to serve as a bulwark against fruitful comparison.

One point of divergence from the experience of other post-colonial states lies in Timor-Leste's recent experience of occupation. While Sierra Leone, following its period as a part of the British Empire, devolved into civil strife, and Cambodia's era of French rule was (though not immediately) succeeded by the horror of the Khmer Rouge, arguably neither bore the marks of wholesale invasion. The persistence, and coherence, of colonial legal cultures is still very pronounced in the latter countries. This can outwardly be seen in the continued insistence, in the tropical heat of Sierra Leone, on courtroom attire of wig, gown, and jabot—a mode of dress increasingly out of favor in its originating jurisdiction. Likewise, an anachronistic reverence for the Napoleonic Code is still in evidence among senior Cambodian practitioners.

Such affectations and touchstones signal the emergence of the legal profession as an identifiable social presence. With such collectivization often comes a system of inclusion and exclusion. Timor-Leste's loose coalition of lawyers could do well to note, and guard against, this phenomenon. In Cambodia, political allegiance has a very strong correlation to professional membership, with entry into courses of tertiary education, and later acquisition of legal posts, both reportedly dependent on

---

[40] Geoffrey Robinson, *East Timor 1999: Crimes against Humanity* (Los Angeles, CA: United Nations Office of the High Commissioner for Human Rights [OHCHR], 2003), p. 228.

[41] JSMP, *Overview of Justice Sector 2009*, p. 36.

[42] Stephen Golub, "Rule of Law and the UN Peacebuilding Commission: A Social Development Approach," *Cambridge Review of International Affairs* 20,1 (2007): p. 48.

[43] United Nations Development Program, *Access to Justice Practice Note* (New York, NY: UNDP, 2004), p. 2.

partisan connections (and money).[44] While it is not impossible to evade such obligations, those whose practices thrive financially are widely acknowledged to do so by means of political patronage. Explicitly pro-government factions for a long time appeared to control the bar association, but an increasingly vital civil society element has threatened this status quo. The recent election of a renowned public-interest lawyer as president of the bar prompted an uncharacteristically blunt response from government, which, through the (dubious) authority of the responsible ministry, blocked the appointment.[45] Issues of independence accordingly remain sensitive.

In Sierra Leone, tribal heritage is the analog. With the Freetown-based Krio privileged in access to education under the British, Krio dominance of the professions has continued into independence. Although there is now some representation of other tribes at both bench and bar, their engagement is still rare enough to be remarked upon. Lecturers and administrators of the country's sole law college are all Krio and, as gatekeepers of the profession, have come under fire for discriminating against those of differing tribal background.[46] Similarly, alleged collusion between lawyers and judicial actors has been blamed for impeding the establishment of legal practices by, for example, Mende and Temne practitioners, who must compete for clients against established, Krio-dominated chambers. While demographic change will eventually shift these dynamics, for the time being, the law is almost exclusively the province of a tribal elite.

There is yet time to halt the formation of such an exclusionary culture within Timor-Leste's justice system. Its mosaic of colonial, occupation-era, and indigenous influences does not give the upper hand unequivocally to any one group. The risk is, however, already apparent that language of instruction may come to serve in this context as a shibboleth in the same way that partisan allegiance or tribal heritage do elsewhere. Divisions between Lusophone and predominantly Bahasa Indonesia-speaking practitioners threaten to derail attempts at producing a representative professional body and coordinating inputs to education and policy. Further emphasizing the use of Tetum as a common language of the courts would go some way to producing a more open and inclusive legal culture.

Greater use of a shared language might go some way to erasing the dividing lines within Timor-Leste's justice system, but it will not directly counterbalance emerging political associations. The experience of other post-colonial contexts suggests that, as the law becomes recognized as a useful political tool, two outcomes are likely. The first is that legal actors come increasingly under pressure to conform to political doctrine. This is seen in the incarceration of key members of the bar in Zimbabwe,[47] and of civil-society legal activists in Cambodia.[48] Conversely, as lawyers

[44] Cambodia Office of the High Commissioner for Human Rights (COHCHR), *Continuing Patterns of Impunity in Cambodia* (Phnom Penh: COHCHR, 2005), p. 20.

[45] United Nations Human Rights Council (UNHRC), *Seventh Session, Agenda Item 10: Report of the Special Representative of the Secretary-General for Human Rights in Cambodia* (New York, NY: UNHRC, 2008), p. 11.

[46] Vivek Maru, "Between Law and Society: Paralegals and the Provision of Justice Services in Sierra Leone and Worldwide," *Yale Journal of International Law* 31 (2006): 451.

[47] International Bar Association (IBA), "Outrage at the Arrest of President and Executive Secretary of the Law Society of Zimbabwe," IBA Press Release, June 6, 2002, p. 1, available at www.ibanet.org/Article/Detail.aspx?ArticleUid=6a9b60b7-3385-4cce-8713-5e313a5cd9b4, accessed May 16, 2012.

rise in status and gain resources, there is a risk of political co-option, or at least acquiescence. The claims from some segments of the Sierra Leonean judiciary that they ought effectively to be exempt from anti-corruption legislation because any accusation against them would bring the system into disrepute suggest a similar example.[49]

The role of advocacy, as a function of legal practice, is still an uncertain one in Timor-Leste. Many qualified practitioners are employed directly by the state as prosecutors or public defenders, and so feel disengaged from the profession in an independent sense. Private lawyers thus form the majority of those identifying with a legal collective. This group, however, encompasses wildly divergent views, with the activist background of some members an influence, and the employment of others by government requiring caution. The prevailing mind state, then, has been of confusion. Though the 2008 law regulating the profession includes an unusually clear mandate to speak out against perceived injustices,[50] the AATL, and its individual members, have to date proven reticent to contribute to critical public debate, other than to reiterate published government positions. Especially with judicial independence seemingly subject to executive predation, there is a need for the legal profession to operate as a watchdog against political excesses.

With institutions across transitional justice contexts historically taking limited account of local conditions, a considerable responsibility has been vested in legal personnel to communicate knowledge of formal processes. Lawyers and other court actors, traversing their roles as representatives of state infrastructure and as members of the community in their own right, have become unwitting players in the nation-building exercise. In Timor-Leste, with relatively few consistent channels for the transmission of information from the national to the local, lawyers are translators of "foreign" concepts into the vernacular and, often by association, ambassadors for the program of government. Other post-colonial jurisdictions have sought to capitalize on this informal expertise by outsourcing legal awareness-raising to the profession, and by expanding on problem-solving authority through licensed avenues of mediation and arbitration. While such measures (though already beginning) will, in Timor-Leste, require extensive training and probably dedicated legislation to take root, they also promise to foster a more fluid and inclusive approach to formal justice.

INTERNATIONAL CONTRIBUTIONS

While the period of post-independence UN administrative command has given way to the authority of the Constitutional Assembly and successive Timorese governments, the continuing role of the international community in justice has been difficult to pin down. The government of Timor-Leste, in its various incarnations, has previously been comfortable in devolving much of its technical responsibilities in policy development, consultation, and drafting to the United Nations (and other international organizations, to a lesser extent). Recently, however, it has begun to

---

[48] Lee Berthaulme and Yun Samean, "Yeng Virak is Released from Prison on Bail," *Cambodia Daily*, January 12, 2006, p. 1.

[49] Mohamed Sesay, "In Defence of the Anti-Corruption Commission of Sierra Leone," *Patriotic Vanguard*, September 3, 2009, p. 2.

[50] JSMP, *Private Lawyers Statutes*, p. 10.

take a more proactive stance, though seemingly not always with the purest of intentions. As the specter of corruption has loomed larger over Timor-Leste's political arena, resistance to international oversight has been more evident.[51]

With investments to recover and treaty obligations to uphold, the international community serves (albeit only persuasively) as a checks-and-balances mechanism on government action. While some have criticized its apparent reticence to take Timorese leadership to task, there are inevitably diplomatic considerations to weigh. Furthermore, the United Nations, in particular, has occasionally departed from its customary caution and delivered a rebuke against perceived justice-sector missteps. The Bere case, for example, prompted the expression of "grave concerns" from the United Nations[52] in respect of impunity and derogation from international law.

The actions and practices of the international community are themselves, of course, not always above reproach. With adviser and contractor salaries lucrative even by developed-world standards, there has reasonably been speculation that such individuals are not overly keen to build the capacity of their local peers and so to hand over responsibility. Some government figures have gone so far as to claim that international advisers have ingratiated themselves inside ministries in order to advance foreign (and allegedly corporate) agendas. The reliance, in the justice system, on Lusophone expertise has left some bemoaning a relatively small pool of potential applicants, and led to concerns over collusive and nepotistic hiring.

Within the UN system especially, anxiety has been expressed over the risk of depleting the legal profession in smaller, Portuguese-speaking states such as Cape Verde, many of whose lawyers are drawn to Timor-Leste by the lure of profitable consultancies. Recourse to other jurisdictions in this way has, over time, built up discrete expatriate communities within legal institutions. Portuguese nationals are reportedly well represented among the judiciary, Cape Verdeans in the prosecutor-general's office and Brazilians in public defense. While the drip-feed of Timorese practitioners into the sector will undoubtedly assuage this reliance over time, there remains an interim risk of insular, exogenous cultures becoming entrenched in an already factionalized justice system.

The vagaries of funding cycles and shifting institutional priorities have also seen criticism leveled at the international community as a whole. In the context of a global financial crisis, aid budgets have shrunk and private philanthropy decreased. Accordingly, donors and implementers alike are under pressure to show measurable results. In the justice sector, where progress is typically subtle and incremental, gains are not so easily quantified. The rubric of security-sector reform, encompassing police and armed forces, is seemingly gaining traction as a marketable alternative,[53] potentially at the expense of continued focus on thorny problems of law.

---

[51] United Nations Independent Comprehensive Needs Assessment Team (ICNA), *The Justice System of Timor-Leste* (New York, NY: United Nations, 2009), p. 9.

[52] JSMP, *Overview of Justice Sector 2009*, p. 36.

[53] International Centre for Transitional Justice (ICTJ), *Security Sector Reform in Timor-Leste* (Dili: ICTJ, 2009), p. 12.

Conclusion

Despite the avowedly forward-looking attitude of its current leaders, Timor-Leste remains strongly tied to its past, both through the persistence of custom and the memory of conflict. Public acceptance of formal justice will accordingly depend on institutional capacity to offer a timely and durable alternative to traditional dispute resolution, and the practical mandate to pursue historical injustices free from political intervention. Extension of appropriate resourcing and acknowledgement of judicial independence would both represent substantial milestones for Timor-Leste as an emerging democracy.

As post-colonial comparisons show, actors in the legal sphere can play an important role in the nation-building endeavor. Especially with language policy so fraught, care will need to be taken in order to ensure that Timor-Leste's nascent legal culture develops in as egalitarian and inclusive a fashion as possible. This will likely require greater recourse to Tetum as a shared idiom, and increased efforts to incorporate the views and needs of citizens outside of more easily traversed urban centers. Only then can Timor-Leste's justice system legitimately claim to represent its people.

POLITICAL PARTIES

Dennis Shoesmith

INTRODUCTION

A competitive party system is the indispensable condition for a consolidated democracy. Political parties are the indispensable agents of democratic representation. As Moisei Ostrogorski observed well over a century ago, "Wherever this life of parties is developed, it focuses the political feelings and active wills of its citizens."[1] This chapter reviews the development of a multiparty system in Timor-Leste and the capacity of that system to deliver effective political representation. This will involve, first, a comparative discussion of the origins of contemporary party politics from the emergence of FRETILIN (Frente Revolucionária de Timor-Leste Independente, Revolutionary Front for an Independent Timor-Leste) and its rivals in 1974 and 1975 and, then, a critique of the multiparty system in operation since independence in 2002. I will argue that, while Timor-Leste has a functioning multiparty system, the electoral system, which is one of voting for closed party lists in a single national constituency, encourages the proliferation of small parties and, since 2007, the apparent necessity for coalition governments. The claim to be tested is that this tends to undermine coherent political representation in the National Parliament. Further, I will argue that the aggressive pursuit in recent years by the current prime minister of an ambitious strategy of state-led development, funded by large withdrawals from the Petroleum Fund, is changing the dynamics of national politics, encouraging a style of political patronage that may further weaken party representation.

New states, and particularly new states that have emerged from episodes of major conflict, find establishing a robust party system highly problematic. In common with almost half of the world's post-conflict states,[2] Timor-Leste has experienced a pattern of recurrent political crises, a condition that tends to provoke political extremism rather than to support democratic pluralism. Following the failure of the initial experiment with multiparty politics, the trend among first-

---

[1] Moisei Ostrogorski, *Democracy and the Organisation of Political Parties* (London: Macmillan, 1902).

[2] Paul Collier, Anke Hoeffler, and Måns Söderbom, *Post-Conflict Risk* (Oxford: Centre for the Study of African Economies, University of Oxford, 2006).

generation African new states was toward one-party and dominant party systems.[3] The former Portuguese colonies in Africa were no exception, typically adopting Marxist–Leninist ideologies and creating one-party systems that allowed the party leadership to capture the state apparatus in each case,[4] leading to a confluence of party and state, characteristic of communist regimes. Multiparty politics has returned to a number of African post-colonial states since the 1990s, but very few have achieved open, competitive democracy. In this context, Timor-Leste, since independence, has achieved some success in the transition to democratic consolidation. It is not yet, however, a consolidated democracy where "democracy is the only game in town."[5] Indeed, Timor-Leste is described variously as a "flawed democracy" and "partly free."[6] The issue here is whether the multiparty system promotes or undermines the transition to full and free democracy.

ORIGINS

The historical development of political parties in Timor-Leste went through three stages. The first was the establishment in Portuguese Timor in 1974–75, following the Carnation Revolution and the overthrow of the dictatorship in Portugal. The second was the twenty-four-year period of Indonesian occupation and the resistance struggle waged by FRETILIN. The third stage is the current development of multiparty politics since independence.

One-party rule was a real possibility in Timor-Leste in the first phase of political development. In 1974, following the overthrow of the dictatorship in Portugal, the governor in Portuguese Timor called for the establishment of political parties in preparation for an end to Portuguese rule. The most successful of these, FRETILIN, began in May 1974, as the ASDT (Associação Social Democrática Timorense, Timorese Social Democratic Association). It immediately attracted widespread support from young educated Timorese and "conditional" support from Timorese university students pursuing studies in Lisbon. The students' reservation was that social democracy was a bourgeois doctrine that did not represent the real interests and aspirations of the common people.[7] In 1975, ASDT moved to a more radical position, was renamed FRETILIN, and adopted the "revolutionary African nationalism" of its mentor, FRELIMO (Frente de Libertação de Moçambique, Liberation Front of Mozambique).

[3] G. M. Carter, *African One-Party States* (Ithaca, NY: Cornell University Press, 1962); Giovanni Sartori, *Parties and Party Systems: A Framework for Analysis* (Colchester: ECPR Press, 1976, 2005).

[4] Octavio Amorim Neto and Marina Costa Lobo, "Between Constitutional Diffusion and Local Politics: Semi-Presidentialism in Portuguese-Speaking Countries," paper presented at American Political Science Association's Annual Meeting, Washington, DC, July 10, 2010, available at http://ssrn.com/abstract=1644026, accessed July 2, 2012.

[5] Juan J. Linz and Alfred C. Stepan, *Problems of Democratic Transition and Consolidation* (Baltimore, MD: Johns Hopkins University Press, 1996), p. 5.

[6] *Democracy Index 2010, Democracy in Retreat—A Report from the Economist Intelligence Unit* (2011), Table 2, p. 4 (East Timor ranked 42 of 167 countries), http://graphics.eiu.com/PDF/Democracy_Index_2010_web.pdf, accessed August 6, 2012; *Freedom in the World 2011*, Freedom House, table "Combined Average Ratings—Independent Countries," at www.freedomhouse.org/report/freedom-world/freedom-world-2011, accessed August 6, 2012.

[7] José Ramos-Horta, *Funu, Unfinished Saga of East Timor* (Trenton, NJ: Red Sea Press, 1987).

FRETILIN's principal rival, also founded in 1974, was UDT (União Democrática Timorense, Timorese Democratic Union). UDT was founded by Mário Carrascalão, whose political experience was as a member of the Portuguese Timor branch of Accão Nacional Popular (ANP, National Popular Action), described by José Ramos-Horta as "a sort of fascist action group, the only political party allowed in Portugal."[8] UDT favored a continued association with Portugal. It attracted conservative support from professionals and Portuguese-speaking *assimilados* (assimilated persons) and from some influential traditional chiefs (*liurai*). UDT opposed integration with Indonesia. As it became clear that Portugal had no interest in retaining East Timor, Mário Carrascalão, and his brother João Carrascalão, changed the UDT platform to support independence but under their conservative control. There was a brief but violent civil war between UDT and FRETILIN in August 1975 in which FRETILIN prevailed. On November 28, 1975, the FRETILIN leadership unilaterally declared independence from Portugal and briefly governed as the Democratic Republic of East Timor (RDTL, República Democrática de Timor-Leste) until the Indonesian military invasion nine days later (see Ramos-Horta's firsthand account[9]).

All the indications were in late 1975 that, if it had continued in power, FRETILIN would have demanded an exclusive right to rule, following the precedent of FRELIMO.[10] In negotiations with the Portuguese government in 1975, FRETILIN demanded "recognition of FRETILIN as the only legitimate representative of the people of East Timor."[11] In the resistance struggle, the Marxist faction in 1977 took control of the FRETILIN Central Committee. It imposed a Leninist model of the vanguard party under a secretary-general presiding over a Department of Political Orientation and Ideology and a Central Committee.[12] The party was renamed the FRETILIN Marxist–Leninist Party (Partido Marxista-Leninista FRETILIN, PMLF). The armed struggle against Indonesia was to be a "protracted people's war" guided by Marxist–Leninist ideology as defined by Mao Zedong. Relentless action by the Indonesian military made this strategy unsustainable.[13]

In exile in Mozambique, the FRETILIN leadership was aware that where multiparty systems had been established in Africa, they had failed. New post-colonial states were confronted with rebellion, insurrection, civil war, and military takeovers.[14] One-party regimes, military juntas, or personal dictatorships were the prevailing pattern.[15] FRELIMO provided the FRETILIN leaders with a working model of a revolutionary, one-party regime. The Indonesian occupation, however,

---

[8] Ibid., p. 29.

[9] Ibid., p. 25–28.

[10] Jill Jolliffe, *East Timor, Nationalism and Colonialism* (St. Lucia: University of Queensland Press, 1978).

[11] Bill Nicol, *Timor, the Stillborn Nation* (Melbourne: Visa, 1978), p. 79.

[12] Ben Kiernan, *Genocide and Resistance in Southeast Asia: Documentation, Denial and Justice in Cambodia and East Timor* (New Brunswick: Transaction Publishers, 2008).

[13] Ibid., p. 172.

[14] Stephen Brown and Paul Kaiser, "Democratisations in Africa: Attempts, Hindrances and Prospects," *Third World Quarterly* 28,6 (2007); Sola Akinrinade, "Single or Multi-Party System: What Option for Africa?" (Africa Economic Analysis 2000), www.afbis.com/analysis/party.htm, accessed April 25, 2012.

[15] John Ishiyama and John James Quinn, "African Phoenix? Explaining the Electoral Performance of the Formerly Dominant Parties in Africa," *Party Politics* 12,3 (2006): 319–20.

precluded the possibility of installing such a regime in Timor-Leste. At the same time, the leaders in exile lost control of their revolutionary force, the armed movement, FALINTIL (Forças Armadas de Libertação National de Timor-Leste, Armed Forces for the National Liberation of Timor-Leste). By the 1980s, FALINTIL was conducting a defensive guerrilla war increasingly independently of the FRETILIN leadership. FALINTIL's commander, Xanana Gusmão, as president of the political coalition created in 1986, the National Council of Maubere Resistance (Conselho Nacional da Resistencia Maubere,CNRM), effectively removed FALINTIL from FRETILIN's control. On December 7, 1987, Gusmão condemned the Central Committee for "enormous and excessive political errors" and promised that FALINTIL would not permit the installation of a leftist regime.[16] The separation between Gusmão and the FRETILIN Central Committee has divided East Timorese national politics ever since.

By the late 1980s, the African pattern had begun to change. In the post–Cold War era, international donors applied pressure on a number of African states to liberalize their political systems.[17] Multiparty politics reappeared.[18] FRETILIN's leaders observed this process firsthand in Mozambique when, in the early 1990s, FRELIMO abandoned Marxist–Leninism, introduced a new constitution, and installed a competitive multiparty system. From a position of strength, FRELIMO won the first parliamentary elections in 1994 and continued ruling over a de facto one-party regime legitimized by a multiparty elections.

FRETILIN, in this instance, had anticipated its mentor. It repudiated its Marxist constitution in 1984 and formally withdrew its claim to be the sole legitimate representative of the East Timorese people in 1987.[19] By 1998, when FRETILIN drew up a constitutional model for an independent Timor-Leste, it sanctioned a pluralist, multiparty system, subsequently the basis for the national politics of the new state when the constitution was promulgated in 2002. FRETILIN's leaders, probably with the Mozambique experience in mind, assumed that the East Timorese people would support the party that had won the struggle for independence, recognize that FRETILIN was the party historically entitled to govern, and accept that the party would permanently preside over a "dominant party" system.

FRETILIN's conversion to multiparty democracy, in any case, was a condition of the international intervention in Timor-Leste in 1999. The unquestionable requirement was that the new state would be a liberal, multiparty democracy. In 2000–2002, the United Nations was involved in the creation of the Democratic Republic of Timor-Leste in a direct and unprecedented way. During its short period of sovereignty, the United Nations Transitional Administration in East Timor (UNTAET) began the process of installing a liberal democratic state system.[20] The continuing UN presence after independence was premised on the assumption that pluralist multiparty democracy was the only political system that would operate in

---

[16] Sarah Niner, *Xanana, Leader of the Struggle for an Independent Timor-Leste* (North Melbourne: Australian Scholarly Publishing, 2009), p. 112.

[17] Brown and Kaiser, "Democratisations in Africa."

[18] Ishiyama and Quinn, "African Phoenix?"

[19] Pat Walsh, "From Opposition to Proposition: The National Council of Timorese Resistance in Transition," *Back Door Newsletter on East Timor* (November 8, 1999).

[20] Oliver P. Richmond, "De-Romanticising the Local, De-mystifying the International Hybridity in Timor-Leste and the Solomon Islands," *Pacific Review* 24,1 (2011).

Timor-Leste. In government, FRETILIN instituted that system. Law No. 3/2004 on Political Parties and Law No. 6/2006 on the Election of the National Parliament established the liberal democratic system required by the constitution and expected by the international community.

MULTIPARTY POLITICS IN PRACTICE

At first, FRETILIN's expectation that it alone should govern was realized; as the majority party in the Constituent Assembly after the 2001 elections, FRETILIN assumed the government of the RDTL when the Constituent Assembly was transformed, in May 2002, into the first National Parliament. In government, Prime Minister Alkatiri exhibited little tolerance for the political opposition.[21] With fifty-five of the eighty-eight seats, FRETILIN formed a single-majority government, against a fragmented opposition of some eleven parties with between two and seven seats each. FRETILIN members of the National Parliament tended to be contemptuous of the opposition parties, dismissing them as "irrelevant."[22] This situation was reversed after the 2007 parliamentary elections. A coalition of four parties then formed a government and FRETILIN, with twenty-one of the parliament's sixty-five seats (the largest single party bloc of seats), formed a disciplined opposition.

The record of democratic multiparty politics in Timor-Leste since independence is a mixed one. In comparative terms, Timor-Leste has been relatively successful in establishing a working multiparty system. This is despite major episodes of political crisis, most seriously the breakdown of state order in 2006. In 2007, national elections delivered a change of government, a significant achievement for a new, post-conflict state. Certainly, the party system may not have survived the crisis of 2006 without the intervention of an international peacekeeping force, but the 2007 national elections were held and a new government did assume office. If Timor-Leste does not yet have a fully mature, consolidated multi-party system, it has made significant progress in that direction.

There are, however, organizational and systemic constraints that hinder the consolidation of a mature party system. These include the limited role of the National Parliament in the formal and informal political system. The parties themselves, with the exception of FRETILIN, struggle for organizational coherence. The key political actors, most notably the current prime minister, Xanana Gusmão, tend to operate as individuals rather than as party leaders. Again, Marí Alkatiri, former prime minister and continuing secretary-general of FRETILIN, is the exception. His personal authority is institutionalized in his party's highly centralist organizational structure. It is his position as party secretary-general that confirms his authority. In a single national electorate, parties struggle to establish reliable constituencies in the districts and *sucos* (villages). The first (FRETILIN) and fourth (Parliamentary Majority Alliance [Aliança para a Maioria Parlementar, AMP]) constitutional governments have each struggled to ensure stable, effective, and representative government in the context of weak state capacity, entrenched rivalries within the national elite, and episodes of serious civil unrest, rebellion, and communal violence.

---

[21] Damien Kingsbury, "Political Development," in *East Timor: Beyond Independence*, ed. Damien Kingsbury and Michael Leach (Clayton: Monash University Press, 2007), p. 20.

[22] Interviews in Dili by the author, April 2006.

FRETILIN, publicly, did not accept its loss of power following the 2007 parliamentary elections (although it acted as a normal opposition in the National Parliament). Its successor, the Parliamentary Majority Alliance government, is an uncomfortable coalition of parties with long-standing differences. Xanana Gusmão, former leader of the resistance movement, first president at independence, and now prime minister in the AMP government, inclines to operate as the charismatic leader, operating independently of his own party, the National Congress for Timorese Reconstruction (Congresso Nacional da Reconstrução Timorense, CNRT). His attitude toward his other coalition partners has often been overbearing and, in the case of the PSD (Partido Social Democrata, Social Democratic Party of East Timor), has demonstrated elements of outright hostility (this is discussed below). Despite serious fractures within the coalition government, the FRETILIN opposition resisted the temptation in 2010 to exploit these divisions to force a vote of no confidence in parliament and provoke an early election.

Within its institutional limitations, the party system provides some response to public interests. Parties do offer real choices, governments can be elected into and out of office, and alternative public policy programs can be put before the electorate. The indications are that the national elections in 2012 will take place and that political parties (and their leaders) will participate in the election within a system of accepted rules. A free and generally accepted outcome of the 2012 elections will substantially advance the democratic consolidation of the new state. Much more uncertain is the larger challenge for political parties, in government and opposition, to promote shared values and norms in an emerging civil society. In terms of the debate on the "New Institutionalism," the party system in Timor-Leste is semi-institutionalized.[23]

POLITICAL PARTIES AND ELECTIONS

Over the past decade, the East Timorese have developed a fairly robust engagement with the electoral process. The electoral history of Timor-Leste began in July 1975, when the Portuguese Decolonization Commission organized local elections to select *liurais* (chiefs) to form an executive council to prepare for a constituent assembly that was planned for October 1976. Most of those elected were FRETILIN members or FRETILIN supporters, although the degree of that support was a matter of contention.[24] As residents of an Indonesian province from 1976, under direct and severe military control, the East Timorese experienced most intensely the authoritarianism of the New Order regime. Given their country's history of colonialism and occupation, the East Timorese were unfamiliar with democratic participation when they were finally given the opportunity to decide on their political future with the end of Indonesian rule.[25]

The ballot on autonomy or independence held on August 30, 1999, was, with the partial exception of the local elections in 1975, the first experience for the East Timorese of a free democratic expression of their political will. The result was an

---

[23] Karol Soltan, Eric M. Uslaner, and Virginia Huafler, "New Institutionalism: Institutions and Social Order," in *Institutions and Social Order,* ed. Karol Edward Soltan, Eric M. Uslaner, and Virginia Haufler (Ann Arbor, MI: The University of Michigan Press, 1998).

[24] Sarah Niner, *Xanana, Leader of the Struggle,* p. 47.

[25] Ibid., p. 220.

overwhelming rejection (78.5 percent) of the Indonesian offer that East Timor retain autonomy while remaining in Indonesia. The violence and destruction inflicted by the militias and the Indonesian army as punishment for that outcome provoked an urgent international response, the deployment of the International Force in East Timor—INTERFET—and the transition to the United Nations Transitional Administration in East Timor. UNTAET organized elections for an eighty-eight-member constituent assembly, which were held in August 2001.

The 2001 Constituent Assembly elections were contested by sixteen parties and five independents.[26] By far the best organized party, FRETILIN, was easily the most serious contender. Alkatiri went into the campaign confident his party would win by a landslide. In the event, FRETILIN won forty-five of the seventy-five seats decided by nationwide proportionality and the thirteen district seats, a total of fifty-five of the eighty-eight seats. FRETILIN's 57.3 percent share of the vote was well below its predicted 80 percent support.

The Democratic Party (Partido Democratico, PD) won seven seats in the Constituent Assembly with 8.7 percent of the vote. Established in June 2001, PD gained support from young political activists from the student and youth movements and included some ex-FRETILIN and resistance members. Led by Fernando "Lasama" de Araújo and Mariano Sabino Lopes, PD appealed to East Timorese who had resisted Indonesian rule but felt that FRETILIN, controlled by the 1975 leadership returned from exile, discounted their contribution to the struggle.[27] They were encouraged in their opposition to FRETILIN by Xanana Gusmão, who attended their rallies during the campaign.

On the political spectrum, PD occupied the center left. The Social Democrat Party occupied the center right. PSD was led by Mário Viegas Carrascalão. Carrascaláo was the founding leader of the Timorese Democratic Union party, founded in 1974, and FRETILIN's opponent in the 1975 civil war.[28] He had been appointed as governor of the province under the Indonesians from 1992. PSD gained 8.18 percent of the vote, giving it six seats. The Timorese Association of Social Democrats, with 7.84 percent, won another six seats. ASDT was regenerated in April 2001 by Francisco Xavier do Amaral. He was the original president of the short-lived Democratic Republic of East Timor in December 1975, and was a founder of FRETILIN, but was expelled for his later negotiations with the Indonesians, particularly the military. He was formally reaccepted by FRETILIN, but decided not to rejoin the party. His ambition was to see the original RDTL government restored. The party takes its name from the organization that preceded FRETILIN in 1974. Another five parties accounted for another 11 percent of the vote in 2001, with thirteen seats between them.[29]

Political parties in Timor-Leste represent, of course, modern systems of politics that have to operate within traditional social systems that coexist with—and tend to appropriate—modern political institutions at the *suco* and *aldeia* (hamlet) levels (see Cummins and Leach, this volume). Local communities operate according to

---

[26] Dwight Y. King, "East Timor's Founding Elections and Emerging Party System," *Asian Survey*, 43,5 (2003): 747.

[27] King, "East Timor's Founding Elections"; see also Gavin Ryan, *Political Parties and Groupings of Timor-Leste*, second edition (Sydney: Australian Labor's International Projects Unit, 2007), pp. 21–22.

[28] Ramos-Horta, *Funu*.

[29] King, "East Timor's Founding Elections," pp. 745–57.

traditional belief systems *(lisan)*. The state and its political leaders somehow have to bridge the gulf between politics based in Dili and politics based in the local community.

Despite their inexperience with free elections, East Timorese voters in 2001 held clear preferences. They may not have understood the purpose of a Constituent Assembly, but they wanted a strong president, and, mistakenly, believed the election would provide this.[30] A survey of voter knowledge carried out by the Asia Foundation in 2001 found that 61 percent thought the 2001 election was for the presidency.[31] While 54 percent of respondents were interested in politics, there was little clear understanding of democracy. (None of those polled identified elections as a characteristic of a democratic country). A significant majority of 64 percent believed political party competition was a bad thing and that it could provoke violence.[32] Given such concerns, voter participation in 1999–2001 was very high: 98 percent in the 1999 referendum and 91 percent in the Constituent Assembly elections.[33]

In 2002, East Timorese were able to vote for a president. Xanana Gusmão received 82.7 percent of the vote. His only competitor, Francisco Xavier do Amaral, conceded that he contested the election simply "to give Xanana someone to run against."[34] Within weeks of assuming the presidency, Gusmão put FRETILIN on notice that he would use his limited constitutional powers, but his considerable personal standing, to subject the Alkatiri government to critical scrutiny.[35]

East Timorese again went to the polls in 2004–05 to elect local *(suco)* councils. Candidates were required to belong to one of the national political parties. FRETILIN won 60.62 percent of the local government positions with 56.98 percent of the vote.[36] At the same time, independent candidates won 134 (or 30.3 percent) of the 442 positions of *chefes de suco* (village chiefs), highlighting the importance of personal politics at the local level.[37] In the *suco* elections held in 2009, changes to the electoral law forbade candidates for *chefes de suco* and *suco* council positions to have affiliations to a political party. Despite this, Alkatiri claimed that FRETILIN candidates attracted 55 percent of the votes and, together with FRETILIN allies, won more than 70 percent of voters' preferences. Although candidates were forbidden to identify their party affiliations, voters knew candidates' party affiliations. Arguing

---

[30] Ibid., p. 749.

[31] The Asia Foundation, *East Timor National Survey of Voter Knowledge* (Dili: Asia Foundation, May 2001), p. 4.

[32] Ibid., p. 3.

[33] King, "East Timor's Founding Elections," p. 747.

[34] Xavier do Amaral had been chosen by FRETILIN as president of the RDTL in 1975. In 1977, when the revolutionary faction took control, Xavier do Amaral was expelled from FRETILIN and placed under arrest. He revived ASDT as a rival, "third way" party in 2000. Although, from 2007, ASDT was a member of the governing AMP coalition, ASDT has broken with Prime Minister Gusmão and negotiated an agreement with the FRETILIN opposition.

[35] Dennis Shoesmith, "Timor-Leste: Divided Leadership in a Semi-Presidential System," *Asian Survey* 63,2 (March/April 2003), pp. 231–52.

[36] Michael Leach, "The 2007 Presidential and Parliamentary Elections in Timor-Leste," *Australian Journal of Politics and History* 55,2 (June, 2009): 219–32.

[37] Andrew McWilliam, "Customary Governance in Timor-Leste," in *Democratic Governance in Timor-Leste: Reconciling the Local and the National,* ed. David Mearns (Darwin: Charles Darwin University Press, 2008), p. 138.

that the outcome of the local elections represented a rejection of the AMP parties, Alkatiri called for the AMP government to resign and hold an early election.[38] FRETILIN's claims were probably exaggerated. Incumbents tended to retain their position in 2009 as *chefe de suco,* and a majority of incumbents from the 2004–05 local elections were aligned with FRETILIN. The result was often an endorsement for a capable *chefe* in office, rather than of FRETILIN as a national party. A survey of voters undertaken in five districts immediately before and after the October 2009 vote found that voters did know the candidates for *chefe* quite well, including their political affiliations, but the general view was that the ban on political parties was an improvement on the earlier local elections. The survey results did not suggest that the vote was an endorsement of FRETILIN and a repudiation of the AMP government at the national level.[39]

FRETILIN's share of the vote nationally was 29 percent, a steep fall from the 57 percent it attracted in the 2001 Constituent Assembly elections. This represented, however, the single largest bloc of votes, delivering to FRETILIN twenty-one seats in the new sixty-five-seat parliament. Its nearest rival, CNRT with 24.1 percent of the vote, held 18 seats. FRETILIN could only form a government if the party was able to negotiate a coalition with other parties.

ASDT formed a coalition with PSD to contest the 2007 elections. The ASDT–PSD support base was highest in Aileu (47.3 percent), Ainaro (29.13 percent), and Manufahi districts, the heartland of the Mambai-speaking East Timorese. In the "eastern" districts, ASDT–PD attracted 12.51 percent of the vote in Lautem, 5.94 percent in Viqueque, and 4.6 percent in Baucau.[40] As a *Loromonu* coalition, ASDT–PSD was unwilling to consider joining a coalition government led by FRETILIN.

The election campaign was marred by violent incidents, including the killing of two CNRT activists in Viqueque.[41] Post-election violence followed the president's announcement authorizing the CNRT-led coalition to form a government as the Parliamentary Alliance. The violence was most intense in Baucau,[42] a city that was a major FRETILIN stronghold. The violence in Baucau and Lautem, and in Manatuto (which has a mixed population of FRETILIN supporters and opponents), reflected political frustration and rejection of the election outcome by FRETILIN voters.

The key factor in determining the outcome of the 2007 parliamentary elections was Xanana Gusmão's decision not to seek reelection as president but to form a new political party, the National Congress for Timorese Reconstruction (Conselho Nacional de Reconstrução de Timor, CNRT) and to seek control of the government as prime minister. The acronym CNRT was deliberately chosen to recall the umbrella organization, the National Council for Timorese Resistance (Conselho Nacional de Resistência Timorense, also abbreviated CNRT), created by Gusmão at the National

---

[38] Marí Alkatiri, "East Timor Opposition Claims Success in Village Polls," Agence France Press (AFP) (October 16, 2009), reprinted in *East Timor Law and Justice Bulletin* (October 17, 2009), http://easttimorlegal.blogspot.com/2009/10/east-timor-opposition-claims-success-in.html, accessed August 8, 2012.

[39] David Mearns and Dennis Shoesmith, unpublished survey of voter attitudes in selected *sucos* in Alieu, Maliana, Ermera, Baucau, and Manatuto, conducted from October 6–10, 2009.

[40] Ibid.

[41] Leach, "2007 Elections in Timor-Leste."

[42] TLVA (Timor-Leste Armed Violence Assessment), "Electoral Violence in Timor-Leste: Mapping Incidents and Responses," Issue Brief No. 3 (June 2009).

Timorese Convention held in Peniche, in Portugal, in April 1998. The original CNRT, which included FRETILIN as well as UDT, was dissolved to establish a multiparty system in advance of the 2001 elections.[43]

The new party's secretary-general, Dionisio Babo Soares, an academic with a doctorate in anthropology from the Australian National University, was instrumental in drawing up a comprehensive party platform for the CNRT. Rejecting the "right to rule" mentality of FRETILIN, the CNRT promised transparent and accountable government and a program of economic development, decentralization, and reconstruction:

> We began this election the way we will finish this election, on a unilateral promise to stop the current undemocratic nature of the parliament, establish a sound democratic government on all levels that is regulated through checks, balances, and systemic regulations in line with other internationally acclaimed democracies. We promise to decentralize government to the district, local, and village level, and while we put this in place we will ensure that services are delivered. We will build a modern, progressive and democratic state where the peoples' voices are heard.[44]

Of the eight parties that won seats, reaching or exceeding the 3 percent threshold to be eligible for seats, two originated in the 1974–75 era: FRETILIN and the Association of Timorese Heroes (Associação does Heróis Timorenses [Klibur Oan Timor Asuwain, KOTA]). PSD, through its leader, Mário Carrascalão, was in line of succession from UDT, FRETILIN's opponent in 1975. FRETILIN, ASDT-PSD, PD, and the AD alliance (KOTA-PPT [Partido do Povo Timor, People's Party of Timor]) all held seats in the previous parliament. The important newcomer was CNRT.

With no party receiving a majority of the vote, only a coalition could form government, though Alkatiri argued that FRETILIN should form a minority government. Both FRETILIN and CNRT opened negotiations with the minor parties. Gusmão was able to persuade ASDT–PSD and PD to form a post-election coalition, but no agreement had been reached on the formation of a government when parliament was sworn in on July 30. In electing PD leader Lasama as president of parliament over the FRETILIN candidate by forty-four votes to twenty-one, the legislature made it clear that FRETILIN could not expect its support if it were to attempt to govern in its own right.[45] On August 6, President Ramos-Horta invited Xanana Gusmão to be sworn in as prime minister and form a government. FRETILIN declared that the new government was unconstitutional and called for a campaign of civil disobedience.

Presidential elections were held a third time in 2012. In the first round, in March, the FRETILIN candidate, Francisco "Lu Olo" Guterres, received 28.7 percent of the vote, followed by guerrilla leader and former commander in chief of the army, José Maria Vasconcelos (Tuar Matam Ruak), with 25.7 percent. Ramos-Horta, with 17.5

---

[43] Leach, "2007 Elections in Timor-Leste," p. 224.

[44] Dionisio Babo Soares, "CNRT Campaigns on Solid Policy for the Reconstruction of East Timor" (June 25, 2009), available at the East Timor Students' Association blog, http://groups.yahoo.com/group/ETSA/message/7110, accessed August 8, 2012.

[45] Leach, "2007 Elections in Timor-Leste," pp. 227–28.

percent, was eliminated.[46] Ruak's candidacy was supported by Xanana Gusmão and the CNRT and, in the second round in April, Ruak won the presidency with 61.2 percent of the vote against Lu Olo's 38.7 percent. All three presidential elections—in 2002, 2007, and 2012—were won by "independent" candidates, although Ruak benefited from the CNRT endorsement.

In the July parliamentary election, CNRT, with 36.6 percent of the vote, increased its seats in parliament from 18 to 30. FRETILIN, with 29.8 percent, increased its parliamentary seats from 21 to 25. PD, with 10.3 percent, held eight seats, and the new party, Frenti-Mudança, with 3.1 percent, won two. PSD and ASDT, with a combined total of eleven seats in the old parliament, failed to win a single seat.[47] There were violent incidents in both the presidential and parliamentary elections. The most serious violence was in July, when, following the election, during live television coverage of a CNRT conference, delegates denounced FRETILIN and announced their intention to form a coalition government with PD and Frenti-Mudança, excluding FRETILIN from any role in government.[48]

AN UNSTABLE COALITION

The parties that made up the AMP coalition government were uncomfortable partners This, in part, reflected long-standing personal rivalries between leading political actors in the coalition who belonged to the generation of 1975. In turn, the instability of the AMP coalition was a consequence of the imperfect institutional grounding of the coalition parties themselves. The leading party, the CNRT, despite the efforts of its party secretariat, has operated more as a political vehicle for its leader, Xanana Gusmão, than as a source of political direction in its own right. The other, smaller parties that made up the Parliamentary Majority Alliance (AMP), also revolved around their respective leaders rather than operating as autonomous political organizations. Interviews with senior party officials of the PSD, the PD, and the CNRT in 2010 confirmed that they were aware of the need to strengthen the organizational clarity and discipline of their parties. The major parties have women and youth movements and, with varying success, have attempted to build a solid support base in the districts and subdistricts.[49] Regional and national party conventions by FRETILIN, the CNRT and the smaller parties in 2011 and 2012 positioned them to compete in the July 7, 2012, parliamentary election.

The AMP coalition was an uneasy partnership from the beginning. While the four parties shared in their common opposition to FRETILIN, and generally occupy the center and the center right of the political spectrum, they lack a coherent and

---

[46] Tribunal de Recurso (Court of Appeal), Democratic Republic of Timor-Leste, Proclamation Proc.01/PEP/Geral/2012/TR, April 23, 2012, available at: http://www.cne.tl/includes/publications/Rezultadu%20definitivo%20segunda%20volta%20eleizaun%20presidencial.pdf, accessed August 8, 2012.

[47] Secretário Técnico de Administração Eleitoral (Technical Secretariat for Electoral Administration, STAE), Dili, July 2012. Provisional Results of the Parliamentary Election 2012, available at: www.stae.tl/elections/2012/rezultado/parlamentar/, accessed August 8, 2012.

[48] Sarah Everingham, "Violence as East Timor Moves towards Coalition Govt," *PM*, ABC Radio (Australian Broadcasting Corporation), July 16, 2012.

[49] Interview with Marito Magno, secretary-general of the Social Democratic Party (PSD), Dili, August 25, 2010.

stabilizing policy agenda.[50] Published party platforms of the CNRT, PSD, and PD include the expected commitments to development and social progress, to the rule of law, and to democratic governance. Rhetorical agreement on broad objectives, however, did not equate to actual mutual political commitment. The alliance is founded on convenience and the distribution of political offices rather than a specific and shared political agenda.

When FRETILIN was in government, there was a convergence between a disciplined party agenda and the agenda of the prime minister. The FRETILIN party constitution requires that a FRETILIN prime minister must be simultaneously secretary-general of the party. Marí Alkatiri's role as leader of the FRETILIN government was conditional on his position as leader of the party. Under the coalition arrangements for the AMP government, Prime Minister Xanana Gusmão has been the leader of the largest party in the coalition, the CNRT, but his control of government is personal, rather than determined by his office in the CNRT. He acts on his own initiative, although there are party rules requiring him to consult the party's National Political Council and the secretary-general on every significant political-policy decision. The CNRT secretary-general has conceded that the prime minister prefers to operate independently of his party machine.[51] Gusmão began as he meant to continue: He personally drew up the final party list of CNRT candidates at the last moment before the 2007 elections.[52]

Gusmão sees his role as the leader, not as a member of a team of ministers representing their own political parties. He is alleged by his opponents to be "contemptuous" of his coalition partners.[53] He has certainly demonstrated a willingness to humiliate publicly coalition members of his Council of Ministers. Serious tensions in the AMP coalition appeared by early 2008. Francisco Xavier do Amaral announced on May 5, 2008, that his party, ASDT, would leave the coalition because of "nepotism and corruption" and establish a "solid coalition" with FRETILIN to build "the next constitutional government of East Timor."[54] ASDT contested the 2007 elections in coalition with the PSD, securing five seats alongside the PSD's six. The agreement with FRETILIN was actually to consider an alliance to contest the 2012 elections; in the meantime, ASDT has continued to support the government in practice.[55]

Divisions between the prime minister and PSD have been even more acrimonious. In 2010, the prime minister recalled the country's ambassadors to Dili to attend the Development Partners meeting, scheduled to begin on April 7. This action overrode Foreign Minister Zacarias da Costa's order that the ambassadors should remain at their posts. The foreign minister sent a text message to the prime

---

[50] Leach, "2007 Elections in Timor-Leste," p. 229.

[51] Dionisio Babo Soares, Secretary-General of CNRT, interview with the author, Dili, August 24, 2010.

[52] Interview with Dionisio Babo Soares, interview with the author, Dili, June 25, 2009.

[53] Interview with José Teixeira, Dili, August 26, 2010. It should be noted, however, that while Teixeira might be correct in this assessment, he is a regular spokesman for and former minister of FRETILIN, so his views are not unbiased.

[54] Patrick O'Connor, "East Timor: Xanana Gusmao's Coalition Government in Crisis," Reuters, June 11, 2008, available at World Socialist Website, http://www.wsws.org/articles/2008/jun2008/dili-j11.shtml, accessed August 6, 2012.

[55] Leach, "2007 Elections in Timor-Leste," p. 230.

minister's office, threatening to resign. Da Costa is chairman of PSD and was one of three PSD ministers in the AMP government. Gusmão attacked the text message as immature, "intolerable," and "intimidating." At a meeting of the Council of Ministers on March 31, which da Costa did not attend, the prime minister called on the foreign minister to act quickly on his threat to resign. On April 13, PSD leaders warned that the party would leave the AMP government if Gusmão expelled da Costa. The next day, at a meeting of the Council of Ministers that da Costa *did* attend, the prime minister launched a long personal attack against him. Da Costa was forced to apologize. The meeting was open to media, and the attack was filmed and later made available on the Internet.[56] The public release of the video, through the state radio and television corporation, RTTL (Radio-Televisão Timor-Leste), was a deliberate move to humiliate da Costa and force his resignation, which he declined to do.

Subsequently, charges of corruption were laid against da Costa, involving allegations that he had signed off on the appointment in 2006 of the wife of then RDTL ambassador to the United Nations, José Luis Guterres, to a well-paid position with the embassy in New York. Guterres belongs to Mudança, the faction that broke away from FRETILIN in 2006 and supported the CNRT in the 2007 elections.[57] He was made deputy prime minister in the AMP government. He was also charged with corruption. Da Costa finally appeared before the Dili District Court, which on November 23 dismissed the case against him.

The prime minister simultaneously pursued the founder and elder statesman of PSD, Mário Carrascalão. In 2009, Carrascalão was appointed second deputy prime minister for state administration, with responsibility to oversee measures to combat corruption. A dispute arose between the second deputy prime minister and the prime minister over a contract for road infrastructure. Carrascalão's allegation was that three million dollars had gone missing as part of the referendum package infrastructure program for which the Ministry of Finance was responsible.

In August, the Council of Ministers removed by a decree the powers given the deputy prime minister to oversee government procurement. On September 2, the secretary of state for the Council of Ministers issued a statement condemning the deputy prime minister's "erroneous and misleading" assertions regarding the roads contract. On the same day as the Council of Ministers' statement, the prime minister used a public consultation in Dili to attack the deputy prime-minister, calling him "stupid" and a "liar."

> This person who has been making statements about these three million dollars in the Ministry of Finance is a stupid person and does not have an understanding of the system.[58]

---

[56] Augusto da Silva, Jr., "This Zacarias da Costa Story Tells a Thing or Two about Timor Leste Politics," *Timor Hau Nian Doben* (April 20, 2010), http://timorhauniandoben.blogspot.com.au/2010/04/this-zacarias-da-costa-story-tells.html, accessed July 2, 2012.

[57] FRETILIN Mudança (Change) was renamed Frenti-Mudança in 2011 in order to gain registration for the 2012 elections.

[58] "Xanana's Calling Mario Carrascalao Stupid Shows Emergence of a Crisis of Trust in AMP Government," *Tempo Semanal*, September 3, 2010.

The prime minister ridiculed Carrascalão's record as an "Indonesian propagandist" while Gusmão was leading the independence struggle: "I do not accept that some people who before made a lot of money from the spilling of our blood, today come and yell criticism at me."

On September 8, Carrascalão resigned. In his letter of resignation, addressed to the prime minister, Carrascalão listed twenty-nine issues of corruption and bad government. He protested that the prime minister had not made himself available for consultations with his deputy prime minister, that he had only managed one cordial meeting with him in August, but that at a later meeting of the Council of Ministers the prime minister had "screamed at [Carrascalão] loudly," when Carrascalão protested against misinformation included in a speech by the prime minister. The personal attack at the Dili public consultation was deliberate and intended to humiliate him:

> At the age of seventy-three, this is the first time anyone has ever called me *"beikteen"* [stupid] or *"bosokteen"* [liar] … the PM of an AMP government supported by the PSD, will not have the opportunity of repeat [sic] these insults or slander as he did.[59]

Despite these attacks against its two most prominent leaders, the PSD did not leave the government coalition. According to Secretary-General Marito Magno, the PSD strategy is to stay with the government until the 2012 elections and then reconsider its alliances.[60] PSD reportedly did hold talks with FRETILIN in 2010 on a possible agreement but any plans for an alliance were put on hold until 2012. Alkatiri has refrained from taking advantage of the divisions in the government to turn the parliament against it and perhaps force an early election. FRETILIN was concentrated, instead, on preparing for July 2012.[61]

Meanwhile, the prime minister has made it clear that he had no interest in maintaining the governing coalition. In 2010, in a speech during a CNRT national congress, Gusmão challenged his own coalition partners, declaring, "We have experienced living together with alliance parties and also other parties. It is enough for us." After the 2012 elections, CNRT would rule as a single governing party, he promised.[62] The *Dili Weekly* observed in an editorial that the prime minister's strategy was to strengthen the CNRT's popularity. Gusmão toured all the sub-

---

[59] Carrascalão, resignation letter to His Excellency Mr. Kay Rala Xanana Gusmão, printed in "Former Vice Prime Minister Mario Carrascalao Resignation Letter: English Translation," *Tempo Semanal,* September 8, 2010.

[60] Interview with the author, Dili, August 25, 2010.

[61] A more cynical view circulating in Dili is that there is a more mundane and practical explanation for the survival of the coalition. Under the provisions of "Monthly Life Pension and Other Privileges for Former Members of Parliament" rules (National Parliament, Law No. 1/2007), members of parliament who first sat beginning in July 30, 2007, in the National Parliament would become eligible for a lifelong pension, equivalent to their full parliamentary salary, after forty-two months of consecutive service. This benefit came into operation in 2011 for MPs first elected in 2007. The collapse of the government and an early election before then would have put at risk their lifelong pension.

[62] Gusmão, quoted in editorial titled "CNRT the Only Rulling [sic] Party in 2012," *Dili Weekly,* no. 104 (October 2010), p. 3.

districts in 2011 to promote the National Development Strategic Plan and distributed contracts for local infrastructure projects. He announced pensions for veterans, seniors, and the disabled; and he announced a referendum package and funding programs for roads, education, and health.[63]

FORMAL PARTY POLITICS

Party systems operate within formal and informal contexts. The balance between formal and informal political processes is a good indicator of the extent to which the political system has been institutionalized. The relative capacity of the state to provide stable, as well as representative, governance is conditional on institutionalized political competition. Leaders whose power is personal and independent of a representative party weaken long-term political stability and undermine state capacity.

The formal, multiparty political system in Timor-Leste is broadly defined by the constitution adopted by the Constituent Assembly in 2001, by supplementary legislation (Law No. 3/2004, Political Parties), and by an electoral system operating on proportional voting for closed party lists in a single, national electorate. (Electors vote for a single party list of candidates who gain a seat according to their order on the list and the percentage of the vote the party attracts.) The Fundamental Principles of the Constitution include recognition of universal suffrage and a multiparty system (Section 7.2). Section 65 of the constitution enjoins that the conversion of votes into a mandate "shall observe the principle of proportional representation" (Section 65.4). Broad rules for the election and composition of the National Parliament are set out in Section 93 of the Constitution.

Law No. 3/2004 provides that the purpose of political parties is to "democratically participate in the life of the country and to contribute to the formation and expression of the political will of the people" (Section 1.1). Their role includes the definition of government programs (Section 2 (c)). They are to "critically appraise the actions of the government and the public administration" (Section 16 (e)).

The electoral system may appear unusual to those familiar, for instance, with the Westminster system and its plurality of single-member electorates. Section 93.3 of the constitution requires that "the law shall establish the rules relating to constituencies, eligibility conditions, nominations and electoral procedures." These rules were encoded in Law No. 6/2006, the Law on the Election of the National Parliament. Law No. 6/2006 rules that "there shall be only one single constituency in the election of the National Parliament, corresponding to the entire national territory, headquartered in Dili" (Article 9). Members of parliament "shall be elected through pluri-nominal lists, presented by political parties or party coalitions, and each voting citizen shall be entitled to one single vote in the list" (Article 11). Lists of candidates must include at least one woman per every group of four candidates (Article 12.3).

Both the single, national electorate and closed, proportional party lists are established by legislation and not by constitutional requirements. Presumably both

---

[63] Ibid.; and see also Dennis Shoesmith, "State-led Development or 'Runaway State-building'?" in *New Research on Timor-Leste*, ed. Michael Leach, Nuno Canas Mendes, Antero B. da Silva, Bob Broughton, and Alarico da Costa Ximenes (Hawthorn, Vic.: Swinburne Press, 2012).

could be rescinded and replaced by alternative electoral and voting systems. Party-list systems have advantages: They provide better opportunities for the legislature to include a range of party representations, with a place in the parliament for smaller parties, and they can ensure (as the Timor-Leste system does) that women candidates are given a proportion of the seats in the legislature. The disadvantages include the result that the link between representatives and constituencies is entirely broken—members of parliament represent everyone and no one. Party leaders can decide who appears where on their party lists, ensuring that otherwise unpopular or compromised candidates can be assured of a place in the legislature. Parties become heavily centralized because aspiring parliament-members are dependent on the party leadership for any hope of election.[64]

INFORMAL PARTY POLITICS

The informal political system is defined by the personal authority of a handful of national leaders whose careers began in the 1970s. Marí Alkatiri and Xanana Gusmão operate as leaders in their own right with the important difference that Alkatiri's personal power is grounded in his office as secretary-general of FRETILIN, while Gusmão's authority is identified with the charismatic individual and not with his position in CNRT. In making the transition from president to prime minister, Gusmão inevitably had to engage in the daily grind of party politics, but his instinct remained patently presidential.

The informal political system is still shaped by the origins of party politics in the 1974 to 1975 era. Ramos-Horta, president until 2012; Gusmão, former president and the prime minister since 2007; and Alkatiri, former prime minister and the FRETILIN Secretary-General, as well as a number of other significant political players, all belong to that generation. Political rivalries are long-standing and ideological as well as personal. The rivalry between Alkatiri and Gusmão led to a final split in the 1980s and culminated in the crisis of 2006, when President Gusmão forced Alkatiri to resign the prime ministership.[65]

The institutional framework of the state has not provided the most encouraging environment for the development of robust multiparty politics in Timor-Leste. In common with a number of former Portuguese colonies, Timor-Leste adopted a broadly Portuguese model of the state, a semi-presidential system in which political parties operate within the parameters of an elected president, an elected national legislature, and a government—the Council of Ministers—which operates separately from the National Parliament and can issue its own decree laws.

Octavio Amorim Neto and Marina Costa Lobo provide a comparative discussion of party systems in a set of Lusophone states: Angola, Cape Verde, Guinea-Bissau, Mozambique, São Tomé, Principe, and Timor-Leste.[66] They argue that there is a Lusophone "brand" of semi-presidentialism (Brazil, alone, has a presidential system). This sets the broad parameters for the way the party system interacts with heads of state, heads of government, and parliamentary majorities. In contrast to

---

[64] Andrew Heywood, *Politics*, third ed. (Houndmills: Palgrave Macmillan, 2007), p. 263.

[65] International Crisis Group, *Resolving Timor-Leste's Crisis*, Asia Report No. 120 (October 10, 2006).

[66] Neto and Costa Lobo, "Between Constitutional Diffusion."

Mozambique (the state system most familiar to key members of the FRETILIN leadership due to their twenty-four years of exile there), actual power in Timor-Leste is concentrated in the prime minister. East Timor has one of the lowest levels of constitutional presidential powers in the Lusophone set of states.[67] The president lacks the crucial power to appoint or dismiss the prime minister and cabinet. The president has limited power to dissolve parliament (Section 86f). Neto and Lobo rank Timor-Leste's presidency a the weakest constitutionally, relative to other Lusophone semi-presidential systems. FRETILIN, in control of the Constituent Assembly that decided Timor-Leste's Constitution, deliberately limited Presidential powers based on the calculation that Gusmão, regarded by them as a serious political enemy, would win the presidency.[68]

While the formal arrangement of political institutions and institutional processes do not, of themselves, determine the way a political system works in practice, these formal arrangements do make a difference. "Presidential-parliamentary regimes," where cabinet ministers are dependent upon a powerful, directly elected president, obviously weaken the role of political parties, particularly when a president is not reliant on party support. "Premier-presidential regimes" concentrate legislative power in the government. How this power is then distributed between the political executive and the legislature varies. Premier-presidential regimes may or may not strengthen the role of the parliament and the parties that populate it. Timor-Leste is identified here as a premier-presidential regime (see the Feijo and Kingsbury chapters in this volume).

In terms of Steven Roper's comparative analysis of premier-presidential regimes,[69] legislative powers in Timor-Leste are the prerogative of the political executive and the parliament. However, when presidential power is assessed beyond the formal aspects of the constitutional role, Timor-Leste emerges with a much stronger presidency, according to the measurements, rating a high 7 on the Siaroff Scale of Presidential Power.[70] Both President Gusmão (2002–07) and then President Ramos-Horta (2007–12) acted to expand the non-legislative powers of the presidential office. Their formidable personal standing has meant that the constitutional weakness of the presidency may disguised the actual role of the president who, while excluded from day-to-day government, can exercise significant influence in some areas of general policy direction. José Maria Vasconcelos (Taur Matan Ruak, "Two Sharp Eyes"), elected president in April, 2012, and who is the former head of the defense force and a former senior guerrilla leader, evidently sees the presidency as a force in government.

During the FRETILIN government (2002–07), parliament and the opposition parties were relatively impotent, sidelined by a government in control of a centralist party in control of a parliament that was, in any case, overshadowed by the Council of Ministers. Government and party were under strict discipline by the party secretary-general/prime minister, Marí Alkatiri. Parliament has become more

---

[67] Ibid., p. 16.

[68] Paulo Gorjão, "The Legacy and Lesson of the United Nations Transitional Administration in East Timor," *Contemporary Southeast Asia* 24,2 (August 2002).

[69] Steven D. Roper, "Are All Semipresidential Regimes the Same? A Comparison of Premier-Presidential Regimes," *Comparative Politics* 34,3 (April 2002), pp. 253–72.

[70] Reproduced in Neto and Costa Lobo, "Between Constitutional Diffusion," Table 3.

assertive since the 2007 elections, but its powers remain limited by a state system that concentrates power in the political executive at the expense of the legislature.

THREATS TO DEMOCRATIC CONSOLIDATION: "RUNAWAY STATE-BUILDING"

By and large, Timor-Leste has so far escaped the threat of retreating into an "illiberal" (or solely procedural) democracy. The experience of new party systems in the post-communist states of eastern Europe confirms that this is a real danger: Weak party systems manipulated by self-serving political elites disempower constituents. Political parties in illiberal democracies do not represent public interests.[71] Conor O'Dwyer has identified "runaway state-building,"[72] driven by patronage politics, as a characteristic of party politics in these new, post-communist states. Parties operate as vehicles of personal advantage rather than as autonomous agents of popular representation. Patronage creates a population of clients dependent upon state patronage. State capacity remains underdeveloped where the state is merely an arena for self-interested contests between competing patron-client networks. Patricia Young and Anna Grzmala-Busse have drawn on O'Dwyer's work to uncover a pattern by which leaders use parties in post-communist eastern Europe to employ "direct extraction of state resources" to support clientalism.[73] A similar pattern developed in Latin America.[74] Competition between rival elite political actors, of course, does not equate to democratic politics. The associated argument is that clientalist politics and consequent low accountability to the constituency vitiate state capacity through poor and corrupt governance.[75]

Uncontrolled or unfocused state-building is a potential problem in Timor-Leste, and there are some recent indications that this sort of state-building may be beginning to happen. The tempting source of government largesse is the Petroleum Fund. Timor-Leste is "the most petroleum-dependent country in the world, with 95 percent of state revenues coming from petroleum receipts."[76] As Timor-Leste moves into a pre-election environment, the prime minister drew heavily on the Petroleum Fund to distribute largesse to the subdistricts and *sucos*. By late 2011, the fund had accumulated some US$9 billion. The prime minister explained his strategy for the fund in a speech delivered in 2010.[77] Previously, government had adopted a

---

[71] Rod Hague and Martin Harrop, *Comparative Government and Politics, An Introduction*, eighth ed. (Houndmills: Palgrave Macmillan, 2007), pp. 224–255.

[72] Conor O'Dwyer, *Runaway State-Building: Patronage Politics and Democratic Development* (Baltimore, MD: Johns Hopkins University Press, 2006).

[73] Patricia T. Young, "Political Parties and Democratic Governance in Romania," paper presented at the American Political Science Association Meeting, Toronto, September 2009; Anna Grzmala-Busse, *Rebuilding Leviathan: Party Competition and State Exploitation in Post-Communist Democracies* (New York, NY: Cambridge University Press, 2007).

[74] Barbara Geddes, *The Politician's Dilemma* (Berkeley, CA: University of California Press, 1994).

[75] Young, "Political Parties in Romania."

[76] La'o Hamutuk, "Timor is Getting Closer to the 'Resource Curse,'" submission to Committee C, RDTL National Parliament, regarding the Proposed State Budget Rectification for 2010 (June 16, revised June 22, 2010).

[77] Xanana Gusmão, "Speech by His Excellency the Prime Minister Kay Rala Xanana Gusmão on the Occasion of the Petroleum Fund Management Seminar," Dili Convention Centre, Mercado Lama, Dili, May 10, 2010, available at http://timor-leste.gov.tl/wp-content/uploads/2010/06/Speech-Petroleum-Fund-Management-Seminar-10.5.101.pdf, accessed April 25, 2012.

"prudent and simple investment strategy" for the fund; now, he said, was the time to move on from this "limited" and "conservative" strategy and diversify and maximize the fund. He announced that

> … if the needs of the country require fast and sustainable growth, we have to invest in basic infrastructure, and for this to be possible, we need to unblock the mistaken policy of savings in order to invest those revenues in the best way.[78]

The fund underwrites the prime minister's very ambitious National Strategic Development Plan, "On the Road to Peace and Prosperity." According to the strategy, Timor-Leste will join the ranks of upper-middle-income countries by 2030.[79] In 2010–11, the government reviewed the fund's investment strategy and introduced amendments to the Petroleum Fund Law that expanded the limits on annual withdrawals from the fund from 3 percent to 5 percent. Some withdrawals from the fund could now be made without parliamentary authorization.[80] The government then decided to increase the proportion of the Petroleum Fund invested in the international share market, raising the limit from 10 to 50 percent, a move that was opposed by the Consultative Council for Petroleum Fund and was made at a time of serious instability in global share markets. A former Australian adviser to the CCPF, Dr. Tim Anderson, warned that "substantial changes proposed for East Timor's Petroleum Fund law will expose the nation's finances to high risk and open the door to corruption."[81] The National Parliament approved the proposal for greater flexibility in investments from the Petroleum Fund in August 2011. The prime minister exercises increasing discretion over special project funds such as the Decentralisation Development Package (Pakote Dezenvolvimentu Desentralizadu, PDD) and the earlier referendum package (Pakote Referendum, PR) of the previous year. PR funding was not included in the state budget and was not subject to parliamentary scrutiny.

Despite efforts to contain corruption, Timor-Leste continues to score poorly on international corruption indicators.[82] The resignation of Deputy Prime Minister

---

[78] Xanana Gusmão, "Speech by His Excellency the Prime Minister Kay Rala Xanana Gusmão at the start of the Timor-Leste and Development Partners meeting," Dili, April 7, 2010, p. 19.

[79] National Strategic Development Plan, 2010. The final version of the strategy was presented to parliament in 2011, and published as *Timor-Leste Strategic Development Plan 2011–2030*, available at: http://www.tls.searo.who.int/LinkFiles/Home_NATIONAL_STRATEGIC_DEVELOPMENT_PLAN_2011-2030.pdf, accessed July 2, 2012.

[80] La'o Hamutuk. "Regarding the Proposed General State Budget for 2012," submitted to Committee C: Economy, Finances and Anti-Corruption, National Parliament, RDTL (October 21, 2011), www.laohamutuk.org/econ/OGE12/LHSubComCPNOJE2012En.pdf, accessed April 25, 2012.

[81] Tim Anderson, "East Timor's Petroleum Fund Is in Danger," *Timor Hau Nian Doben*, July 7, 2011, http://timorhauniandoben.blogspot.com.au/2011/07/east-timors-petroleum-fund-in-danger.html (accessed July 2, 2012) and reprinted in *Green Left Weekly*, July 17, 2011.

[82] Transparency International, *2011 Corruption Perceptions Index*, available at: http://cpi.transparency.org/cpi2011/ (accessed July 2, 2012), ranked Timor Leste as 143rd out of 183 countries, that is, the 40th highest index of perceived corruption. See also USAID, *Corruption Assessment: Timor-Leste*, Washington, DC, September 15, 2009.

Mário Viegas Carrascalão in September 2010 was provoked, according to the deputy prime minister, by "corruption, nepotism and collusion ... with the corrupt protecting one another, in an increasingly sophisticated way."[83] This affair will be discussed further below. The inability to control patronage politics provided some of the most serious challenges to Asia's new and restored democracies in the 1980s and 1990s, as the Philippines and Indonesia vividly illustrated. The capture of democratic politics by family dynasties through patron networks, so characteristic of local and national politics in the Philippines, has not developed to that extent in Timor-Leste.[84] However, the potential for "money politics" to subvert the party system is evident as the recent generous and loosely regulated disbursement of government funds for local development programs suggests.

THREATS TO DEMOCRATIC CONSOLIDATION: THE "EASTERN"–"WESTERN" DIVIDE

National, much more than local, elections reflect the political geography of a Timorese electorate that votes in elections for the National Parliament across a significant east–west divide. The origins of this divide are debated.[85] That it provokes inter-communal violence was evident in the house-burning and gang fighting during the political crisis of 2006. Some explain this persistent division by arguing that regional differences acquired a new political edge during the Indonesian occupation.[86] After independence, "westerners" (*Loromonu* or *Kaladi*) were perceived by some FRETILIN supporters as having a history of collaboration with the Indonesian invaders. "Easterners" (*Lorosa'e* or *Firaku*) were, according to this view, the true resistance supporters. Prime Minister Gusmão, in a provocative speech in March 2006, addressed the "*loromonu-lorosa'e*" issue, identifying it as a political problem that had long existed in the Timor-Leste defense force, the F-FDTL (FALINTIL-Forcas de Defesa de Timor-Leste, FALINTIL-Defence Forces of Timor-Leste) and that needed very careful resolution.[87] In January, 159 soldiers had presented a petition to the president and the chief of the defense force claiming discrimination by eastern-originating officers against personnel from western districts. The "Petitioners" staged a strike, leading to the dismissal of 595 soldiers (one-third of the F-FDTL), which provoked a full-scale rebellion.

The parliamentary elections held on June 30, 2007, and in July 2012 clearly reproduced the eastern–western divide. As Michael Leach observed, "Highly regionalised party affiliations [suggested] wider problems of national unity."[88] In

---

[83] Mário Viegas Carrascalão, "Letter to His Excellency Mr. Kay Rala Xanana Gusmão, Prime Minister of the Government of the RDTL," September 6, 2010, reproduced in *Tempo Semanal*, September 8, 2010.

[84] Alfred W. McCoy, ed., *An Anarchy of Families, State and Family in the Philippines* (Quezon City: Ateneo de Manila University Press, 1994); Jose F. Lacaba, ed., *Boss: 5 Case Studies of Local Politics in the Philippines* (Manila: Philippine Center for Investigative Journalism, 1995).

[85] See Shawn Donnan, "East Timor's Ethnic Violence Puzzles Analysts," *Financial Times* (June 10, 2006).

[86] José Trindade and Bryant Castro, "Rethinking Timor Identity as a Peacebuilding Strategy: The Lorosa'e-Loromonu Conflict from a Traditional Perspective" (Dili: European Union Rapid Reaction Mechanism Programme, 2006).

[87] Xanana Gusmão, Message to the Nation on F-FDTL, Palace of the Ashes, Dili, March 23, 2006.

[88] Leach, "2007 Elections in Timor-Leste," p. 227.

2007, FRETILIN won in only four of the thirteen districts, including their three eastern strongholds. The party gained 46 percent of the vote in Lautem, 60 percent in Viqueque, and 62 percent in Baucau. In the other nine districts, FRETILIN's vote ranged between 8 percent in Ainaro to 28 percent in Covalima, where it strongly outperformed the Democratic Party (PD), with 20 percent, and CNRT, with 15 percent.[89] In 2012, FRETILIN again won in only four of the thirteen districts: Baucau (51.3 percent); Lautem (43.8 percent); Viqueque (59.5 percent), and Manufahi (31.8 percent, just ahead of CNRT's 31.3 percent).

Threats to Democratic Consolidation: Party Fragmentation

The proliferation of small parties since independence, alongside the survival or parties and leaders from 1974 to 1975, determine the character of multiparty politics in Timor-Leste. The proportional voting system, which offers the single, national electorate pluri-nominal party lists from which to choose their representatives, encourages the divergence of multiple parties; this procedure contrasts with plurality voting systems that encourage the convergence of multiple parties into a two-party system.[90] A party must reach a threshold of 3 percent of votes cast to be entitled to a seat in the National Parliament.[91] There were twelve parties represented in the 2002 National Parliament, nine in the National Parliament elected in 2007 and twenty-two parties registered to contest the 2012 election by July 2011. With the exception of FRETILIN and perhaps the CNRT, parties struggle to establish reliable constituencies across the thirteen districts, sixty-five subdistricts, and 442 *sucos*. FRETILIN remains the broadest, nationally established party, but, as noted earlier, its support is concentrated in the three eastern districts.

States aspiring to democratic consolidation require broad-based political parties operating in government and opposition. Timor-Leste's multiparty system and the proliferation of small parties pose challenges to coherent governance.[92] Two-party systems usually deliver clear, national policy choices and usually deliver a clear rotation of power. Two-party systems tend to converge on the political center in order to attract an outright majority to form a government. "Catch-all parties" seek to consolidate their support with a broad constituency, rather than depend upon sectoral groups or special interests. Timor-Leste has adopted a proportional representation (PR) system that works against convergence on the center. There is a degree of political fragmentation. Some parties in the National Parliament represent quite local or minority interests. KOTA defends the status of the *liurai* families, the customary rulers. UNDERTIM (Unidade Nacional Democrática da Resistência Timorense, National Democratic Unity of Timorese Resistance), which is in the governing coalition, is a veterans' party with links to a folk religious movement. The trend elsewhere in Southeast Asia has been away from PR to plurality. Indonesia, in contrast to East Timor, introduced electoral laws in 1999 and 2004 that radically

---

[89] Faustino Cardoso, *Eleisaun Parlamentar Sira* (Dili, National Electoral Commission, 2010).

[90] Maurice Duverger, "Factors in a Two-Party and Multiparty System," in *Party Politics and Pressure Groups* (New York, NY: Thomas Y. Cromwell, 1972), pp. 23–32.

[91] Law No. 6/2006 on the Election of the National Parliament.

[92] Larry Diamond, Juan Linz, and Seymour Martin Lipset, eds. *Politics in Developing Countries: Comparing Experiences with Democracy*, second ed. (Boulder, CO: Lynne Rienner, 1995).

reduced the number of parties registered to contest parliamentary elections, requiring that they demonstrate a significant presence in at least two-thirds of the country's provinces.[93]

Multiparty systems tend to produce short-lived or unstable coalition governments, even in stable democracies. Italian coalition governments in the latter part of the twentieth century averaged terms of less than one year.[94] In post-conflict new states, such as Timor-Leste, the risk of political instability and fragmentation is real in a multiparty system that produces uneasy coalition governments. The question is whether a successful democratic system can function if the party system is diffuse and fragmented. Multiparty politics in neighboring Papua New Guinea have been described as ineffectual: "Politically the nation has no real party system, merely shifting alliances of support in Parliament for the country's leading political figures."[95] Although it has a more disciplined party system, Timor-Leste faces a similar risk to that faced by the multiparty system of Papua New Guinea: "disorderly democracy" and political "dysfunction."[96]

CONCLUSION

Party politics remains alive and fairly well in Timor-Leste. This is a creditable outcome given the record of most other post-conflict states. In terms of Scott Mainwaring and Timothy Scully's four criteria for party system institutionalization, Timor-Leste has achieved a degree of political stability in interparty competition.[97] In opposition, FRETILIN has refrained from taking advantage of serious divisions in the coalition government to provoke a political crisis. The parties have some degree of local organization outside the capital city, although, in the cases of the minor parties, support is localized in just a few of the thirteen districts. Parties and elections are generally considered legitimate and operate within an accepted system of rules.

The degree of rule stability and organizational discipline within parties is less certain, perhaps with the exception of FRETILIN. The country, with help, has managed one national election that resulted in a change of government, and the prospects for an orderly national election in 2012 are promising. The competitive party system allows the East Timorese electorate to support those leaders and those

---

[93] Benjamin Reilly, "Democratisation and Electoral Reform in the Asia-Pacific Region," *Comparative Political Studies* 40,11 (November 2007), pp. 1350–71.

[94] Daniel Diermeier, Hülya Eraslan, and Antonio Merlo, "Coalition Governments and Comparative Constitutional Design" *European Economic Review* 46 (2001): 893–907.

[95] Antony Green, "Candidate Elected with just 7.7% of the Vote under FPTP," *Antony Green's Election Blog* (April 16, 2011), http://blogs.abc.net.au/antonygreen/2011/04/candidate-elected-with-just-72-of-the-vote-under-fptp, accessed June 28, 2012.

[96] Ronald J. May, "Sir Michael Somare and PNG Politics," *Development Policy Blog* (May 20, 2011), http://devpolicy.org/sir-michael-somare-and-png-politics, accessed April 25, 2012; Philip Dorling, "Australia, US Damn PNGs Rotten Political Practices," *Saturday Age*, September 3, 2011. For a more extended discussion of small party politics in Timor-Leste, see Dennis Shoesmith, "Is Small Beautiful? Multiparty Politics and Democratic Consolidation in Timor-Leste," *Asian Politics and Policy* 4,1 (January 2012), pp. 33–51.

[97] Scott Mainwaring and Timothy R. Sculley, eds., *Building Democratic Institutions, Party Systems in Latin America* (Stanford, CA: Stanford University Press, 1995).

parties they perceive to best grasp and represent their interests, although there is evidence that many voters are alienated from Dili politics.[98]

There are, however, significant constraints on the party system that have been identified in this discussion. These constraints include the weakening of the role of the National Parliament by the proliferation of small parties and an electoral system that denies representative accountability to the local electorate, and which, in 2007 and 2012, did not deliver one party a majority to form a government in its own right. The 2012 parliamentary election did reduce the number of parties in the national parliament from eight to four, with a much stronger CNRT, but whether the coalition formed in July 2012 is effective depends on the compliance of PD, which now clearly exercises the balance of power. Based on an assessment of the past, we can predict that coalitions of political parties may be unstable and lacking in political clarity. Dysfunctional multiparty politics in Papua New Guinea represent a warning to Timor-Leste's political leaders that they should consider electoral reform that restrains the proliferation of small parties, in large part because such parties are able to claim exaggerated, disproportionate bargaining power if they gain representation in parliament, where coalition governments must be negotiated.

The parties themselves require stronger organizational development and less dependence upon a handful of leaders who remain the survivors of 1975. There are signs that "runaway state-building" and associated patronage politics are emerging and that this trend is accelerating in the leadup to the 2012 elections. In an economy dependent solely upon petroleum revenues, political parties in government and their leaders will find it difficult to resist the opportunity to buy support in the name of "development," which has previously produced the political element of the "resource curse" in other energy rich, but otherwise poor, countries. The politics of patronage, such as those experienced in the post-communist states of eastern Europe and elsewhere, undermine representative party politics and threaten to implant and foster illiberal multiparty systems. Reform of the party system may not by itself ensure the consolidation of democratic governance in Timor-Leste, but without it that consolidation will remain problematic.

---

[98] David Hicks, "Centre and Periphery in Contemporary Timor-Leste," paper presented at the conference Nation-Building Across Urban and Rural Timor-Leste, RMIT University, Dili, July 8–10, 2009.

THE NEED FOR A RESHAPED FOREIGN POLICY

Pedro Seabra

INTRODUCTION

Having apparently overcome some of the internal strife that scarred the nation-building process in 2006 and 2008, Timor-Leste now appears to be experiencing a period of relative political stability and social order, albeit with several unresolved issues still looming on the horizon. Nonetheless, in this rather steady context, Timor-Leste has become increasingly vocal and assertive on a range of topics with significant potential implications for the country's foreign policy agenda. This indicates an existing political will to enhance or diversify its role in the region, with sometimes unpredictable results. The potential ripple effects across the region—given the level of international focus, Timor-Leste's strategic geographic locations, and its vast but still mostly untapped natural wealth—are also unforeseeable, warranting greater attention and analysis.

Accordingly, as Timor-Leste's assertiveness grows, new questions and doubts will also arise with regard to the intended course the country seeks to pursue in the coming years. With that in mind, this chapter will start by examining the current context of Timor-Leste's foreign policy, identifying its main external partners and the goals it has set since officially joining the international community, with a detailed focus on relationships with four key actors: Australia, China, Indonesia, and Portugal. A study of the relationships with these countries—while not exhausting Timor's foreign policy agenda—will allow a better understanding of Timor-Leste's current foreign policy positioning in the world. This chapter will then examine some particular and instructive episodes in Timor's foreign policy development that have raised concerns among its traditional partners, now confronted with this independent actor. Finally, a prospective analysis will be offered, highlighting the country's options in the middle term and potential courses of action to be taken, particularly with respect to these key four relationships. Conclusions will then be drawn regarding Timor-Leste's current regional stance and what lies ahead for the Southeast Asian nation in terms of its still-nascent foreign policy.

STARTING FROM ZERO

After the destructive post-referendum violence in 1999 subsided, United Nations (UN) multinational forces were suddenly in charge of a massive program of state-building, seeking to create the institutions necessary to a democratic and stable state—despite the common belief that international assistance would be needed for years to come.[1]

As the newest inexperienced player in the international arena, Timor-Leste quickly found itself in the position of having to formulate a foreign policy that would simultaneously guarantee its worldwide recognition as a viable state, which was therefore, worthy of continuing international assistance, and, also, establish the country as a credible actor in the regional setting—all this, while not neglecting its nearest neighbors. The challenge for the Timorese leadership was thus considerable, especially given the meager resources available and the various choices that had to be made concerning where to allocate them. Opting to balance significant international donors with historically and culturally important affinities, while investing in a secure and stable regional scenario, constituted a bold and ambitious agenda. But given Timor's own context, the decision was, in itself, inescapable, as the country's variety of needs demanded considerable heterogeneity with respect to sources of international support.

In that sense, a careful diversification of the country's foreign policy goals was duly required, despite the constraints that could impede those seeking to follow such a path. Indeed, despite the various commitments of the international community on the ground, certain international hurdles still threatened to jeopardize prospects of internal and regional stability. Right from the start, relations with Indonesia were bound to hold the key. After more than two decades under Indonesia's authoritarian rule and the tumultuous and violent independence process, Timor-Leste was faced with the necessity of establishing a working bilateral relationship with its former ruler, if the new nation was ever going to succeed internally or externally. Understanding this challenging scenario, and in the interest of state survival, Timor-Leste's authorities—including the most prominent independence leaders, such as José Alexandre "Xanana" Gusmão, José Ramos-Horta, and Marí Alkatiri—recognized the necessity of normalizing ties with Indonesia. In this new relationship, the human rights violations perpetrated by the Indonesian military were considered the most sensitive issue. Indeed, already in 2001 and still under the UN administration, a Commission for Reception, Truth, and Reconciliation (CAVR, Comissão de Acolhimento, Verdade e Reconciliação) was established with the aim of investigating human rights violations during the Indonesian-ruled period, from 1974

---

[1] Through UN Security Council Resolution (UNSC) 1246 (1999), the United Nations Mission in East Timor (UNAMET) was established on June 11, 1999, to organize the national referendum and to lead the peacekeeping mission known as International Force East Timor (INTERFET). The peacekeeping mission was authorized by UNSC Resolution 1264 (1999) and deployed on September 20, 1999, to restore local order. With the backing of UNSC Resolution 1272 (1999), on October 25, 1999, the United Nations Transitional Authority for East Timor (UNTAET) was established and would be succeeded, in May 17, 2002, by the United Nations Mission of Support in East Timor (UNMISET)—the two were authorized by UNSC Resolution 1410 (2002). Afterwards, through UNSC Resolution 1599 (2005), the United Nations Office in Timor-Leste (UNOTIL) was installed on May 20, 2005. In the wake of the 2006 crisis, UNSC Resolution 1704 (2006) led to the deployment of the United Nations Integrated Mission in Timor-Leste (UNMIT).

to 1999.[2] Likewise, under international pressure, Indonesia set up a human rights court to investigate Indonesia's own military accountability for the atrocities of 1999.

Predictably, both attempts essentially failed to meet every generalized expectation. The CAVR came to produce a 2,500-page–final report recognizing that the occupation was directly responsible for the deaths of an estimated minimum of 102,800 East Timorese, but the Timorese government fell short in following the CAVR's recommendations for further action. For its part, the ad hoc Indonesian court indicted eighteen individuals, but only one was actually convicted—the former East Timorese militia leader Eurico Guterres. A sense of widespread frustration was then felt by both the Timorese population and by the international community as it became clear that justice would have a hard time being served.

In the interest of dealing with this issue while protecting bilateral relations, Timor-Leste and Indonesia then created in 2005 a bilateral Truth and Friendship Commission (CVA, Comissão de Verdade e Amizade) with the goal of turning the page on their troubled common history, and setting the tone of their relationship for years to come. But since the TFC had no indictment or prosecution powers, it was widely considered a toothless and ineffective instrument that "instead served to render some already conclusive truths inconclusive."[3] From the start, it was clear that the East Timorese government was more interested in rebooting relations and appeasing its neighbor than actually digging up, once again, the past crimes that could jeopardize the objective of achieving good relations between the two countries. The constant visits to Timor-Leste and Indonesia from both countries' respective highest authorities evidenced this same concern and motive. The visit by Indonesian President Susilo Bambang Yudhoyono in 2005 to the Santa Cruz Cemetery—where in 1991 more than 250 protesters were shot and killed by Indonesian troops—exemplified, and symbolized, these shared attempts to reinforce ties between both parties.[4] Likewise, after he assumed office in May 2007, President Ramos-Horta's first state visit abroad was to Jakarta. Afterwards, when former President Suharto died in January 2008, Prime Minister Gusmão and other senior Timorese officials proved once more their intentions to seek full reconciliation by traveling to Indonesia to pay their respects. The humanitarian assistance provided by Timor-Leste to the victims of the 2004 tsunami that hit Indonesian shores was, equally, considered symbolically important for the relationship.

On the other hand, Timor-Leste also had to deal with Indonesia's fears of its former province becoming a staging ground for other regional powers and of a diminished role reserved for Indonesian influence. But even those apprehensions were somewhat laid to rest when the East Timorese government declared its intention to seek full membership in the Association of Southeast Asian Nations (ASEAN)[5]—as opposed to joining the Pacific Islands Forum, a goal once envisioned

---

[2] Paulo Gorjão, "The East Timorese Commission for Reception, Truth and Reconciliation: Chronicle of a Foretold Failure?" *Civil Wars* 4,2 (2001): 143.

[3] Megan Hirst, "Too Much Friendship, Too Little Truth—Monitoring Report on the Commission of Truth and Friendship in Indonesia and Timor-Leste," report from International Center for Transitional Justice, 2008, p. 37.

[4] "Yudhoyono Prays at Site of Dili Massacre," *Associated Press*, April 9, 2005, available at www.smh.com.au/news/World/Yudhoyono-prays-at-site-of-Dili-massacre/2005/04/09/111 2997218540.html, accessed September 20, 2010.

[5] ASEAN currently consists of Indonesia, Malaysia, Singapore, Philippines, Thailand, Brunei, Cambodia, Vietnam, Laos, and Myanmar (Burma).

by then Foreign Minister José Ramos-Horta in 1999.[6] Indeed, by choosing the former multilateral institution over the latter—which includes Australia, New Zealand and the majority of the Pacific islands—Timor-Leste exhibited its self-proclaimed allegiance to Southeast Asia while demonstrating the nation's willingness to participate in the region's leading integration process. It is not as if Timor-Leste entirely closed the door to the possibility of belonging to the Pacific Islands Forum, but it did provide some clues as to the country's intentions in the region. For all intents and purposes, Timor-Leste saw its future as primarily tied to developments in Southeast Asia, even though it also signaled an intention to join as many international forums as it could, to better secure its longer-term diplomatic relations. The potential for opening new relations with vibrant and prosperous economies, as well as for contributing to a neighborly stability, were considered the main reasons behind the push to join ASEAN. Nonetheless, this particular goal has so far been on hold, as Timor-Leste has been limited to observer status in ASEAN since 2002 due to a number of structural constraints in the accession process and to some members' doubts about Timor-Leste's ability to meet the organization's requirements. Burma, in particular, appeared to be blocking Timor-Leste's bid to joint the organization in the first years, in response to Timor-Leste's public support of Aung San Suu Kyi as Burma's rightful leader and its ongoing criticism of Burma's military regime. In this context, Timor-Leste's membership in the ASEAN Regional Forum, granted in 2005, although officially understood as a first step to membership in ASEAN, ended up a mere consolation prize while the country waited for further developments on this front.

But while Indonesia and ASEAN are crucial to Timor-Leste's security and political stability, the country's foreign agenda also grants considerable attention and focus to its other predominant neighbor, Australia. Given Australia's contribution to the latter stage of the independence process—through both its leadership of the INTERFET (International Force East Timor) forces and its bilateral aid program, larger than any other country's—and the close geographic proximity of the two countries, Australia has come to regard Timor-Leste as a country situated within its sphere of influence, which has occasionally caused some bilateral tensions. One particular difficult issue concerns the exploration of the vast natural resource reserves lying beneath the Timor Sea and previously regulated by the Timor Gap Treaty of 1991 between Australia and Indonesia—later replaced by the Timor Sea Treaty when the newly independent Timor-Leste became a contracting party in 2002. While it was possible to work out an agreement regarding the sharing of the proceeds from the Joint Petroleum Development Area (JPDA), itself a result of the latter treaty, the same cannot be said about the efforts to come to an agreement regarding sovereignty and the establishment of a definite maritime boundary between Australia and Timor-Leste; resolution of this latter issue has been essentially deferred for fifty years in recognition of the likely revenues that both parties can draw in the interim period.

Additionally, beyond the significant amounts of development aid it has provided to Timor-Leste in the past decade—AU$930 million (US$933 million) from

---

[6] Nuno Canas Mendes, "Dilemas identitários e fatalidades geopolíticas: Timor-Leste entre o Sudeste Asiático e o Pacífico-Sul" (Identity dilemas and geopolitical fatalities: Timor Leste between Southeast Asia and South Pacific), in *Understanding Timor-Leste*, ed. Michael Leach et al. (Hawthorn: Swinburne Press, 2010), p. 37.

1999 to 2010 in official development assistance (ODA), coupled with an annual aid budget in 2011–12 of just over AU$80 million—Australia also continues to play a decisive role in Timor-Leste's internal security. In the wake of the 2006 crisis, peacekeepers were once again needed to pacify the country, and Australia promptly contributed 1,000 men, 390 of whom are still stationed in Timor-Leste, alongside a small policing force working closely with the United Nations.

For its part, Portugal retains a historical and continuing bond with Timor-Leste. Since the Indonesian invasion in 1975, and especially through the 1990s, Portugal has argued Timor-Leste's case and became a decisive actor in securing the referendum leading to independence. Furthermore, during the series of UN-led operations, Portugal consistently stood out as the second highest contributor of troops on the ground, behind Australia, actively participating in the nation's stabilization. In 2006, as violence erupted, Portugal contributed 126 members of the National Republican Guard (GNR, Guarda Nacional Republicana) to the peacekeeping effort.[7] Furthermore, Portugal has also maintained its international commitments, having disbursed more than €400 million (US$525 million) in aid from 1999 to 2006 while allocating another €60 million (US$79 million) through the latest Indication Cooperation Program for 2007–10. Particular investments have been made to support the teaching and learning of the Portuguese language throughout the country. Timor-Leste's prompt insertion into the Community of Portuguese-speaking Countries (CPLP) was considered another way of gaining international recognition for the young nation, as it implied that Timor-Leste had established alliances with interested regional powers, like Brazil and Angola, and influential multilateral organizations, like the European Union, through Portugal.[8]

China has also increasingly positioned itself as an increasingly close partner for Timor-Leste, even though it has provided significantly lower aid amounts when compared to Western donors (less than US$53 million from 1999 to 2009). It was the first country officially to recognize Timor's independence, at a time when Beijing and Jakarta did not have diplomatic relations, and since then China has gradually become an invaluable help for local plans of reconstruction and development.[9] Indeed, the construction of the presidential palace, the foreign ministry, and the military residential quarters in Metinaro are just a few visible examples of Chinese presence in Timor-Leste, showcasing a growing foreign influence in the country. Considering its aid and assistance efforts, coupled with other contributions—such as scholarships and training programs for civil servants or, for example, the donation of 8,000 tonnes of rice during the 2009 food crisis—China is sending a clear public message regarding the seriousness of strengthening bilateral ties with the tiny but strategically important Southeast Asian state.

It is also worth mentioning some of Timor-Leste's other important partners in international aid, of which the country is still a significant recipient, though the scale of such assistance does not match that provided by the countries described above. As

---

[7] Reinaldo Saraiva Hermenegildo, "O Papel da GNR em Timor-Leste: Um contributo para a Política Externa de Portugal" (The role of GNR in Timor-Leste: A contributor to Portugal's foreign policy), *Revista Militar* (2008): 783–812.

[8] José Palmeira, "O potencial de Timor-Leste na geopolítica da CPLP" (The potential of Timor-Leste in CPLP geopolitics), in *Understanding Timor-Leste*, ed. Michael Leach et al. (Hawthorn: Swinburne Press, 2010), p. 43.

[9] Ian Storey, "China's Inroads Into East Timor," *China Brief* 9,6 (2009): 7.

an important player in the international process back in 1999, the United States has consistently disbursed funds in support of local development and sustainable state structures, totaling more than US$300 million since 2000. The European Union (EU) has provided close to €47 million (US$62 million) in emergency assistance and is currently following through its Country Strategy Paper/National Indicative Programme for 2008–13 with another €63 million (US$83 million) focused on stabilization and dialogue, fighting poverty, and humanitarian support. For its part, Japan continues to play a vital role as a major donor, having contributed with ¥15 billion (US$181 million) between 2002 and 2009, while currently cooperating in training local police officers in Timor. It is equally worth mentioning the role of Cuba as a significant provider of medical aid, either through the presence of Cuban doctors on the ground or through hundreds of scholarships provided for East Timorese students to study medicine in Cuba. Finally, one cannot leave out Malaysia and New Zealand—which have actively contributed to the country's security throughout the past decade through the provision of police and soldiers—as Timor-Leste's remaining relevant foreign partners with an interest in its development and security, partly because both of these nations recognize the regional fallout that could potentially result from a deteriorating situation in Timor-Leste.

Increasingly Vocal

Among Timor's external partners, it is the relationship with Australia that has most frequently commanded attention in recent years, with a series of episodes straining ties. First and foremost, both countries' attention is focused on the Timor Sea, and especially on the Greater Sunrise block, where oil and natural gas reserves are estimated at 5.13 trillion cubic feet and 226 million barrels, respectively. Unlike the remaining area—regulated by the above-mentioned Timor Sea Treaty of 2002—this particular section is under the Sunrise International Unitization Agreement (Sunrise IUA) and the Treaty on Certain Maritime Arrangements in the Timor Sea (CMATS), signed in 2003 and 2006, respectively. Although the Sunrise IUA initially foresaw that proceeds from the Sunrise block would be unevenly distributed (with the lion's share going to Australia) for the sake of speedy development and exploitation, the CMATS treaty amended those disproportionate assignments, essentially providing that any revenues from this particular area were to be shared fifty-fifty between Timor-Leste and Australia.[10] To that end, a joint-venture consortium—led by Australian Woodside Petroleum (with a 33.4 percent investment share) and including ConocoPhillips (30 percent), Royal Dutch Shell (26.6 percent), and Osaka Gas (10 percent)—was formed to expedite the planning and consequent extraction of the natural resources under water.

However, in January 2010, the intended plan was stopped when Woodside disclosed its intention to go ahead with the building of a floating platform to process the untapped liquefied natural gas (LNG) available in the Greater Sunrise block—a choice confirmed the following April, with a combined announcement by all Sunrise joint-venture partners. This option was immediately and bluntly opposed by Timor-Leste's government, which said it preferred to see a new LNG processing plant built

---

[10] The CMTAS also put on hold any claim to sovereign rights and did not establish any local seabed boundary, the final definition of which was postponed until the treaty's expiration in fifty years, more precisely, in 2057.

on its southern coast, near Suai, as it had insistently indicated throughout the negotiation process. In its defense, Timor-Leste officials pointed out that an LNG floating platform had yet to be tested—it would be the second of its kind in the world—and that the technological risk may not pay off in terms of costs and benefits, especially when considering the geographic adversities of the surrounding Timor Trough. Furthermore, Timor-Leste also argued that the establishment of an onshore plant would help fight its 30 percent unemployment rate, with the consequent economic and social benefits that one could expect from such a massive project at a local level. In addition to all this, Woodside's move was branded by the Timorese government as reflecting an unacceptable level of "arrogance" because it had not taken into consideration Timor's interests in this matter.[11]

As for the Australian government, it was accused of not pulling its weight in influencing one of Australia's major companies in the pursuit of a commonly beneficial solution, even though it had clearly stated that the decision about the location of the LNG processing plant was a purely commercial one, that the previous agreement stipulated the most economically viable option, and that the Australian government would not interfere in private commercial decisions. On the other hand, Woodside's position was that the cost of laying a pipeline from the gas field to Timor-Leste's south coast was prohibitive as well as technologically unfeasible.

Angered by these developments and apparently willing to test bilateral relations, Prime Minister Xanana Gusmão took this opportunity to dig deep into the past and escalated his rhetoric when, during an international donors' conference, he accused Australia of sacrificing the lives of 60,000 Timorese in World War II and secretly plotting in 1963 for Indonesia to take over what was then Portuguese Timor.[12] Given the visible military contribution to Timor-Leste's security and the high level of effort and aid allocated to the island by Australia, this declaration raised considerable official concern in Australia and was widely seen as further fueling bilateral tensions.

But if the bilateral relationship was already rocky, a change in leadership in the Australian government added another seemingly difficult topic to the agenda. Among new Prime Minister Julia Gillard's policy ideas was the possibility of building a regional "asylum-seeker processing center" in Timor-Leste. For his part, then Deputy Prime Minister Mário Carrascalão promptly declared that Díli was "nobody's puppet."[13] The fact that Gillard only initially discussed her intentions with President Ramos-Horta and not with Prime Minister Xanana Gusmão, who held the real authority, did not assist her case. While the proposal grew into one of the major debating points in the Australian federal elections, the subject attracted extra regional concern, as other countries—such as Indonesia, which hosts around 14,000 refugees from Afghanistan who were intercepted on their way to Australia—worried about the lack of consultation in a matter that inevitably affected the entire region. Timor-Leste's positioning then became crucial, with Gillard actively seeking a

---

[11] Xavier La Canna, "East Timor May Derail Woodside Project," *Australian Associated Press*, April 30, 2010, available at http://news.smh.com.au/breaking-news-business/east-timor-may-derail-woodside-project-20100430-tyvc.html, accessed September 20, 2010.

[12] Lindsay Murdoch, "Gusmao Lashes Australia for Duplicity," *Sidney Morning Herald*, April 9, 2010, available at www.smh.com.au/world/gusmao-lashes-australia-for-duplicity-20100408-rv6e.html, accessed September 25, 2010.

[13] "E. Timor Deputy PM Rejects Australian Asylum Fix," *Agence France-Press*, July 14, 2010, available at http://www.asiaone.com/News/Latest+News/Asia/Story/A1Story20100714-226961.html, accessed September 22, 2010.

compromise that she could present to her constituents as an effective solution to what was, fundamentally, a domestic Australian political problem.

Amid these disputes, another episode attracted media attention because of its alleged geostrategic implications. On May 20, 2010, Timor-Leste finally received the two Chinese Shanghai III patrol boats—*Jaco* and *Betano*, designed in the 1960s and equipped with 30-millimeter cannons—bought two years prior through a US$28 million contract with Poly Technologies, a defense company with close links to China's People Liberation Army (PLA). Officially, these vessels are needed to police illegal fishery activities in Timor-Leste's exclusive economic zone—illegal fishing deprives the state of an estimated US$45 million a year in revenues—and to provide some security assurance against smuggling and drug trafficking along 870 kilometers of coastline.[14] Further seeking to fix Timor-Leste's lack of naval capabilities, Portugal had already donated two ageing Albatoss-class patrol vessels— *Atauro* and *Oecussi*—back in 2002, armed with twenty-millimeter cannons, though the growing need for repairs to these old boats and the US$500,000 a year required to keep them running probably weighed heavily in the country's decision to renew its fleet. Although Timor-Leste's reasons for purchasing the patrol boats were understandable, the fact that the Chinese-made vessels were apparently ill-suited for the maritime conditions common in the Timor Sea, combined with the presence of a Chinese crew to man the boats while their Timorese counterparts are trained, have served to increase regional wariness of China's growing influence in the country.

This wariness was intensified when, on August 24, 2010, at the beginning of the construction on the vast complex of the Ministry of Defense and Security and of the headquarters of Timor-Leste's Defense Forces (F-FDTL, Falintil-Forças de Defesa de Timor Leste)—backed yet again by US$8.9 million in Chinese funding—Prime Minister Gusmão took the opportunity to declare that Timor-Leste was "firmly committed to incrementing bilateral cooperation in the military area with friendly countries that provide us with uninterested support. Our Chinese brothers and sisters are clearly part of this group." Through such words, warnings were sent out that it would not be legitimate for anyone to "seek to constrain our options," which was then understood as a clear message to Gusmão's Australian counterparts.[15]

Timor-Leste's newfound confrontational posture was not only brought to bear on its dealings with the Australian government or Australian companies. Although on a different level, another example concerned the situation of Timor Telecom— majority held by Portuguese Portugal Telecom (PT)—which, in 2002, invested in the nascent nation in return for the monopoly over local telecommunications for fifteen years. Accordingly, Portugal Telecom was caught off guard when on May 15, 2010— seven years before the contract's expiration—Deputy Prime Minister José Luis Guterres announced that the sector would be liberalized by 2011 in a bid to fulfill one of Xanana Gusmão's main electoral promises, to reduce the high cost of

---

[14] Nuno Cana Mendes, "The Dragon and the Crocodile: Chinese Interests in East Timor," *Portuguese Journal of International Affairs* 1 (2009): 8.

[15] Xanana Gusmão, "Address by His Excellency the Prime Minister on the Occasion of the Turning of the First Stone for the Construction of the Ministry of Defence and F-FDTL Headquarters Building," August 24, 2010, available at http://timor-leste.gov.tl/wp-content/uploads/2010/08/Lan%C3%A7amento-da-1%C2%AA-pedra-do-MD-e-QG-F-FDTL-24.8.pdf, accessed October 30, 2010.

telecommunications.[16] Timor Telecom's strategic plan of investments, disclosed just six months prior to this news, was thus put on hold, awaiting further official clarification.

The relationship between Indonesia and Timor-Leste, despite all the goodwill rhetoric of the Timorese leadership, has also faced some hurdles along the way. First, the definition of their commonly shared border has proven difficult to agree on, even though the necessity of a comprehensive agreement on the issue has topped the bilateral agenda for years. Indeed, while Indonesia still continues to go slowly on tackling the final demarcation of their territory, Timor-Leste also does not appear capable of pushing forward with a consensual compromise that its neighbor can accept. The situation is even more critical with regard to the Oecusse enclave, located within Indonesian West Timor, and the inherent challenges regarding the regulated and unregulated movement of people and goods across the border.[17] Meanwhile, local tensions increased throughout 2010, fueled by small skirmishes and veiled threats from the Indonesian military, persistently confronted with ongoing civil construction by East Timorese citizens in supposedly "neutral" areas at the undefined border. Even if limited and rather sporadic, these incidents threatened to taint the current rapprochement process, especially given the apparent lack of political will from both sides finally to move forward with establishing a clear demarcation.

Furthermore, the latent ramifications resulting from the murky handover of former Laksaur militia leader Maternus Bere to Indonesian authorities in 2009 are still felt within East Timorese civil society. The daunting pressure that Indonesia applied to the Timorese leadership in order to achieve Bere's release and freedom soured the supposedly renewed relationship and, in that sense, reminded the country of the ongoing issues with its neighbor and how obstacles from their common past still keep appearing to impede a mutually respectful working relationship. When coupled with other unclear decisions—like the release in 2008 of another militia leader, Joni Marques, who saw his thirty-three-year–prison sentence commuted—it is commonly agreed that the memories of the Indonesian occupation period still continue to disrupt prospects for establishing good will between the two nations.

WHAT LIES AHEAD

With so many "combat fronts," one is left to speculate as to whether the above-mentioned episodes indicate Timor-Leste's intention to modify seriously its foreign positioning and adapt the balance of its international relationship— perhaps to garner more regional attention to its owns interests in the long run—or whether these actions have merely been part of the nation's evolution, as it learns to assert itself as a truly independent country; if the latter theory is true, then perhaps these actions are ultimately not of concern. However, even though these episodes appear

---

[16] "East Timor Government to Liberalize Telecommunications by Start of 2011," *Macauhub*, May 12, 2010, available at www.macauhub.com.mo/en/news.php?ID=9414, accessed on September 22, 2010.

[17] International Crisis Group, "Timor-Leste: Oecusse and the Indonesian Border," *Asia Briefing* 104 (May 20, 2010): 4.

disconnected from each other, it is impossible to deny their sequencing in time, as if substantiating a growing trend in Timor-Leste, calling for the revision of its foreign policy options. The choices that will be taken in the future on a number of important issues will undoubtedly help clarify the issues at stake, and provide a realistic guide to better understand Timor's aspirations in the world at large.

The case of the Greater Sunrise exploration is the most pressing. Indeed, according to CMATS Article 12, if a development plan is not approved by 2013, or if extraction does not take place by 2017, then either Australia or Timor-Leste could cancel the existing arrangements and thus "set the project back decades, undoing all the [progress of the] strained negotiations."[18] The CMATS treaty is widely viewed as having been forced upon the Timorese leadership by former Australian Foreign Minister Alexander Downer, who threatened to withhold a final agreement on Sunrise's income—which would have blocked any likely revenues and strangled Timor-Leste's incipient economy—if the CMATS were not approved by Timor-Leste's parliament. But, in any given scenario, Timor-Leste's consent will always be required before the site can be developed. While there have been semi-official approaches to other potentially interested companies, to date none has taken up Timor-Leste's option of being an alternative development partner.[19] Additionally, if the Timorese government insists on consistently and publicly presenting its case as a "David/impoverished nation vs. Goliath/ruthless Australian mega-corporation," it increasingly runs the risk of being perceived as an unfriendly or unreliable business partner and site for potential international investment. Indeed, the tense relationship with Woodside and, to a lesser extent, with Portugal Telecom, may end up proving counterproductive for the foreign investment the country so desperately needs. In the case of Woodside, the change in the company's executive leadership has provided an opportunity to renew negotiations over the development of the Timor Sea Greater Sunrise field, although at the time of writing there was no indication of a substantive shift of position by either party.

On the other hand, the Australian proposal to set up an asylum-seeker processing center amounted to nothing more than a poorly conceived and executed policy that created an unnecessary hurdle in the relationship between Timor-Leste and Australia. As events unfolded, it soon became clear that such a project was essentially "dead in the water," as explicit East Timorese opposition made the proposal impracticable at every level.[20] Hopes that negotiations could provide an acceptable solution, either under a bilateral agreement or under a regional framework—such as the Bali Process, for example[21]—were also quickly discarded as it became clear that Timor-Leste would not grant final approval and support for the center. In that sense, once the fiery rhetoric was over, the quiet abandonment of the project allowed for a certain amount of breathing room in the bilateral relationship. However, the fast escalation in political acrimony throughout this entire episode

---

[18] "The Greater Game of Greater Sunrise," *Petroleum Economist,* September 22, 2011: 4.

[19] In the beginning of 2010, Malaysian Petronas was frequently pointed out as the frontrunner for an exploration alternative, but it has, since then, detached itself from the process.

[20] "Dead in the Water," *The Economist,* April 1, 2011, available at www.economist.com/blogs/banyan/2011/04/australias_processing_centre, accessed October 2, 2011.

[21] The Bali Process, involving more than fifty nations (including Australia, Indonesia, and Timor-Leste), was established in 2002 as a regional diplomatic grouping to combat transnational crime and people-smuggling.

serves as an acute example of how Timor-Leste and Australia are easily susceptible to unexpected flare-ups.

Be that as it may, if Timor-Leste truly seeks to maintain a fruitful working environment with its neighbor, reiterated accusations against Australia of "bullying" tactics are likely to bear little fruit.[22] As a recognizable preponderant actor in the region, Australia is bound to assume an overreaching and regionally protective attitude regarding smaller neighbors, of which Timor-Leste is unavoidably one; indeed, its security, stability, and cohesion have already been upgraded to a national strategic interest in Australian defense policy,[23] and it is not too far-fetched to assume that "a smaller, less intrusive but better coordinated aid, policing and military assistance program" linking the two countries will eventually be needed.[24] As easy as it is to rebuff what can be seen as Australia's over-protective stance, Timor-Leste recognizes how intertwined its present and future stability is with its neighbor's willingness effectively to support it. If Timor-Leste truly desires an equal and effective working relationship with Australia—as it should—toning down the usual inflammatory rhetoric might prove to be a useful meaningful step toward a more sustainable relationship.

With the International Stabilisation Force due to depart Timor-Leste in the second half of 2012, the overly ambitious goals the East Timorese authorities have outlined for their own military (proposed in the 2007 defense blueprint *Force 2020* report and later confirmed by the 2011 Strategic Development Plan and by the F-FDTL 2011–15 Development Plan) do not appear to match strategic needs and are unlikely to come to fruition in the foreseeable future. Indeed, by proclaiming the need for a 3,000-person-strong armed forces, backed by a national conscription process and missile-equipped warships—including the purchase of the Chinese vessels previously mentioned[25]—Timor-Leste has only tended to reinforce the arguments of its critics, who often target the disparities and inconsistencies of the government's priorities, complaining that the government's grand schemes do not take into account the country's still underdeveloped status. Although presented in a long-term timeframe, the plans to build up the country's defense structures can thus be understandably hard to explain and justify to the local populace, which still faces many social and economic challenges after ten years of independence.

Timor-Leste's eagerness to build up its defense forces also concerns the international community, and especially those countries and organizations invested in Timor-Leste's stability, which wonder about the current security apparatus the country requires, and the seriousness of the East Timorese government in providing the appropriate means, capabilities, and orientations for its sometimes only poorly controlled security sector. Even though the ongoing United Nations Integrated Mission on Timor-Leste (UNMIT) will end its mandate in 2012—coinciding with the country's own electoral calendar—calls for some kind of extended presence by

---

[22] Jose Belo, "Proud Timorese Are Fed Up with Canberra's Bullying," *Sidney Morning Herald*, June 15, 2010.

[23] Australian Department of Defence, "Defending Australia in the Asia Pacific Century: Force 2030—Defence White Paper 2009" (Commonwealth of Australia, 2009).

[24] Damien Kingsbury, "The ADF and Timor-Leste: Looking Towards 2020," in *A Reliable Partner: Strengthening Australia-Timor-Leste Relations*, a special report from Australian Strategic Policy Institute, April 2011, p. 20.

[25] Afterwards, on September 2011, Timor-Leste also received another three South Korean retired patrol vessels as part of Timor-Leste's growing naval contingent.

international security forces have already been heard.[26] In that sense, though Timor-Leste clearly has the right to provide for its own national defense, these overly ambitious designs and the apparent political will to pursue them may, in the short-term, become counterproductive and complicate longer-term training and other military-to-military relationships.

The next international partner to leave, after the withdrawal of the International Stabilisation Force, could well be Portugal. Given the long duration of its commitment to and involvement in the development of Timor-Leste, the Portuguese authorities must be wondering if the conditions on the ground are finally ripe for a low-profile withdrawal of their GNR forces. After several years of contributing physically to the country's security, and with the harsh effects of the global financing crisis in mind, Portugal will certainly prefer a diminished role in Timor-Leste, through which development aid will trump—if not substitute entirely—any "boots on the ground." Furthermore, as local stability in Timor-Leste becomes more consolidated, the chances of Portugal withdrawing its security forces will understandably increase. On the other hand, calls for Portugal's greater economic presence in Timor-Leste—made by President Ramos-Horta during his last trip to Portugal in October 2010 and again by Prime Minister Xanana Gusmão in September 2011—will face some obstacles before materializing as Portuguese investors will inevitably recall their past mistreatment. The experience with Timor Telecom remains a case in point. Even though the "introduction of competition in the telecommunications sector" and the attendant reduction in telecommunications costs[27] represented a mainstay priority for the Gusmão cabinet, only in March 2012 was it possible to reach an agreement that effectively ended Timor Telecom's monopoly.[28] The lengthy negotiation process involved thus serves as a stark reminder that unless guarantees of a stable legal framework are provided, any future economic investor will most likely think twice before risking venturing into Timor-Leste.

Nevertheless, the country's cooperation with Portugal is likely to remain cordial as new joint ventures and opportunities continue to emerge. The latest, for example, concerned the East Timorese contingent that joined Portugal's own military assignment with the United Nations Interim Force in Lebanon (UNIFIL) at the beginning of 2012. Likewise, the Lusophone domain will most certainly retain significance in Timor-Leste's agenda as the organization of the CPLP's third Parliamentary Assembly in Díli on September 21–23, 2011, clearly exemplifies.

---

[26] See, for example, "Presidente de Timor-Leste quer acordo bilateral com Portugal para manter GNR depois de 2012" (East Timorese president wants bilateral agreement with Portugal to maintain GNR after 2012), *Lusa* (October 4, 2011), available at www.pub lico.pt/Pol%C3%ADtica/presidente-de-timorleste-quer-acordo-bilateral-com-portugal-para-manter-gnr-depois-de-2012—1515034, accessed October 5, 2011.

[27] Xanana Gusmão, "Address by His Excellency the Prime Minister Kay Rala Xanana Gusmão at the Chamber of Commerce & Industry of Timor-Leste Regarding Telecommunications Liberalization," August 18, 2011, available at http://timor-leste.gov.tl/wp-content /uploads/2011/08/Telecom-Liberalisation-18.8.pdf, accessed October 5, 2011.

[28] Hugo Paula, "Timor Leste antecipa liberalização do mercado de telecomunicações/Timor-Leste anticipates the liberalization of the telecommunications market" *Jornal de Negócios*, March 27, 2012, available at http://www.jornaldenegocios.pt/home.php?template= SHOWNEWS_V2&id=547321, accessed April 2, 2012.

With regard to its Southeast Asian strategy, Timor-Leste is equally and increasingly looking to Thailand and the Philippines as potential players in the region, in the hopes of gaining further support for Timor-Leste's ASEAN accession. Surprisingly enough, this objective was given new momentum with the organization's ministerial meeting in Hanoi in July 2010, in which a consensus appeared to emerge regarding Timor-Leste's candidacy.[29] Indeed, in a rather politically ambiguous move, President José Ramos-Horta even welcomed Burma's Foreign Minister Nyan Win to Dili the following month, while professing the desire to encourage strong business ties and develop the once-stagnant bilateral relations with Burma—after the mandatory formal establishment of diplomatic relations back in 2006.

Given Ramos-Horta's past criticism of Burma's human rights record, many were left to wonder if he was ready to trade his internationally acclaimed activism for a full membership in ASEAN. As the accession process drags on, it will almost certainly be the case that Timor-Leste realizes that in order, finally, to elicit action regarding its aging bid, its leaders will eventually have to tone down their rhetoric and continue to engage Burma on a bilateral basis, before being able to work together in a common multilateral forum.

However, the ultimate regional goal of joining ASEAN was also further advanced when on March 4, 2011, Timorese Foreign Minister Zacarias Albano da Costa delivered his country's formal membership application to his Indonesian counterpart, Marty Natalegawa, thus taking another step along the road to full accession. Still, although 2012 was mooted as the initial target date for final entry, the amount of work required by the Timorese government—in terms of human resources, English-speaking officials, coordination among various ministries, and overcoming the inherent difficulties in adapting and harmonizing the necessary legislation—as well as new doubts about Timor-Leste's application by some members like Singapore, inevitably forced a delay. Therefore, 2015 is increasingly being identified as the most probable date for a final resolution on Timor-Leste's entry.

But a different consideration can be deduced from these latest developments. Indeed, although Timor-Leste's campaign to join ASEAN unequivocally substantiates its decision to adhere to the Southeast Asian preferential framework, these efforts also come at a time in which the country is not too coy in reaching out to other regional institutions. The Melanesian Spearhead Group (MSG), for example, received ample attention from Timorese authorities throughout 2011 in exchange for group's agreement to grant Timor-Leste the status of observer.[30] Likewise, Timor-Leste continues to work steadily with the Pacific Island Forum in a similar fashion; Prime Minister Xanana Gusmão even attended the group's summit in Auckland on September 2011 with promises to "step up the engagement."[31] In other words,

---

[29] Kavi Chongkittavorn, "Is an ASEAN 12 Possible—with Timor-Leste?" *Nation*, September 20, 2010, available at www.nationmultimedia.com/home/2010/09/20/opinion/Is-an-Asean-12-possible--with-Timor-Leste-30138306.html, accessed September 20, 2010.

[30] The MSG currently comprises Fiji, Papua New Guinea, Solomon Islands, and Vanuatu. During Xanana Gusmão's last visit to Vanuatu, in September 2011, he pledged US$500 for the group's permanent secretariat, established in that country's capital, Port Vila.

[31] Xanana Gusmão, "Address by His Excellency the Prime Minister Kay Rala Xanana Gusmão to the Pacific Islands Forum 2011," September 7, 2011, available at http://timor-

despite the manifested will to adhere to ASEAN, Timor-Leste has undoubtedly assumed the "inescapable impact of geography"[32] in its foreign designs and is now trying to diversify its neighborly reach while awaiting the consecration of its primary regional objective.

On the other hand, regarding Indonesia, the fact that such a country held ASEAN's rotating chairmanship during 2011 also helped to underscore the level of the current state of relations with its former twenty-seventh province. The timing of the presentation of Timor-Leste's membership application was not randomly chosen, as both parties sought to present an image of full reconciliation and affinity in common regional matters, while highlighting Indonesian support for the Timorese candidacy. Furthermore, the necessary cohabitation in the island of Timor has never looked more feasible, even with pending issues still looming in the rear view. Indeed, though worrisome, with regard to the aforementioned obstacles, the way may soon be cleared through political compromise. As the need for a stabilized and permanently defined border grows, so will national public pressure after more than ten years of indecision that has curbed the development and growth of the corresponding regions. Ultimately, it is a matter of common interest to resolve quickly the bilateral imbroglio, which stands in the way of full amicable relations. However, the possibility of further "incidents" cannot be simply cast aside, since local animosities and tensions hardly ever follow political dictates from the respective leaderships and are more susceptible to any triggering situations. The continuing unlawful construction just over the border and uncontrolled transit of people could very well serve as motives for local reaction and will, therefore, require greater attention to keep tension levels at bay. But even if the border issue is eventually met with a swift resolution, the matter of undefined maritime borders— probably even more intricate and complex than the territorial boundaries themselves—will surely provide enough reason for more prolonged talks between both countries' authorities in years to come.

As for the matter of human rights violations and the persistent calls for justice, these issues will require an even more sensitive approach. It is clear by now that most of the Timorese leadership favors a controversial amnesty as an immediate "fix," in order to turn over a new leaf—for example, President Ramos-Horta went as far as to pardon the people responsible for the assassination attempt in 2008 on his own life. Nonetheless, the political and public costs of taking and standing by that kind of far-reaching pardon are not easily dismissed. One can try to explain the benefits of focusing the country's energies on the future, and on a healthy relationship with Indonesia—with no "historic baggage" attached—but inevitably, the local population will always be left with a sense of disappointment if the perpetrators elude punishment, as well as with a growing feeling of dissatisfaction toward its government and state structures, with unpredictable social consequences. Likewise, international public opinion that supported and eventually assisted Timor-Leste's rise as an independent nation will also surely question the merits of any political decision to grant a generalized amnesty, as it involves overlooking atrocities that, in similar cases, would usually constitute grounds for the application of

---

leste.gov.tl/wp-content/uploads/2011/09/Pacific_Islands_Forum_Speech-7.91.pdf, accessed October 5, 2011.

[32] Pedro Seabra, "A Road Far from Finished: Timor-Leste and ASEAN," *IPRIS Lusophone Countries Bulletin* 17 (2011): 4.

international justice. Either way, it is an issue that will surely continue to divide civil society and the international community. Given that a national reparations program or an "Institute for Memory"—two projects proposed both by the CAVR and the CVA reports—have been put on hold due to bureaucratic obstacles, calls for either a general amnesty,[33] or an international tribunal,[34] are thus likely to continue as the only proposals on the table that could finally put the past to rest.

Regarding China, the Asian juggernaut is set to play a major role in any future Timor-Leste foreign policy scenario. Initially, China's approach to the country was mainly understood as a preemptive measure, intended to block any possible Taiwanese influence, but China's response is increasingly viewed as part of a larger strategy that aims to insert Chinese influence in the remaining Portuguese-speaking countries and consolidate its influence in Southeast Asia. Indeed, the news disclosed on August 2010 that the Chinese government was preparing to give complete customs tax exemption to products from companies based in Timor-Leste only reinforced this view of a partnership that has grown closer, with China seeking a prominent role in the young nation's development. Likewise, a special interest in Timor-Leste's vast natural wealth is not to be completely ruled out, as China's energy needs appear unquenchable. One expects that China will, however, fall short of actually declaring an express wish to participate in the exploration of the untapped resources and instead opt for a low-profile posture, since it has no interest in directly confronting Australia in this matter—at least while the issues with Woodside are unresolved.

Preferable economic relations, increasingly aid flows, and, of course, military/security assistance are therefore likely to comprise the various components of the strategy the world's second largest economic power will undertake to formalize and consolidate its relation with Timor-Leste. This strategy is by no means novel if we consider the larger picture: Aware that its influence in Southeast Asia has to remain unchallenged in a fast-growing region, China will undoubtedly resort to a soft-power approach, courting several small and underdeveloped states—where it can easily establish a significant economic foothold—as a way to counter possible opposing or discordant influences. China's culture, diplomacy, businesses, and arts, rather than its rising military strength, increasingly figure as key features in its grand designs regarding Southeast Asia, and have proven irresistible for many countries.[35]

For its part, Timor-Leste will welcome such interest, probably convinced that it can maintain an ambiguous foreign positioning, without any kind of political or economic fallout, especially from within its own region. In the name of its future growth and sustainable development, Timor-Leste will be more than willing to continue down such a road. Moreover, these growing ties and the public perception they imply will also be increasingly and skillfully brought into focus by the Timorese authorities whenever a regional dispute arises, especially with Australia, where officials are particularly sensitive to any semblance of Chinese presence in this area. The impact that such relationships can have in any regional diplomatic quarrel is

---

[33] Paulo Gorjão, "Timor-Leste: An Amnesty Is Needed Once and for All," *IPRIS Lusophone Countries Bulletin* 1 (2009): 5.

[34] Amnesty International report, "Timor-Leste: International Criminal Court: Justice in the Shadow," Amnesty International Publications, 2010.

[35] Josh Kurlantzick, "Chinese Soft Power in Southeast Asia (Part I)," *Global List*, April 2, 2007, available at www.theglobalist.com/StoryId.aspx?StoryId=6240, accessed September 25, 2010.

undeniable, and although Timor-Leste will definitely refrain from explicitly using the influence that comes from its growing ties with China—as doing so would signal the final passing to the other side of the diplomatic barricade—it is unlikely to refrain from indirectly employing the inherent advantages of such positioning as leverage with nearby regional powers.

CONCLUSION

Ultimately, the relatively complicated relationships between Timor-Leste and some of its major foreign partners are emblematic of underlying problems for every small state. Indeed, it is not uncommon that, instead of forging a long-term–foreign policy strategy, such states—frequently "new," "weak," or "fragile"—focus on "intensive bursts of crisis management."[36] Their goals shrink and ultimately focus on the search for a neutral status, for an alliance with a greater power, or an emphasis on collective security. In Timor-Leste's case, none of these options has been that clear cut since its apparent diversification strategy does not currently enable analysts to discern—or Timorese leaders to follow—a clear and precise framework through which Timorese foreign policy could be easily categorized or evaluated. But by combining good neighborliness, engagement within regional frameworks, and the courting of international donors and traditional partners, the Southeast Asian nation has managed to maintain a considerable level of consistency in its foreign approach.

However, in this context, a range of voices have begun pointing to a growing detachment from previous policy positions, with Timor-Leste apparently seeking to exhibit a degree of autonomy that the predominant players in the region are simply not used to. Indeed, the willingness to demonstrate foreign policy maturity also carries the inherent risk of damaging Timor-Leste's own external goals in the long run, many of which were designed and decided in the post-referendum euphoria. Certain political choices taken since independence have only helped to reinforce perceptions of disarray within the East Timorese leadership with regard to its foreign positioning, and to its relationship with crucial actors that remain instrumental in its independence and future.

The need for greater freedom to establish independent policy is inherent in any state's growth, and, since Timor-Leste is a young nation, it is only natural that some hard choices and decisions have to be taken in the name of state survival and development. Nonetheless, it is a fact that the country not only remains considerably dependent on foreign assistance and goodwill from the international community, but also deeply intertwined with the fate of a necessary cohabitation with Indonesia and Australia.

It is therefore difficult to understand why long-running territorial disputes are allowed to be drag on; why the choice for a full-blown amnesty for past crimes—if indeed, it is the choice to be taken—is not finally assumed by Timorese officials; why a country so in need of further international investments presents itself as an often inflexible negotiating party with little attention to the consequent fallout in terms of the business environment; and why the country appears keen on wooing political and economic giants when it most certainly knows it will risk damaging in return the delicate regional balance of stability upon which it unavoidably depends.

---

[36] Anthony Smith, "Constraints and Choices: East Timor as Foreign Policy Actor," *New Zealand Journal of Asian Studies* 7,1 (2005): 16.

Ultimately, it is expected that Timor-Leste will take these important variables into account when setting the course of its own future foreign policy. The impulse to address these challenges will only intensify as the end of the United Nation's mission draws near and as the country absorbs the impact of a new electoral cycle. Above all, despite an admirable and growing confidence in its future, Timor-Leste's leadership cannot ignore the fact that, in order to assume its rightful place as a credible and reliable suitor in the international and regional arena, the country has to adopt a stable foreign policy course that can simultaneously conciliate the nurturing of confidence ties with its international partners and the protection of its foreign interests. Accordingly, a careful evaluation of the country's agenda appears to be inevitable, so that the image and credibility of Timor-Leste abroad is not dealt any permanent damage in Timor-Leste's quest to assert itself as a nation in the making.

DEMOCRACY OLD AND NEW: THE INTERACTION OF MODERN AND TRADITIONAL AUTHORITY IN LOCAL GOVERNMENT

Deborah Cummins and Michael Leach

INTRODUCTION

This chapter examines the evolving relationship between traditional and modern forms of political authority in local government in Timor-Leste.[1] The "clash of paradigms" between traditional and liberal democratic ideas of legitimacy in Timor-Leste is widely considered to be an important issue for the stability of the nation-state as a whole.[2] Creating a durable balance for this relationship is also considered integral to engaging local communities in nation-building, peace-building, and democratization.[3] Negotiating the interactions between local council administration and traditional authority has been a fraught task since 2002, particularly given the administration system inherited from the United Nations Transitional Administration for East Timor (UNTAET), which continued the same highly centralist approach as the former Indonesian and Portuguese authorities. There are also critical and ongoing issues for government authorities to consider in the continuing decentralization process, and in regulating aspects of customary law.

---

[1] An earlier version of this chapter was published as Deborah Cummins and Michael Leach, "Democracy Old and New: The Interaction of Modern and Traditional Authority in East Timorese Local Government," *Asian Politics and Policy* 4,1 (2012): 89–104.

[2] Tania Hohe, "The Clash of Paradigms: International Administration and Local Political Legitimacy in East Timor." *Contemporary Southeast Asia* 24,3 (2002): 569–90; Josh Trindade and Bryant Castro, "Rethinking Timorese Identity as a Peacebuilding Strategy: The Lorosa'e-Loromonu Conflict from a Traditional Perspective," in Final Report for GTZ/IS (Dili: GTZ, European Union's Rapid Reaction Mechanism Programme, 2007), www.indopubs.com/Trindade_Castro_Rethinking_Timorese_Identity.pdf, accessed June 18, 2012.

[3] Alexandre Gusmao and Anne Brown, "Polítika Komunidade no Harii-Dame iha Timor Leste," in *Understanding Timor-Leste*: *Proceedings of the Timor-Leste Studies Association Conference*, ed. Michael Leach, Nuno Canas Mendes, Antero da Silva, Alarico Ximenes, and Bob Boughton (Hawthorn: Swinburne Press, 2010), pp. 21–25.

Here we focus on the relationship between modern and traditional authority in local government,[4] examining the ways elected *chefes de suku* (village chief) and *chefes de aldeia* (hamlet chief) interact with traditional authorities and communities at the local level. Fieldwork was conducted by the authors in various areas of Baucau, Los Palos, Viqueque, Venilale, and Ainaro in 2008–09.[5] In general, our findings suggest that the interaction of modern and traditional systems at the local level has produced several hybrid models of local political authority and legitimacy. Specifically, we identify three hybrid modes of authority: two "co-incumbency" models and an "authorization" model, emphasizing a separation of power between traditional and modern authorities.

BACKGROUND

In the 1960s and 1970s, the concept of nation-building in post-colonial states was commonly premised on the notion of a transition from "pre-modern" local and traditional identities to a modern, unified national identity. In Timor-Leste in the 1970s, for example, the architects of modern nationalism, while drawing on unifying traditional identities of *"maubere,"* or common people, essentially saw traditional political systems and legitimacy as feudal and backward.[6] More recently, the existence—and potential—of hybrid models of liberal and customary government have become the subject both of empirical attention and theoretical inquiry.[7] In Timor-Leste, the tensions between modern and traditional administration and notions of political authority remain a key challenge for nation builders. As Josh Trindade and Bryant Castro argue, one broad background factor of the 2006 crisis lay in the imposition of a modern state, from Dili, without a supporting concept of the "nation" capable of resonating with collective visions of community and identity in the regions. For these commentators, many East Timorese "[felt] that they [were] lacking a sense of ownership of current governance processes. They mistrust[ed] the current government and [perceived] that the idea of the nation-state ... [was] imposed on them just as the colonial system [had been]."[8] Ten years on from the first elections, this disconnection continues to be felt. For example one, elder stated:

---

[4] *Konsellu de suku,* or *suku* councils, are not officially regarded as part of the East Timorese governmental structure, but, rather, are legally defined "community authorities." Nonetheless, we refer to them here as part of the "government" in recognition of their key role in local administration.

[5] Fieldwork interviews in Venilale and Ainaro were conducted by Cummins from August 2008 to February 2009. Interviews in Baucau, Los Palos, and Viqueque were conducted by Leach between January and March 2008.

[6] Jill Joliffe, *East Timor: Nationalism and Colonialism* (St Lucia: University of Queensland Press, 1978).

[7] Deborah Cummins, "Democracy or Democrazy? Local Experiences of Democratisation in Timor-Leste," *Democratization* 17,5 (2010): 899–919; David Butterworth and Pamela Dale, "Articulations of Local Governance in Timor-Leste: Lessons for Local Government Under Decentralization," Justice for the Poor, World Bank, Washington, DC (2010), http://documents.worldbank.org/curated/en/2010/10/12836440/articulations-local-governance-timor-leste-lessons-local-development-under-decentralization, accessed June 18, 2012.

[8] Trindade and Castro, "Rethinking Timorese Identity," p. 14.

The democracy that we did in 2001, we chose the members of the parliament for the Constitution. Everyone raised their hands ... we closed our eyes and we supported [the Constituent Assembly] but we knew that this was wrong for our country ... why don't we use the [traditional] system from before?[9]

Sentiments such as these were often repeated during the authors' fieldwork.[10]

In the wake of the 2006 political-military crisis, then Prime Minister Ramos-Horta's government promised to review local administration, to allow traditional political authority mechanisms to be accorded greater status in local and regional administration, and to review the processes of district elections. This commitment did not, however, make it into the 2009 *konsellu de suku* (Suco Council) legislation introduced by the AMP (Aliança Maioria Parlamentar, Parliamentary Majority Alliance) government to replace the previous 2004 legislation (Decree Law 3/2009). Despite this lack of formal recognition, an informal integration of traditional and modern spheres of administration continues to occur in *suku* level politics, evident in the migration of notions of legitimacy from the spiritual and traditional realms to the temporal and modern. Specifically, the findings suggest that those with *liurai* (political authority) or *lia-na'in* (ritual authority) heritage have proven more effective in modern local-government roles and have greater "speaking power" than those candidates from modern political parties without local traditional legitimacy. The challenges for those without customary "speaking power" are considerable, and both the appointed (district and subdistrict administrators) and elected officials (members of *konsellu de suku*, including *chefe de suku* and *chefes de aldeia*) from these backgrounds have commonly failed in their roles.

The critical issues of decentralization and the reformulation of local and municipal administration are clear sites in which to examine the tensions and negotiations between modern and traditional authority in Timor-Leste.[11] As the program of the Fourth Constitutional Government noted, these issues were to have priority over the 2007–12 term of the government:

> Decentralized participation is accepted as an essential condition for the exercise of citizenship, and, therefore, with the national limitations, local administrations will be ensured, *in strict partnership with traditional administration*, the means and resources needed for it to perform its attributions and competences.[12]

While modified *konsellu de suku* election legislation was passed in 2009, the process of creating municipalities and reformulating district government—including district assembly elections—has been delayed until at least 2014.

---

[9] Interview with Venilale *katuas*, Venilale, Baucau district, November 21, 2008.

[10] Tensions between modern and traditional authority at the local government level are by no means an exclusively rural phenomenon. Nonetheless, the relative "distance" that citizens feel from the state in rural areas make these complex relationships especially salient in decision-making processes.

[11] Butterworth and Dale, "Articulations of Local Governance"; Hohe, "Clash of Paradigms."

[12] Democratic Republic of Timor-Leste RDTL, *Program of the Fourth Constitutional Government Program, 2007–2012*, p. 5, www.laohamutuk.org/misc/AMPGovt/GovtProgramEng.pdf, accessed June 18, 2012.

HISTORICAL DIMENSIONS

Contemporary local administration in Timor-Leste needs to be understood in context of the longer history of interactions between external power and traditional authorities. While some traditional Timorese kingdoms had suzerainty over extensive territories,[13] others were much smaller—often the size of a single *suku*. When the Portuguese consolidated their rule in the late nineteenth century, the larger kingdoms were broken up to better facilitate colonial rule, leaving many smaller, less powerful kingdoms intact (though sometimes with lesser nobles installed as *liurai* by the Portuguese in exchange for loyalty). The core locus of traditional power in Timor-Leste lies at the level of the *suku*, where the traditional house of the *liurai* continues to command authority and allegiance in most communities. In this context, traditional authority tends to be localized authority extending over recognized domains of the traditional house.

Until the late colonial era (1910s), the colonial touch was relatively light, especially in the interior, leaving aside the military enforcement of loyalties against hostile *liurai* and the payment of *fintas* (tributes) to the Portuguese. *Fintas* were typically raised by the *liurai* themselves, leaving their internal authority largely intact. As Geoffrey Gunn notes,[14] the shift in the early twentieth century to a head-tax regime, collected directly by the Portuguese colonial authorities themselves, represented a fundamental intervention in traditional authority and lay behind the various uprisings of that era, most notably, the Dom Boaventura rebellion of 1911–12.[15]

During the Indonesian interregnum, local Timorese structures were brought into line with those of other parts of Indonesia.[16] The Indonesians largely adopted pre-existing district, subdistrict, and *suku* boundaries, integrating them into Indonesian local government structures. In addition to this, the Indonesians formally incorporated the previously unrecognized governing unit at the level of *aldeia*.[17] On the other hand, the creation of security hamlets resulted in the wholesale relocation of numerous villages. Nominally democratic elections were introduced for *suku* chiefs in 1982. However, in line with the militarized administration of the territory throughout this period, the most powerful people at every level of administration continued to be the military commanders.

Running parallel to the Indonesian local government were the clandestine structures introduced by the Timorese resistance, present in every *suku* across Timor-Leste. As Andrew McWilliam relates,[18] key to the clandestine movement were the *suku*-based networks known as the *nucleos de resistencia popular* (*nurep*). *Nurep* were popularly elected by *aldeia* representatives, with the election conducted by a Falintil (Forças Armadas de Libertação Nacional de Timor-Leste, Armed Forces for the National Liberation of East Timor) commander. The clandestine subdistrict chief,

---

[13] Geoffrey C. Gunn, *Timor Loro Sae: 500 Years* (Macau: Livros do Oriente, 1999), pp. 17–28.

[14] Ibid., pp. 96, 124.

[15] See also Katharine Davidson, "The Portuguese Consolidation of Timor: The Final Stage, 1850–1912" (doctoral dissertation, University of New South Wales, 1994), p. 19.

[16] James Dunn, *Timor: A People Betrayed* (Milton: Jacaranda Press, 1983), p. 301.

[17] João Saldanha, *The Political Economy of East Timor Development* (Jakarta: Pustaka Sinar Harapan, 1994), pp. 102–3.

[18] Andrew McWilliam, "Houses of Resistance in East Timor: Structuring Sociality in the New Nation," *Anthropological Forum* 15,1, (2005): 27–44, 35.

secretario do zona, was chosen by Falintil commanders. These figures were often considered to have more legitimacy than those recognized by the Indonesians, and in many *sukus* the *nurep* went on to become the *chefe de suku* when Timor-Leste became independent.

Throughout both Portuguese and Indonesian rule, traditional authorities and law continued to operate and guide the daily lives of most rural East Timorese. These administrative structures ran parallel with those of the external rulers, at various times being reinforced or undermined by the overarching structure of the state, which impacted upon local communities and their self-regulating practices (for example, when the Portuguese changed traditional *suku* boundaries for the sake of administrative convenience, or their insistence on dealing with "blood crimes"). These enduring structures received little recognition in the UNTAET period, and did not figure in their state-building agenda.[19] This left the complex questions of local administration to the newly independent government of Timor-Leste in 2002.

The coexistence of modern and traditional administration has a long history, and the set of political hybrids that have resulted remain an important context for understanding contemporary local governance in Timor-Leste. While "traditional" administration cannot be regarded as fixed or unchanging, it has never been subsumed or displaced by the various incarnations of the external state. The interpenetration of state-based and traditional modes of decision making and dispute resolution continue to generate hybrid models that impact upon the daily lives of people in the rural areas and hold important implications for the legitimacy of elected local leaders.

THE CENTRALITY OF *LISAN*

The place of traditional authority figures is defined in terms of their connection with *lisan*,[20] or customary law. The ongoing importance of *lisan*, particularly in the rural areas, is well-recognized as an important facet of contemporary Timorese political, social, ecological, and spiritual life. From the perspective of most Timorese, traditional institutions, while unwritten, are highly formalized. *Lisan* is for many community members the central body of law through which their lives are guided and social structures understood.[21] Traditional leaders are intimately connected to *lisan*, and hold spiritual and ritual responsibilities alongside temporal responsibilities to lead the community and resolve disputes. *Lisan* is implemented through complex hierarchical relationships that guide local dispute resolution, and also provide for other needs within and between family groups.

The principle of maintaining communal balance through exchange is fundamental to *lisan*. The material world inhabited by living things, and the cosmos inhabited by the spirit and ancestors must be kept in balance through rituals of exchange. Failure to observe these rituals leads to imbalance, which can have serious consequences, such as the spread of disease, harvest failure, or natural disasters (e.g., earthquakes). Because of its importance, the principle of exchange for the Timorese

---

[19] Hohe, "Clash of Paradigms."

[20] *Lisan* is also commonly referred to by the Malay term *adat*.

[21] Tanja Hohe and Rod Nixon, *Reconciling Justice: 'Traditional' Law and State Judiciary in East Timor* (Washington, DC: United States Institute of Peace, 2003), www.gsdrc.org/go/display &type=Document&id=813, accessed June 18, 2012.

people is described by Forman as "the idiom of life, symbolically, ideologically, and pragmatically."[22] Disruption or imbalance can also be seen as a background factor to social conflict.

It is in this local political environment that the actors and institutions of modern local government are interpreted and incorporated. This generates significant interaction and overlap between modern and traditional spheres of administration at the local level. Key examples include hybrid conceptions of legitimacy and practices of local political leadership in local settings. Political hybridity is also evident in the way state-based and customary institutional structures are used alternately to resolve different types of intracommunity disputes and in the way projects are coordinated within a *suku*. The composition and structure of local communities along family lines can also have important implications for how external resources are distributed.

The significance of *lisan* lies, not only in the spiritual realm, but also in the temporal and practical ordering of intragroup relations. As has been noted in previous studies,[23] while different in form from liberal democracy, *lisan* continues to enjoy legitimacy within the community because it displays many characteristics that people describe as "democratic." With its emphasis on maintaining balance in the community, *lisan* has helped maintain community cohesion in the face of massive social upheavals. With the lack of state penetration in rural areas as a perennial backdrop, customary institutions continue to provide opportunities for community participation in decision making over the issues that affect community members between elections, something liberal democratic institutions have been unable to provide. One elder in Venilale described the institution of *nahe biti boot*[24] as the "old democracy" of Timor, designed to involve everyone affected in resolving an issue through reaching consensus. This, he argued, was preferable to the "new democracy," which he saw as disconnected from the Timorese who live in the rural areas and, the preserve of Dili-based elites. While there are distinct conceptions of democracy at play here, the ongoing popular legitimacy of customary institutions such as *nahe biti boot* underscores the need to take customary practices of dispute resolution seriously. Where the "new democracy" has often been equated with divisive conflict between different political parties, the "old democracy," embodied in rituals such as *nahe biti boot*, is seen to encourage consensus and communal cohesion.

LOCAL ADMINISTRATION IN DEMOCRATIC TIMOR-LESTE

Conversely, of course, there are clear limits to the extent that customary institutions can satisfy the requirements of a liberal, citizenship-based democracy. While *lisan* is central to a traditional understanding of political community, customary law must inevitably accommodate liberal democratic conceptions of

---

[22] Shepard Forman, "Descent, Alliance and Exchange Ideology Among the Makassae of East Timor," in *The Flow of Life: Essays on Eastern Indonesia*, ed. James Fox (Cambridge, MA: Harvard University Press, 1980), p. 153.

[23] For example, see Cummins, "Democracy or Democrazy?"

[24] Interview with Venilale *katuas*, November 21, 2008. "*Nahe biti-boot*," or "spreading out the mat," is a customary method of resolving issues or disputes by consensus, presided over by a *lia-na'in* (traditional dispute resolution authority).

citizen equality. Notions of class, masculine authority, and hierarchical leadership are deeply embedded in *lisan*, privileging certain family lines that have access to the "ritual words" that are essential to holding traditional leadership. Equally, in patrilineal areas (the majority of Timor), women are normally not permitted to speak in a traditional ceremony. Certain aspects of the legislation that shapes modern *suku* administration are clearly designed to address these issues, including the requirement for women and youth representatives on *konsellu de suku*. However, a combination of factors, including the underresourcing of *konsellu de suku* and the norms of *lisan*, have meant that women and youth representatives are rarely empowered by the other members of *konsellu de suku* to take active roles in local community decision making.[25] The challenge of transforming gender and youth quotas into more than a political "numbers game" is clearly an important area of focus for the East Timorese government. Such a task will require particular focus on the distinct challenges that women face when exercising local leadership.

For FRETILIN particularly—though by no means exclusively—modern citizenship rights were understood from the 1970s onward as the remedy, not only to colonial domination, but also to "feudal" forms of traditional authority. Of course, in the twenty-first century, few political parties can countenance the idea of gender and age inequality common to traditional institutions. But in rural communities, both *lisan* and "modern" democracy are often proudly proclaimed as the joint inheritances of the independence struggle. A common phrase, repeated to the authors throughout their fieldwork, was that *lisan* and democracy must "walk together."

These engagements between traditionally legitimated and democratically elected leaders take place in the context of geographical local administration units that have changed very little since the Portuguese colonial era. The smallest geographical unit is the *aldeia*, led by the *chefe de aldeia*. A *suku* area comprises several *aldeia* and is headed by the *chefe de suku*. The *chefes de aldeia* and *chefe de suku* are directly elected positions. Moving geographically outward from the *suku*, the subdistrict comprises a number of *suku*, administered by an appointed subdistrict administrator, who is in turn accountable to Dili via the government-appointed district administrator.

The principal institutions of local democracy are the *konsellu de suku*, established under Decree Law 5/2004. Since replaced by Decree Law 3/2009 (promulgated following consultations conducted around the country in late 2008), the legislation provides the legal basis for *konsellu de suku* in each of the 442 *sukus* across Timor-Leste. Each *konsellu* is directly elected by eligible voting members of the *suku* using the *pakote* (package) system,[26] and is headed by the popularly elected *chefe de suku*. Other *konsellu* members include each of the elected *chefes de aldeia* in the *suku* area, one elder (*ferik* or *katuas*), two women's representatives, and two youth representatives, one man and one woman (Decree Law 3/2009). In addition to the elected *suku* elder, there is, since the 2009 law, a provision for one *lia-na'in* to be appointed by the *konsellu de suku* members at their first meeting following an election. This more recent development makes explicit the hybrid constitution of the *konsellu de suku*, discussed further below, as the *lia-na'in* sits by appointment rather than election, and in addition to the elected *ferik* or *katuas* (elder).

---

[25] Deborah Cummins, "The Problem of Gender Quotas: Women's Representatives on Timor-Leste's *Suku* Councils," *Development in Practice* 21,1 (2011), pp. 85–95.

[26] This refers to the system in which an entire council of candidates seeks to be voted in as a single block.

Notably, the 2009 law proscribed political parties formally running candidates at *suku* elections. This appears to be a response to concerns—well founded in many cases—over the divisive effect of political party campaigning in some local communities in the 2004–05 round of *suku* elections. The relationship between *konsellu de suku* and a proposed new level of municipal administration remains under review.

HYBRID AUTHORITY IN LOCAL ADMINISTRATION

While the democratically elected *konsellu de suku* is the principal local governing body recognized by the state, the reality of power relations within the *suku* is somewhat different. Fieldwork findings suggest that the establishment of democratically elected *konsellu de suku* has resulted in hybridized forms of local administration, with a strong traditional-authority presence on the councils, as communities endeavor to reconcile traditional notions of political legitimacy with modern institutions. Primarily, this takes the form of electing candidates who are either traditionally legitimated to rule, or who have the explicit support of traditional authorities. In addition, elected *chefes de suku* tend to share authority and work closely with non-elected traditional figures in the *suku*. These processes may be seen as a form of "re-traditionalization" of local government. Yet, while these new hybrid forms draw strongly on traditional sources of legitimacy, the interaction with state-based institutions and central authorities is also potentially transformative, casting into doubt, for example, customary inequalities of gender and class, or, in the alternative tension, undermining formal notions of citizenship equality through the reproduction of customary power relations.

Elected local leaders on the *konsellu de suku* are expected to fulfill many local government functions. Strictly speaking, these positions are defined under Decree Law 3/2009 as "Community Authorities," and council members essentially work as volunteers, being paid a small amount per month to offset expenses. Resources are scarce and it is a common complaint that project proposals rarely receive a positive response—an unsurprising outcome in a small developing nation with 442 *sukus*. State reach in rural areas is extremely limited and *chefes de suku* tend to act as a political "contact point" for the state, providing necessary statistics and information to the East Timorese government, subdistrict administrators, and other service providers. To fulfill these tasks, and the broader roles of resolving disputes and "administering" their populations, *chefes* commonly work in tight, networked arrangements with the non-elected traditional leaders of the community. Local authority and power is generally shared among elected *chefes de suku* and non-elected traditional authorities, and there are many instances where *chefes de suku* engage more closely with the traditional leadership than with other members of *konsellu de suku*, who are regarded locally as possessing less authority. These governing dynamics were common across all *sukus* in which fieldwork was conducted.

For *chefes de suku*, a key relationship is with the subdistrict administrator—an appointee of the Dili-based government who coordinates activities and works closely with all the *chefes de suku* in the subdistrict.[27] Alongside their other duties, the

---

[27] Also commonly referred to by the Portuguese term *"posto"*—the subdistrict administrator is often referred to as *Chefe de Posto*, and in some places referred to by the Indonesian term *"camat."*

subdistrict administrator ensures that government policy agendas are carried out smoothly within the *suku*, which may involve "reminding" *chefes* of their responsibilities as an elected official. In most cases, the subdistrict administrator does not have direct contact with the Dili-based government—these communications occur via the district administrator, who is also a government appointee.

MAPPING THE LOCAL POLITICAL ENVIRONMENT

Unlike *sukus*, *aldeias* are not officially mapped. Accordingly, while they may correspond with particular geographical areas, *aldeias* tend to be defined by traditional understandings of community, which are in turn based on family relations and *uma lulik*.[28] Beneath the *aldeia* level of administration are a number of extended family groups referred to as *uma kain*, related to each other via *uma lulik* in a structured system of Wife Giver and Wife Taker houses. Even in *aldeias* where there are new family groups (often due to resettlement in Indonesian times), respect for the traditional owners and of the local *uma lulik* in guiding social relations continues to be important.[29]

The various *uma kain* are governed by complex social norms that regulate relations within and among them in any single *aldeia*.[30] It is these family networks that form the first layer of communal governance experienced by individuals. The state-recognized layers of local administration (*aldeia, suku*, and subdistrict) thus overlap with those that have significance through *lisan*: the *uma kain, aldeia*, and *suku*. It is rare for an average community member to have direct interaction with the subdistrict administrator in his or her official capacity, with most interaction between *suku* and subdistrict levels occurring via the *chefe de suku*.

These relationships are best illustrated by tracking how local disputes are resolved. In the hierarchy of local authority, conflict is first addressed at the level closest to the disputants. When a person commits an offense, he or she is pushing the community out of balance; the role of *lisan* is to restore balance to the community.[31] As such, it is important that the offense is dealt with quickly. Depending on the issue and the community, there are accepted hierarchies to follow in resolving disputes, involving three levels: the traditionally legitimated *chefe de uma kain* and *lia-na'in* at the *uma kain* level; the elected *chefe de aldeia* and traditionally legitimated *lia-na'in* at the *aldeia* level; and the elected *chefe de suku* and appointed *lia-na'in* at the *suku* level.[32]

The exact mode of dispute resolution varies. Some *aldeias* follow a strict hierarchy, described as "climbing a ladder" from one level to the next if the resolution process proves difficult. Other *aldeias* may approach disputes with a variant but accepted hierarchy. For example, in village Telega in *suku* Ainaro, the

---

[28] "*Uma lulik*," or sacred house, is both a physical construct and a spiritual focal point through which people relate to each other and to the ancestors.

[29] For example, *lia-na'in* from the Wailacama aldeia of Vemasse are still invited to speak at the *chefe de aldeia* inauguration ceremonies in Ostico, despite having no formally shared territory since Portuguese times, following a relocation of the population in 1979.

[30] McWilliam, "Houses of Resistance in East Timor."

[31] Dionisio Babo-Soares, "Nahe biti: The Philosophy and Process of Grassroots Reconciliation (and Justice) in East Timor," *Asia Pacific Journal of Anthropology* 5,1 (2004): 15–33. See also Hohe and Nixon, "Reconciling Justice"; Trindade and Castro, "Rethinking Timorese Identity."

[32] Since 2009, a *lia-na'in* from each *suku* may be specially appointed to the *konsellu de suku*. It is worth noting that some *suku* have more than one *lia-na'in*.

chefe de aldeia and *aldeia lia-na'in* resolve disputes together as a council. If they are unable to resolve the dispute, it is then taken to the *chefe de suku* to resolve in conjunction with the *chefe de aldeia* and the *suku lia-na'in*. If it is a civil matter, and remains unresolved at the *suku* level, it may then go to the subdistrict administrator for mediation. This particular pattern often occurs in complicated land disputes. Similarly, if it is a criminal matter and remains unresolved, the authorities may refer the matter to the police. In this way, the disputants move simultaneously "outward" from the *uma kain* to the *aldeia, suku,* or subdistrict, and ideologically from customary to state law. Elected and non-elected leaders work together in a structured fashion that signals the central role of *lisan* but also recognizes the elected local leadership. Significantly, certain *konsellu de suku* members (for example, women's representatives) are rarely integrated in this local "hybrid" hierarchy.

Communal administration starts with the *uma kain*, where spiritual obligations are maintained, disputes are settled, economic patron-client relations sustained, and family policing is carried out. Relationships among family groups are maintained at the *aldeia* level, involving the resolution of disputes and the collection of information and statistics for the *chefe de suku*. As community needs become more complex at the *suku* level, the extent of external involvement increases, in the form of police, health centers, schools, the church, NGOs, and other actors. New power bases and networks become available to *chefes de suku*, outside their usual remits. Managing these networks requires leadership skills, and the ability to coordinate modern and traditional authorities in developing community responses. For example, it is commonly accepted that police are required to deal with criminal matters where "blood is spilled," and in practice police will often work closely with the local leaders. As effective police authority is somewhat constrained in rural areas, however, police often rely on and sometimes participate in *nahe biti boot* ceremonies rather than formally address disputes under the criminal code. The limited capacity of the police and the courts is therefore an important context for the ongoing importance of customary dispute resolution.

OBTAINING AUTHORITY

While traditional ritual and spiritual authority is conferred via *lisan*, local political authority in post-independence Timor-Leste is conferred through the state-regulated process of *suku* elections. The democratization of local administration requires traditional leaders to engage with the electoral processes of the state if they wish to exercise political power. Interview findings suggest that as a result of this engagement, a hybrid system has formed at local government levels, particularly in relation to patterns of candidature. Those candidates with traditional authority are more effective in local-government roles and have greater "speaking power" than those from political parties who lack traditional legitimacy. The challenges for those without traditional "speaking power" are considerable, and such appointees (district and subdistrict administrators) and elected officials (*konsellu de suku, chefes de suku* and *aldeia*) have commonly failed in their roles.

Though successful candidates for *chefes de suku* are elected because they are considered capable of performing a "modern" governing role, local leadership involves the ability to command, coordinate, and resolve disputes within the community—tasks that are significantly easier if one is a recognized traditional leader. *Chefes de suku* must also work closely with non-elected traditional leaders, which is likewise significantly easier if one is also a recognized traditional authority.

The influence of traditional notions of legitimacy varies significantly from one *suku* to the next, depending on patterns set by the local history of traditional-external relations. Below we identify three models characterizing the relationships between traditional and modern authority at the local level: two "co-incumbency" models, and an "authorization" model emphasizing a "separation of powers."

Two types of "co-incumbency" models can be identified: a strict co-inheritance approach, and a "traditional house candidate" approach. An example of the first approach may be found in *suku* Uai Oli in the subdistrict of Venilale, where the *liurai* is required by his community to stand for election as *chefe de suku*. Many in the community believe that if they are not led by the *liurai* the spiritual balance will be upset and the community will become "sick." When the *liurai*'s father and older brother died in 1999, the new *liurai* was required to leave a lucrative job in Dili to return to the *suku* to take on the role of *chefe*. This community has effectively created a hereditary *chefe de suku* system that is legitimated through elections and parallels the traditional inheritance of authority in the *liurai* family line. However, this mode of "co-inherited" traditional and modern authority appears to be fairly rare. Indeed, in this *suku* community expectations appear to be shifting. In the 2009 elections, the *liurai* was reelected with just 49 percent of the vote, narrowly beating another candidate from the same *liurai* house, but not immediately in the line of succession, who received 43 percent. For the role of *chefe de aldeia*, however, the "co-inherited" traditional and modern authority model was far more common. For example, all *chefes de aldeia* within *suku* Ainaro openly described their position as one that is inherited, but legitimated through popular election.

For the role of *chefe de suku*, the more common "co-incumbency" model is the "traditional house candidate" practice of selecting "modern" local leaders from the *liurai* house. Relative to the co-incumbency model, this approach opens the field to a wider range of candidates with traditional legitimacy and allows scope for the position to change hands frequently. A common way communities seek to secure legitimacy within both spheres is by electing the most capable and "savvy" candidates from the *liurai* house, thus incorporating an element of meritocratic competition within the traditional leadership pool. There are interesting variations on these hybrid arrangements, with sometimes surprising outcomes. For example, in the *suku* of Soro in the subdistrict of Ainaro, the *chefe de suku* was one of the few women in this position in Timor-Leste.[33] As she explained, traditionally she would have been required to "stay in the kitchen" and considered an unsuitable candidate for the role of *suku* leader. However, the political party she belonged to viewed her as a good candidate, in part because she came from the *liurai* house. This highlights the importance of traditional considerations in the candidate-selection processes of political parties themselves—and, equally, the potential (though rarely realized) influence of modern institutions on traditional notions of political leadership. As she explained, beyond her perceived ability to perform the requirements of the role, it was important that she came from the right family and enjoyed the necessary support and connections:

---

[33] She has since (in the 2009 elections) been voted out of office.

> From our ancestors they say that the biggest *uma lulik* in this *suku* is this one [so] I became *chefe de suku* partially because of my *uma lulik*. As I said before, my family, in terms of the traditional, is the most important in this *suku*. But it was not only because of the culture that I could be *chefe de suku*. It is based on my behavior and the behavior before, the connection with the community, who the people trust to be *chefe de suku*.[34]

There are variations throughout local communities in Timor-Leste, often unique to the history of each *suku*. The nature of the allegiance to *liurais* has also turned on the expectation that they deal fairly with the people. Through the early twentieth century, and particularly in the late colonial era, there were *suku* in which the *liurai* had "lost" his authority, and the subject population had transferred their allegiance to another *liurai* or become independent.[35] With the new pressures and opportunities that arose as the Portuguese prepared to decolonize, and an emerging Timorese political elite prepared for independent rule, the authority of the *liurais* was further undermined, particularly in *sukus* where the *liurai* had been more brutal in the enforcement of labor provisions.[36] Later, under Indonesian occupation, many children of the *liurai* became active in the Timorese resistance, and the leadership of many *liurai* was critically important in maintaining community cohesion and resilience. As one *lia-na'in* from the village of Teliga in *suku* Ainaro put it, "self-determination and democracy was why we fought ... [but] we only came out on top because of *lisan* and the ancestors, and the spiritual guidance of the *liurai*."[37] In other cases, *liurai* authority was challenged by the mass mobilization and literacy campaigns of the early FRETILIN era. This complicated relationship with the authority of the *liurai* continues in post-independence Timor-Leste and varies significantly from one *suku* to the next.

While membership of the *liurai* house remains a highly influential factor in determining legitimate candidature, communities across Timor-Leste are also creatively interpreting traditional requirements in order to confer legitimacy upon local leaders who do not emerge from the "right" house. In some *sukus*, elected *chefes* without traditional authority have nonetheless satisfied traditional requirements by obtaining the symbolic support of the old *liurai*. This may be termed an "authorization" model of hybrid local administration. As the subdistrict administrator of Los Palos explained:

> Culturally they believe that to be a *liurai* you rule people and have a *rota*.[38] And they say the *rota* is heavy. Someone holding the *rota* must be a *liurai*, because it's too heavy otherwise. It will cause lot of problems if a leader

---

[34] Interview with *chefe de suku* Soro, subdistrict Ainaro, December 19, 2008.

[35] Kevin Sherlock, "East Timor: *Liurais* and *Chefes de Suco*: Indigenous Authorities in 1952" (an unpublished study of indigenous political units in Portuguese Timor in the mid-twentieth century, 1983), online at http://trove.nla.gov.au/work/17827299?selectedversion= NBD23589452, accessed June 18, 2012. See also Davidson, "Portuguese Consolidation of Timor."

[36] See, for example, Jose Ramos-Horta, *Funu: The Unfinished Saga of East Timor* (Trenton, NJ: Red Sea Press, 1987), pp. 32–34.

[37] Interview with *lia-na'in* Teliga, *suku* Ainaro, January 2, 2009.

[38] "*Rota*," or rattan stick, is symbolic of the *liurai's* rule.

cannot carry it. When they elect the *chefe de suku*, they have a ceremony, and they invite these old *liurai* to come and to give support, to speak. Here it's very important to speak because of the verbal culture. So the *chefes de suku* have a shadow placed behind them by old *liurai*.[39]

The "shadow" cast by the *liurai* over the *chefe* is especially important in relation to any responsibilities that overlap with traditional administration or the spiritual or ritual life of the community. Some *chefes* explicitly portray the relationship with the *liurai* as one of principal and agent; they act *for* the *liurai*, except perhaps in relation to a very narrow band of modern administrative tasks. This "authorization" is reflected in the ceremonies that follow *suku* and *aldeia* elections. As the *chefe de aldeia* of Caicua village in Vemasse put it, when he was elected, the *liurai* and *lia-na'in* came to speak to legitimize his authority:

> They spoke at the ceremony. Because we want keep the old system. We still respect them. The *chefe de aldeia* was elected to do a government job, but traditional matters will be in their hands. The *chefe de aldeia* is just like the "hands and legs" of the *liurai*. I am only a servant.[40]

This "authorization" of modern *chefe* power by traditional authorities is a key feature of political hybridity in the rural areas of Timor-Leste. As noted above, in some regions—for example, the *aldeias* in *suku* Ainaro—traditional authorization of modern local government is implicit in "co-incumbency" models, in which the traditional leader is routinely elected to the *chefe de aldeia* position. This is felt to be an obligation **of** traditional leaders, and is not always welcomed. For example, the *chefe de aldeia* of Hatumera, in *suku* Ainaro, felt the role was "too heavy,"[41] with insufficient recognition or support from the government. Nonetheless, he stood again in the 2009 *suku* elections, noting that until the community decided to vote for someone else, he would not be relieved of this obligation.

In cases of the traditional "authorization" of elected leaders, there are nonetheless many areas of ritual communal life in which the elected *chefe de suku* cannot play a role. As such, the balance between modern and traditional authority is often expressed in terms of a strict separation of powers. This is the case in the *aldeia* of Caicua, Vemasse:

> I was elected as *chefe de aldeia* only, and my job is to deal with the administrative matters to bridge people and government ... In regard to the traditional matters, I call the descendants of *liurai* to deal with matters. I considered them as a *rotan-na'in*. They are *lia-nain*. The *chefe de aldeia* is only administrative position. I organize all the activities in relation to state matters, and the traditional matters I leave to the descendants of *liurai* to deal with.[42]

---

[39] Interviw with Jacinto da Costa, subdistrict administrator, Los Palos, January 29, 2008.

[40] Interview with Geraldo da Silva; *chefe de aldeia* Caicua, Vemasse, Baucau, March 3, 2008.

[41] Interview with *chefe de aldeia* Hatumera, Ainaro, January 31, 2008.

[42] Interview with Geraldo da Silva; *chefe de aldeia* Caicua, Vemasse, Baucau, March 3, 2008.

Even so, in some important symbolic matters regarding the relationship between a local community and the state, the traditional authorities take the fore. As *chefe de aldeia* of Caucui explained, when the village received its national flag from Dili, it was the *liurai* who represented the *aldeia* in receiving it, not the *chefe de aldeia*. The fact that flags are often *sasaan lulik* may be a strong factor in this practice.[43]

While traditional sources of legitimacy are critical, the modern local-government structure itself opens up networks and resource bases that can bestow legitimacy on those who "deliver." For example, during the 2004–05 *suku* elections, affiliation to political party became an important consideration as it was generally felt that those allied to the party leading the national government would have a better chance of securing resources for the *suku*. Equally, an individual's involvement in the resistance offers an important source of "modern" political legitimacy in Timor-Leste—especially at the national level of politics. Indeed, as one interviewee noted, it is possibly an irony that where the "modern" political legitimacy enjoyed by resistance veterans would assist someone to become prime minister, it would often be insufficient to ensure their election as a *chefe de suku*. While involvement in the resistance is one important source of legitimacy at the local level, it must also be balanced against the requirements of *lisan* and customary sources of legitimacy.[44]

It is clear that local people are negotiating the two systems in ways intended to confer legitimacy through both worldviews. This act of negotiation is a pragmatic one, seeking to find local leaders who will be able to fill a diverse range of community needs that encompass the temporal and the sacred. However, this act of negotiation carries internal tensions that become increasingly important when considering how authority is exercised.

MAINTAINING AUTHORITY

While *suku* elections are an important moment in the negotiation between customary and state-based authority, the more critical test lies in the day-to-day exercise of authority between elections. Experience since independence suggests that those *chefes de suku* without traditional legitimacy have struggled in their roles. Almost without exception, interviewees noted that the responsibilities of the *chefe de suku* in coordinating and leading the people within the *suku* are significantly easier if the elected leader is of *liurai* heritage. Traditionally, it is important that leaders know "how to speak" the ritual forms of language that command authority. In a culture in which the oral tradition has primacy, and authority is often measured against eloquence, a traditionally legitimated leader has a much better chance of being viewed as an effective leader than one who does not. Those with *liurai* heritage as the holders of ritual words clearly possess greater "speaking power" than those lacking traditional legitimacy. One respondent referred to this as the "secret voice" possessed only by traditional authorities, which authorizes and gives the protection of the *lia-na'in* to the new *chefes*.[45] As the district administrator of Viqueque explains, this is an important issue for *chefes de suku* who are elected on grounds other than their traditional legitimacy:

---

[43] "*Sasaan lulik*" means "sacred items.

[44] Interview with the subdistrict administrator, Los Palos, January 29, 2008.

[45] Interview with Carlos Rodrigues, *lia-na'in* and *chefe de aldeia* of Wailacama, Vemasse, Baucau, March 2, 2008.

> We have *suku* here who elected the *chefe de suku* from the *liurai* house. And experience tells us that these *suku* don't have a problem. But those who elected people from outside, elected some people because they think they are clever—they can read, they can write—or have tradition in politics—those *suku* have problems all the time. It doesn't matter what they do—*even if they do the same thing.* The *chefes de suku,* if not descendants of the *liurai,* have a lot more problems. So I think this needs to be put into consideration, the psychology—I say that we need change to be gradual.[46]

More broadly, the interviewees suggest that traditional leaders elected to *chefe* positions face lower expectations, particularly in terms of their ability to connect with external networks. By contrast, *chefes de suku* without traditional legitimacy need to demonstrate successes to justify their continuing position. Success or failure is often measured against the ability to deliver communal resources such as schools, medical services, or better roads. However, such successes are heavily dependent on the capacity and willingness of external actors, such as the government or NGOs, to invest in the *suku.* This remains a constant challenge, given the generalized lack of state investment in rural areas. As *chefe de suku* of Uma Ana Icu, in subdistrict Venilale, explains, the *chefe* is often held to account for these failures, rather than the Dili-based government. As the perceived failures of the *chefe de suku* accumulate, the community's faith in the *chefe* as an effective leader diminishes.[47] In effect, *chefes* who cannot claim customary authority through *lisan* must perform in a manner more analogous to the "Big Men" leaders of Melanesia, and demonstrate material success in a manner not necessarily expected of traditional leaders.

Other difficult issues for *chefes* include negotiating the boundaries between traditional and modern forms of dispute resolution. As *chefe de aldeia* of Caucui explains, local communities alternate between different modes, depending on the context:

> We solve most problems using traditional way, even political problems. If there is a fight, police will come and make the situation calm. Sometimes the police have to detain those who are involved. After police normalize the situation, they will hand over the case to *lia-na'in.* For example, in this *aldeia,* when the militants of some political parties fought each other during the campaign, they were detained. But later on I took them from the detention center and brought them back to our village. Then I gathered *lia-nain* and leaders of political parties to come together to fix the problem using the traditional method.[48]

A similar pattern was also evident in the aftermath of a murder involving two *sukus* in Venilale, which caused violence among youths that lasted almost a week. Throughout this time, the *chefes de suku, chefes de aldeia,* the police, the parish priests, and other local leaders worked together to restore peace. The chief offender was detained by the police and formally charged, while the "smaller" offenses of assault

---

[46] Interview with Francisco da Silva, district administrator, Viqueque, January 30, 2008 (emphasis added).

[47] Interview with *chefe de suku* Uma Ana Icu, Baucau District, October 10, 2008.

[48] Interview with *Chefe de aldeia,* Caicua, Vemasse, Baucau, March 3, 2008.

were dealt with first by the police and then resolved through *lisan*, with the offenders being restored to their communities. As the parish priest of Venilale explained,[49] this murder represented payback for another murder that had occurred many years before and the challenge was to break the cycle of violence. While resolution via *lisan* allowed for the offenses to be put in historical context, the modern legal system could only deal with the offense at hand. The focus in resolving the "smaller" offenses of assault via *lisan* was to promote reconciliation by acknowledging this historical context and restoring balance to the community, with the hope that this would avoid similar murders occurring in the future.

IMPLICATIONS OF A HYBRID POLITICAL ENVIRONMENT

This article has examined the interaction of traditional and modern authority in *suku* administration in rural Timor-Leste, identifying three hybrid modes of authority at the local government level: two "co-incumbency" models and an "authorization" model emphasizing a separation of powers. Clearly, the third model offers scope for leaders who cannot claim authority through *lisan* to play effective roles in *suku* administration, though it was noted that the challenges facing these leaders are considerable. It was also noted that for the role of *chefe de aldeia*, possessing traditional authority appears to be even more critical. In general, the scope for nontraditional leaders to exercise authority appears to increase with the distance from local traditional communities, offering increased scope for other sources of political legitimacy, for example, participation in the resistance to the Indonesian occupation.

As with previous systems of local administration instituted in the Portuguese and Indonesian colonial eras, traditional administrative structures have continued to be adapted to externally imposed requirements in the post-independence era, while maintaining core aspects of the traditional practices of *suku* administration. The "co-incumbency" and "authorization" models of local authority outlined here are an inherent feature of contemporary local politics and need to be understood in the context of limited state reach into rural communities. The new nation of Timor-Leste is also, however, in a state of rapid change. Just as the last ten years have seen substantial change in social and political structures, particularly in the urban center of Dili, so, too, it is likely that the next decade will see further significant development across the rural areas of Timor-Leste. The potential role of the East Timorese state as an agent of development means that the existing balance negotiated through local politics could change very quickly, creating new challenges and opportunities for different actors at the local level. The challenge for the East Timorese government is to shape local politics within this changing political environment by acknowledging the centrality of *lisan* in rural communities, while also working to address those areas where gender and class inequalities are reproduced through the "re-traditionalization" of modern local administration.

---

[49] Interview with parish priest, Venilale, November 10, 2008.

THE POLITICS OF SECURITY-SECTOR REFORM

Bu V. E. Wilson

INTRODUCTION

This chapter considers security-sector reform in Timor-Leste from 2006 to 2011, including both the broader security-sector reform "project" and the process of reforming the police. The political and security crisis of 2006, with its origins found in conflicts within and between the uniformed forces, evidenced the necessity of reforming Timor-Leste's police and military and their respective oversight ministries. Yet the reform project—premised on cooperation between international and national actors—has stumbled, faltered, and, arguably, even failed. In this chapter, I examine how an ill-defined project, contests over sovereignty, shortcomings in capacity, and incompatible international and national agendas have worked to produce poor outcomes for long-term security in Timor-Leste. I also discuss how these opposing agendas and stances have worked synergistically, in an expression of regulatory ritualism, to obscure the lack of progress made, with all actors having a stake in *appearing* to reform the security sector in Timor-Leste.

THE POST-CONFLICT SECURITY-SECTOR REFORM PROJECT

Security-sector reform (SSR) is now regarded as a cardinal component of post-conflict state-building and stabilization efforts. This acknowledgment recognizes that particular states may not be able to provide basic security for their citizens, that the apparatus of those states may be the cause of that insecurity, and that both the welfare and human rights of a state's citizens are integral to any calculation of security.[1] Although the term SSR is comparatively new, most of the component parts of SSR, such as military and police reform or development of civilian oversight capacity, were already part of donor development programs before the term SSR was first used in 1998.[2]

---

[1] Global Facilitation Network for Security Sector Reform (GFN SSR), *A Beginner's Guide to Security Sector Reform* (Birmingham: GBN SSR, 2007).

[2] Michael Brzoska, *Development Donors and the Concept of Security Sector Reform*, DCAF Occasional Paper, no. 4 (Geneva: Geneva Centre for Democratic Contol of the Armed Forces, 2003).

A range of benefits is claimed to result from SSR, including that it facilitates holistic thinking about a set of interrelated issues and enables coordination of reform efforts both within a country and with external donors. It is also claimed to be a necessary prerequisite for achieving both development and stability in post-conflict states.[3] Achieving or sustaining success in SSR undertakings has, however, proved particularly elusive. SSR is complex, and achieving consistency and coordination within a multifaceted program is difficult. It is also an expensive and human-resource-intensive process, and maintaining donor interest and commitment over the long time frames required is challenging.[4] SSR efforts have also suffered from a shortage of institutions and personnel familiar with the complexity of such an undertaking. In addition, a small number of commentators have raised concerns about the capacity of international actors who carry out SSR, with Gordon Peake, Eric Scheye, and Alice Hills noting that:

> The organisations charged with implementing reform usually lack appropriate structures and capacity, while many of the international personnel engaging in field-based activities—the link between policy goals and policy achievement—do not possess the necessary skills.[5]

In addition to these practical considerations, SSR is often criticized for being an ad hoc process, lacking in coherent definition and strategy, manifesting as a "grab bag" of previously separate activities repackaged as an SSR program.[6] SSR is sometimes characterized as a "modernizing" project informed by Western liberal values, seeking to introduce the concept, and model, of security organizations subject to democratic civilian control. This modernizing project carries with it an assumption that reforming the security sector will produce broader cultural, governance, and societal change.[7] The SSR project also carries other assumptions about the way change is effected in institutional settings. SSR programs tend to be rationalist in nature, having an outcome that implementers want to achieve and a series of activities planned in advance for achieving that outcome. Programs assume that the implementing agencies and personnel will wield a high degree of influence. Characteristically, however, those engaged in efforts to implement SSR have not anticipated what will happen to those programs when introduced into the particularly unpredictable context of a post-conflict environment.[8] Ultimately, SSR is about engineering change and rearranging power relationships within the most

---

[3] Sean McFate, *Securing the Future: A Primer on Security Sector Reform in Conflict Countries* (Washington, DC: United States Institute of Peace, 2008); Heiner Hänggi and Vincenza Scherrer, "Recent Experience of UN Integrated Missions in Security Sector Reform (SSR)," in *Security Sector Reform and UN Integrated Missions: Experience from Burundi, the Democratic Republic of Congo, Haiti, and Kosovo*, ed. Heiner Hänggi and Vincenza Scherrer (Geneva: Geneva Centre for the Democratic Control of the Armed Forces [DCAF], 2008).

[4] GFN SSR, *A Beginner's Guide.*

[5] Gordon Peake, Eric Scheye, and Alice Hills. "Conclusions," *Civil Wars* 8,2 (2006): 251.

[6] R. Egnell and P. Haldén, "Laudable, Ahistorical and Overambitious: Security Sector Reform Meets State Formation Theory," *Conflict, Security & Development* 9,1 (2009): 27–54.

[7] E. Scheye and G. Peake. "To Arrest Insecurity: Time for a Revised Security Sector Reform Agenda," *Conflict, Security and Development* 5,3 (2005): 297–99.

[8] V. Piotukh and P. Wilson, *Security Sector Evolution: Understanding and Influencing How Security Institutions Change* (London: Libra Advisory Group, 2009), pp. 4–5.

sensitive areas of governance, and, characteristically, such reform efforts must contend with resistance from individuals and institutions.

Although donor agendas commonly revolve around governance and accountability issues, their agendas may be very different from those of ordinary people, for whom tangible improvements in everyday security may be far more pressing. It is often overlooked that very different programming will be required to achieve these disparate outcomes and that one cannot assume that security will "trickle down" from "good governance."[9] Additionally, in situations where the reach of the state is (and may always have been) incomplete, human, logistical, and financial capacity is limited and the legitimacy of state security institutions is compromised. Thus, it will also often be the case that most security (and justice) services will be provided principally by nonstate actors.[10] In these circumstances, focusing primarily on strengthening state-based institutions will not deliver improved security outcomes to most of the population.[11]

IDENTIFYING THE NEED FOR SSR IN TIMOR-LESTE

In April and May 2006, Timor-Leste experienced a major political and security crisis. This included widespread fighting between, and within, the two uniformed security forces, the almost complete cessation of government functionality, the resignation of multiple government ministers, widespread violence, the displacement of approximately 150,000 people, extensive destruction of housing stock, and the deaths of at least thirty-eight people.[12] By late May 2006, the situation became so serious that the government of Timor-Leste called for international military and police intervention from Australia, New Zealand, Portugal, and Malaysia. Initially, 2,200 personnel were deployed. Subsequently the government requested the establishment of a new UN mission.

The proximate cause of the crisis was the sacking of 591 members (or approximately one-third) of Timor-Leste's military (the FALINTIL–Forças Defesa de Timor-Leste, or F-FDTL) in March 2006, a group that came to be known as "the petitioners." The petitioners were almost exclusively from western districts, and they alleged that members of the organization from the east of the country had discriminated against members of F-FDTL from the west. Failures of the security institutions were central to this crisis. Members of both Timor-Leste's police force (Polícia Nacional Timor-Leste, PNTL) and F-FDTL and their respective oversight ministries, the Ministry of the Interior and the Ministry of Defence, were directly involved in the violence of April and May 2006. Problems within the police force and the Ministry of the Interior had been apparent for some time, but the crisis served to bring to international attention major developmental, legitimacy, and performance issues. It also highlighted the divisions within and between PNTL and F-FDTL.

---

[9] Scheye and Peake, "To Arrest Insecurity," pp. 300–301.

[10] Finn Stepputat, Louise Andersen, and Bjørn Møller, "Introduction: Security Arrangements in Fragile States," in *Fragile States and Insecure People? Violence, Security, and Statehood in the Twenty-First Century*, ed. Louise Andersen, Bjørn Møller, and Finn Stepputat (Houndsmill and New York, NY: Palgrave McMillan, 2007), pp. 8–9.

[11] Ibid., pp. 6–8.

[12] United Nations, *Report of the United Nations Independent Special Commission of Inquiry* (2006), p. 3.

Subsequently, many PNTL officers and the Minister of the Interior were recommended for prosecution or further investigation by a UN commission of inquiry (COI). The PNTL general-commander was not recommended for prosecution, but the COI found that he had bypassed institutional procedures by irregularly transferring weapons and had committed a serious dereliction of duty by deserting his post.[13] Members of the F-FDTL—including Brigadier General Taur Matan Ruak,[14] Chief of Staff Colonel Lere Anan Timor,[15] Colonel Rate Laek Falur, and Major Mau Buti—and the then Minister for Defence Roque Rodrigues were recommended for prosecution by the COI for illegal weapons transfer. Seven other F-FDTL officers were recommended for prosecution for murder, six of them for the murder of unarmed PNTL officers.

The failures of PNTL and F-FDTL were inextricably connected. This was recognized in the report of Special Envoy Ian Martin, who had been sent by the UN secretary-general to Timor-Leste in June 2006 to explore the scope of tasks that could be carried out by a mission that would follow the United Nations Office in Timor-Leste (UNOTIL) mission. Martin recommended a comprehensive review, which would include a threat assessment and options for development of the sector that would address the tensions between the PNTL and F-FDTL, as well as options for addressing the relationship between the two institutions.[16] The United Nations Integrated Mission in Timor-Leste (UNMIT) commenced on August 25, 2006, with a broad mandate that included restoring and maintaining public security, providing assistance to further develop the PNTL, and providing support for a security-sector review.

However, in the process of developing the UNMIT mandate, a number of things began to be lost in translation. The proposal to review the security sector as a whole and the need to reform the police—processes that should have been integrally connected—became separated. In addition, addressing the problems inherent in the F-FDTL completely fell by the wayside. The United Nations had existing "policing" capacity in the form of United Nations Police (UNPOL), but no personnel, bureaucratic units, or strategy dedicated to security-sector reform. There were no personnel within the Department of Peacekeeping Operations detailed to military development.[17] Furthermore, Timor-Leste's political leadership made it clear very early in the process that the F-FDTL would not be subject to the same kinds of review and accountability as it was prepared to contemplate for the PNTL.

---

[13] Ibid., p. 75.

[14] Taur Matan Ruak was subsequently elected president of the Republic in Timor-Leste's 2012 presidential elections.

[15] Brigadier General Lere Anan Timor became commander of F-FDTL in September 2011, after Taur Matan Ruak resigned to run for the post of president.

[16] United Nations, *Report of the Secretary-General on Timor-Leste Pursuant to Security Council Resolution 1690 (2006), S/2006/628* (2006).

[17] Gordon Peake "A Lot of Talk but Not a Lot of Action: The Difficulty of Implementing SSR in Timor-Leste," in *Security Sector Reform in Challenging Environments*, ed. Hans Born and Albrecht Schnabel (Geneva: Geneva Centre for the Democratic Control of the Armed Forces [DCAF], 2009), pp. 213–38.

RECONSTRUCTING THE PNTL

Under the UNMIT mandate, UNPOL reassumed the role of executive policing normally reserved for the sovereign state, something it had previously done in Timor-Leste until 2004. This placed Timor-Leste's police under UN control. The goals of restoring public security and reconstructing the police were premised on the presence of UNPOL. Yet, as with other UN missions, UNPOL was slow to arrive. The organization's officers did not arrive until November 2006, UNPOL was not properly functioning until the following year, and it took almost a year to reach 80 percent of authorized strength.[18] As with its previous attempt to construct the PNTL between 2000 and 2004, UNPOL had difficulty recruiting officers of adequate caliber in sufficient numbers and in a timely fashion. The "national balance" model of deploying forty or more different nationalities of police to supervise an already weak and poorly structured police institution was once again found to be wanting. Once again, it became apparent that "cops on the beat" alone do not have the capacity to establish a public-service organization.

At the heart of UNMIT's plan for reconstruction of the police was a process for vetting PNTL members, to be followed by provisional certification, training, and mentoring, and, then, final certification. Vetting is most frequently used in security- and justice-sector institutions where human rights abuses have diminished the legitimacy of state institutions.[19] However, vetting processes carry inherent risks. If vetting is not done well, it can undermine or unnecessarily complicate other transitional justice processes, and the vetted institutions may end up with an even more compromised legitimacy than they had prior to the process.[20]

The greater detail outlining how the public security and reform tasks were to be carried out was contained in a Supplemental Arrangement (SA) that was concluded between UNMIT and the Timor-Leste government in late 2006.[21] In January 2007, UNPOL completed an assessment of the technical and administrative competencies of the PNTL, including internal accountability mechanisms.[22] This formed the basis for preparing an Organizational Strategic Plan for Reform, Restructuring, and Rebuilding the PNTL (hereafter the RRRD plan). UNPOL completed several versions of the RRRD with little or no input from the PNTL. None of the versions was translated into any language that would have made it accessible for East Timorese recipients. None of the versions was ever agreed to by the government. Rather, then minister of the interior, Alcino Bárris, in a letter to UNPOL Commissioner Rodolfo Tor dated April 24, 2007, extensively criticized the plan. Minister Bárris noted,

---

[18] United Nations, *Report of the Expert Mission to Timor-Leste on Policing, 17 to 27 March 2008, S/2008/329 Annex* (2008), p. 8.

[19] Roger Duthie, "Introduction," in *Justice as Prevention: Vetting Public Employees in Transitional Societies,* ed. Alexander Mayer-Rieckh and Pablo de Grieff (New York, NY: Social Science Research Council, 2007), p. 21.

[20] Pablo De Greiff, "Vetting and Transitional Justice," in *Justice as Prevention: Vetting Public Employees in Transitional Societies,* ed. Alexander Mayer-Rieckh and Pablo De Greiff (New York, NY: Social Science Research Council, 2007), 527–28.

[21] UNMIT and Democratic Republic of Timor-Leste, *Arrangement on the Restoration and Maintenance of Public Security in Timor-Leste and on Assistance to the Reform, Restructuring and Rebuilding of the Timorese National Police (PNTL) and the Ministry of Interior Supplemental to the Agreement between the United Nations and the Democratic Republic of Timor-Leste on the Status of the United Nations Integrated Mission in Timor-Leste (UNMIT),* 2006.

[22] United Nations, *Report on Policing.*

among other things, that the plan lacked costings; had considerable duplications, inconsistencies, and weaknesses; and was not oriented to the local context. Perhaps most damningly, he alleged he had found extensive plagiarism in the plan. He demonstrated that parts of the plan were taken, without acknowledgement, from sources as diverse as Wikipedia and documents of the Feinberg School of Medicine, Northwestern University, in the United States.[23] The RRRD was also criticized extensively by members of an expert UN policing mission, who noted that the plan did not reflect the SA. The mission also expressed concern regarding "national ownership of the plan, since it had not been prepared with the active participation of local stakeholders" and concluded that "the document [could not] be used as a basis for the reform, restructuring and rebuilding of the national police in its current format and [would] require substantive changes."[24] The SA anticipated that benchmarks for the staged handover of policing from the UN, back to Timorese authorities, would be determined by the RRRD plan. As the government never approved any versions of the plan, it was not clear for a number of years how various benchmarks and performance targets would be recognized.

Despite being responsible for supervising the PNTL, UNPOL struggled to exert any day-to-day command and control over the PNTL, particularly within the "special units" such as the UIR (Unidade Intervenção Rápida, or Rapid Response Unit), URP (Unidade de Reserva da Polícia, or Police Reserve Unit) and UPF (Unidade Patrulhamento Fronteira, or Border Patrol Unit).[25] These units were all significantly involved in different ways in the unraveling of the security forces and associated violence in 2006.[26] However, rather than making reforming these units a priority, the suspect organizations received a "hands off" treatment by UNMIT, with no UNPOL officers co-located with any of them.

This lack of effective command and control was also evidenced in the many critical decisions that were taken by PNTL from 2006 onward without the agreement, or sometimes even the knowledge, of UNPOL. This included the development of the Dili Task Force in 2007 and, more critically, the creation of the Joint Military Police Command in February 2008. The ability of UNPOL to supervise PNTL was undermined by factors including a failure to co-locate UNPOL and PNTL, resulting in parallel command structures; the variable—and sometimes high—turnover of UNPOL officers; language and other communication difficulties; and failure to deploy UNPOL officers to most subdistricts due to harsh living conditions.

In addition to the challenges posed by the UN's lack of practical control over the PNTL, it also appears that the executive policing function of UNPOL and,

---

[23] Minister of Interior, Alcino de Araújo Bárris, *Letter to Mr. Rodolfo Tor, Police Commissioner, UNMIT, Office of the Police Commissioner, Dili, 24 April 2007* (2007).

[24] United Nations, *Report on Policing*, p. 9.

[25] Under Decree Law 9/2009, *Organic Law of Timor-Leste's National Police* (PNTL), the URP became the Special Police Unit (Unidade Especial de Polícia) and the UIR became the Public Order Battalion (Batalhão Orden Publico, BOP). Although this law was promulgated in February 2009, the original special units were still in evidence in July 2009.

[26] The Special Commission of Inquiry (COI) recommended both named and unnamed UIR and URP officers for prosecution and further investigation. The COI also noted that members of the UIR and URP deserted with Alfredo Reinado, members of the URP were involved in supporting east–west confrontations and subsequent attacks in Fatu Ahi, members of the UIR were involved in the attack at the Comoro Market, and that significant irregular distribution of URP weapons also occurred.

consequently, their supervision of PNTL had no legal basis. On December 9, 2008, in a little-publicized Court of Appeal decision, it was found that because the SA was not ratified by parliament and promulgated, as required by the constitution of Timor-Leste, with publication in the official gazette, *Journal da Republica*, the SA did not have the force of law.[27] Curiously, it appears to have suited both the Timor-Leste government and the United Nations to ignore the court's decision and ignore the legal limbo that this decision created. How this squares with the UNMIT mandate to promote the rule of law, or Article 1(1) and 6(d) of the RDTL constitution that determines that Timor-Leste is a rule-of-law state, is unclear.

The cornerstone of the police-vetting process, as determined by the SA, involved screening and certifying individual PNTL officers. This was to prove challenging. Initially, there was confusion about who was carrying out the processes of registering and screening members of the PNTL. The poor communication between the government and UNMIT was highlighted when it became apparent that serving PNTL members were required to register both with UNPOL and the Ministry of the Interior. For quite some time, senior UN officials would not believe their own staff who told them the government was running a parallel process. Following initial certification, PNTL members were required to undergo five days of training. This was to be followed by six months of mentoring by UNPOL. Although UNPOL handled some of the five-days' training sessions, during 2007 the training was subcontracted to the Australian-based Timor-Leste Police Development Program (TLPDP), as UNPOL did not have the capacity to carry out the program. There was initial difficulty in getting PNTL members to attend the course, and absenteeism was high. Ambivalence about the screening and certification process from then minister of the interior Alcino Bárris contributed to the difficulty of getting PNTL members to attend training. It goes without saying that serious limitations are inevitable in any course that is limited to five days.

UNPOL originally intended that PNTL members who had undergone police training would each be allocated an UNPOL mentor on a one-to-one basis, but this proved impossible to implement. The mentoring program suffered from serious problems, and there is every indication that it ultimately amounted to a "box ticking" exercise. The failure to recruit UNPOL officers who had training and mentoring experience undoubtedly contributed to this problem. In 2007, the practice of mentoring was described by UN officials and bilateral advisers I interviewed as "the weak link in the chain," "a bit dysfunctional," and "hit and miss." It is apparent that, for a considerable part of the mission period, much effort went into creating the impression that the police-reform process was proceeding better than it really was. In interviews with the UNPOL commissioner in 2007, he claimed that every PNTL member was being mentored every day with a daily written summary, something that clearly was not happening.

In 2007 and 2008, these observations regarding the poor state of UNPOL's training and mentoring program were confirmed during two important visits from New York–based UN officials, who were sent to assess the realities on the ground in Timor-Leste. Members of a Security Council mission visited Timor-Leste in 2007 and expressed disquiet about the effectiveness of UNPOL. Subsequently, the 2008 expert

---

[27] Bu V. E. Wilson, "Timor-Leste: The Curious Case of the Fake Policemen," *East Timor Law Journal* (February 2009), www.Eastimorlawjournal.Org/Articles/2009/Timor_Leste_the_Curious_Case_of_the_Fake_Policemen_Bu_Wilson_2009.Html, accessed June 26, 2012.

police mission noted in relation to PNTL that "tremendous institutional gaps [persisted], including weak management and command and control, lack of core capacities (e.g., investigations), and an almost total absence of logistics and systems maintenance capacity."[28] The expert mission also expressed "reservations about the mentoring process ... in particular the qualifications of UNMIT personnel deployed in such a capacity and the lack of advisers at the sub-district level," and concluded that the process was "relatively unsystematic." [29]

Sustained pressure from the Timor-Leste government, eager to see UNPOL hand over policing responsibilities to the PNTL, culminated in a letter from the Timor-Leste secretary of state for security to the UN deputy special representative of the secretary-general (SRSG) dated December 16, 2008, outlining a proposal for advancing a full resumption of responsibility by the PNTL, commencing on March 27, 2009. Although the letter indicated a wish to advance the process, it also proposed a comprehensive independent assessment to gauge the administrative, institutional, and operational readiness of the PNTL. The independent assessment would then be used to determine whether the PNTL was "fully reconstituted." The secretary of state's proposal for an independent commission was predicated on an acknowledgement that "the United Nations and Timorese authorities have both been deeply involved in the reform process, which [meant] that neither [enjoyed] the necessary remove to look at the readiness of the PNTL in a dispassionate manner."[30]

However, there was no enthusiasm within UNMIT for an independent assessment, and UNMIT representatives reiterated their preference for joint UNMIT/PNTL assessments. A joint technical team (JTT) and joint field assessment teams (JFATs), comprising equal representation from UNMIT, UNPOL, PNTL, and the government of Timor-Leste, were set up to evaluate the readiness of the districts/units based on jointly agreed upon criteria: (a) ability of PNTL to respond appropriately to the security environment in a given district; (b) final certification of at least 80 percent of the eligible PNTL officers in a given district/unit slated to be freed from UNPOL's supervision and granted its own authority; (c) availability of initial operational logistical requirements; and (d) institutional stability, which included the ability to exercise command and control, and community acceptance.

During this time, it became apparent that senior United Nations personnel and Timor-Leste government personnel viewed the handover process, and the basis upon which the handover process was proceeding, very differently, and that tensions were building as a result. When interviewed, the UN Police commissioner, Luis Carillho, said that the handover was being carried out according to the RRRD plan—a plan described by the UN policing mission as unfit to be used as a basis for the reform, restructuring, and rebuilding of the national police in its current format. The secretary of state for security, Francisco Guterres, expressed a contrary view. He said the handover was not being carried out according to the RRRD plan but according to the government's Five-Year Plan. He added that, if they followed the RRRD plan, "what would be the point of having independence?" Empirically, however, the handover did not proceed according to either plan.

---

[28] United Nations, *Report on Policing*, p. 2.

[29] Ibid.

[30] Secretary of State for Security, Francisco Guterres, "Letter to Mr. Takahisa Kawakami, Deputy Special Representative of the Secretary General for Security Sector Support and Rule of Law, United Nations Integrated Mission in Timor-Leste, December 16, 2008" (2008).

Ultimately, the course of the handover was determined by political rather than technical considerations. Interviews carried out in Timor-Leste between 2008 and 2010 suggested that commencement of the handover came about not because the PNTL had been reconstructed or because it fully met the criteria, but due to the fact that the government of Timor-Leste was tiring of the relationship with UNMIT; consequently, the government had pressed UNPOL for more than a year, asking for handover to commence. On May 14, 2009, the district of Lautem was the first district to be handed back to Timorese authorities for "everyday policing," with the handover of full executive policing responsibilities and authority to occur at an undetermined date in the future. Lautem was perceived as an "unproblematic" district, although it was still dependent on UNPOL resources to function. With the United Nations having worked its way through the less challenging districts and police units, the handover process became increasingly difficult for the United Nations, as more problematic and dysfunctional districts and the special units were considered. Pressure upon the United Nations, from Timorese authorities, to bring forward the handover of executive policing authority resulted in what could be considered unseemly haste—characterized by less and less evidence-based decision making. One senior UN official told me that he asked the SRSG, Ameera Haq, if she really wanted to be photographed with the Liquica police when that district was handed over, as it comprised so many uncertified officers and officers with criminal charges pending against them.

By the end of March 2011, the PNTL celebrated the eleventh anniversary of the founding of the organization, and full executive policing responsibility was handed back to the Timorese authorities. Unfortunately, despite a UN mandate that was supposed to be primarily focused on police reform, the PNTL had not been reconstructed since the crisis. The extensive vetting process of individual police officers that took more than four years was effectively abandoned, as was a comprehensive process for determining when individual districts had met criteria enabling them to be handed over. The final handover appeared to be based on nothing in particular.

The vetting process, which focused on individual officers rather than the institution as a whole, was of minimal benefit in addressing institutional issues. The four criteria that were used to evaluate later-stage trainees prior to final certification were not well suited to evaluating the capacity or integrity of individual police officers, and indicated nothing about the capacity and integrity of the institution. The ineffectiveness of the vetting process is evidenced by the continuing lack of accountability that PNTL enjoys concerning human rights violations and abuses of authority, a sorry condition that worsened during and following the operations of the February 2008 Joint Command.[31] The excesses of the Joint Command were replicated in a special police operation in 2010 to deal with putative "ninjas" in Bobonaro and Covalima districts, which resulted in widespread human rights abuses, leading a prominent human rights organization to question the authorization

---

[31] Bu V. E. Wilson, "Joint Command for PNTL and F-FDTL Undermines Rule of Law and Security Sector Reform in Timor-Leste," *East Timor Law Journal* (February 2008), http://easttimorlawjournal.wordpress.com/2012/05/24/joint-command-for-pntl-and-f-fdtl-undermines-rule-of-law-and-security-sector-reform-in-timor-leste/, accessed June 19, 2012.

process for, and the necessity of, the extended paramilitary operation involving both the police and the military.[32]

The disciplinary mechanisms within PNTL are still unsatisfactory and ad hoc in nature.[33] The disciplinary regulation, copied from its Portuguese equivalent, contains complex formulae running to several pages that even for a Western-educated science/math graduate is almost impossible to understand. Professional Standards and Discipline Office (PSDO) officers[34] in each district are appointed by the district commander and are frequently low-ranking agents who have little real authority and are beholden to the district commander.[35]

A credible and fair (but complex) career regime with transitional provisions has been legislated for, promulgated, and ostensibly "socialized." However, rank-and-file PNTL members are either unaware of its existence or don't understand it. Considerable anxiety exists among PNTL members about forthcoming changes in relation to career structure, with concern expressed that the new arrangements "will make trouble in the future." This reflects a broader problem within the institution: that is, in the absence of regular, credible internal communications about what is going on within the PNTL, members are left to assume the worst.

UNPOL has had two opportunities now to (re)construct the PNTL, and many of the mistakes that marred the first attempt were repeated the second time around. Many of the important tasks, identified by the special envoy in 2006, necessary to reform and reconstruct the PNTL have not been completed (or, in some cases, commenced). It also appears that many of the serious shortcomings of both UNPOL and PNTL, identified by the expert policing mission in 2008, were not addressed.

REVIEWING THE SECURITY SECTOR

In addition to reforming, restructuring, and rebuilding the PNTL, UNMIT was also mandated to provide assistance to the Timor-Leste government to carry out a security-sector review. As noted above, this undertaking initially had no obvious "home" in the mission, and in response the Security Sector Support Unit (SSSU) was established with responsibility for the review. UNMIT's difficulty in recruiting and deploying sufficient numbers and caliber of UNPOL officers also affected civilian deployments. It took two years for the SSSU to fill the positions it had identified. This made the work of setting a direction for the unit and establishing critical relationships with government interlocutors very difficult.

When the author met with SSSU staff more than a year after commencement of the mission, in November 2007, it was clear that the staff felt excluded from any real processes having to do with the security sector. The staff members were approaching the review with some trepidation and sense of pointlessness, as they felt that the government was acting independently, preempting the review and not informing

---

[32] Perkumpulan Hak, "HAK Report: Human Rights Situation in Covalima and Bobonaro," February 15, 2010 (English-language edited version of HAK Association's report), available at http://fundasaunmahein.wordpress.com/2010/02/23/hak-report-human-rights-situation-in-covalima-and-bobonaro, accessed April 30, 2012.

[33] Interviews conducted with UN officials July 2009, Timor-Leste.

[34] Now referred to as "Department of Justice," not to be confused with the Ministry of Justice within the Government of Timor-Leste.

[35] Interviews conducted with UN personnel and bilateral advisers, Dili, July 2009.

them of what was being done. SSSU advisers responded by refocusing their role on sourcing advisers to be placed within the F-FDTL and ministries of interior and defense, assistance that had been previously requested by then-president José Ramos-Horta.[36] However, the decision to focus on this task posed a serious "sequencing" problem, as the SSSU staff was sourcing advisers when there was no clear process or policy framework to establish what these recruits should be advising upon or what skills they should have. Given that the SSSU staff seemed to be so lacking in confidence about their role, it was interesting that they described themselves as being involved in a process of "confidence building" for the government that included the convening of educational seminars. In 2007, three of these seminars were convened on the topic of SSR. During these seminars, East Timorese leaders expressed skepticism about the United Nations' capacity to assist with reform, given its track record on building security institutions to date.[37] Meanwhile, the United Nations reported back positively on the outcomes of the seminars.[38]

It was not until June 2008, almost two years after the beginning of the UNMIT mission, that the prime minister signed a project document worth US$1,223,226 in support of a review of the security sector. Until this stage, the project document had been through at least three iterations. The Security Sector Review Project, under the joint auspices of UNMIT and the United Nations Development Program (UNDP), included the following activities: (a) a functional analysis of governance institutions and state and nonstate security institutions, (b) a gap analysis of institutional and regulatory gaps relevant to the security sector, (c) a threat analysis, and (d) a strategic environment review.

In interviews in July 2009, both the head of the SSSU and the UNDP project manager for the review agreed that the review, as such, would not happen. However, in 2010, a short ritualistic review was produced, with factual assistance and corrections contributed from other parts of the mission but no input from Timor-Leste's authorities. The draft review, produced only in English, was then passed from hand to hand through the Office of the Secretary of State for Security, then languished a while in the president's office.

In January 2011, the report of the secretary-general effectively put the security-sector review to rest:

> The finalisation of the draft document on the comprehensive review of the security sector has been delayed. Currently, the Government and the Office of the President are reviewing the document, in consultation with UNMIT. While it appears unlikely that the document will be finalized in the near future, many of the elements identified in the draft document have already

---

[36] Interviews conducted with UN personnel, Dili, November 2007.

[37] International Crisis Group (ICG), *Timor-Leste: Security Sector Reform* (Dili and Brussels: ICG, 2008). The ICG also recounts how a high-level East Timorese official, in a subsequent interview, was "explicit in his distaste" about the utility of the United Nations in relation to the security sector review. In an interview with ICG Roque Rodrigues, presidential adviser on SSR, he was critical of UNMIT, claiming it was displaying arrogance in the way that it was allocating its security-sector advisors to East Timorese bodies. Ibid., p. 11.

[38] United Nations, *Report of the Secretary-General on the United Nations Integrated Mission in Timor-Leste, for the Period from 27 January to 20 August 2007*, S/2007/513 (2007).

been addressed ... and, once finalized, it will serve as a useful reference document.[39]

In May 2012, the review was finally presented to the Council of Ministers, who described it as "the first phase of an ongoing process."[40] Given the difficulties that staff members of the SSSU had in establishing relationships with the Timor-Leste government, it is likely that the review bears little correspondence to the considerable and significant process of decision making that has been carried out by Timorese structures of power and networks not visible to international actors.

One of the difficulties facing the SSSU in relation to the review was that it had always been clear that the review itself was the responsibility of the Timor-Leste government and that the role of the UN mission was to "assist." As long as the government was unwilling to commit to the process of a review and to involve the United Nations, the "assistance" framework was always going to encounter obstacles. The 2006 crisis further sensitized the political elite to security issues, and they became very reluctant to engage in the review. However, several factors made the government want to seem to be committed to security reform, despite evidence to the contrary. One of these factors was the severity of the crisis, which included the unraveling of the security forces and security in general and led to the necessity to invite international forces to restore order and to ask the United Nations to reestablish a mission. That the Timor-Leste government needed help and needed it quickly in May 2006 is something upon which all parties would probably agree.

Whether the Timor-Leste government was quite as enthusiastic about an SSR process that was unfamiliar and implied a further loss of control and effective sovereignty is more doubtful. However, the government was in no position to reject the package of measures that was being offered. The agreement, however, has proved to be particularly unstable and arguably superficial, and the gap between design and implementation was substantial.

On the international side, UNMIT, generally, and the SSSU, more specifically, were unsure how to proceed, how to establish the difficult relationship with a sovereign government that had to play a fundamental role in order for the review to commence. To compound these issues, UNMIT and the SSSU did not have enough people with the right skills to actually carry out the work.[41] In addition, the SSSU had no money in its 2007–08 budget to support the review. Further reasons for difficulties in getting the security-sector review to "take hold" in Timor-Leste have been highlighted by Gordon Peake:

> The phrase "SSR" has little traction within Timor-Leste. Profound uncertainty remains as to what the phrase actually means. The phrase may

---

[39] United Nations, *Report of the Secretary-General on the United Nations Integrated Mission in Timor-Leste, for the period from 21 September 2010 to 7 January 2011*, S/2011/32 (2011), p. 10.

[40] Press Release, Government of Timor-Leste Council of Ministers, May 2, 2012.

[41] Jim Della-Giacoma, "The UN's Lame Security Review for Timor-Leste," *The Interpreter*, Lowy Institute for International Policy, February 17, 2009, www.lowyinterpreter.org/post/2009/02/17/The-UNs-tame-security-review-for-Timor-Leste.aspx, accessed June 19, 2012.

be intimately familiar to headquarters-based policymakers, but it is still somewhat alien to those on the ground actually engaging in reform.[42]

Previous UN failures in Timor in the area of security development have similarly made UNMIT feel a need to seem to be getting on with the job of carrying out/supporting a security-sector review in the same way that the Timor-Leste government feels compelled to appear to be doing so. As the UN-sponsored review foundered, a range of parallel security-sector-reform structures established by the East Timorese government also produced little.

POLITICAL CONTEXT

Although surveys indicate that very few people regard police as being primarily responsible for maintaining law and order,[43] there is, historically in Timor-Leste, an inordinate interest among the political elite and associated aspirants in gaining control of various parts of security institutions such as the police and the army. The political elite are suspicious of the motives and capacities of internationals charged with assisting with police-building and security-sector reform, and are nervous about the incursions into sovereignty that international assistance represents. Timor-Leste's leadership across the political spectrum has been reluctant to work with the United Nations. Timor-Leste leaders have been reluctant to cooperate not only because they are suspicious of the process, but also because successive Timor-Leste governments have had no experience in constructing state-based security systems or in carrying out processes that lead to formal institutional change and accompanying policy and legislative development.

From the beginning of the UNMIT mandate, there have been tensions between successive Timor-Leste governments' purported support of police reconstruction and security-sector review and those same governments' desires to demonstrate sovereignty and independence around such a flagship issue. Consequently, reconstruction of the PNTL has not run smoothly, with both technical and political challenges evident. Similarly, the mandated security-sector review did not really run at all. During these processes, it became clear that the Timor-Leste government had tired of the international security presence, with Secretary of State for Defence Julio Pinto stating that "what we do know is that if we compare the character, self-confidence and performance of some PNTL members with some UNPOL members, ours are much better."[44] Similarly, in 2009, then-chief of the F-FDTL, Brigadier General Taur Matan Ruak, Chief of the F-FDTL, stated that foreign forces should have left Timor-Leste by now.[45]

---

[42] Global Facilitation Network for Security Sector Reform, "SSR in Timor-Leste," *SSR Bulletin* 20 (2008): 2.

[43] The Asia Foundation, *Law and Justice in East Timor: A Survey of Citizen Awareness and Attitudes Regarding Law and Justice in East Timor* (Dili: The Asia Foundation, 2004); Silas Everett, *Law and Justice in Timor-Leste: A Survey of Citizen Awareness and Attitudes Regarding Law and Justice* (Dili: The Asia Foundation, 2009).

[44] Júlio Tomás Pinto, "SSR in Timor-Leste—Reforming the Security Sector: Facing Challenges, Achieving Progress in Timor Leste," *Tempo Semanal,* August 18, 2009, http://temposemanal timor.blogspot.com.au/2009/08/ssr-in-timor-leste.html, accessed June 22, 2012.

[45] Lusa News Agency, August 27, 2009.

The profound ambiguities in the SA contributed to a range of power struggles around the contested nature of who would own and control such an intrinsically political process as police reform, and who, ultimately, would decide about who stays and who goes. This ambiguity, together with the significant incursion into the boundaries of the sovereignty of the Timor-Leste government that the SA represented, contributed to the palpably poor relationship between the UN mission and the government, and between UNPOL and PNTL. Through the course of the mission, there were pressures on UNMIT and UNPOL from the government to have PNTL deployed "back on the street" with little regard for the certification process.

Both UN headquarters and the Timor-Leste government have expressed concerns about the reform process, including the methods and the integrity of the process of reconstructing the Timor-Leste security organizations. Although many problems with the international police reconstruction process were identified by both UN headquarters and the Timor-Leste government, this shared recognition of the problems appeared to occasion little change to the trajectory that the poorly conceived and executed project was taking. Most mistakes made in the first construction of the PNTL were rigorously reproduced in the second attempt.

Increasingly, international actors have been sidelined in police reconstruction and security-sector development processes. One of the most obvious manifestations of this state of affairs is the emerging divide between an international agenda that favors the separation of the police and the military and the practice and policy development of the Timor-Leste government that demonstrates an increasing blurring of the roles of the police and military, something familiar to East Timorese from both the Indonesian occupation and the Portuguese colonial period. This development marks both an East Timorese preference for an organizational model that has police and military working closely together, and it has emerged as a point of resistance by the East Timorese political leadership against international control.

From the beginning, there has been conflict between the East Timorese police and army. The way each institution recruited its members contributed to the perception that F-FDTL carried the mantle of the armed resistance, whereas PNTL was associated with the Indonesian occupation. The predominance of easterners in the first F-FDTL battalion and a perception that westerners were dominant in the PNTL accentuated this perceived division. Since the formation of PNTL and F-FDTL, there have been attempts by F-FDTL officers to interfere in police investigations involving their members and serious assaults by F-FDTL officers on PNTL officers.[46] In January 2004, following a dispute between an F-FDTL soldier and civilians, F-FDTL stormed a police station and a hospital, fired shots, destroyed property, and took ten PNTL officers hostage, detaining them at an F-FDTL base.[47]

Initially, PNTL were much better resourced than the F-FDTL, causing tensions that were exacerbated by an unclear division of responsibilities between the police and the military. Although the Timor-Leste constitution is clear on the different

---

[46] United Nations Economic and Social Council, *Question of the Violation of Human Rights and Fundamental Freedoms in Any Part of the World—Situation of Human Rights in Timor-Leste,* Report of the United Nations High Commissioner for Human Rights, E/CN.4/2003/37 (March 2003), p. 4.

[47] United Nations Economic and Social Council, *Report of the United Nations High Commissioner for Human Rights on Technical Cooperation in the Field of Human Rights in Timor-Leste,* Report of the United Nations High Commissioner for Human Rights, E/CN.4/2005/115 (March 2005), p. 7.

responsibilities of the PNTL and the F-FDTL, subsequent developments have made this division much less clear. Although international actors have been keen to differentiate the role of the police from that of the military, this idea has not been so compelling for successive East Timorese governments. Rather, the police have become increasingly militarized, the military are increasingly involved in everyday policing, and the two organizations are now regularly deployed together for everyday policing.

Although former Interior Minister Rogerio Lobato was the first to develop heavily armed paramilitary units within the police, the attacks on the president and prime minister in February 2008 marked a significant new direction for how the PNTL and F-FDTL would work together in future. Following the attacks, the government established a joint military–police command that placed the PNTL under the control of the F-FDTL at a time when the PNTL was ostensibly under the control of UNPOL. The Joint Command was established in the first instance to hunt down those involved in the attacks, but after that task had been completed, there was considerable reluctance to wind up the new arrangements. An odd assortment of tasks was found for the group, including resettling IDPs (internally displaced persons), searching for weapons, and controlling martial arts groups, although these activities appeared to have been invented in order to provide justification for the Joint Command after the fact. Extraordinarily, even when the Joint Command had been formally wound up, it continued to operate for many months. The period of the Joint Command was notable for an escalation of human rights abuses by the uniformed forces and a corresponding expansion of impunity for abuses committed by the police and military.

It became apparent that the Joint Command fulfilled a number of functions apart from chasing rebels. The government hoped that collaboration between the two institutions would enable some reconciliation of previous enmities, a point made explicitly by the secretary of state for security. However, of possibly more significance was that the creation of the Joint Command reasserted East Timorese control of the uniformed forces and the accompanying security reform agenda. The Joint Command became valorized by many politicians and even found its way into the new security legislation as a point of nationalistic pride.

THE EMERGENCE OF REGULATORY RITUALISM

In examining the police reconstruction and security-sector review process, it is apparent that issues of relationship and capacity and contests over sovereignty have affected the processes of police reconstruction. The process has also been gripped by a peculiar torpor. In this section of the chapter, it is suggested that the paralysis that has gripped the process can be understood in terms of "regulatory ritualism." This ritualism serves to obscure a vast gulf between the parties. The United Nations has a stated commitment to importing a Weberian model of state security, although it has a manifest incapacity to carry out such a venture even if the Timor-Leste leadership were a willing partner. Timor-Leste's leadership is committed to the personalized exercise of power and is suspicious of models of impartial security forces. As a result of this impasse, both sides have merely pretended to carry out police and broader security-sector reform.

The phenomenon of pretending to do something rather than actually doing it has been referred to as *regulatory ritualism*. This concept was initially developed by John

Braithwaite, Toni Makkai, and Valerie Braithwaite in relation to nursing home regulation.[48] In developing their analysis of regulatory ritualism, the authors use Robert Merton's typology of individual adaptation to a normative order—which may include conformity, innovation, ritualism, retreatism, and rebellion.[49] Rather than carrying out a process of security-sector review/reform and police reconstruction, both the Timor-Leste government and the United Nations have been engaged in a mutually reinforcing process of regulatory ritualism. It is not only in Timor-Leste that postconflict governments say what they think donors want to hear. They do this in order to be accorded the status of a "functioning" rather than a "failed" state, which in turn ensures that the state in question will receive continued diplomatic and financial support. Alice Hills has noted, in relation to Rwanda, that

> The regime consistently used the language donors wanted to hear ... and provid[ed] training courses on subjects such as stress management, trauma counselling, and gender-based violence, while tolerating extrajudicial killings by government soldiers, the deaths of thousands of unarmed civilians.[50]

Evidence of this form of regulatory ritualism in relation to police reconstruction and SSR in Timor-Leste is found in the way the United Nations has ignored an increasing failure to distinguish between the role of the police and that of the military, in the decision to hand back responsibility from the United Nations to an unreconstituted PNTL, and in the failure to produce a meaningful review of the security sector for more than five years—despite the allocation of more than one million and possibly as much as four million dollars to support the process.[51]

The alternating use of ritualism and rebellion by the Timor-Leste government, and ritualism and retreatism by the United Nations, has served to obscure the ambivalence of all parties regarding a security reform agenda in Timor-Leste. The government has gone through the ritualism of publicly expressing support for the SSR process and setting up various security-related bodies. It has also participated, albeit tepidly, in the evaluation of the PNTL as part of the reconstruction process. The ritualism of the United Nations follows the same path.

Where the organizations diverge is in the "rebellion" or hostility toward the UN presence and role that is intermittently displayed by Timor-Leste figures such as the prime minister, the secretary of state for security, the secretary of state for defense, and the former and current commander-general of the PNTL. This hostility will sometimes manifest in decisions taken, and decisions thwarted by, the Timor-Leste government. It also manifests in the steady stream of negative statements about foreign forces, including UNPOL and the International Stabilisation Force.

---

[48] J. Braithwaite, T. Makkai, and V. Braithwaite, *Regulating Aged Care: Ritualism and the New Pyramid* (Cheltenham: Edward Elgar Publishing, 2007).

[49] Robert King Merton, *Social Theory and Social Structure* (New York, NY: Free Press, 1968).

[50] Alice Hills, *Policing Post-Conflict Cities* (London and New York, NY: Zed Books, 2009), p. 145.

[51] República Democrática de Timor-Leste, UNMIT, and UNDP, "Project Document: Security Sector Review in Timor-Leste" (Dili: June 2008). This figure should, however, be viewed in the context of the larger expenditure on UNMIT, with one of its central mandated activities being the security sector review.

For the United Nations, it can be argued that, in addition to engaging in the ritual of merely appearing to be carrying out a support role to the security-sector review and police reconstruction, UN agents are also engaging in retreatism. The United Nations' frequent invocation of "local ownership" allows it to avoid responsibility for failing to advance outcomes and allows UN personnel to respond passively when the Timor-Leste government behaves in ways contrary to the mandates of the mission and the ideals of the United Nations. This retreatism was manifest when the United Nations failed to insist on seeing through the disciplinary and legal processes that should be visited on errant PNTL—theoretically under UN control—or when UN staff members defer to local ownership in expressing approval for the establishment and conduct of the Joint Command, although its establishment contravened the terms of the SA. UN retreatism was also evident in the reluctance of the UNMIT mission to speak out in protest when Timor-Leste's authorities released indicted war criminal Martenus Bere in August 2009. His extrajudicial release violated international law and undermined the rule of law and the constitution of Timor-Leste, all things that should be at the forefront of UNMIT's agenda.

CONCLUSION

In this chapter, I have described how, rather than cooperating in a reform process, both the Timor-Leste government and the United Nations have carried out a process of mutually reinforcing ritualism designed to obscure a lack of engagement with, or capacity to carry out, police reform and reform of the security sector. I describe how three of Merton's identified responses to a normative order—ritualism, rebellion, and retreatism—are used in particular combination by actors in Timor-Leste's police reform. Although the agendas of the government and the United Nations differed they had congruent interests in the enactment of a police reform ritual, sustained by believable fictions.

Timor-Leste's authorities are mostly keen for international forces to leave, as evidenced by the rebellious stances they have adopted and criticisms they have leveled in reaction to an international presence. Their resistance was tempered, however, by the fact that Timor-Leste needs continued access to the material resources that accompany international intervention and that its leaders wish their nation to be considered a successful rather than failed state. Timorese leaders have exhibited great ambivalence toward the notion of impartial and accountable state institutions, evidenced by the ongoing personalized exercise of power in contravention of Timor-Leste's constitution and laws. The United Nations was mindful of the need to address its own shortcomings in building the PNTL the first time and was, consequently, highly focused on producing a police-reform success story. By using the rhetoric of local ownership and engaging in retreatism, the United Nations sought to absolve itself of failure to reform the PNTL.

The consequences of such an enactment of regulatory ritualism are serious. All poorly executed reform attempts leave legacies of suspicion and disengagement that are difficult to undo. The ritualism has served to institutionalize fragility further in an already weak sector. Meanwhile, extensive resources that could have been used in more creative ways to improve public safety and security have been misallocated.

INFORMAL SECURITY GROUPS AND SOCIAL MOVEMENTS

James Scambary

INTRODUCTION

In the years since the intense conflict of 2006–07, there has been a widespread hope that the death of Alfredo Reinado,[1] the demobilization of the Petitioners, and a change in government would bring an end to an almost Wild West era of violence and vigilantism in Timor-Leste. That hope is now looking increasingly fragile. In May 2010, an unidentified armed group exchanged fire with a unit of the national police in the mountainous western district of Ermera. After a comparative lull in the eighteen months following the joint attacks on the president and the prime minister in February 2008, there was also a marked rise in informal security-group-related violence nationally, particularly among martial arts groups, peaking in the period just before Christmas 2011. While such levels of conflict could in no way be compared with the intensity of 2006 and 2007, this renewed violence serves to demonstrate the troubling persistence of informal-security-group conflict in Timor-Leste today.

Informal security groups have long been part of Timor's cultural and political landscape, dating back to the Portuguese era. There are more than three hundred of these groups in contemporary Timor-Leste, which include rural-based millenarian groups, protest movements and veterans groups; mass-scale, national martial arts groups; political-front groups; and street-corner gangs. Predominantly male, these groups span a wide range of ages and often transcend ethnolinguistic boundaries. Their hybrid nature and often overlapping memberships with other groups makes categorization both difficult and contentious.[2]

Most of these groups were formed under the Indonesian occupation and it would be expected that with independence these groups would have largely

---

[1] Major Alfredo Reinado deserted the F-FDTL in May, 2006 to lead a paramilitary group comprising former police, soldiers and civilians opposed to the FRETILIN government. Although the precise circumstances of Reinado's death are still unclear, he was killed during an attack in February 2008 while at the residence of the then-president, Jose Ramos Horta.

[2] James Scambary, "Groups, Gangs, and Armed Violence in East Timor," Issue Brief No. 2, Geneva Small Arms Survey, April 2009, available at www.timor-leste-violence. org/pdfs/Timor-Leste-Violence-IB2-ENGLISH.pdf, accessed June 6, 2012.

disbanded. Unfortunately, past experience in other post-conflict states, like South Africa, Guatemala, and Angola, has proved that this is rarely the case. In Timor-Leste, a series of political and social upheavals in the post-independence period has served to reopen old wounds (or created new ones) and to ensure that these groups have both reemerged and remobilized.

The diversity and endurance of these groups in contemporary Timor-Leste also reflects the challenges faced by wider East Timorese society in adapting to a number of rapid transitions from war to peace, dictatorship to parliamentary democracy, and perhaps tradition to modernity, among many other changes. These transitions are reflected in the transformation of some of these groups, as they have changed their structure, objectives, and tactics to suit a changing political and social landscape.

These groups have often been reductively portrayed as products of poverty, social disintegration, or a weak state, but they are much more complex than that. Each has its own unique provenance, and each plays an integral role within East Timorese society, history, and politics. Renewed activism by these groups, or intensified conflict among them, has always occurred at critical junctures in East Timor's post-independence history. It is therefore vital to understand the nature and origins of these groups, as they can serve as important barometers of popular discontent and social tensions. Focusing on the nationally based and overtly politicized informal-security groups, this chapter will examine the origin and nature of these groups, their impact on the independence-era political landscape, and their interactions with contemporary political parties in Timor-Leste.

THE VETERANS GROUPS

The first of the post-independence upheavals was the demobilization of the old resistance army, the Armed Forces for the National Liberation of East Timor (FALINTIL), and the creation of the new national army (F-FDTL) and the national police force (PNTL). On February 1, 2001, FALINTIL was officially disbanded and the F-FDTL was born. About 650 FALINTIL members were selected to constitute the first battalion of the F-FDTL, while the remaining 1,300 were demobilized under the FALINTIL Reinsertion Assistance Programme (FRAP).[3]

Inevitably, there were many genuine applicants to this program who missed out and who felt that the process was neither fair nor transparent. By its own admission, FRAP did not adequately distinguish between actual FALINTIL veterans, numbering around thirteen hundred—from FALINTIL/OPS (operations), FALINTIL FBA (Forcas Bases De Apoio or support)—and clandestine resistance operatives numbering around eighteen thousand.[4] There were many who served bravely in the clandestine resistance and saw their schooling and family life destroyed, and who hoped for some reward or recognition for their sacrifice through employment in the new national army. In addition to this perceived affront, in a devastated, war-torn economy, secure state-sector employment was a highly contested resource.

---

[3] Edward Rees, "Under Pressure FALINTIL—Forças De Defesa De Timor Leste: Three Decades of Defence Force Development in Timor Leste, 1975–2004" (Geneva Centre for the Democratic Control of Armed Forces [DCAF] Working Paper, No. 139, Geneva, 2004).

[4] World Bank, "FALINTIL Re-Insertion Assistance Program Evaluation" (Dili, 2002), internal document.

Many of those who were not selected for F-FDTL then turned their attention to being recruited into the new police force, only to be rebuffed again. Frustration turned to anger with the revelation that around three hundred former police under the Indonesian regime had secured posts, and the stage was set for confrontation, which was not long in coming. In response, small autonomous groups of veterans, sometimes referred to as *"isolados,"* led by former guerrilla leaders, began to appear in remote areas of the rural districts, confronting and sometimes attacking the police. Many of these groups were loosely connected under the umbrella of the Association of Ex-Combatants 1975 (AC75), under the leadership of Rogerio Lobato (later to become FRETILIN Minister for the Interior).[5]

CPD-RDTL

In addition to the veterans' groups, there were also a number of larger, more organized groups, formed during the resistance period, that mobilized this disaffection into substantial national movements. The most militant, and arguably the largest of these groups, was the Council for the Defence of the Democratic Republic of Timor-Leste (CPD-RDTL). Like many of the groups to emerge in this turbulent period, the CPD-RDTL had a long history. The CPD-RDTL claims their group was founded back in 1974 at the birth of the Asosiasaun Social Democratica Timorense (ASDT)[6]. Others claim it was more recent, around the time of the May 5, 1999, accord between Indonesia and Portugal to hold a referendum in East Timor.[7] The group's stronghold is the Viqueque area (the natal region of two of its founders, Cristiano Da Costa and Olo-Gari Asswain), and parts of the neighboring Baucau district, but members of the group can be found throughout the country, especially in the border regions of Bobonaro and Cova Lima districts in the west. The CPD-RDTL general coordinator, Antonio Da Costa (aka Ai Tahan Matak),[8] claims that the group has about fifty-two branches nationally, is represented in all thirteen districts, and has around five hundred members.[9]

The CPD-RDTL's main platform is that the original declaration of independence of November 28, 1975, and the original Constitution be reinstated. Given that its members feel that the original independence declaration still stands, they also claim that UNTAET's mandate to implement independence was illegitimate, as Timor was already independent. They also claim that the CPD-RDTL is the only true umbrella body for all the different parties and resistance groups, not FRETILIN or the CNRT. They maintain that FRETILIN itself is merely a party and that the CPD-RDTL is the real FRETILIN movement. They consistently use the national flag and other FRETILIN emblems as their own, drawing denunciation from FRETILIN leaders and harassment from FRETILIN supporters.[10]

---

[5] Dionysio Babo Soares, "Branching from the Trunk: East Timorese Perceptions of Nationalism in Transition" (PhD dissertation, Australian National University, Canberra, 2003), p. 295.

[6] Interview with CPD-RDTL Coordinator Antonio Da Costa, Ai Tahan Matak, Dili, November 16, 2006.

[7] Babo Soares, "Branching from the Trunk," p. 175.

[8] Referred to hereinafter as Ai Tahan Matak to avoid confusion with Cristiano Da Costa.

[9] Interview with Ai Tahan Matak.

[10] Babo Soares, "Branching from the Trunk," p. 167.

Although CPD-RDTL may officially have been founded around the time of the May 5 accord, it has its historical roots in what is often referred to as the "Hudi Laran tragedy." In May 1977, FRETILIN changed from a nationalist movement into a left-wing movement, the Marxist-Leninist Front (MLF), resulting in acrimonious divisions within FRETILIN. When, at a meeting of the FRETILIN Central Committee (CCF) in Hudi Laran, Manatuto District, in 1984, the MLF changed its name to the Conselho Revolucionario da Resistência Nacional (CRRN), a new division appeared. One faction in favor of the change, which included Xanana Gusmão, opposed another led by Reinaldo Freitas Belo (aka Kilik Wae Gae), then FALINTIL chief of staff, and Commander Paulino Gama (aka Mauk Moruk). Belo and Gama were dismissed from their positions at the conference.[11]

Belo and some of his friends then disappeared. Xanana's opponents have accused his faction of having killed them, although it is equally possible they were killed by Indonesian forces. Gama, who became CPD-RDTL vice president, escaped to the Netherlands and Olo-Gari Asswain, CPD-RDTL leader and a member of the opposing faction, was later captured by the Indonesians. While circumstances of the actual event remain obscure, this incident has certainly bred a deep antipathy among the CPD-RDTL to the FRETILIN leadership and Xanana.[12]

The CPD-RDTL's propensity for violence is probably exaggerated. During the period 2000–01, serious clashes erupted among CPD-RDTL and FRETILIN supporters when the CPD-RDTL tried to raise the flag in a number of districts, but such violence has generally occurred only on a sporadic and limited basis since 2001. Nonetheless, the CPD-RDTL effectively marshaled the anger of disaffected ex-guerrillas over their exclusion from the new defense forces, and their mass public rallies drew thousands of supporters. This group had such a following that, for at least three years, CPD-RDTL celebrations of national holidays were better attended than government celebrations. A CPD-RDTL–organized independence rally on November 28, 2002, for example, attracted three thousand supporters, humiliating the prime minister at the official ceremony, which only about three hundred people attended.[13]

Press reports and public statements by then Interior Minister Rogerio Lobato invariably blamed the CPD-RDTL for incidents that were later proved to be the work of other groups. Having earlier supported the CPD-RDTL and other such groups, the relationship soured once he became minister; there is a widespread belief that the rift arose from a conflict over shares of illegal logging proceeds, in which Lobato was widely believed to be heavily involved. One such incident was the Molotov cocktail attack on a Baucau police station on November 12, 2005. Initially blamed on the CPD-RDTL, members of a martial arts group were later found to be the perpetrators.[14] The coordinator of CPD-RDTL, Ai Tahan Matak has been a victim of a number of attacks, including one in Venilale on December 7, 2000, in which CPD-RDTL members were attacked by FRETILIN supporters. Ai Tahan Matak was stabbed in the melee and spent several weeks in a hospital.[15] CPD-RDTL members

---

[11] Ibid., p. 183.

[12] Ibid., p. 186.

[13] Dennis Shoesmith, "Timor-Leste: Divided Leadership in a Semi-Presidential System," *Asian Survey* XLIII,2 (March/April, 2003): 245.

[14] *Timor Sun*, "Baucau Case: Lobato Condemnation of New Group," November 14–20, 2005.

[15] Babo Soares, "Branching from the Trunk," p. 195.

were also attacked in Vemasse on June 21, 2002, by a group paradoxically named Youth Against Violence.[16] Ai Tahan Matak has consistently alleged arbitrary police violence toward his group in the Viqueque district, a claim backed up by other sources.[17] The Dili riots of December 4, 2002, have sometimes been blamed on CPD-RDTL, following the group's earlier Independence Day rally on November 28.[18] The group Colimau 2000 and others have made highly credible claims that the CPD-RDTL has attempted to force people to join or donate to its group.

Currently, the CPD-RDTL hardly seems to constitute a threat. Largely driven underground by intimidation and harassment, it has also been overtaken by events. It has been thirteen years since the referendum, and UNTAET has finished its mandate; most of the trappings of the original independence declaration have been assumed, including the celebration of November 28 as Independence Day. Once CPD-RDTL could attract thousands to parades and demonstrations. By comparison, its demonstrations in Dili in the 2010 to 2012 period rarely attracted more than about a hundred people at most. The reduction in their militancy can partly be attributed to one of the group's founders and a driving force, Cristiano Da Costa, joining UNDERTIM (Unidade Nacional Democrática da Resistência Timorense, National Democratic Unity of Timorese Resistance National Democratic Unity of Timorese Resistance), the new party set up by Cornelio Gama (aka L-7), which is part of the AMP coalition government. Ai Tahan Matak claims Da Costa still supports CPD-RDTL's ideals, but his absence has undoubtedly curbed the CPD-RDTL's militancy.

While being largely dormant during the 2006–08 period, the CPD-RDTL reappeared in 2009 with a number of small public demonstrations in Dili and small bands of its members erecting road blocks in Bobonaro district. According to one source, a group of CPD-RDTL members still occupy a former FALINTIL encampment in a remote area of Bobonaro.[19] In the first half of 2010, a joint police and military operation was carried out against the CPD-RDTL in the western border region, where members have been accused of being ninjas and responsible for two murders, although this was never proved.[20] This operation bears a remarkable resemblance to persecution of the group under the Lobato regime, when they were inevitably blamed for any social unrest and harassed and hunted down by police.

Still, the CPD-RDTL continues to cleave to the same issues, especially that it is the true FRETILIN and resistance umbrella body and that Timor is not yet ready for a multiparty electoral system. Ai Tahan Matak believes that the party system should in fact be closed down until Timor is ready—that Timor should first develop its agriculture system and all its institutions—and that an interim government of national unity composed of eminent people including veterans, academics, and

---

[16] "Antonio Ai Tahan Matak: Youth Against Violence Threaten CPD-RDTL Members," *Suara Timor Lorosae,* June 21, 2002.

[17] "Justice Demanded in Viqueque Case," *Timor Sun*, November 21–27, 2005).

[18] Shoesmith, "Divided Leadership," p. 251.

[19] Interview with RTTL District Coordinator, Dili, June 7, 2009.

[20] During the Indonesian occupation, ninjas were the black-clad masked intruders, many of them drawn from the criminal underworld, hired by the Indonesian military to harass and kill independence supporters. Nowadays, they are feared criminal gangs with reputed magical powers that help them evade detection or capture.

political leaders (in which he includes Xanana, Fransisco Amaral, and even Mario Carascalao) should be formed.[21]

Ai Tahan Matak also believes that the semi-presidential-style system adopted by Timor has contributed to the 2006 crisis through indecision and conflict between the president and the prime minister, which is not an isolated viewpoint.[22] Dennis Shoesmith, for example, argues that this system has institutionalized the friction between Xanana and Alkatiri.[23] Ai Tahan Matak says he would prefer to see a system by which the president has executive power. Despite this difference, he claims that the CPD-RDTL has warm relations with Xanana, Alkatiri, and the F-FDTL, and that although he rejects elections as premature and wants to see a reunification first, he says he still respects the institution of government.[24]

Sagrada Familia

Another group to reemerge as a consequence of dissatisfaction over the F-FDTL recruitment process was Sagrada Familia. Like the CPD-RDTL, Sagrada Familia has been portrayed as a dangerous sect-like anti-government group. Like the CPD-RDTL, Sagrada Familia had its genesis in the Hudi Laran incident. Paulino Gama (aka Mauk Moruk) is the brother of Sagrada Familia's Cornelio Gama (more popularly known as L7, or Elle Sete). A junior FALINTIL commander at the time, Elle Sete was briefly ousted from FALINTIL following Mauk Moruk's fall from favor with the FALINTIL leadership. Despite being later reintegrated into FALINTIL, Elle Sete consistently clashed with FALINTIL High Command, finally breaking away in 1985 to form an independent armed movement in the hinterland of Baucau, which became known as Sagrada Familia.[25]

Elle Sete claims to have been given a *"fita mean"* (red ribbon) by the Holy Family, to protect him from danger. All Sagrada Familia members wear this, although some are also said to wear amulets containing a potion that gives them magic powers. Although the group claims to have members all over Timor-Leste, the bulk of its support is in Elle Sete's birthplace of Laga, in the Baucau district.

After the arrival of international peacekeeping forces in September 1999, some 1,000 to 1,300 FALINTIL forces, by agreement with FALINTIL High Command, were confined to a cantonment in Aileu district.[26] Angered by his exclusion from the new national army, and its dominance by Xanana and Taur Matan Ruak loyalists, Elle Sete left the cantonment in February 2001. Like his brother Mauk Moruk in exile, Elle Sete expressed his resentment of the FALINTIL High Command by calling for the investigation into the wartime activities of Brigadier General Taur Matan Ruak, Chief of Staff Colonel Lere Anan Timor, and First Battalion Commander Lieutenant Colonel Falur Rate Laek.[27]

---

[21] Interview with CPD-RDTL coordinator, Antonio Da Costa, Dili, November 16, 2006.

[22] Ibid.

[23] Shoesmith, "Divided Leadership," p. 250.

[24] Interview with Ai Tahan Matak.

[25] Shoesmith, "Divided Leadership," p. 248

[26] Rees, "Under Pressure FALINTIL," p. 45.

[27] Ibid., p. 42.

From his power base in Laga, Baucau, beginning in August 2000, Elle Sete organized a series of mass demonstrations and, like the CPD-RDTL, his group became a focal point for many disaffected veterans. Recognizing the political influence wielded by Sagrada Familia (at least in its power base in Baucau), FRETILIN courted its members in the run-up to the October 2001 general election. A number of younger Sagrada Familia activists were elected to the FRETILIN Central Committee in August 2001, one of whom was appointed national security adviser to the chief minister.[28]

It was, however, the minister of the interior, Rogerio Lobato, who would actually win their allegiance. Lobato was at the time also president of one of the main veterans associations, the Association of Ex-Combatants 1975, and a spokesperson for disaffected veterans.[29] Lobato moved to appoint Cornelio Gama as his department's security adviser in July 2002, in an attempt perhaps to counterbalance Xanana FALINTIL loyalists and at the same time strengthen his own faction within FRETILIN against Alkatiri.[30] It was probably this alliance that prompted charges of Sagrada Familia involvement in the December 4 Dili riots that targeted Alkatiri properties.

Sagrada Familia members then became involved in a series of clashes, most notoriously, an attack on a Baucau police station in November 2002, where Elle Sete himself was sighted. Sagrada Familia members were also involved in a series of Dili street brawls—although these could have been over private matters or part of ongoing east–west tensions. In addition to the security concerns raised by such aggressive behavior, Sagrada Familia was identified as an eastern group, and it has been argued that this helped spark the rise of other geographically based "security groups" in reaction, especially those based around former guerilla leaders in the west.[31]

Little has been heard of Sagrada Familia since 2004. According to most accounts, it was not involved in the 2006–07 violence crisis, at least not as an organization, although many people expressed fear that Sagrada Familia's "Laga boys" would one day be unleashed. However, there were renewed tensions between the veterans and the PNTL after the confiscation of Elle Sete's truck in July 2010, on suspicion of smuggling tires from Indonesia.[32]

This decrease in militancy could be partly attributed to the creation by presidential decree, in response to growing agitation and debate around the veterans issue, of three commissions—the Commission for the Issues of Former Combatants (CAAC) in 2002 and, later, the Commission for the Issues of Veterans of FALINTIL (CAVF) and the Commission on Cadres of the Resistance, both in 2004—and associated nationwide public discussions around the issue.[33] These initiatives, plus a law passed in 2006 to award pensions to veterans, undoubtedly took a lot of the heat out of the ex-combatants question.

Another reason for the decreased militancy is that Sagrada Familia appears to have opted for a more peaceful, political approach. In June 2005, Sagrada Familia set

---

[28] Ibid.

[29] Ibid., p. 47.

[30] Shoesmith, "Divided Leadership," p. 249.

[31] Babo Soares, "Branching from the Trunk," p. 297.

[32] "L-7 Calls on PNTL to Explain Motive of Seizing His Car," *Timor Post*, July 13, 2010.

[33] World Bank, "FALINTIL Re-Insertion Assistance Program Evaluation."

up a political party, UNDERTIM. Among the founders are former guerrilla leaders Samba Sembilan and Renan Selak and, from the CPD-RDTL, Cristiano Da Costa. UNDERTIM could almost be described as a veterans' party, although UNDERTIM spokesperson Andre da Costa Belo argues that UNDERTIM's mission is to represent the districts' needs, which he felt had been ignored by the overcentralization of the FRETILIN government.[34]

Da Costa Belo is keen to dismiss the notion that UNDERTIM was merely Sagrada Familia in another guise, saying Sagrada Familia, although it still exists, is just a resistance movement, implying it is a thing of the past.[35] Despite its historical antipathy to Xanana, however, UNDERTIM is part of the current AMP government coalition, although the relationship has not always been harmonious.

Colimau 2000

While the overall security climate in the period 1999 to early 2006 was relatively stable, there were numerous small security incidents. The arrival of families trickling back from West Timor, for example, proved a common trigger for communal conflict: In many cases, the land of returnees had been assumed by other families, who often justified this as "compensation" for alleged involvement in militia activities or pro-autonomy allegiances.[36] There were also numerous cases of small bands of former militia crossing the border to harass border communities, frequently in reprisal, over just such land disputes.

One such case was the Atsabe incident of January 4, 2003. On that night, armed groups simultaneously attacked Tiarlelo and Laubuno villages in the Atsabe area of Ermera district, leaving seven people dead. The F-FDTL was called in, in a policing role (and in contravention of their constitutional mandate), and apprehended fifty-nine people, including some children, with very little investigation and without warrant, and handed them over to the police. As it turned out, nearly all of the adults arrested were members of Colimau 2000. Twenty-eight out of the thirty-one presented in court were later freed for lack of evidence.[37]

There is considerable evidence that militia were responsible for these killings. One news report even claimed it was a coordinated militia attack planned by rogue members of the Indonesian Army, the TNI (Tentara Nasional Indonesia). This claim is supported by the group's use of automatic weapons and the discovery immediately after the incident of bullet casings from Indonesian-issue SKS rifles.[38] Another source claimed the assailants were wearing TNI uniforms (without insignia). The Atsabe incident was followed by an attack on a bus on February 24, involving a smaller group of armed men, with another group attacking a PKF patrol

---

[34] Interview with Andre da Costa Belo, Dili, November 30, 2006.

[35] Ibid.

[36] Daniel Fitzpatrick, "Mediating Land Conflict in East Timor," in the report *Making Land Work*, vol. 2 (Canberra: Australian National University, USAID, 2008).

[37] Jill Jolliffe, "Threatened Timorese Town Seeks Troops," *Sydney Morning Herald*, February 1, 2003, available at www.smh.com.au/articles/2003/01/31/1043804520387.html, accessed June 11, 2012.

[38] Ibid.

on February 27, 2003. There were numerous (though unofficial) reports of similar incidents in Bobonaro and Cova Lima districts.[39]

Nonetheless, the Atsabe incident became etched in public memory as the work of Colimau 2000, and has made it an object of fear and mystery ever since—a mystique compounded by its reputation for syncretic ritualism. This incident also, however, created a bitter grudge among Colimau 2000 members against both the F-FDTL and FRETILIN. The grudge was to find its outlet in the April 2006 riots, where Colimau 2000 members were prominent in the anti-government demonstrations and riots that ensued. Many of the Petitioners, including their leaders Gastao Salsinha, are said to be Colimau members.[40]

Except for two journal articles, by Andrea Molnar and Douglas Kammen,[41] there is very little historical information on this group beyond their own account. According to Kammen, Colimau 2000 (Colimau is a compound abbreviation of Comando Libertasaun Maubere) had its origins in a religious group called Sagrada do Coração de Jesus (Sacred Heart of Jesus). The group was formed in the mid-1980s by Martinho Vidal, in the Hatu Builico area of Ainaro district.[42] According to anthropologist Mathew Libbis doing field work in the Manufahi area, Colimau is the name of a Bunak village in Bobonaro. In Kammen's account, it was a name given to the clandestine resistance by the Bobonaro District Military Command. The number 2000 is derived from a dream Martinho had that Indonesian occupation would end in the year 2000. According to Kammen's account, while the founding members became inactive, a new generation arose in 2000.[43] This new generation is led by Osorio Mau Lequi, Gabriel Fernandez, and Bruno da Costa Magalhaes, who attained a master's degree in theology in Indonesia.[44]

Colimau 2000's followers have been characterized as poor, illiterate peasants from rural areas and some ex-guerrillas. Colimau has strongest local support in its power base around the Kemak *suco* of Leimea Kraik in Hatolia, in the district of Ermera, Gabriel Fernandez's natal area. It also has branches in the neighboring district of Bobonaro, where Mau Lequi was born, and in Turiscai, Manufahi district, where Magalhaes was born, but maintains a presence throughout all the western districts. Although itself a distinct group, Colimau 2000 also claims to have members throughout the other clandestine groups such as Seven-Seven, Five Five, Bua Malus, and ORSNACO (which claims to be an umbrella organization for these groups).

While Colimau 2000 is still the main organization, since independence it has formed a number of offshoots. In 2003, according to Mau Lequi, after a violent clash with the martial arts group PSHT (Persaudaraan Setia Hati Terate, Faithful Fraternity of the Lotus) in Maliana, Colimau decided it needed to enter the political mainstream, to launch itself as a political movement instead of a clandestine group.[45]

---

[39] Damien Kingsbury, "The Political Economy of Cross-Border Relations: The TNI and East Timor," *South East Asia Research* 11,3 (2003): 284.

[40] Interview with Colimau 2000 leader, Osorio Mau Lequi, Dili, December 1, 2006.

[41] Andrea Molnar, "An Anthropological Study of Atsabe Perceptions of Colimau 2000," *Anthropos* 99 (2004): 365–79; Douglas Kammen, "Fragments of Utopia: Popular Yearnings in East Timor," *Journal of Southeast Asian Studies* 40,2 (June 2009): 385–408.

[42] Kammen, "Fragments of Utopia," p. 400.

[43] Ibid., pp. 400–402.

[44] Interview with Colimau 2000 leader, Osorio Mau Lequi, Dili, December 1, 2006.

[45] Ibid.

It formed the Colimau Communication Forum in 2003 and then registered its party, the Democratic Party of the Republic of Timor (PDRT), in September 2004. Gabriel Fernandez, listed by Colimau as its coordinator for the Ermera and Bobonaro regions, is the PDRT president.[46]

In 2006, Colimau 2000 launched the Movement for National Unity (MUN, Movimento Unidade Nasional-MUN),[47] which Mau Lequi describes as a sort of promotional vehicle for Colimau's principles of justice, unity, democracy, and peaceful change through elections. The main demand of the MUN is that the national flag be changed as, according to the MUN, it should not be the flag of FRETILIN, a political party, but should promote recognition of all political parties involved in the independence movement, the Church, and East Timorese cultural emblems.[48]

Colimau 2000 has also established an NGO, Maromun, the goals of which are to "increase agricultural production through capacity building, to improve water and sanitation and implement a plantation based logging industry."[49] Mau Lequi, who has previously worked for a number of international aid agencies, is the prime author of this initiative.[50]

Colimau 2000 has been variously described as a millenarian movement and an animist cult. One source of this reputation for animism, is the belief of some of its members that fallen independence fighters, in particular slain resistance leader Nicolau Lobato, will be reborn to lead them. One of Colimau's leaders, Bruno Magalhaes, espouses such a view, claiming that in 1982 Xanana lied to Bishop Belo that Nicolau Lobato was dead. According to Magalhaes, Lobato was seen as a communist, so if the United States thought he was dead, it would take their planes back and would support Timor-Leste in the post-independence period. According to Magalhaes, Nicolau Lobato is hiding in a secret mountain city, bigger than Dili, with an international airport, waiting, along with representatives from MI5, the CIA, and Mossad, until the time is right for his reemergence. Magalhaes also claims that people deliberately created the 2006 crisis to "bring back the Australians" so as to create greater political freedom and prosperity.[51]

Another of Magalhaes's claims is that Colimau ruled all Timor until it lost power to the Portuguese in 1512. He claims to still have some of the sacred objects from this time and that they have been moved from one place to another for safety. Now Colimau wants to bring them to Dili, build an *uma adat* (house of culture) to store them, and show people the greatness of the "people of Maubere." Magalhaes maintains that the west of Timor Leste is the center of the world and all the problems of the world can be solved there.[52]

---

[46] "Democratic Party of the Republic of Timor (PDRT) Political Manual," Dili, 2004 (limited printing).

[47] The Movement for National Unity is unrelated to the Movement for Justice and National Unity (MUNJ).

[48] Interview with Osorio Mau Lequi.

[49] "PDRT Political Manual," p. 96.

[50] One Colimau 2000 member, Domingos Gomes, has also written and self-published a cultural and political history of East Timor; see *"Budaya Dan Tradisi: Dale Timor Leste"* (Culture and Traditions of Timor-Leste), limited printing.

[51] Interview with Dr. Magalhaes, conducted together with interviewer Douglas Kammen, Dili, November 2006.

[52] Ibid.

This last belief is a central tenet of Mambai cosmology; the Mambai believe Mt. Tatamailau, in Ainaro, is at the center of the world, and all other countries are founded by descendents of the original *uma lulik* (sacred house) built there.[53] The belief in the dead coming back to life is a common feature of Melanesian millenarian or revitalization movements, as is a belief in restoring lost traditions from an imagined golden era and an attempt to effect the return of perceived former benefactors, in this case, the UNTAET Administration.[54] Certainly, Colimau 2000 would not be the first such movement. As Andrea Molnar points out, there have been three other significant movements in Timor Leste since the end of the nineteenth century taking the form of religious sects, and these, too, were primarily political movements against dominant authority.[55]

Osorio Mau Lequi, however, dismisses the idea that Lobato or any other dead resistance heroes will come back to life. Mau Lequi distinguishes between the old animist Colimau 2000 by referring to it as the "Old Testament Group" and the new Colimau 2000 as the "New Testament Group." He says that the new, "official" Colimau 2000 members wear crucifixes, that they support the Roman Catholic Church, and that they no longer practice their ancestors' syncretic ritual belief systems. They now call for "peace, love, and unity." According to Mau Lequi, FRETILIN's policies take Timor back to its past, to 1975 and disunity, and are thus also "Old Testament."[56] This belief in breaking with past tradition to formulate a new social order is also an aspect of millenarian belief, although this label is too reductive for a movement as diverse as Colimau 2000.

Colimau is often accused by its detractors of links to former militia. Anthropologist Andrea Molnar conducted fieldwork on Colimau in Atsabe, in 2002 and 2003. She remarks that the main composition of Colimau 2000 in Atsabe is former resistance fighters. She believes there are a number of reasons for this identification of Colimau with militia. One reason is that members of criminal or former militia may use Colimau's name when involved in extortion and violence. Another is that Colimau might have hired former militia from time to time to carry out petty extortion, in the same way as the Indonesians did and local politicians sometimes do during elections. She argues that people knew that Colimau 2000 members were innocent of the charges, but nevertheless identified Colimau followers to the army to be rid of Colimau's petty theft and extortion activities. According to Molnar, many other attacks are blamed on Colimau, when, in fact, they are really just family disputes or payback enacted on returning former militia or their families.[57]

Molnar also argues that Colimau is not homogenous, that in Atsabe it is only loosely organized at the local level. According to Molnar, fringe elements attach themselves to Colimau, including criminals and disaffected former guerrillas; and it is mainly these groups that carry out violent acts in Colimau's name.[58] Colimau is

---

[53] Elizabeth Traube, *Cosmology and Social Life; Ritual Exchange among the Mambai of East Timor* (Chicago, IL: University of Chicago Press, 1986).

[54] Roger Keesing, *Cultural Anthropology: A Contemporary Perspective* (New York, NY: Holt, Rhinehart and Wilson, 1981).

[55] Molnar, "Atsabe Perceptions," p. 371.

[56] Interview with Osorio Mau Lequi.

[57] Molnar, "Atsabe Perceptions," p. 374.

[58] Ibid., p. 376.

also said to engage in the issuing of identification cards, forcing people to join and pay a membership fee. While this does not excuse Colimau, it is not the only group to indulge in this behavior, and this was a standard tactic of the major political parties as far back as 1975.[59]

Osorio Mau Lequi himself is described in the 2006 UN Commission of Inquiry (COI) Report as having made inflammatory anti-government and anti-eastern speeches on April 28 that year, implying some responsibility for the ensuing violence.[60] Mau Lequi disputes this, maintaining that he only stated the Petitioners' case alleging discrimination. He further claims that he wanted to be on the list of those recommended by the COI report for investigation or prosecution, so that he could then argue his case in court.[61]

Colimau 2000's involvement in that protest was as part of a larger anti-government movement known as the National Front for Justice and Peace (FNJP), which later became the Movement for Justice and National Unity (MUNJ), led by Vital Dos Santos. Dos Santos became a Democratic Party (PD) member of parliament in the 2007 election. The FNJP split after then Prime Minister Mari Alkatiri stepped down, with one faction pushing for the collapse of the government and the other faction wanting to give the interim prime minister, Ramos-Horta, a chance and awaiting the outcome of democratic elections. Thus, when the FNJP led a pro-Alfredo protest outside the International Forces Detention Centre in Caicoli, which turned violent on July 27, 2006, Colimau 2000 members camped close by in Matadouro remained uninvolved. As a sign of Colimau 2000's disaffection with that movement and the involvement of opposition parties and, perhaps, of his own mercurial nature, Mau Lequi endorsed FRETILIN's claim to government in the August 2007 elections.[62]

Colimau, however, then became involved in a number of subsequent violent incidents. On November 15, 2006, fighting between Colimau and the martial arts group PSHT killed four people in Estado, in the Atsabe subdistrict of Ermera, resulting in a conflict that rapidly spread from village to village before flowing to Bobonaro and Cova Lima districts, leading to the deaths of seven people.[63]

Molnar argues that tension between Colimau's stronghold of Leimea Kraik and neighboring *sucos* such as Estado has been simmering since Portuguese times, due to historic antagonisms between the former kingdoms of Tiar Lelo and Lemia. According to Molnar, various attacks attributed to Colimau 2000 have been against villages aligned with the former kingdom of Tiar Lelo and its allies, which she claims usurped the kingdom of Lemia and its lands when the Portuguese apportioned parts of Atsabe, Ermera, into the new district of Ainaro. The Lemia region, along with the Boboe region, has traditionally been the heartland of Colimau. Molnar claims that those aligned with the Tiar Lelo ruling house have also received the highest proportion of jobs in the local administration and the local police force, most of the productive farming land, and the biggest coffee plantations. Molnar believes,

---

[59] Truth and Reconciliation Commission (CAVR), *The History of the Conflict,* Part Three, Dili, 2005, p. 29.

[60] UN Commission of Inquiry (COI) for Timor-Leste, 2006, Geneva, p. 23.

[61] Interview with Osorio Mau Lequi.

[62] *Jornal Nacional Diário*, Dili, June 6, 2010.

[63] "Kolimau 2000 Group Attacks Martial Arts Group," *Suara Timor Lorosa'e,* from UNMIT Media Monitoring Service, November 17, 2006.

therefore, that the Atsabe conflict is to some degree a power struggle for authority and economic advantage.[64]

It seems plausible that this conflict has been replicated in contemporary divisions in Dili. One resident of Bebonuk, a site of constant tensions and intense fighting in 2007 between Seven-Seven[65] and PSHT, claims that conflict between the two groups started when his own father was killed in an ambush by PSHT in Lemia Kraik, in November 2006, then spread to Dili. According to that resident, his family belonged to the vanquished family and the opposing family still enjoyed superior social standing and privileges.[66]

Whether this historical tension has simply been reproduced in a contemporary division between Colimau 2000 and PSHT warrants further study. A number of sources have suggested that the conflict between these two groups that began in Estado village was actually a land dispute between two extended families over a coffee plantation. There is certainly substantial evidence to suggest that purely local communal disputes, sometimes over a century old, often assume the form of a political conflict when rival communities appropriate the names of rival political parties or martial arts groups to further their cause, or as security against attack. For example, as Molnar points out, the most feared Atsabe militia leaders came from villages and houses that had historically challenged the authority of the Atsabe king or had some grievance with the ruling families. This suggests that in some cases residual communal antipathies or class antagonism are as much, or more, a motivation in militia violence than any strongly held political belief.[67]

According to press reports, however, in an incident in Maubisse on November 20, 2006, Colimau 2000 members actually fought each other, which resulted in one death and a number of injuries.[68] Unconfirmed news reports attributed the clash to Colimau 2000 trying to get residents to join its group. One source claimed that this was due to antagonism between Julio Metamalik, a Colimau founding member, and the faction led by Mau Lequi.[69] Mau Lequi himself claims that this region is not under the control of his central organization but, rather, under a faction of Colimau 2000. Mau Lequi contends that there is another faction led by Ameu van Damme in Ermera that he can't control, and that these groups, including small splinter groups in Atabae, Bobonaro, Same, and Ainaro, are predominantly anti-government, whereas the "official" Colimau 2000 is committed to stability and peaceful change through the electoral process.[70]

---

[64] Molnar, "Atsabe Perceptions," p. 373.

[65] Seven-Seven is one of a number of former clandestine groups; the other main ones are Five-Five, Twelve-Twelve, and Bua Malus. These groups' members are distinguished by a series of scars on their arms corresponding to the number of the group. The scars are caused by a potion they insert under their skin that members believe will give them magical powers. Seven-Seven is the only group still active, although the other networks may still be reactivated sometimes, as they were in 2006 violence and anti-government protests.

[66] Interview with Bebonuk resident, Dili, December 3, 2008.

[67] Molnar, "Atsabe Perceptions," p. 373.

[68] "One Killed, Two Injured in Fresh E Timor Violence," *Agence France Presse*, November 22, 2006.

[69] Interview with UN Political Affairs, January 21, 2008. Individuals requested anonymity.

[70] Interview with Osorio Mau Lequi.

Another group that incorporates elements of all these groups and associated disaffected clandestine groups is ORSNACO (Organisasaun Resistencia Social Nacional Cooperativa). This group, formerly called the Former Combatants of the Orsnaco Base (ACBO), was a movement of former FALINTIL combatants and their families, originally said to have about a thousand members led by former guerrilla leader Marcos Da Costa (aka Ruin Falur). After demobilization of FALINTIL in 2000, the group established itself as an agricultural cooperative in the village of Orsnaco, in the Turiscai subdistrict of Manufahi.[71]

ORSNACO members say they used the name of the village, Orsnaco, as an acronym for the organization. This group also claims to include all the clandestine groups such as Fitar Bua Malus, Five-Five, Seven-Seven, Twelve-Twelve, and others. Marcos Da Costa is the local leader, but a man called Ananias da Calma (also known as Sanamear), one of the leaders of the Seven-Seven group, appears to be the leader of the clandestine groups. Like other veterans' groups, ORSNACO members were angry with the FRETILIN-led First Constitutional Government, especially former president, Xanana Gusmão, for not awarding veterans benefits for former military service, and felt that the government did not look after them. When Gusmão went to visit ORSNACO for the inauguration of its community hall in September 2003, it was feared that he would be attacked and even killed, but the visit proceeded without incident.[72]

Although a USAID Conflict Assessment listed this group as a potential threat to national security,[73] little has been heard of this group since 2003 (although there are occasional rumors that the ORSNACO base still remains on its original site). Given that the base is at least three-days walk from the nearest road, the rumors are hard to verify. Most of the members seem to have either left or joined other groups such as Colimau 2000. Nonetheless, this mountainous region, in the west of the country—and also a stronghold for Alfredo and his followers and a number of other key leaders in the 2006 violence—has been a hotbed of rebellion and millenarian and of syncretic belief systems since Portuguese times, and is likely to produce similar groups in the future. The appearance of a new group in Ermera is testament to the volatility of this region and its tradition of rebellion.

A host of new organizations have appeared since 2009, in both the city and rural areas, such as the Asociação dos Combatentes no Veteranos da Luta de Libertação Nacional (Association of Veterans and Combatants of the National Liberation Struggle), claiming to represent veterans and demanding benefits of some kind. Some have also been accused of extorting membership fees from local populations, much as the groups described above once did. Whether these groups will, in time, become more militant and violent will depend on the government's skills in negotiating such demands and effectiveness of the national security forces.

---

[71] Babo Soares, "Branching from the Trunk," p. 308.

[72] Ibid.

[73] USAID, "Timor-Leste Conflict Vulnerability Assessment," MSI Assessment Team, produced for USAID/East Timor and USAID Office of Conflict, 2004.

MARTIAL ARTS GROUPS

While veterans' groups have largely faded from view, violence among opposing martial arts groups (MAGs) has continued to present substantial security challenges in Timor-Leste. While periodic violence has occurred between almost all informal security groups, conflicts among MAGS appear to be the most prevalent. Based on data from the Ministry of Interior, prior to the 2006 violence, between the period 2002–04, registered cases of violence increased from seven to thirty-seven, spreading from four (out of thirteen) districts in 2002 to eleven districts in 2004.[74] Most districts in East Timor continue to suffer from sporadic violence to some degree, particularly Dili.

The violence continues to be prevalent in five districts: the three western highlands districts of Bobonaro, Ermera, and Ainaro and the eastern districts of Baucau and Viqueque. The figures give no indication of the seriousness of the clashes. A riot among martial arts groups in March 2001, for example, almost entirely destroyed two villages in Viqueque,[75] and in August 2004, fifty houses were burned down in Ainaro district.[76] On November 14, 2006, in Ermera district, local conflict between PSHT and Colimau 2000 claimed the lives of seven people and destroyed up to one hundred houses.[77] This conflict then rapidly spread from village to village in Ermera district, to Bobonaro and Suai districts, and then to Dili, where it sparked a larger conflict that was to last for over a year.

The prime minister's office negotiated a peace agreement among the warring groups that lasted almost until late November 2006,[78] at which time renewed conflict flared between the largest MAG, PSHT, and the largest of the clandestine groups, Seven-Seven. This conflict was to rage for most of 2007. Then, after a lull lasting some eighteen months, MAG conflict reemerged in both the capital, Dili, and in outlying rural districts. Most recently, MAG violence in 2011 claimed the lives of about a dozen people and the destruction of over one hundred houses, leading to an official government ban on MAG training in December that year. As the violence of 2006–07 showed, MAG conflict always has the capacity to flare into a wider conflagration.

MAGs in Timor-Leste have a mixed provenance. They are certainly not a new phenomenon, or a product of youth alienation or unemployment as they are often portrayed. Martial arts practices could have been originally inherited from China, which has long had its own strong MAG culture, via contact with Chinese traders or Malay traders influenced by Chinese martial arts traditions. Some of the names of contemporary East Timorese MAGs bear strong similarity to the names of Chinese martial arts groups or sects, such as the sixteenth-century White Lotus sect.[79] There

---

[74] Lene Ostergaard, "Timor-Leste Youth Social Analysis Mapping and Youth Institutional Assessment" (Dili: World Bank, 2005).

[75] "East Timor: Clashing Youths Burn 30 Houses, Cars Near Viqueque Dili," *LUSA,* March 12, 2001.

[76] "One Dead, Seven Missing in E. Timor after Gangs Clash," *Associated Press,* August 16, 2004.

[77] "Kolimau 2000 Group Attacks Martial Arts Group," UNMIT Daily Security Briefing, November 17, 2006.

[78] "Martial Arts Leaders Pledge to End Gang Violence," TL Government Media Release, November 25, 2006, available at www.etan.org/et2006/november/25/25mrtial.htm, accessed June 11, 2012.

[79] Daniel Overmyer, "Alternatives: Popular Religious Sects in Chinese Society," *Modern China* 7,2 (1981): 153–90.

is, however, little evidence to suggest that there were any organized groups or competitions until the Indonesian occupation, during which time the establishment of such groups became a feature of the Indonesian military's counter-insurgency strategy.

In Indonesia, the practice of martial arts, or *pencak silat*, became increasingly associated with the military and nationalism, especially after the end of the Japanese occupation in 1945.[80] The association of MAGs with the state and the military became most pronounced under the New Order regime of Suharto, whose family as well as the military were strong patrons of the Indonesian MAG national governing the Indonesian Pencak Silat Association.[81]

In East Timor, as in Indonesia, sport—in this instance, martial arts—was implicitly viewed by the New Order regime as a tool of social control.[82] According to one account, the Indonesian military began to recruit and train East Timorese youth into martial arts groups as early as 1975, the year Indonesia invaded East Timor.[83] The strategy, by most accounts, continued throughout the Indonesian occupation, complemented by an associated strategy of organizing youth sporting clubs, much as they had in Indonesia.

The strategy of organizing Timorese youth into martial arts groups for the purposes of indoctrination is undoubtedly the main reason for the sheer size and variety of MAGs currently in existence in Timor-Leste. Another reason for being a member of one of the MAGs associated with the Indonesian military was the prospect of benefiting from patronage networks. Membership in a MAG was a pragmatic step to gain access to scholarships, jobs, and, most importantly, protection from the military and militias.[84]

Although dominated by two major groups, Kmanek Oan Rai Klaran (KORK, Wise Children of the Hinterland) and PSHT, there are some fifteen to twenty martial arts groups. The number of registered members is probably around twenty thousand, with as many as forty-five thousand unregistered members. Although most of the groups were established during the Indonesian period as part of larger Indonesian national or regional organizations, they have since become autonomous, local organizations. Several organizations have members in all thirteen districts, with branches down to the village and hamlet level.[85]

There is considerable demographic variation in martial arts groups. While the bulk of MAG members would certainly be young, unemployed males, membership appears to transcend age, gender, and class boundaries. High-ranking leaders are often highly educated and employed in senior positions in government (some are ministers) and international NGOs, including UN agencies. Group members can also be found throughout civil society organizations, including human rights and conflict-resolution NGOs. Many of their members can be found on rosters for security companies, the police force, and the army, as well.

---

[80] Ian Wilson, "Continuity and Change: The Changing Contours of Organized Violence in Post-New Order Indonesia," *Critical Asian Studies* 38,2 (2006): 204.

[81] Ibid., p. 212.

[82] Ibid., p. 213.

[83] Interview with former clandestine resistance leader, Dili, May 23, 2010.

[84] Interview with senior PNTL member, Dili, January 23, 2008.

[85] Ostergaard, "Timor-Leste Youth Social Analysis Mapping," p. 41.

For young, unemployed men, especially migrants new to a city, martial arts groups provide a welcome source of structure in the absence of family support, protection, sport, and companionship. Many people also say that being a member of a group is part of Timorese male identity, which may explain these groups' broader and continuing popularity. As a consequence, martial arts groups have become an entrenched and ubiquitous feature of the Timorese social and political landscape.

The infiltration of martial arts groups into the security forces is a major concern. Abilio Massoko, for example, was a police commander, as well as a leader, or *warga*, of PSHT. Massoko (aka Abilio Mesquito or Abilio Audian) was arrested for distributing guns during the 2006 crisis and subsequently named in the UN Commission of Inquiry Report as having initiated the attack on F-FDTL Brigadier Taur Matan Ruak's house on May 24, 2006.[86] Police are often accused of siding with one group against another during martial arts clashes and, unsurprisingly, given policemen's access to firearms, a number of shootings in gang fights have been committed by serving police officers who are members of MAGs. In one martial arts clash just before Christmas 2011, which resulted in two fatalities, as many as twenty PNTL members were accused of being involved in the skirmish.[87]

Particular MAGs are popularly perceived as being allied with particular political parties. While alliances do exist, they are organic and informal and rely on traditional clan-based ties or other allegiances between individual MAG leaders and politicians. PSHT, for example, is often linked to the Democratic Party (PD). Jaime Lopes, the leader of PSHT during the 2006–07 period (before his imprisonment), is the blood cousin of the PD leader Fernando Lasama de Araujo. However, there are FRETILIN PSHT members, too, including at least one Dili village chief, but such linkages between FRETILIN and PSHT are unusual.

The most widely known link, however, is that between KORK and FRETILIN. Nuno Soares, appointed as KORK leader after the imprisonment of Naimori in 2005 for arson, hails from Ainaro in the west. Soares was responsible for affiliating KORK with FRETILIN, and although this alliance is much cited as being proof of political-party–gang alliances, this decision to affiliate was highly unpopular with large sections of KORK's membership. In KORK's heartland, Ainaro, for example, FRETILIN received only 10 percent of votes cast in the first round of the 2007 presidential election.[88] After Naimori was released from prison, he promptly expelled Soares from KORK and disaffiliated KORK from FRETILIN.[89]

Like Colimau 2000 and Sagrada Familia, many MAGs, particularly those of Indonesian origin influenced by Javanese mysticism, incorporate ritual as part of their practice. Some members believe these rituals give them magic powers, such as invincibility, invisibility, and healing abilities. There is also a certain element of syncretism in MAG rites. Even PSHT, whose members often scorn other self-proclaimed "indigenous" MAGs, such as KORK, as backward bush-dwellers, believed that the wall at their former headquarters, destroyed during the fighting in

---

[86] UN Commission of Inquiry (COI) for Timor-Leste, p. 49.

[87] "Twenty PNTL Officers May be Sacked over Martial Arts Conflict," *Daily Media Monitoring Service*, December 22, 2011.

[88] "Presidential Election Results a Worrying Portent for East Timor," *Canberra Times*, April 20, 2007.

[89] Declaration by KORK leadership, obtained January 2008.

2007, is imbued with sacred significance. The KORK leader Naimori believes he has invented a secret language and script, passed down to him through a dream.[90]

This appropriation of traditional East Timorese animist belief systems has therefore further enmeshed these groups into East Timorese society. Indeed, in rural areas and some urban areas with a history of communal conflict, MAG membership runs along kinship lines, so conflict becomes a family affair, with whole villages sometimes being members of or allied to a particular MAG, and opposed to a neighboring village allied to another MAG. Sometimes a whole village is affiliated with the same political party as well, so that frequently there are conflicts among PSHT/PD villages and KORK/FRETILIN villages, or other MAG/political party symmetries. The dovetailing of family disputes with MAG disputes and political affiliations has rendered some communal conflicts particularly intractable and has considerably complicated mediation efforts.

CONCLUSION

The range of informal security groups still active in contemporary, post-independence Timor-Leste is potent testament to a multitude of unresolved current and historical issues. However, the complexity and adaptability of these groups, as they have emerged at different points in time, in response to different social and political upheavals, demands a deeper understanding than those represented by reductive portrayals of the groups as "gangs" and as threats to security.

In little over a decade, between 1999 to 2012, a number of these groups changed from resistance movements to protest vehicles and, sometimes, into political parties. For many, such movements are the only way to influence a centralized development and political process they feel they have little participation in or control over. As Sahlins contends, such movements should be considered as patterns of resistance within societies that are confronted with rapid and drastic social change.[91] Rooted in East Timorese cultural traditions and history, rather than being fringe elements alienated from society, they play an integral role within their communities as a means of voicing the demands, aspirations, and identity of community members. In the absence of an effective police force, especially in remote mountain villages, they are often their community's sole source of security.

While some groups may fade with time as they reshape their identity, their leaders grow old, or the issues become redundant, new issues will certainly breed new groups. The recent appearance of a number of new urban and rural-based protest movements is testament to this. The combination of an inefficient justice system with an ineffectual and divided police force means that communities will continue to look to informal security groups for protection, and for "summary justice" or retribution. Their utility to political parties as "rent-a-crowds" during the 2006–07 violence has also further entrenched their popularity and power. Rather than disappearing with the onset of the "modernizing" forces of economic development and democracy, informal security groups are therefore likely to remain a feature of life in Timor-Leste for quite some time to come.

---

[90] Interview with UN Political Affairs former Gang Task Force member, Dili, January 21, 2008.

[91] Marshall Sahlins, "The Economics of Develop-man in the Pacific," in *The Making of Global and Local Modernities in Melanesia*, ed. Joel Robbins and Holly Wardlow (Aldershot: Ashgate, 2005), pp. 23–42.

DEVELOPMENT STRATEGY

Tim Anderson

Development strategies have consequences. They affect socioeconomic relationships, the priorities of government budgets, and views of the future. For those reasons, it is worth reflecting on the general approach a country takes to development.

Since independence, Timor-Leste has formed its own hybrid development strategies, through a National Development Plan (NDP) and the distinct practices of two different governments. These hybrids incorporate mixed ideas from economic liberal, developmental state, and human development traditions. Yet the language and practice of development strategy have not always matched, and both are changing. This chapter identifies the main contemporary approaches to development strategy, then links those to experience in Timor-Leste since independence. It concludes with some observations on the neglected sectors of education, health, and agriculture.

Timor-Leste faced enormous challenges at independence. As well as the violence, infrastructure destruction, and mass dislocation of 1999, the little country was left with environmental degradation, the flight of professional classes, virtually no effective governmental institutions, and a variety of international agencies and experts with their own ideas on development. In this context, administrations had to formulate their own approach to development. This chapter suggests that the strategic differences between the FRETILIN-led (Frente Revolucionária do Timor Leste Independente, Revolutionary Front of Independent East Timor) and AMP (Aliansa Maioria Parlamentar, Parliamentary Majority Alliance) administrations cannot be determined by their policy statements alone but, rather, require a study of their respective practice.

DEVELOPMENT STRATEGIES

Three broad development strategies can be defined: the private-investor-led "market economy" approach, the "developmental state" model; and those approaches that emphasize human development. This section identifies the distinct underpinning ideas and views on sectoral development (education, health, agriculture, infrastructure, the economy), some notable international experiences, and the challenges facing each approach.

The Private "Market Economy" Approach

The private investor led "market economy" approach to development—commonly advocated by Western powers—often expresses a unified economic goal, such as "broad-based growth." It draws on the notion of "comparative advantage,"[1] which encourages specialization and trade, and the "open market" ideas of the nineteenth-century European neoclassical economists,[2] supplemented by mid-twentieth-century ideas on the "macroeconomy" and its management.[3] These "economic liberal" ideas are promoted by the international financial institutions. The World Bank,[4] for example, developed the ideas of "pro poor growth" and "inclusive growth," in response to criticisms that the poor do not benefit and are excluded from growth strategies; but the World Bank's emphasis remains on economic growth.

Broad-based growth arose in recognition of the dangers of extreme specialization, as in the so-called banana republics, which had faithfully followed comparative-advantage strategies but suffered economic crisis when prices for their single cash-crop fell. So the need for some diversification was accepted by economic liberals. However, they continue to emphasize trade, suggesting that specialization in competitive markets indicates enhanced potential economic gains. Nevertheless, the developmental prospects of comparative advantage are limited, as the idea is based on comparative statics and only addresses a short-term opportunity. It does not explain how a country might actually improve its productive capacities.

Economic liberals speak of a minimal economic role for the state and oppose public investment that might crowd out (compete with) private investment.[5] Community or customary land should be registered and commercialized, according to this view. This approach has led to calls for the state to merely create an "enabling environment" of laws, security, and infrastructure to suit the needs and interests of private investors.

The economic liberal view of education, health, and social security is that the state should minimize its commitments and introduce "user pays" and privatized services to encourage consumer participation and market formation. Social services might be offered as a minimal safety net, in recognition of the exclusion of poor people; but open market ideas oppose systems of social guarantees or comprehensive public welfare systems.[6] Increasing commercialization of services

---

[1] David Ricardo, *On the Principles of Political Economy and Taxation* (London: John Murray, 1817).

[2] William Stanley Jevons, *The Theory of Political Economy* (London: MacMillan, 1871); Carl Menger, *Grundsätze der Volkswirtschaftslehre* [Principles of Economics] (Vienna: Wilhelm Braumüller, 1871); Léon Walras, *Éléments d'économie politique pure* [Elements of Pure Economics] (Paris: Corbaz, 1874–1877).

[3] John Maynard Keynes, *The General Theory of Employment, Interest and Money* (London: Palgrave MacMillan, 1936).

[4] World Bank, "What Is Inclusive Growth" (2009), http://siteresources.worldbank.org/INTDEBTDEPT/Resources/468980-1218567884549/WhatIsInclusiveGrowth20081230.pdf, accessed May 24, 2012.

[5] For example, Roger W. Spencer and William P. Yohe, "The 'Crowding Out' of Private Expenditures by Fiscal Policy Actions," *Federal Reserve Bank of St. Louis Review* (October 1970): 12–24.

[6] For example, Charles W. Calomiris, *The Post-Modern Bank Safety Net: Lessons from Developed and Developing Economies* (Washington, DC: AEI Press, American Enterprise Institute, 1997).

leads to employment and economic growth. Free services, on the other hand, are said to create among individuals laziness and a dependent mentality. The behavioral assumption here is that it is good for people to feel some pressure to participate in markets, so that they may value and more effectively use the goods and services that they purchase (relative to those who are handed goods and services for free).

A major problem with this approach is the unaffordability of (or uneven access to) basic services for large sections of the population, particularly children. Reliance on open markets always favors wealthy people and, in developing countries, excludes large sections of the population. Aid programs aim to fill this gap, but bring their own problems, including inflationary bubble economies, dependency, and "aid trauma" through failures in capacity-building and great inequality.[7]

In more recent times, the market economy approach has insisted that the state should assist the most dynamic sections of the economy, in particular, the export sector, as these sectors can contribute much to the growth of the formal economy and, so, stimulate (create spin-off benefits for) other private investors. Successful private investment creates employment, the principal means by which benefits are said to trickle down to wider sections of the community. An important implication is that infrastructure improvements, such as roads and ports, paid for by the government, are prioritized to encourage export enterprises to expand. Also, preferential (e.g., tax free) treatment for private investors, including foreign investors, is a by-product of a market-economy approach.

States that engage in social-infrastructure development, public enterprise, and provision of free services are moving outside the bounds of the economic liberal view of what used to be called sound economic policy, but is now often included in notions of good governance. Such public institution-building may compete with private investment, which is said to be "more efficient."[8]

Despite being a hallmark of powerful economies, open market strategies have never led to the industrial development of any country. Such a model was not used in the industrialization of Europe, North America, or Japan. There have been some economic liberal attempts to prove the contrary,[9] but the evidence is very poor.

Development in Europe was backed by a substantial economic surplus from colonialism and slave-based economies, absorbed into commerce and industry.[10] European, North American, and Japanese capitalist development then grew their human resources and technologies with state sponsorship and financial assistance, public-private collaborations, and little competition.[11] After World War Two, the United States suggested that Japan pursue its "comparative advantage" as a provider of cheap labor in basic industry. The Japanese, building on their strength in human resources—in a war-devastated, resource-poor, and disempowered nation—

---

[7] Neil Middleton and Phil O'Keefe, *Disaster and Development: The Politics of Humanitarian Aid* (London: Pluto Press, in association with ETC [UK], 1998); Tim Anderson, "RAMSI: Intervention, Aid Trauma, and Self Governance," *Journal of Australian Political Economy* 62 (December 2008): 62–92.

[8] World Bank, "Bureaucrats in Business" (New York, NY: Oxford University Press, 1995).

[9] Walt Rostow, *The Stages of Economic Growth: A Non-Communist Manifesto* (Cambridge: Cambridge University Press, 1960).

[10] Eric Williams, *Capitalism and Slavery* (Chapel Hill, NC: University of North Carolina, 1944).

[11] Nancy Ettlinger, "The Roots of Competitive Advantage in California and Japan," *Annals of the Association of American Geographers* 81,3 (September 1991): 391–407.

preferred to upgrade their productive capacities, building a successful industrial economy within a relatively short space of time.[12]

Open market ideas these days suit, and are promoted by, those nations that have already achieved some degree of "market" dominance. But it may also be said that the failure of open market models is what drives the principal alternatives, that is, developmental state and human development (or human-resource-focused) approaches.

The principal challenges for a market economy strategy are how to prevent: a collapse in basic services; the leakages (overseas and in elite consumption) in investment and income generation; and widening inequality and social exclusion. Some formal-sector industries may boom (e.g., natural-resource extraction), but international experience suggests that the benefits of such industries will be poorly distributed. The best evidence of this can be found in resource-rich developing countries, such as Nigeria and Bolivia. Yet inequality does not concern economic liberals; rather, it is seen positively, as a spur for market participation.

The "Developmental State"

East Asian versions of the "developmental state" represent the most prominent and successful examples of developing countries (and in some cases former colonies) upgrading their productive capacities. We can see capitalist and socialist variants, looking at Japan, South Korea, Taiwan, Singapore, Venezuela, and the Peoples' Republic of China. In both the capitalist variant (where private investors dominate) and the socialist variant (where social investment dominates), strong political will is required, so that the state has a degree of autonomy with respect to private investors. A developmental state implies that the state leads the process of development, whether by forming councils to coordinate the production and trade strategies of large, private companies (as in Japan), by developing long-term plans beyond the agenda of existing industries (as in Singapore), or by building strong public enterprises (as in Venezuela). As this requires struggling with large private corporations, it has been said that an authoritarian state is required.[13] Indeed, authoritarianism was prominent in militarized South Korea and civilian-led Singapore. However, developmental states have been described in relatively strong democracies, too, such as contemporary Venezuela, and in small island nations, such as Mauritius.[14]

---

[12] A. Johnson Chalmers, *MITI and the Japanese Miracle* (Stanford, CA: Stanford University Press, 1982).

[13] A. Johnson Chalmers, "Political Institutions and Economic Performance: The Government-Business Relationship in Japan, South Korea, and Japan, in *The Political Economy of the New Asian Industrialism*, ed. F. C. Deyo (Ithaca, NY: Cornell University Press, 1987); and Eun Mee Kim, *Big Business, Strong State: Collusion and Conflict in South Korean Development, 1960–1990* (New York, NY: State University of New York Press, 1997).

[14] Thomas Meisenhelder, "The Developmental State in Mauritius," *Journal of Modern African Studies* 35,2 (June 1997): 279–97.

The World Bank's "East Asian Miracle" report gives some idea of the developmental state's challenge to the open market model.[15] It raised a huge controversy in the United States, amongst economic liberal opponents of state "intervention" in the economy. The report drew attention to the coordination required in industrial development and the key economic role of East Asian states. However, as Joseph Stiglitz reminds us,[16] this report was watered down due to resistance from the United States, and only appeared at all because Japan funded the report.

Institutional ideas help explain the conventional success of the developmental state model, including in the United States. Economist John Kenneth Galbraith saw the key features of North American capitalism as little to do with markets and more to do with the planned sector, where large corporations backed by states administer systems and prices.[17] The idea of comparative advantage was challenged by that of competitive advantage, where it was recognized that local advantages were created and not static.[18] The technical-industrial centers of both Japan and California have been described as developing under long-term influences of joint ventures, a strong human-resource base, linkages with other states, state–corporate coordination, and "complementary strategies of import substitution and export promotion."[19]

In a similar way, the institutional idea of "circular and cumulative causation," with its discussion of the development and decay of institutional linkages,[20] has been used to explain industrial "cluster development" in developing countries. The United Nations Commission on Trade and Development has discussed criteria for regional clusters, including technological development, innovation and trust, cooperation as well as competition, and the learning involved in industrial clusters. The most successful subregional example of this model is the engineering and information-technology cluster in Bangalore, India. This large industrial zone was built on strong central-government investment in colleges and defense industries, as well as on coordination with and among private firms.[21]

Many of the examples of developmental states have been large, strong countries. However, examples also include small island states such as Singapore[22] and Mauritius.[23] In the latter case, the former colony managed to escape dependency on plantation sugar and moved into a diversified, capitalist model, with strong

---

[15] World Bank, *The East Asian Miracle: Economic Growth and Public Policy*, World Bank Policy Research Reports (Washington, DC: World Bank, 1993).

[16] Joseph Stiglitz, *Globalization and Its Discontents* (New York, NY: Norton and Co., 2002).

[17] J. K. Galbraith, *The New Industrial State* (Boston, MA: Houghton Mifflin, 1967).

[18] For example, R. J. Johnston, "Extending the Research Agenda," *Economic Geography* 65 (1989): 338–47; and Michael Porter, *The Competitive Advantage of Nations* (New York, NY: Free Press, 1990).

[19] Ettlinger, "Roots of Competitive Advantage."

[20] Philip Toner, *Main Currents in Cumulative Causation: The Dynamics of Growth and Development* (London: MacMillan, 1999).

[21] UNCTAD, "Promoting and Sustaining SMEs, Clusters, and Networks for Development," Issues Paper, UN Conference on Trade and Development, New York, NY, 1998.

[22] Kevin Grice and David Drakakis-Smith, "The Role of the State in Shaping Development: Two Decades of Growth in Singapore," *Transactions of the Institute of British Geographers* 10,3 (1985): 347–59.

[23] Richard Sandbrook, "Origins of the Developmental State: Interrogating Mauritius," *Canadian Journal of African Studies* 39,3 (2005): 549–81.

development of education and health. The process was said to require a "capable and relatively autonomous state bureaucracy."[24] However, the role of the state in planned institutional development and the various linkages within a developmental state do not of themselves provide the full picture. This process also depends on the substantial development of human resources and, in particular, a firm basis in education and health. Challenges for a developmental state approach include a clear vision, a well-educated population, and political will alongside popular support.

Human Development

Focusing on education and health sits alongside the emphases on other human capabilities in what might now be called a human development approach. To the extent that this can be called a distinct strategy of development, it requires emphases on core capabilities such as education, health, and gender equality and participation. In development this should be seen as strong and sustained efforts to build not just human resources but a healthy, well-educated population. In this approach, education and health are key goals of development, not just the means to create skilled workers.

It is notable that several resource-poor island states have made great advances through building their human resources. Japan, for example, became an industrial power despite being crushed by war, and despite the absence of energy resources. Singapore, a former colony with hardly any physical resources (it even has to import fresh water), is now a high-income country. Likewise Cuba, with few physical resources, has the best health indicators in the developing world and is the major provider of health-aid programs to other developing countries. These three very different countries have one thing in common: They built a distinct future by investing in their own people.

While the human development concept is relatively new, the approach is not. Sweden, for example, led the world in maternal care in the late nineteenth century, through its network of midwives. Though a fairly poor country at that time, its well-organized and well-distributed system of birth assistants gave it better maternal mortality outcomes than other European countries.[25] Sweden's early success in maternal health was not due to economic wealth. Indeed, research commissioned by the World Bank tells us that, across all developing countries, the education of women has a more powerful impact on critical health indicators (adult and child mortality, fertility rates) than does earning a high income.[26] Yet market economy approaches always stress high incomes.

---

[24] Thomas Meisenhelder, "Developmental State in Mauritius."

[25] Wim Van Lerberghe and Vincent De Brouwere, "Of Blind Alleys and Things that Have Worked: History's Lessons on Reducing Maternal Mortality," *Studies in Health Services Organisation and Policy*, no. 17 (Antwerp: ITG Press, 2001), www.jsieurope.org/safem/collect/safem/pdf/s2929e/s2929e.pdf, accessed May 24, 2012.

[26] Jia Wang et al., *Measuring Country Performance on Health: Selected Indicators for 115 Countries* (Washington, DC: World Bank, 1999).

Table 1 Development Strategies			
	Private Market Economy	**Developmental State**	**Human Development**
Ideas, strategies, emphases	Open markets, broad-based growth, comparative advantage	State-led planning, competitive advantage, institution-building	Participation, human capabilities, human resources
Sectoral implications (education, health, infrastructure, economy)	Minimal free services, safety net, export infrastructure, privatization, enabling environment	Coordination of human resources and industry, state investment, capitalist or socialist versions	Strong push in education, health, and equality
International experience	Western model (selectively applied), favored by corporations	East Asia (Japan, South Korea, China, Singapore), Venezuela	Japan, Kerala, Cuba, Venezuela, Singapore
Challenges	Weak strategic plan, excludes the poor	Human resources, political will, and popular support	Coordination, mobilization of human resources

The focus on human capabilities and improved outcomes allows for a wide view of development. For example, it seems likely that customary or community land, in some countries, serves as a powerful basis for food security, employment, and social security. Where land is widely distributed, as in the Melanesian countries (Papua New Guinea, the Solomon Islands, Vanuatu), it serves as a great "hidden" reserve of wealth, nutrition, and potential income. The land also provides the distribution mechanism for those benefits.[27] Market economies, by contrast, will always demand the commercialization of land.[28] This will be followed by land rationalization and greater reliance on cash economies, with all their distribution problems.

A human development emphasis faces challenges of effective coordination and mobilization of its human resources. Nevertheless, the focus remains on building human capacity for the future.

---

[27] J. Fingleton, ed., "Privatising Land in the Pacific: A Defence of Customary Tenures" (Canberra: Australia Institute, 2005), https://www.tai.org.au/index.php?q=node%2F19&pubid=80&act=display, accessed on April 30, 2012; and Tim Anderson, "Land Registration, Land Markets, and Livelihoods in Papua New Guinea," in *In Defence of Melanesian Customary Land*, ed. Tim Anderson and Gary Lee (Sydney: Aid/Watch, 2010), http://aidwatch.org.au/publications/publication-in-defence-of-melanesian-customary-land, accessed April 30, 2012.

[28] For example, S. Gosarevski, H. Hughes, and S. Windybank, "Is Papua New Guinea Viable?" *Pacific Economic Bulletin* 19,1 (2004): 134–48.

STRATEGIES IN TIMOR-LESTE

The post-independence development strategy in Timor-Leste began with a National Development Plan (NDP), launched upon independence in May 2002. Since then we have seen the differing approaches of two main administrations: the FRETILIN-led government of 2001–06, and the AMP coalition of 2007–10. We must have regard to the language of strategy, but we also have to look at practice. Let's start with the NDP.

The National Development Plan, 2002

Timor-Leste's National Development Plan[29] is a complex document and is difficult to characterize because the process of its development required that it contain a variety of influences. It is necessarily a hybrid. In the first instance, the process of developing the NDP added elements of a human development character: inclusiveness and participation. Economic liberal approaches see economic policy as a "technical" matter, best left to the experts. As in any elitist process, programs are formulated "from on high" and delivered. Yet, in the formulation of Timor-Leste's NDP, then chief minister and chair of the planning commission, Mari Alkatiri, pointed to

> the open, participatory and inclusive nature of our planning … we invited representatives of the Church and members of Civil Society, national and international NGOs, the private sector and public interest groups … to help debate and formulate policy options, program priorities and implementation strategies for the National Development Plan.[30]

The president-elect, Xanana Gusmão, agreed:

> The process of preparing the Plan [NDP] gave thousands of East Timorese, from school children to elderly people, the opportunity to think about the kind of future they want for themselves and for future generations.[31]

This level of participation helps include a wide range of voices, adding both relevance and ownership to the development process, thus enhancing human capabilities. The human development emphasis is present, but more muted, in the rest of the document. There is some emphasis, in education and capacity building (skills development), on "reducing imbalances in education" and addressing urban-rural gaps.[32] This emphasis on eliminating inequalities takes the NDP beyond the more limited market economy commitments to publicly funded basic education, usually followed by a push to privatize secondary and technical education.

---

[29] Planning Commission, *East Timor: National Development Plan* (Dili: Planning Commission, May 2002).

[30] Ibid., p. xvii.

[31] Ibid., p. xvi.

[32] Ibid., pp. 4, 9, 31.

There are other hints of a human development emphasis, through the NDP's commitment to ongoing participation in governance—to the "participation of all citizens in economic, social, and political processes and activities" and to promoting "gender equality and the empowerment of women."[33] The plan's commitment to the Millennium Development Goals (MDGs) maintains this same emphasis, as the first few MDGs are based on human development measures. There is an emphasis on institution-building in the NDP, as one might expect of a new nation that requires the basic institutions of a new state, that is, law, policy, and infrastructure. Institution-building in itself would not reflect a developmental state approach unless it was preparing a leading role for the state, especially in investment planning and resource management.

A market economy approach would focus institution-building on creating an enabling environment of law and institutions for private economic activity. Indeed, the NDP does this repeatedly.[34] It thus incorporates some of the market economy approach into its institution-building. However, it goes further than that. Despite the market economy language on institutions, the NDP is heterodox in maintaining a strong role for state planning, state involvement in resource control, and some hints of greater planning in the areas of agricultural development and rural development.[35] These provide hints of a modest developmental state approach.

Despite the fact that the NDP is said to cover eighteen years (2002–20), Mari Alkatiri, in his introduction, suggests that the plan relates mainly to "the next five years."[36] The plan itself refers to an ongoing monitoring and evaluation process that includes "most importantly, improvement in the plan in itself."[37] As such, both participation and state direction are to be maintained.

A market economy, or economic liberal, approach to resource management would leave this to the private sector, with the state simply collecting taxes and license fees. This is indeed the case in Australia, for example, where the state has no equity at all in natural-resource or processing industries. The NDP, by contrast (building on Article 139 of the Constitution, which requires the state to own and fairly manage natural resources), calls for strong state management and, in particular, for "sound administration and sustainable utilization of the oil and gas revenues to benefit present and future generations" and to "curb the temptation to squander the windfall in ostentatious consumption."[38] This contrasts with the strong tendency of market economy approaches to "discount the future value" of assets (e.g., environmental assets) and to emphasize current market transactions.

However, the NDP has other strong economic liberal elements, to some extent, due to outside influences such as the World Bank. This plan was created before independence, at a time when Timor-Leste did not quite have its full sovereign voice, and when development banks and international donors had a stronger say. The language of economic liberal institutions (particularly the World Bank) is apparent, and has been incorporated into this sovereign document. The NDP repeatedly emphasizes the themes of private-sector-led development, with a diminishing

---

[33] Ibid., pp. 20–24.

[34] Ibid., pp. 2, 20, 22, 24, 28, 29.

[35] Ibid., pp. 10, 20, 31.

[36] Ibid., p. xvii.

[37] Ibid., p. 5.

[38] Ibid., pp. 24, 30.

economic role for the state. It is notable, though, that the "private sector" of the NDP is a wide concept, mixing informal farming with private-formal-sector businesses, domestic or foreign.

The NDP suggests that "successful private sector development will be a key driver of economic growth and poverty reduction ... the Government has committed itself to a market-based economy ... [including] an open approach to foreign investment and foreign trade."[39] It calls for "an open market system but with important strategic and regulatory roles for government,"[40] saying that Timor-Leste will develop:

> a market economic system with strategic and regulatory roles for government, including the provision of social safety nets ... [and] a strong role for the private sector in development ... [as well as] an enabling environment ... and [will arrange] for the delivery of essential support services for the private sector to gain confidence and strength ... [and will] provide a growth enabling policy and legal environment ...[41]

There are many emphases on private investor led growth, including an openness to foreign investment.[42] The market-based economy approach is also applied to agricultural development, although here the private sector is said to include informal-sector farmers.[43] An outside reader of the NDP might say that, in terms of economic development strategy, economic liberal influences are strong to dominant, but moderated by some developmental state influences in the areas of planning and natural resource management and by some human development emphases in terms of participation and a more equitable approach to education, women, and rural development. However we must look at practice to better understand national strategy.

FRETILIN-Led Heterodoxy, 2001–06

The practice of the first post-independence government, a coalition led by FRETILIN, built on the NDP, but was, in practice, more heterodox. What follows is not an assessment of that government, but, rather, some illustrations of its distinct themes in the fields of agriculture, fiscal autonomy, and education and health.

With very little money in the first budget and with the task of constructing the institutions of a new state—a parliament, criminal and civil law, a police service, public services, language policy—there was much to address. Prime Minister Alkatiri stressed the need to construct democratic institutions but also to address key human development objectives, such as nutrition, health, and education. Poverty would be reduced by "rapid, integrated, equitable and sustainable economic

---

[39] Ibid., p. 11.

[40] Ibid., p. 6.

[41] Ibid, pp. 22, 28–29.

[42] Ibid., p. 31.

[43] Ibid., p. 24.

growth,"[44] to help meet the people's basic needs. He noted the objective of creating an enabling environment for the private sector, but this included "farmers, fishers, investors, micro-enterprise ... traders and others."[45] The government would maintain a market economy but with "a strategic and regulatory role" for government, which would in particular create "the networks and mean by which to guarantee social security during the most difficult times."[46]

One of the first conflicts with international agencies came over agriculture, before independence, and illustrates the challenges that would be faced by FRETILIN and the NDP. In 2000, a World Bank team that included AusAID officials had rejected proposals by the United Nations Transitional Administration (UNTAET) and East Timorese leaders that aid money be used for agricultural service centers, a public abattoir, and public grain silos. The agencies did not support the move to rehabilitate irrigated rice fields, either. This opposition was evidently ideological, motivated by a prescriptive economic liberalism: "Such public sector involvement [in agricultural services] has not proved successful elsewhere,"[47] and "the government should not own revenue generating enterprises, such as meat slaughterhouses, warehouse facilities, grain storage facilities ... [This] would be costly and would inhibit private entrepreneurship."[48] Given that these proposals were linked to concerns arising from the country's prior food crises, the World Bank's interventions were acts of extraordinary insensitivity, and a denial of self-determination.[49]

After independence, the government proceeded with its planned rehabilitation of rice fields, but without World Bank or Australian help. Australia, a major grain exporter, had made clear that its assistance with food security would focus on export crops and agribusiness.[50] With some assistance from the United Nations' Food and

---

[44] Mari Alkatiri, *Timor Leste: a Caminho do Desenvolvimento: os primeros anos de governação* (East Timor: The path of development: The first years of government), 2a edição actualizada (Lisboa: Lidel, 2006).

[45] Ibid.

[46] Ibid., p. 45.

[47] World Bank, "Project Appraisal Document on a Proposed Trust Fund for East Timor Grant in the Amount of US$6.8 Million Equivalent and a Second Grant of US$11.4 Million to East Timor for an Agricultural Rehabilitation Project," Rural Development and Natural Resources Sector Unit, Papua New Guinea/Pacific Islands Country Unit, East Asia and Pacific Region, Report no. 20439-TP, June 14, 2000, p. 14.

[48] IDA, "Agriculture in East Timor: A Strategy for Rehabilitation and Development" (Dili: International Development Association/World Bank Mission Report, May 2000), pp. 3–4.

[49] See Tim Anderson, "Self-determination after Independence: East Timor and the World Bank," *Portuguese Studies Review* 11,1, Special Issue on East Timor (July 2003): 176–77.

[50] DFAT, "Food Security and Trade: A Future Perspective," Department of Foreign Affairs and Trade (Canberra, 1996), Summary (vii–xi). Despite Australia's economic liberal approach to food security ("rely on trade, not self-sufficiency"), the country did offer support for a "Seeds of Life" program, which was aimed at developing appropriate domestic seeds (including rice) for Timor Leste's conditions; see: ACIAR, "Seeds of Life—East Timor," http://aciar.gov.au /project/cim/2000/160, accessed May 24, 2012; see also E. L. Javier, G. San Valentin, P. Kapukha, B. Monaghan, B. Palmer, C. Piggin, F. Tilman de Benevides, D. Da Silva, and A. De Oliveira, "Selection of Better Rice for East Timor," in *Agriculture: New Directions for a New Nation—East Timor (Timor Leste)*, ed. Helda Da Costa, Colin Piggin, Cesar J. da Cruz, and James J. Fox, ACIAR Workshop Proceedings, No. 113 (2003), pp. 79–83, http://aciar.gov.au/ files/node/512/pr113.pdf, accessed May 24, 2012.

Agriculture Organization (for grain silos) and Japan (in rice production), Timor-Leste maintained an independent course. By 2004, rice production (mostly irrigated fields) had increased strongly from the very low levels of 1998–99 (from 36,000 to 65,000 tonnes), though possibly at the expense of maize and cassava production.[51]

In 2005, a food security policy was introduced that emphasized a fair degree of independence from market economy orthodoxy in agriculture. This policy focuses on support for existing small-scale farming, rather than (as advocated by the World Bank and the Asian Development Bank) a push into large-scale cash cropping, aimed at export markets. It proposed a range of extension services (e.g., seeds, technologies, livestock services), support for farmers' organizations, rural credit, and marketing and infrastructure support for both local and export markets. It speaks of a land use policy, support for community organizations and cooperatives, and roads to provide "market access for isolated sucos [villages]."[52] The food security policy goes beyond agriculture into "early warning systems," grain storage, and relief assistance, "preferably established and managed at community levels through Suco councils."[53] There was no talk of alienation of land to large agribusiness investors. Nevertheless, a proposed biofuel industry, using contracted East Timorese Jatropha farmers, was initiated in mid 2005.[54]

Little of the proposed wide-ranging support to small farmers was achieved. This was in part because of limited budgets, and also due to competing demands on those budgets. The commitment to agriculture in the 2004–05 combined-sources budget was 8.8 percent,[55] down from the 11 percent that had been promised in the Sector Investment Program.[56]

The first government maintained its resolve to pursue cautious and autonomous fiscal policy, carefully managing small budgets and, despite the lack of resources, avoiding debt. Conscious of the debt-based political leverage introduced in the 1980s and 1990s, which had been resisted strongly by many other developing countries, a public campaign backed this move for a "debt free" future.[57] So, despite the virtual absence of oil and gas revenues in the first few years, the government took out no loans.[58] Nor were there significant private takeovers of key services.

The government developed a series of Sector Investment Programs (SIPs), though these tended to be more comprehensive than focused. For example, the private-sector SIP committed itself to the support of "agri-business" and "private

[51] UNDP, "The Path Out of Poverty," *Timor Leste Human Development Report 2006* (Dili: United Nations Development Programme, 2006), p. 84.

[52] MAAF, "National Food Security Policy for Timor Leste," Ministry of Agriculture, Forestry and Fisheries (Dili: República Democrática de Timor Leste, November 16, 2005).

[53] Ibid.

[54] Ortlan Bennett, "Timor Link to Region's Biggest Biofuel Industry," *Sunday Times*, Perth, October 2, 2005.

[55] RDTL, *General Budget of the State 2004-05*, Budget Paper No. 1 (Dili: Ministry of Planning and Finance, Democratic Republic of Timor Leste, 2004), p. 44.

[56] UNDP, "Path Out of Poverty," p. 38.

[57] ETAN, "The World's Newest Country Must Start Debt-Free!" (2003), http://etan.org/action/action2/06alert.htm, accessed May 24, 2012.

[58] IMF, "Staff Report for the 2006 Article IV Consultation, Democratic Republic of Timor-Leste" (Dili: International Monetary Fund, December 27, 2006).

participation in infrastructure, including perhaps power and water supply."[59] There were, however, no large agribusiness projects nor private-investor moves into power or water. Water and electricity, though very limited, were kept in public hands.[60] Telecommunications was handed to a foreign company, but on a build-operate-transfer (BOT) basis, through which the government maintained some equity and future rights.[61]

This was not a market economy approach but, rather, a state-managed effort to retain strategic control and avoid leverage by foreign financiers. Nevertheless, those financiers were managed tactfully. Timor-Leste joined the World Bank, but did not borrow its money. The Bank maintained an advisory role, as well as helping coordinate foreign assistance.[62] At a conference in 2005, the prime minister explained why his government had not engaged in the World Bank's "Poverty Reduction Strategy Paper" (formerly Structural Adjustment Programs) process of conditional loans:

> The PRSP with its concessional loans program increasingly places more burdens on developing nations because they are not based on real feasibility studies ... we have adopted a policy of avoiding such debts because we recognise that our capacity to absorb these funds is still limited, as is our labour force productivity.[63]

The conflict over agriculture and food security provides one example of the leverage Alkatiri's government sought to avoid. The constant demand for foreign investor "participation" in key services was another.[64]

In education and health, the FRETILIN government built on the country's constitutional commitment to education and health as rights, rather than commodities. In this sense, the 2001 Constitution had established and the government had maintained some "human development themes," opposed to the "pay for service" ethos of market economies. The government began with strong commitments, pledging "more than 35 percent of resources" to education and health in its first budget.[65] However, it delivered only 27 percent and 25 percent in the 2004–05 and 2005–06 budgets, respectively (see Table 2 below).

---

[59] Ministry of Development, "Private Sector Development: Priorities and Proposed Sector Investment Program" (Dili: Private Sector Development Sector Investment Program, April, 2006), pp. ix–x.

[60] IMF, "Selected Issues and Statistical Appendix, Democratic Republic of Timor-Leste" (Dili: International Monetary Fund, January 9, 2007).

[61] Alkatiri, *Timor Leste: a Caminho*, p. 53.

[62] IMF, "Staff Report for the 2006 Article IV Consultation, Democratic Republic of Timor-Leste," Annex, pp. 5–6.

[63] Alkatiri, "Keynote remarks at the International Meeting to Review the Implementation of the Program of Action for the Sustainable Development of Small Island Developing States," January 13, 2005, www.un.org/smallislands2005/coverage/statements/sids050113timor-leste.pdf, accessed May 24, 2012.

[64] For example, IMF. "Selected issues and Statistical Appendix," p. 8.

[65] Alkatiri, *Timor Leste: a Caminho*, p. 48.

Table 2					
Public Spending in Key Sectors, Timor-Leste					
Spending as a percentage of combined sources (CS) and state budget	2004–05	2005–06	2006–07	2008	2010
Education (% of CS budget)	14.9	13.4	10.7	11.7	11.3
Education (% of state budget)	15.3	15.1	11.1	13.0	10.2
Health (% of CS budget)	12.2	11.3	9.2	8.2	6.9
Health (% of state budget)	9.0	11.9	8.1	6.9	5.4
Agriculture (% of CS budget)	8.8	4.6	5.8	5.9	3.7
Agriculture (% state budget)	1.5	3.7	4.4	4.8	2.5
Infrastructure (% of CS budget)	n.a.	n.a.	8.8	13.2	26.6
Infrastructure (% of state budget)	n.a.	n.a.	15.8	12.8	28.5

Notes: "Combined sources" is the state budget plus contributions from outside agencies; the Ministry of Education was the Ministry of Education and Culture before 2008; the Ministry of Infrastructure was the Ministry of Public Works in 2006-07 and prior to that was part of transport and communications; prior to 2005, the state budget was divided into CFET (Consolidated Fund for East Timor) and TFET (Trust Fund for East Timor); autonomous agencies are included in combined sources, but not in state budgets.

Sources: RDTL, General Budget of the State 2004–05, Table 8.1; RDTL, General Budget of the State 2005–06, Table 6.5; RDTL 2007, Table 8.5; RDTL, General Budget of the State 2008, Table 7.3.

There were some modest education and health achievements in those first years. Combined school enrollment rates rose from 59 percent in 1999 to 66 percent in 2004, and under-five (years) mortality (deaths per thousand) was said to have fallen from 159 in 1999 to 136 in 2004.[66] Lack of capacity and resources constrained educational development. Nevertheless, a school feeding program was introduced in some districts, again, representing a strong human development theme. The first draft of the food-security policy included reference to the school feeding program, backed by the United Nations' World Food Program, which would both "encourage school attendance and improve nutrition of school age children."[67] For some reason this reference was dropped from the final food-security policy;[68] but the school feeding program itself was maintained.

A significant human development move in health occurred in early 2003, when the country's leadership chose—against the opposition of the United States and Australia—to take on a health-cooperation program with Cuba. This "south-south cooperation" program rapidly became the backbone of the country's primary health care and medical training, dwarfing all other health aid programs in the country, indeed, in the entire region. By late 2005, there was an offer of one thousand medical scholarships, and by 2008 almost nine hundred of the scholarships had been awarded. By 2006, there were almost 300 Cuban health workers in the country, many

[66] UNDP, "Path Out of Poverty."

[67] MAAF, "DRAFT National Food Security Policy for Timor Leste" (Ministry of Agriculture, Forestry and Fisheries, Dili, República Democrática de Timor Leste, July 7, 2005).

[68] MAAF, "National Food Security Policy for Timor Leste."

of them in remote rural areas. Building on the Cuban-model's success with health care, a substantial literacy program, based on a Cuban method, was introduced in 2005.[69] These programs gave strong practical support to the constitutional commitment to health and education as basic human rights, and represent a strong human development emphasis, contrasting with market economy ideas.

The FRETILIN-led government built on the National Development Plan and its Sector Investment Programs, both of which had some strong economic liberal language. Nevertheless, the government pursued some key heterodox policies: in agriculture, finance, education, and health. This was a strong human development approach, at odds with the "user pays" and private-investor "participation" ethos of market economy programs. As the stated economic strategy was wide ranging and had a fair degree of economic liberal language, it attracted support of the international agencies. But in 2006, when a political crisis destabilized the government, the International Monetary Fund (IMF) pressed for stronger measures to support private-sector-led growth, including private investment in agriculture, fisheries, and tourism. It warned of rising wages and, to contain this, urged "greater labour market flexibility."[70] These market economy ideas found greater resonance with the AMP coalition government elected in 2007.

The AMP and Big Money, 2007–2010

The AMP coalition government, led by Xanana Gusmão, introduced some economic liberal emphases. Once again, what follows is not an attempt to assess the AMP government but, rather, a characterization of some important elements of its strategic approach in the fields of fiscal policy, infrastructure, land use, and education and health.

The AMP coalition had access to larger budgets relative to 2001-06, mostly thanks to petroleum revenues, and was also inclined to spend more freely. The state budget almost tripled, from US$120 million in 2005 to $348 million in 2008; by 2010, the budget had risen to US$660 million.[71] Despite rising revenues from the Petroleum Fund, in 2009, the government overdrew the nominal "sustainable" amount (ESI) by US$104 million, taking $512 million instead of $408 million.[72] In that same year, further overspending of the Petroleum Fund, in the name of an Economic Stabilization Fund, was blocked when the courts found such overspending to be unconstitutional.[73] This sharply increased level of spending, justified by references to poverty reduction and a "stimulus" to the economy,[74] identifies the AMP government with a "big money" approach most consistent with economic liberalism.

---

[69] Tim Anderson, "Solidarity Aid: The Cuba–Timor Leste Health Program," *International Journal of Cuban Studies*, Issue 2 (December 2008), pp. 53–65, http://cubanstudies.plutojournals.org/Portals/8/Issues/sissue_2_bw.pdf, accessed May 24, 2012.

[70] IMF, "Staff Report for the 2006 Article IV Consultation."

[71] RDTL, General Budget of the State 2005–06, Budget Paper No. 1, Dili, Ministry of Planning and Finance, Democratic Republic of Timor Leste, 2005; RDTL, General Budget of the State 2008, Budget Paper No. 1, Dili, Ministry of Finance, Democratic Republic of Timor Leste, 2007; RDTL, 2010 State Budget, Dili, República Democrática de Timor Leste, Book 1, 2009.

[72] World Bank, "East Asia and Pacific Economic Update 2010," Vol. 1, Timor Leste, 2010, p. 71.

[73] RDTL, 2010 State Budget, p. 8.

[74] Ibid.

Some foreign advisers and economic liberal agencies[75] had urged this stimulus spending, especially on infrastructure and on improving conditions for foreign investors. "Ramp up public spending," the IMF said.[76] The aim was to "lift [economic] growth to a higher sustainable path."[77] The emphasis here is on current spending, consistent with the market economy approach to development, in which "future value" is discounted. Government spending can stimulate waves of new income and consumption in an economy. Such spending may be more useful if linked to the creation of valuable infrastructure, such as roads and schools, but can also be carried out in a wasteful manner.

The chief stated aim of Timor-Leste's 2010 budget was infrastructure:

> The 2010 budget prioritizes investment in infrastructure. The future of our country depends upon the building of basic infrastructure. We need infrastructure to develop a modern and prosperous Timor-Leste.[78]

Indeed, there was a very strong budget commitment to infrastructure. Planned expenditure rose from US$44.5 million in 2008 to $229 million in 2010, representing a jump from 15.8 percent to 28.5 percent **of** the state budget (see Table 2). However, the potential for waste and corruption is reinforced by the idea that the "stimulus" provided to private businesses is as much a legitimate policy aim as the infrastructure development itself. For example, under the August 2009 "Referendum Package"—comprising some $70 million of mostly infrastructure projects—the aim was to subcontract projects so that private companies would make a profit while constructing public facilities. However, dozens of projects were allocated outside normal government procedures, mostly to private companies, and many complaints of waste and corruption ensued.[79] The secretary of state for public works, Domingos Caero, rapidly acknowledged that "about 60 percent of the Referendum Package Projects are of bad quality" and said he was taking steps to penalize the companies involved.[80] However, it seems likely that a similar pattern of subcontracting will be employed in the 2010–11 infrastructure budget, marked for roads, bridges, power generation, and other facilities.[81]

The concept of a stimulus was developed in wealthy countries with strong formal sectors. The idea was that weak consumer demand in a previously active

---

[75] For example, Jeffrey Sachs, "General Taur Matan Ruak Questions Jeffrey Sachs on International Aid," *Tempo Semanal*, April 5, 2010, http://temposemanaltimor.blogspot.com /2010/04/general-taur-matan-ruak-questions.html, accessed on April 30, 2012.

[76] IMF, "Selected Issues and Statistical Appendix," pp. 2, 5.

[77] Ibid., 2, 8; IMF, "Staff Report for the 2006 Article IV Consultation," pp. 10, 12, 21.

[78] Xanana Gusmão, in RDTL, 2010 State Budget, Dili, República Democrática de Timor Leste, Book 1, 2009, p. 15.

[79] *Tempo Semanal*, "Pakote Referendum Timor-Leste: Exclusive Major Government Document Leak," March 28, 2010, http://temposemanaltimor.blogspot.com/2010/03/pakote-referendum-timor-leste-exclusive.html, accessed April 30, 2012.

[80] FRETILIN.Media, "Government Admits 60% of Public Works Projects of 'Bad Quality,'" Media Release, Dili: Frente Revolucionaria do Timor Leste Independente, June 7, 2010, http://fretilinmedia.blogspot.com/2010/06/media-release-government-admits-60-of.html, accessed April 30, 2012.

[81] RDTL, 2010 State Budget, pp. 15, 29.

formal economy could be reactivated by new spending.[82] However, this was not a developmental concept aimed at building new capacity. Indeed, such demand management was unable to address the structural changes of the 1970s in wealthy countries. Additional problems with such stimulus spending in less developed economies may include the money being captured by elites in the cities and formal sector, leaving little to "trickle down" to those in the rural, informal sector; large leakages to offshore accounts and wealthy consumption spending, which weakens any spin-offs or trickle down to other sectors; and a lack of coordination, undermining new capacity and the creation of new job-creating enterprises, especially when the so-called stimulus is carried out through private contracts. A developmental state emphasis would maintain greater control and coordination of infrastructure development.

An unusual feature of Timor-Leste's fiscal policy in 2008 was the decision to cut a range of taxes, in particular, service taxes, income tax, and tariffs. This was a unilateral, economic liberal move, welcomed, but not really called for, by international agencies. In 2007, the IMF had discussed possible "tax reform" in Timor-Leste, generally favoring tax reductions but admitting there was no strong evidence to indicate benefits. Indeed, the IMF recognized that cuts to the non-oil tax system would "remove a useful discretionary fiscal policy instrument" and that retaining "some level of non-oil tax revenue would be prudent."[83] Nevertheless, President Ramos-Horta called for the country to be "almost tax free," in a bid to attract foreign investment.[84] A law along these lines was passed by the parliament in mid-2008 and was subsequently praised by the World Bank.[85] The immediate effect was to narrow, even further, the "tax base" of the country, making the state even more dependent on the Petroleum Fund. There do not appear to be any offsetting investment dividends from this move. Political stability and improvements in infrastructure and public health would likely do more than the tax cuts did to attract investment in, say, the tourism sector.

In agriculture, the major initiatives of 2008 were proposed biofuel projects. One of these extended the earlier proposal for subcontracted Jatropha farming, near Baucau.[86] The other involved a proposed lease to a foreign company of 100,000 hectares, about 20 percent of the country's arable land.[87] It was argued that a sugarcane plantation on this land would create jobs. FRETILIN spokesperson

---

[82] For example, John Maynard Keynes, *General Theory of Employment*.

[83] IMF, "Selected issues and Statistical Appendix," pp. 19–24.

[84] ABC, "Ramos Horta Calls for Timor to Be Tax Free," May 26, 2008, www.radioaustralia.net .au/international/radio/onairhighlights/ramos-horta-calls-for-timor-to-be-tax-free, accessed May 24, 2012.

[85] World Bank, "Paying Taxes 2010: The Global Picture," 2010, www.pwc.com/gx/en/paying-taxes/pdf/paytax-2010.pdf, accessed May 24, 2012.

[86] RDTL-EDA, "Deed of Agreement for Carabella Bio-Oil Facility, Republica Democratica de Timor Leste and Enviroenergy Developments Australia" (ten-page agreement signed by Avelino da Silva, Secretary of State for Energy Policy and Edian Krsevan, Director EDA, February 13, 2008).

[87] MAP-GTLeste Biotech, "Memorandum of Understanding [concerning proposed sugar cane industry and lease of 100,000 hectares of land]," Dili, Ministerio da Agricultura e Pescas, MOU signed by Mariano Sabino, Minister of Agriculture and Fisheries and Gino Sakiris, Chairman of GTLeste Biotech, January 15, 2008.

Estanislau da Silva (the former agriculture minister) strongly criticized the large lease proposal:

> They say they are going to plant sugarcane ... [This] goes against what we are doing in terms of development and increasing food production and food [self-] reliance ... Two thousand jobs means nothing to me when you give away 100,000 hectares.[88]

This was, indeed, a shift away from an autonomous agricultural and food security policy—based on domestic crops as the core of food security—toward a market economy approach, which emphasizes formal-sector industry, export-oriented cropping, and food security through cash-for-food exchanges. Yet the dangerous volatility of rice markets from 2006 onward should have warned against such an approach. The government sale of subsidized rice imports is said to have created hoarding, speculative markets, and corruption, as well as economic damage to local growers.[89] This is an unstable "solution."

The AMP government's commitment to education and health sounds good, but has not been matched in practice. The prime minister's 2010 Strategic Development Plan presents the admirable goal of "school construction and teacher training to ensure universal secondary school completion through Grade 12 by the year 2020."[90] This would be an achievement above that of most wealthy countries—and is possible; but those developing countries that have made strong advances in education have only done so after many years of strong and consistent investment in education and training.

In contrast, the proportion of both Timor-Leste's state budget and total budget ("combined sources," i.e., state plus donors, especially outside agencies) dedicated to education has fallen steadily since 2004–05. The 2010 state budget dedicates only 10.2 percent to education, down from 15 percent five years earlier (see Table 2). Although the total budgets have grown larger and the absolute dollar amounts spent on education and health have also increased, the relative spending on education and health has fallen. In UNDP (United Nations Development Programme) terms, reducing the percentage being spent represents a weak commitment to education and health.[91]

The Strategic Development Plan (SDP) itself presents as a successor to the National Development Plan of 2002. It is an ambitious and optimistic document,

---

[88] Agence France-Presse, "Massive East Timor Land-for-Biofuel Plan Raises Hackles," Dili, June 24, 2008, http://www.spacedaily.com/reports/Massive_East_Timor_Land_For_Biofuel_Plan_Raises_Hackles_999.html, accessed April 30, 2012.

[89] Douglas Kammen and S. W. Hayati, "Crisis and Rice in East Timor," 2007, http://www.etan.org/news/2007/03food.htm, accessed April 30, 2012; Steve Holland et al., "East Timor PM Accused of Corruption," Radio Australia, June 26, 2009, http://www.radioaustralia.net.au/asiapac/stories/200906/s2610077.htm, accessed April 30, 2012.

[90] OPM, "From Conflict to Prosperity: Timor Leste's Strategic Development Plan 2011–2030," Dili, Office of the Prime Minister, April 7, 2010.

[91] UNDP, *Human Development Report 2007/2008—Fighting Climate Change: Human Solidarity in a Divided World* (New York, NY: United Nations Development Programme, 2008), pp. 247–50, 265–68, http://hdr.undp.org/en/media/HDR_20072008_EN_Complete.pdf, accessed June 11, 2012.

suggesting that Timor-Leste is set for huge increases in per capita income, that petroleum revenues will "provide substantial revenues for decades," and that the big-spending approach—including "withdrawing in excess of the ESI" and additional borrowing—is desirable and necessary.[92] The SDP has some strong human-development language and, in contrast to AMP government practice, is less strong on economic liberal ideas. Nevertheless, it does see private investment as the key element in the petroleum sector, telecommunications, and agriculture.[93] This document does not have the legitimacy of the earlier NDP, being basically a missive from the prime minister's office. After it was published, Prime Minister Gusmão sought "dialogue."[94] In view of this genesis, it seems unlikely that this plan will survive the next change of government.

International financial institutions (IMF, World Bank, Asian Development Bank) seem to have influenced AMP government policy and practice. The IMF took its typical narrow view of development in Timor-Leste, insisting that everything depends on economic growth: "To promote human development and reduce poverty, the growth rate of Timor-Leste's economy will need to accelerate markedly."[95] The AMP government's practical approach has been broadly consistent with this theme. That means that despite enhanced spending, there is less emphasis on those factors or sectors that do not contribute to apparent economic growth: a strong, informal, rural sector and development of human capabilities through participation, education, and health.

MANAGING PETROLEUM FUNDS

Both the FRETILIN-led and the AMP governments have demonstrated strong national will in struggles with the Australian government and Australia-based mining companies over petroleum revenues. There have been drawn-out disputes over maritime boundaries, royalty shares, and a gas refinery location. This political will shows the capacity to support development plans, but the impact of this is undermined, more recently, by reversion to market economy practice. This latter theme has become more pronounced in the AMP government's practice than in that of the former FRETILIN-led government.

We can see this greater AMP government reliance on economic liberal arguments in the 2010–11 debates over changes to Timor-Leste's Petroleum Fund. This crucial fund began as a cautious mechanism for managing anticipated one-off flows of funds from oil and gas fields. Principles established by the Petroleum Fund Law 2005 (in turn, based on Article 139 of Timor-Leste's constitution) require the nation's natural resources to be owned by the state, "prudently managed," and used "in a fair and equitable manner" for the needs of "both current and future generations."[96] The law set up a governance structure for the fund, a regulated

---

[92] Office of the Prime Minister, "From Conflict to Prosperity: Timor Leste's Strategic Development Plan 2011–2030, Summary, pp. 4, 22, www.scribd.com/doc/29934804/TIMOR%E2%80%90LESTE%E2%80%99S-Strategic-Development-Plan-2011-%E2%80%93-2030, accessed May 24, 2012.

[93] Ibid., pp. 16–18.

[94] Ibid, p. 24.

[95] IMF, "Selected Issues and Statistical Appendix," p. 12.

[96] Article 11.4 of the Petroleum Fund Law 2005.

investment regime for its financial assets (mostly US-dollar bonds), and a process for "sustainable" withdrawal of revenues.

Those basic principles enjoyed broad support when there was no money in the fund, but discontent grew as several billions of dollars accumulated. The AMP government drew strongly on the fund for a range of projects, but at a time of global recession when there were limited actual returns on the fund's mainly US-dollar bond investments. Particular risk factors for the fund include the state's extreme dependence on fund revenues. In the 2010 budget, the fund provided more than 90 percent of local revenues.[97] In addition, local financial management capacity was limited and, consequently, there were moves to contract less accountable external managers. In 2010, consulting firm Towers Watson, contracted by the Ministry of Finance, proposed a substantial shift of fund assets into externally managed equities.[98] Later, former World Bank official Jeffrey Sachs backed AMP government moves to draw down and spend more from the fund—a proposal questioned by then armed forces chief, General Taur Matan Ruak.[99]

FRETILIN claimed credit for the initial conservative Petroleum Fund strategy, saying that it had protected the country's assets during the 2008 financial crisis.[100] It continued to criticize the high-spending budgets of the AMP government. In late 2010, the AMP released its proposal for amending the Petroleum Fund Law. Prominent was the enhanced role for the Minister of Finance, the use of external managers, and allowing up to 50 percent of the fund to be invested in stock markets, with the aim of "maximizing the risk-adjusted financial returns" of the fund.[101] FRETILIN opposed this plan, as well as the government for "non-transparent" and excessive spending, especially on infrastructure programs.[102]

Greater spending (which would put at risk long-term revenue streams from the fund) is consistent with an economic liberal emphasis on stimulating the economy (e.g., through infrastructure projects) to produce new rounds of economic activity. This approach heavily discounts future returns in favor of supposed near-term benefits from current spending. It is less consistent with developmental state and human development strategies, which would place greater emphasis on education and training and institutional development, both of which are long-term projects with little short-term economic impact. Going for high-risk investments, hoping for high returns, is also consistent with economic liberalism, with its focus on greater "market participation."

Timor Leste's fund is small, and its managers have limited levels of financial expertise. Nevertheless, the state has rapidly developed an extreme dependence on fund revenue. Countries with higher levels of skilled personnel relative to Timor-

---

[97] RDTL, 2010 State Budget.

[98] Peter J. Ryan-Kane, "Timor Leste Petroleum Fund: From Oil to Financial Assets: Planning for a Sustainable Future for Timor Leste," public presentation by Towers Watson to Finance Ministry, Dili, March 2010.

[99] Sachs, "General Taur Matan Ruak Questions Jeffrey Sachs on International Aid."

[100] FRETILIN, "Fretilin Investment Strategy Protects Timor Leste's Petroleum Fund," Media Release, Dili, Frente Revolucionaria do Timor Leste Independente, October 15, 2008.

[101] Ministry of Finance, "First Alteration to Petroleum Fund Law No. 9/2005 of 20 June," Legislation Proposal, October 20, 2010, Article 14.

[102] For example, FRETILIN, "Timor Leste Government Raids Petroleum Fund Ignoring the Law," Media Release, Dili, Frente Revolucionaria do Timor Leste Independente, January 27, 2011.

Leste's might better manage exposure to risk in volatile financial and equity markets, but the particular developmental features of Timor-Leste otherwise suggest a more cautious approach. Given the poor returns of US bonds and the steady depreciation of the US dollar, a change to the law was necessary. However, rather than an anxiety to maximize returns and spend even more, a move into diversified bonds—along with cautious expansion of direct investment options, while slowly building domestic financial management capacity—would retain most of the prudential aspects of the initial regime.[103]

THE NEGLECTED SECTORS

Development of the key sectors of agriculture, education, and health remains fragile. There are gaps between rhetoric and commitment, such as in the area of agriculture. With most of the population dependent on informal-sector farming—and with the entire population affected by failures in staple-food production—every government has stressed the importance of support for rural farming communities. Yet no government has matched this concern with substantial investment. This sector, which engages and employs as much as 80 percent of Timor-Leste's population[104] has never received more than 5 percent of the state budget (see Table 2). Small farmers have been mostly left to their own devices.

Why is small farming so undervalued? For one thing, it is not "counted" well by economists, nor by those who rely on market economy information. Subsistence production and a great deal of informal work and exchange are simply not added to the national accounts. Even the UNDP—generally more heterodox in economic matters—adopts this misleading approach. For example, in the 2006 Human Development Report for Timor-Leste, the country is said to need "sustained economic growth" for "tackling rural poverty." The report goes on to note:

> Growth will have to start with agriculture, which employs around three-quarters of the labour force. Most farmers are engaged in subsistence cultivation ... average landholdings are around 1.2 hectares. Currently productivity is low: output per worker is less than one-tenth of that in industry and services and, as a result, agriculture generates only one-fifth of GDP.[105]

This is a basic misreading of the agricultural sector. The confusion comes from conflating a large informal sector with formal sector macroaggregates. To put it another way, they have not included proper estimates of subsistence and informal sector production. Production in rural subsistence sectors is often underestimated.[106]

---

[103] See Tim Anderson, "The Petroleum Fund and Development Strategy in Timor Leste" (a Report for Timor Leste's Petroleum Fund Consultative Council, Dili, June, 2010).

[104] ACIAR, "Rebuilding Agriculture in East Timor," Australian Centre for International Agricultural Research, 2011, http://aciar.gov.au/files/node/665/Rebuilding%20Agriculture%20in%20East%20Timor.pdf, accessed April 30, 2012.

[105] UNDP, "Path Out of Poverty," p. 3.

[106] John Gibson, "The Economic and Nutritional Importance of Household Food Production in PNG," in *Food Security for Papua New Guinea*, ed. M. Bourke, G. Allen, and J. Salisbury, Proceedings for the Papua New Guinea Food and Nutrition 2000 Conference (Lae: PNG

It seems likely that agriculture contributes the major part of Timor-Leste's national production, given that more than 75 to 80 percent of the population rely on it for their food and livelihoods.[107]

Understating the economic value of small farming contributes to the logic of governments pushing small farmers from their lands to make way for large export crop plantations. This is precisely what happened with the oil palm developments in Indonesia after the Asian Financial Crisis. The big plantations may increase GDP, but the displacement impact on small farming could easily lower total production, as well as dislocate large communities. Rural poverty could very well increase.

The alternative is to more decisively support rural communities, to help them do better in their current farming and expand their domestic market opportunities, while backing up these communities with essential services. Better estimates of subsistence production can strengthen government commitments to deliver on their promises of extension services, local market facilities, food storage, and improved local roads. Export markets can come second.

Closely related to support for small farming is the recognition of customary land rights, and resisting the temptation to give over alienated or "unused" land to large export crop plantations. Timor-Leste's 2002 Constitution, at section 54.4, specifies that only East Timorese "natural persons" can own land—neither corporations nor foreigners can. There was good reason for this. Community and family control of land for small farming provides the basis for livelihoods, food security, social security, and environmental protection. Export capacity would better build on this basis rather than displace it. The multiple benefits of small farming have only recently been more widely recognized.[108] Large plantations, on the other hand, bring the particular dangers of dispossession, displacement, environmentally damaging monocultures, and food insecurity. The experience of Haiti is one the best recent examples of this.[109]

Another neglected sector under the AMP government has been health care. The apparent decline in commitment to health care—from 12 percent of the state budget in 2005–06 to less than 6 percent in 2010—is alarming, given the health care needs of the country. The Ministry of Health's Mid Term Expenditure Framework, developed in 2007, expected that 12 percent of the state budget would be earmarked for health;[110] clearly, there has been a retreat from this position. The AMP may have become complacent over its commitment to health care, by relying on the huge Cuban health program. While there have been some investments in health, these will have to be scaled up substantially to make good use of the hundreds of medical students returning from Cuba. Failure to do so will risk losing many of those highly trained young people to emigration or other careers. The big surge in trained doctors, expected between 2010 and 2013, is a rare opportunity that needs careful management, and significant investment.

University of Technology, 2000), pp. 37–44; and Anderson, "Land Registration, Land Markets, and Livelihoods in Papua New Guinea."

[107] ACIAR, "Rebuilding Agriculture in East Timor"; and UNDP, "Path Out of Poverty," p. 3.

[108] For example, Marcel Mazoyer, "Protecting Small Farmers and the Rural Poor in the Context of Globalization," Rome, United Nations' Food and Agriculture Organization, 2001, http://www.fao.org/DOCREP/007/Y1743E/Y1743E00.htm, accessed April 30, 2012.

[109] Georges, Josiane, "Trade and the Disappearance of Haitian Rice," TED Case Studies No. 725, June 2004, http://www1.american.edu/TED/haitirice.htm, accessed April 30, 2012.

[110] Rui Araujo, personal communication, May 2010.

The steady decline in the budget commitment to education is also alarming, given Timor-Leste's rapidly growing and relatively young population. Despite expanding budgets overall, and despite Prime Minister Gusmão's commendable goal of universal secondary school enrollment by 2020,[111] the state's commitment to the education sector has fallen from 15 percent to 10 percent of the state budget. This level of funding is inadequate for the stated goal.

Although Timor-Leste's relative performance in education is better than its per capita income would suggest—we have to look thirty places up the HDI (Human Development Index) rankings to South Africa to find another country that has a similar (above 70 percent) combined gross enrollment rate[112]—Timor-Leste's commitment to education is weak and compares poorly to other countries. Moreover, the country's literacy deficit falls more heavily on women than men. In 2004, only 43.9 percent of adult females in Timor-Leste were literate, compared with 56.3 percent of adult males.[113] Developing countries on average commit 14 to 15 percent of their government budgets to education. Those that want rapid progress in human development must do much better than this. Twenty-two developing countries dedicate more than 20 percent of their government budgets to education; and a couple allocate more than 30 percent.[114] Against its low education commitment, Timor-Leste has the fourth highest rate of natural population growth on earth, at 3.1 percent per year.[115] This should prompt a greater commitment to education, not a diminished one. Meeting the universal secondary schooling goal of the 2010 Strategic Development Plan in the next decade would likely require that something closer to 30 percent of the total budget be committed for education.

CONCLUSION

This chapter explained three competing approaches to development strategy: those that emphasize the market economy, those that emphasize the role of the developmental state, and those that emphasize a human development approach. It has been argued that the market economy approach is counterproductive to a genuine development process and, instead, represents the preferred model of large corporations and those countries that have attained a fair degree of market dominance in international trade and investment. The latter two approaches, on the other hand, represent contemporary currents of genuine development strategy, directing the transformation of country capacity and building human resources for such change.

All three strategies are embodied to varying degrees in the various hybrids of Timor-Leste's National Development Plan, the practice of the FRETILIN-led government of 2001–06 and the AMP coalition of 2007–11. The NDP was a necessary hybrid, with distinct influences from international agencies. It has strong economic liberal influences, moderated by some developmental state influences in the areas of planning and natural resource management, and some human development

[111] OPM, "From Conflict to Prosperity," p. 14.

[112] UNDP, *Human Development Report 2007–08* (New York, NY: United Nations Development Programme, 2008), p. 231.

[113] UNDP, "Path Out of Poverty," p. 15.

[114] UNDP, *Human Development Report 2007–08*, Table 11.

[115] UNDP, *Human Development Report 2009*, Table L.

emphases in terms of participation and a more equitable approach to education, women, and rural development.

The adopted strategies of the two post-independence governments were inferred more from their practice than from policy statements, due to the increased inclusiveness of policy language. The Fretilin-led government built on the National Development Plan, but pursued more heterodox, human development policies, with elements of development state ideas in agriculture, finance, education, and health. The AMP coalition had strong market economy influences, consistent with IMF advice. While the AMP asserted some human development themes in its 2010 Strategic Development Plan, its big spending stimulus approach coupled with weak investment in education and health was more indicative of economic liberalism. There are serious implications of such an approach, particularly for the neglected sectors of agriculture, education, and health. It is hoped that this discussion encourages further debate on development strategy, particularly within Timor-Leste.

BETWEEN EARTH AND HEAVEN: THE POLITICS OF GENDER

Sara Niner

In this chapter, I will discuss the central issues surrounding gender in the contemporary post-conflict environment of Timor-Leste. Understandings of what it is to be a man or a woman are central to these issues and underlay the everyday experiences of people's lives. At the heart of the many challenges surrounding gender in Timor is how understandings of female and male in indigenous culture have evolved throughout Timorese history to shape the modern gender roles and relations that exist today. One illustration of indigenous understandings comes from a central myth of the Mambai people, who recount the beginnings of humankind from a union between Mother Earth, or Ina Lu, and Father Heaven, represented by the sun, the god-like Maromak, the Shining One.[1] In this myth, Ina Lu first gave birth to Tata Mai Lau, the highest and most sacred of mountains, and then to all other natural elements and living things. She came to rest with her feet firmly pressing back the waters in the north, calming and controlling the female sea but leaving her back to the unrestrained and wild male sea, which is feared and treacherous.[2] This and other such beliefs provide insight into the complementary relations between men and women that permeate indigenous Timorese thought and what this means for women and men today.

"GENDER" IS ABOUT WOMEN *AND* MEN

The concept of gender has been much misunderstood in Timor-Leste and is often perceived to be associated with aid and development programs that target and favor women, sometimes at the expense of men. The use of the word *culture* is similarly

---

[1] Elizabeth Traube, "Mambai Perspectives on Colonialism and Decolonization," in *East Timor at the Crossroads*, ed. Peter Carey and Carter Bentley (London: SSRC & Cassell, 1995), p. 46.

[2] Elizabeth Traube, *Cosmology and Social Life: Ritual Exchange among the Mambai of East Timor* (Chicago, IL: University of Chicago Press, 1986), p. 39; Patricia Thatcher, "The Timor-Born in Exile in Australia" (master's thesis, Melbourne, Monash University, 1993), p. 64; Elizabete Lim Gomes, "Birth in the Great Mountain Tatamailau," in *Bitter Flowers, Sweet Flowers: East Timor, Indonesia and the World Community*, ed. Richard Tanter, Mark Selden, and Shalom (Lanham, MD: Rowman and Littlefield, 2001), p. 105.

laden with confusion but, here, refers to the beliefs, customs, practices, and social behavior of a people, which are understood to change over time. Education is required to foster better understandings of "gender" as a term referring to the roles and responsibilities ascribed to men and women across different cultures and societies. To implement such an educational program will necessitate much debate and the addressing of different understandings about which human behaviors are "natural," or biologically determined by sex, and which are learned and prescribed by family, society, culture, or religion. Within the field of gender theory, it is generally accepted that gender roles and relations between the sexes are socially constructed and negotiated in those specific environments. Many people will not even be aware of how much their behavior is learned and influenced by the unwritten rules of gendered behavior that influence their particular social group.

The term "gender relations" refers to the hierarchical relations of power between men and women that, all over the world, usually favor men. Social systems that privilege men are called patriarchal, and those that give women social and political power are called matriarchal (these are less common). Traditional gender roles and relations differ enormously throughout the world and across cultures and are forever changing and evolving. Traditions, described simply as "repetitive cultural patterns," are "constantly prone to innovations reflecting specific presents and anticipated futures."[3] Some theorists believe traditions are, essentially, inventions and reinventions based on power hierarchies,[4] and this is particularly true for gender relations. These ideas too need much wider discussion in Timor-Leste.[5]

The contemporary interest in the social construction of gender, both masculine and feminine, has largely been a consequence of the feminist movement and its attempt to make the world a fairer place for women. This interest in improving the lives of women has been broadened to focus not just on women and the inequities they suffer, but on gender roles more generally and how gender relations are created and reproduced. It takes conscious effort to entrench and maintain power and gender hierarchies and cultivate the preferred types of masculinity and femininity that accomplish this process of entrenchment. The success of these efforts can be measured by the outcomes, such as access to political power and resources. New studies, too, have not just focused on the negotiated relationships between men and women but also on those among groups of men and among women, and the crosscutting influences of class and race.

There is no universal form of masculinity or femininity—differences in what constitutes "the masculine" or "the feminine" are determined by a range of variables, including class, ethnicity, age, religion, disability, and sexual orientation. However, one important idea that has developed in this regard is the idea of a "hegemonic masculinity," described as an idealized, dominant, heterosexual masculinity constructed in relation to women, and also in relation to subordinated masculinities such as those marking homosexual men or less powerful men. According to Raewyn

---

[3] Jill Forshee, *Between the Folds: Stories of Cloth, Lives, and Travels in Sumba* (Honolulu, HI: University of Hawaii Press, 2001), p. 8.

[4] Cf. Anthony Giddens, *Runaway World* (London: Profile Books, 2002), p. 40.

[5] CEDAW, "Concluding Observations of the Committee on the Elimination of Discrimination against Women [CEDAW], Timor Leste, 44th Session," July 20 to August 7, 2009, http://daccess-ods.un.org/access.nsf/Get?Open&DS=CEDAW/C/TLS/CO/1&Lang=E, accessed June 13, 2012.

Connell, this idea of hegemonic masculinity has become a "significant critique of the often negative expressions of men's power around the world."[6] It is understood that many men take their privileges (such as access to work and higher incomes, capacity to own land, access to domestic services from women, and decision-making power) for granted, ignorant that these privileges are not natural but are sustained through cultural practices.[7] The analysis of such cultural practices is therefore crucial.

These analyses of gender relations and hierarchies within the broader dimensions of power and social difference are used as tools to challenge inequality. The overriding goal both of feminism and of gender and development programs is gender equity, whereby men and women have similar opportunities—equal access to resources, education, and work and the ability (and freedom) to direct their own lives. The establishment of gender equity usually requires reforms to legislation, equal opportunity advocacy, and programs and economic empowerment initiatives, but it also requires deep-seated changes to culture, a process that has proven much more difficult to induce. New approaches and interventions are more inclusive of men and multifarious, a condition that highlights the need to challenge existing hierarchies and relations and foster the empowerment of oppressed and marginalized groups.

GENDER IN POSTWAR SOCIETY AND TIMOR-LESTE

Observing that violence and war has profound social and psychological impacts on the survivors and the society that emerges from the conflict appears an obvious point to make. Yet these circumstances are now often forgotten in discussions about post-conflict Timor-Leste, as more than ten years have passed since the conclusion of the long and brutal Indonesian occupation (1975–99).[8] It is clear from studies of post-conflict environments that violence, including sexual and gender-based violence, does not conform to "the timelines of peace treaties and ceasefires but endures past them." Those who have fought and committed violence are rarely formally counseled nor are "the deep imprinting of violent masculinities ... and the effects of militarism on the society overall" charted or addressed.[9] This is substantially the case in Timor-Leste.

---

[6] R. W. Connell and James W. Messerschmidt, "Hegemonic Masculinity: Rethinking the Concept," *Gender and Society* 19,6 (2005): 832.

[7] Oxfam, *Gender Equality and Men: Learning from Practice*, ed Sandy Ruxton (Oxford: Oxfam, 2004), p. 8.

[8] J. Modvig, J. Pagaduan-Lopez, J. Rodenburg, C. M. D. Salud, R. V. Cabigon, and C. I. A. Panelo, "Torture and Trauma in Post-conflict East Timor," *Lancet* 356,9243 (2000): 1763. It is safe to assume that this type of trauma affects most families. A study carried out in 2000 documented that nearly all Timorese had experienced at least one traumatic event during the Indonesian occupation. Three-quarters had experienced combat and more than half had come close to death; 12 percent had lost children to political violence; 57 percent had been tortured; and 22 percent had witnessed the murder of relatives or friends. One-third of the population was classified as having post-traumatic stress, and 20 percent of these people believed they would never recover.

[9] Naomi Cahn and Fionnuala Ni Aolain, "Gender, Masculinities, and Transition in Conflicted Societies," *New England Law Review* (2010), George Washington University Law School, Public Law and Legal Theory Working Paper No. 481, pp. 116, 118, http://papers.ssrn.com/sol3/papers.cfm?abstract_id=1516709, accessed June 13, 2012.

The Indonesian occupation of East Timor and the associated trauma have resulted in a brutalized and more violent society. One of the 2005 findings of the East Timorese National Commission for Truth, Reception, and Reconciliation (or Comissão de Acolhimento, Verdade e Reconciliação, CAVR) was a causal link between the period of armed conflict and current high levels of domestic violence and sexual assault: Male survivors of detention and torture, now perpetrators of violence themselves, reported this directly to the Commission.[10] Henri Myrttinen too describes the "domestication" of the violence of the conflict.[11] Outbreaks of national-level violence will be discussed later.

While conflict has profound negative impacts on society and affects women and men differently, war has also often empowered women. The conflict in East Timor shifted women's economic, social, and political roles, as war has done repeatedly around the world, and many women were challenged to act more independently than they had previously. In East Timor, the war forced many women to take up roles outside the domestic sphere for the first time. Not only did women lose husbands, fathers, brothers, and sons to the war, making it necessary for them to provide for their families by entering an economic sphere previously closed to them, but women also played a major part in the resistance fronts: military, political civil, and diplomatic.

In 2001, leading Timorese feminist Milena Pires explained that male combatants were returning home to a changed society. While they had been fighting and hiding in the mountains, Timorese women had been "holding the fort at home" and, in some cases, furthering their education overseas. She continued, "Women were involved at every level ... they helped run the camps, sent supplies, smuggled information. And now as men come out of hiding, the women don't want to return to their traditional roles. It is a very traditional Catholic society which has been frozen by years of war."[12] The war also meant that any modern ideas of gender equity were muted, although not altogether absent.

The pressure in postwar societies for women to return to their prewar status and roles often becomes a site of conflict between men and women, both privately and publicly. A pertinent example of this is the 1950s backlash against women in postwar America.[13] Today in Timor-Leste, in the postwar environment, gender roles are now being renegotiated, creating a tension between the "traditional" role for women and ideas of a more modern, dynamic, and public role for women. This situation is complicated by the facts that the occupation lasted for so long and the population is

---

[10] CAVR, *Chega! Final Report of the Commission for Reception, Truth, and Reconciliation in East Timor* (Dili: CAVR, 2006), http://www.etan.org/news/2006/cavr.htm, accessed May 1, 2012.

[11] Henri Myrttinen, "Masculinities, Violence, and Power in Timor Leste," *Revue Lusotopie* XII, 1-2 (2005): 233. Henri Myrttinen also asserts that the post-conflict period has benefited women more than men, although this may be pure perception on the part of men. He argues that the availability of more jobs for women, in a climate of underemployment, has created men who are "jealous of the non-traditional role of a female breadwinner, or feel threatened in their masculinity as they are not able to fulfil their perceived duties as men." Henri Myrttinen, "Poster Boys No More: Gender and Security Sector Reform in Timor-Leste," Policy Paper No. 31, Geneva, Centre for the Democratic Control of Armed Forces, 2009, p. 13.

[12] Mary O'Kane, "Return of the Revolutionaries," *Guardian*, January 14, 2001, www.guardian.co.uk/world/2001/jan/15/indonesia.gender, accessed June 13, 2012.

[13] Cahn and Ni Aolain, "Gender, Masculinities, and Transition."

so young, so that it is hard to define what this somewhat idealized "traditional" role for women was before 1975.

"Culture" is often given as the reason why women cannot participate in politics or why it is difficult to implement gender equity in Timor-Leste. Although women activists protest against this "cultural relativism," the resistance to change is strong.[14] Moreover, a portion of the senior male political leadership has patriotically promoted a "traditional" indigenous culture while denigrating international "gender equity" policies as foreign impositions.[15] Regarding comparable post-conflict situations, some have argued that a desire for normalcy and healing can make "the certainties of patriarchal institutions and tradition seem therapeutic."[16] Carolyn Graydon documents similar processes of "retraditionalisation" and a backlash against women in contemporary Timor-Leste.[17] One Timorese woman, who was part of the emerging women's movement in the 1970s, states that the claim that the concept of equality for women arrived only with the United Nations in 1999 is simply "an attempt to discredit [gender equality] as a foreign and imposed notion."[18] The view that gender equity is incompatible with traditional culture is disputed not only by Timorese feminists, but also by cultural activists who are offended that some use Timorese culture to justify discrimination and violence against women.[19]

THE EVOLUTION OF GENDER IN TIMOR

Babel

The fixed, "traditional" role for women that I have cited bears closer examination, with an investigation of gender roles in indigenous society. Here an important observation was made in 1944 by the anthropologist Mendes Correa, who described the Portuguese colony of Timor as a "Babel ... a melting pot," referring to the diverse mix of traditions that are still strongly apparent today. Original neolithic peoples were joined by waves of Papuan migrants and Austronesian migrants from Southeast Asia over a period of centuries, so that today approximately eighteen different languages are spoken in Timor-Leste. Although there are many cultural differences between the distinct ethnolinguistic groups—for example, various groups

---

[14] Irena Cristalis and Catherine Scott, *Independent Women: The Story of Women's Activism in Timor-Leste* (London: Catholic Institute for International Relations, 2005), p. 101–2.

[15] Hilary Charlesworth and Mary Wood, "Women and Human Rights in the Rebuilding of East Timor," *Nordic Journal of International Law* 71 (2002): 334–36; Nina Hall, "East Timorese Women Challenge Domestic Violence," *Australian Journal of Political Science* 44,2 (2009): 309–12, 318–19.

[16] Mike Kesby, "Arenas for Control, Terrains of Gender Contestation: Guerrilla Struggle and Counter-Insurgency Warfare in Zimbabwe 1972–1980," *Journal of Southern African Studies* 22,4 (1996): 561–84.

[17] Carolyn Graydon, "Time to Get Serious about Women's Rights in Timor-Leste: Wrestling Change from the Grassroots Up," in *Timor-Leste: Challenges for Justice and Human Rights in the Shadow of the Past*, ed. William Binchy, Asian Law and Human Rights Series (Dublin: Trinity College 2009), pp. 386, 416.

[18] Sofi Ospina, "Participation of Women in Politics and Decision-Making in Timor-Leste: A Recent History" (Dili: UNIFEM, 2006) p. 19.

[19] Jose "Josh" Trindade, "'*Feto Mak Maromak*': Traditional Concepts of Gender in Timor-Leste," paper delivered to "Understanding Timor-Leste: Timor-Leste Studies Association Conference," Dili, University of Timor-Leste, July 2–3, 2009.

may consider themselves as either autochthonous or migratory, or as favoring matriarchal or patriarchal systems—most share similar cosmological beliefs and social structures. According to the 2010 Timor-Leste Government Census, the largest Malayo- or Austronesian-language speaking groups are the Tetun Praca (385,269 individuals), Tetum Terik (63,519), Mambai (131,361), Tokodete (39,483), Kemak (61,969), and Baikenu (62,201). The main groups of Papuan or Melanesian mother-tongue speakers include the Bunak (55,837), Fataluku (37,779), and Makassae (101,854).[20]

Timorese indigenous societies lived according to an ancient animist belief system referred to as *Lulik*. The local hereditary king, or *liurai*, was regarded as having divine attributes. Both women and men of the *liurai* class were, and still are, very powerful. Members of the *liurai's* extended family were part of the *dato*, the nobility; below them were the common farming people and, lower still, a caste of slaves.[21] These kingdoms were linked in complex political alliances renewed by ritual exchange and marriage. A modern or hybrid patronage system that appears to operate in Timor-Leste today has been referred to as *liurai*-ism.[22]

These indigenous societies share qualities, too, in their social and political organization, which revolves around concepts of complementary dualism such as *feto-mane* (male–female), *tasi feto–tasi mane* (north–south), *rai ulun–rai ikun* (east–west), *ema laran–ema liur* (insider–outsider).[23] These dualisms are woven through the hierarchical social system and a social order that establishes precedence and hierarchy. Social status is attributed in continually recurring patterns to persons and groups in relation to one another. In this way, women can be socially superior to men depending on the complementary category to which they are assigned. In cosmology, the visible and tangible secular world, *rai*, lies on the earth's surface and is dominated by men, while the sacred world, *rai laran* (the world inside), is dominated by female ancestral ghosts.

Anthropological accounts confirm the prominence given to women in ritual practices and the centrality of fertility as a powerful and sought after asset, with female symbology of womb and mother earth significant.[24] Jose Trindade highlights the sacredness accorded women across Timorese cultures and the prominence of the divine female element in much indigenous belief.[25] There is very little feminist analysis present in these anthropological works, and the characterization by

---

[20] "Population Distribution by Mother Tongue—Urban, Rural, and District," Timor-Leste Ministry of Finance, Timor-Leste Census 2010, Vol. 2, Table 13, pp. 205–6, www.mof.gov.tl/about-the-ministry/statistics-indicators/statistics-and-census/?lang=en, accessed June 13, 2012. Note that Tetun Praca is a local lingua franca. The full range of languages spoken in Timor-Leste is shown on maps in Frederic Durand, *East Timor, A Country at the Crossroads of Asia and the Pacific: A Geohistorical Atlas* (Chiang Mai: Silkworm Books, 2006), pp. 46–48, 95.

[21] Thatcher, "The Timor-Born in Exile in Australia," p. 48.

[22] Geoffrey Gunn and Reyko Huang, *New Nation: United Nations Peacebuilding in East Timor* (Macao, Tipographica Hung Heng, 2006), p. 123.

[23] Jose 'Josh' Trindade, "*Feto Mak Maromak*: Traditional Concepts of Gender in Timor-Leste," paper delivered to Understanding Timor-Leste: Timor-Leste Studies Association Conference, Dili, University of Timor-Leste, July 2–3, 2009.

[24] James Fox, ed., *The Flow of Life: Essays on Eastern Indonesia* (Cambridge, MA: Harvard University Press, 1980); Traube, *Cosmology and Social Life*; David Hicks, *Tetum Ghosts and Kin: Fertility and Gender in East Timor* (Long Grove, IL: Waveland Press, 2004).

[25] Trindade, "'*Feto Mak Maromak*.'"

anthropologists of the roles of male and female as complementary does not imply symmetry. While myth and belief make up fertile ground for the imagining (or reimagining) of a powerful place for women in Timorese society, today roles are not equal or equitable as we understand these terms in a more prosaic, modern sense (see section on Women and Men's Contemporary Status). Furthermore, while a woman's fertility determines and can extend her social status within both family and society, it appears today that women are severely limited to and by that primary role.

The mythological inner world is feminine, maternal, and sacred, while the outer world is masculine, paternal, and secular, and, according to this indigenous logic, women and girls are consigned to this internal or domestic sphere rather than the external or public sphere. Therefore, women generally have not had a strong public or political voice in Timor but may hold power in a deeper, less obvious way, such as in social exchanges and rituals.[26] Domestic duties, including care of children and preparation of food for private and public events, are the sole domain of women, and men would suffer a loss of status if seen carrying out such tasks. While this may explain the formidable positions many women hold within households, it also means the full burden of domestic chores and childrearing falls to them.

Society in Timor-Leste remains very hierarchical and senior or elite women hold powerful positions, therefore any gender analysis with respect to Timor must be modified with this class awareness. Class, or caste, is so strictly observed in the more traditional sections of Timorese society that elite and middle-class women are invested with much more power and privilege than non-dominant men. Even though there are numerous powerful elite women in Timorese public life today, this does not mean that they all act to increase the power, rights, and authority of Timorese women more generally, or address the deeper structural patterns in society that oppress women. Further implications for political leadership and the women's movement will be discussed later.

Barlake

Indigenous kinship and alliances systems are maintained through marriage. These relations are focused in the Timorese ritual, or sacred, houses (*uma lulik*), which represent the social hierarchies of origin, ancestry, and descent.[27] Customary practices that regulate marriage and relations between the families or clans of the bride and groom are called *barlake* (or *barlaque*), and these are integral to a wider, complex system of social action and ritual exchange that creates social bonds and harmony. *Barlake* customs demonstrate the central importance of women and their fertility in Timorese indigenous society and are another way of reimagining a powerful place for women in society.

Barlake creates relationships involving a lifelong commitment to provide mutual support between the families of the bride and groom and an ongoing exchange of goods and duties in the context of ritual life and death ceremonies. The value of the

---

[26] Sofi Ospina and Tanja Hohe, "Traditional Power Structures and Local Governance in East Timor: A Case Study of the Community Empowerment Project (CEP)" (Geneva: Graduate Institute of Development Studies, 2002), p. 110.

[27] Andrew McWilliam, "Houses of Resistance in Timor-Leste: Structuring Sociality in the New Nation," *Anthropological Forum* 15,1 (2005): 27–44.

barlake exchange is in accordance with the status of the *uma lulik* and that class of the families involved, and, more pragmatically, what they have the capacity to offer. Marked differences exist in *barlake* between matrilineal and patrilineal groups, with the value of exchanges and associated rituals being less in matrilineal communities.[28] Today there are significant changes to these practices, based in part on a shift in gender roles and criticisms that they contribute to domestic violence.

The exchange of goods between a bride's and groom's families is made up of a number of elements of equal value, but this appears, for the most part, to be on a symbolic level only (as the gifts from the bride's family are viewed as symbolically more valuable because they are associated with fertility). Nowadays the bride and groom's families can exchange money (of equivalent value) in place of goods.

Such commodification, along with an asymmetrical exchange of goods, favoring the bride's family, encourages the perception that women and their fertility are being paid for. A central criticism of *barlake* by the modern women's movement is that this exchange, often now reduced and referred to as a dowry, or bride-price, creates in the groom and his family a sense that they own the woman who has joined their family through marriage, a condition cited as a major factor in domestic violence and undue pressure on married women to produce children. These processes of commodification have happened in other parts of the world, such as India, and have had negative effects on women's lives. Yet many women in Timor still speak in favor of *barlake;* they say it values them and is an important part of their culture.[29] One hears women defend the *barlake* particularly in any context that notes its degradation during the Indonesian occupation—a period when women experienced a profound loss of security and status. A key distinction in this debate is between the use of the terms *value* and *price*, and this needs to be explored further. A focus on the original principles of *barlake*, rather than the amounts exchanged, may improve the outcomes for women.

Some recent research reports that domestic violence is as prevalent in matrilineal communities (where *barlake* exchanges are low) as in patrilineal communities, suggesting that *barlake* is only one of several factors that may lead to increased domestic violence.[30] A deeper analysis may be needed to disengage customary practices, like *barlake*, from entrenched socialized practices that have developed in Timor-Leste. However these factors are so interwoven that separating them out will be difficult. Allowing that cultural practices evolve and transform over time, a more fruitful approach may be to work with customary authorities to improve how women are regarded and treated within those systems.

Caravels

The process of studying and understanding what a "traditional" role for women is in Timor-Leste must also take into account the effects of Portuguese colonialism. Xavier do Amaral, one of the original leaders of FRETILIN, the modern nationalist

---

[28] Sofi Ospina, draft report with author, 2009.

[29] Alola Foundation, "Weaving Women's Stories," unpublished booklet, Dili, 2002.

[30] These findings are based on an August 2010 interview conducted in Dili by the author with a researcher from Fokupers (the local and oldest women's NGO in Timor-Leste), who carried out the research into the relationship between *barlake* practices and the prevalence of domestic violence. For various reasons the research report is not available.

movement of the 1970s, attributes a feminist agenda to the most famous rebel against Portuguese colonialism, Dom Boaventura.[31] Boaventura led an armed rebellion against the Portuguese in 1911. While it was far too early in the century for Boaventura to have developed a fully feminist consciousness, Amaral argues that one of Boaventura's grievances was the sexual abuse and exploitation of Timorese women by the Portuguese. The idea of protecting women and keeping them safe at home must have become more firmly entrenched as a result of Portuguese colonialism and Timorese resistance to Portuguese abuse of women.

For most of the twentieth century, eastern Timor was ruled directly from Portugal by the fascist dictatorship of Salazar. The colony remained neglected and closeted from any modern liberal ideas. Colonial society was strictly hierarchically ordered, with the upper echelons peopled by the Portuguese military and civilian officers. Beneath them, Timorese society was ordered according to three main social classes: an upper class of the old, elite, mixed-race persons, *mesticos,* and the *liurai* families; a middle class of *mestico* and educated native Timorese; and a lower class of the mass of uneducated native Timorese. The colonial administration was overwhelmingly maintained by an urbanized and "Portugalized" *mestico* elite. These socially prominent, "white collar patricians" believed it was their duty and right to lead the community, and their attitude toward the native Timorese was "both aloof and paternalistic." One anthropologist commented that most in Timor had "what can only be described as an obsession with social rank."[32] Education was key to class mobility and generally limited to a privileged minority, typically the sons of *liurais* and *mesticos*. However, elite girls too could be educated, typically by orders of nuns, with a heavy emphasis on the students' domestic skills.

Rosa Muki Bonaparte was another founder of FRETILIN and the only woman to hold a position within the central structure of a political party in the 1970s.[33] She was also leader of FRETILIN's Organização Popular Mulher Timorense (Popular Organization of Timorese Women, OPMT). A statement from her from the 1970s reads, "The creation of OPMT has a double objective: firstly, to participate directly in the struggle against colonialism, and second, to fight in every way the violent discrimination that Timorese women had suffered in colonial society."[34] Another OPMT member, Domingas Coelho, recollected in 1991 that "OPMT also encouraged the women to take part in meetings. The Portuguese never encouraged women to work outside the home—they were expected to stay at home all the time."[35] Current female parliamentarian Bi Soi recalled the early days of OPMT, "During Portuguese times and because of Timorese culture, East Timorese women were not allowed to express their ideas and say what they [wanted]. It was a challenge for me to contribute to and fight for women's rights."[36]

---

[31] Ospina, "Participation of Women in Politics," p. 16.

[32] Thatcher, "Timor-Born in Exile in Australia," pp. 60–95.

[33] Ospina, "Participation of Women in Politics," p. 18.

[34] Helen Hill, "FRETILIN: The Origins, Ideologies, and Strategies of a Nationalist Movement in East Timor" (master's thesis, Monash University, 1978), p. 192.

[35] E. Franks, "Women and Resistance in East Timor: 'The Centre, as They Say, Knows Itself by the Margins,'" *Women's Studies International Forum* 19,1/2 (1996): 158.

[36] This comment was made in an interview held with Bi Soi by the author in 2010, in Dili. It should appear more fully in a forthcoming chapter, "Bisoi—A Veteran of Timor-Leste's Independence Movement," in the book *Nationalist Women in South East Asia*.

Catholicism also had an enormous impact on Timorese culture. The colonial society was heavily influenced by the missionary zeal of the Catholic priests who commanded "god-like" respect.[37] Harris Rimmer explains the nature of the Catholic Church in recent times:

> The Church in Timor Lorosa'e was cut off from the outside world at the same time as the changes introduced by the second Vatican Council (1962–65) were beginning to percolate through the Church on a global level. Some trappings of the pre-Vatican II era still remain ... The Church is itself a patriarchal institution wedded to ideas of hierarchy and obedience and has supported the patriarchal structure of East Timorese society.[38]

The paternalism of the Portuguese colonial administration, when combined with its attendant Catholic Church, has had a great effect on women's strength and power in East Timor.[39] No one can measure precisely to what extent Catholicism degraded women's sacred power within the Timorese indigenous religion and replaced it with its own, more demure, version of femininity. I would argue that the late colonial-era status of women, which OPMT was fighting to improve, was inferior to the status Timorese women commanded prior to the advent of the Portuguese and their influence; certainly it was not a better one.

Today Rosa Bonaparte and other women important to the early struggle seem like ghosts: They appear in documents and occasionally in photos but, mostly, they are invisible in the telling of East Timorese history. They do not make an appearance in the Resistance Museum in Dili, where women are startlingly absent. Most of the writing on East Timor is fully focused on the men: the leaders and guerrilla fighters.

War

During the Indonesian occupation (1975–99), the military and police deliberately used violence, including the rape and torture of women and girls, to achieve political and psychological advantage over the population.[40] Peter Carey goes so far as to say that some of these acts of sexual violence appear to have been ritualistic and "designed to eradicate the sexual potency of entire elite families."[41] These abuses have been methodically documented, most comprehensively by the national

---

[37] Geoffrey Hull, "East Timor: Just a Political Question?" Occasional Paper No. 11, North Sydney: ACSJC, 1992, p. 5.

[38] Susan Harris Rimmer, "The Roman Catholic Church and the Rights of East Timorese Women," in *Mixed Blessing: Women, Religion, and the Law in Southeast Asia*, ed. Caroline Evan and Amanda Whiting (Leiden: Brill Press, Martinus Nijhoff Publishers, 2005), pp. 164, 173.

[39] Cristalis and Scott, *Independent Women*, p. 24.

[40] Mario de Araujo, "'Liberation for Everyone, Not Just Men': A Case Study of the Men's Association against Violence (AMKV) in Timor Leste," in *Gender Equality and Men: Learning from Practice*, p. 141.

[41] Peter Carey, "Challenging Tradition, Changing Society: The Role of Women in East Timor's Transition to Independence," *Lusotopie* (2001): 258. See also Sara Niner, "*Hakat klot*, Narrow Steps: Negotiating Gender in Post-Conflict Timor-Leste," *International Feminist Journal of Politics* 13,3 (2011): 413–35, for a discussion of how women who were sexually abused during the war have been rejected by communities and unrecognized in post-war programs; and Graydon, "Time to Get Serious," pp. 389–91, on these same issues.

Commission for Truth, Reception, and Reconciliation.[42] I have noted here previously the brutal effects of such armed conflict and will extrapolate further on how this can affect gender in a postwar society.

Few people have studied and documented a perhaps more surprising effect of the Indonesian occupation: how the Indonesian civilian administration also offered opportunities to women that had never existed under the Portuguese. More women were able to work under Indonesian, as opposed to Portuguese, rule: in the public service sector, a few women rose to senior positions and became involved in NGOs and state-sponsored women's organizations, such as the Dharma Wanita, for wives of civil servants, and the Pembinaan Kesejahteraan Keluarga, which worked to build the capacities of rural women and improve their living conditions. Many current female political leaders worked with the Pembinaan Kesejahteraan Keluarga, which also allowed them to disguise their work for the clandestine resistance. By the later years of the occupation, women also had greatly increased access to basic education and to tertiary education.[43]

However, human rights abuses overshadowed any such development and the national women's council, Rede Feto, estimated that 45 percent of women lost their husbands during the Indonesian occupation, so women were also forced to head households.[44] Women also took up new roles in the resistance structures, with one reliable source quoting a figure estimating the percentage of women among resistance cadres as high as 60 percent.[45] The Rede Feto statement to the United Nations Security Council in 2000 reads:

> From the invasion of 1975, Timorese women have contributed to all aspects of the resistance in the mountains: Timorese women were at once mothers, responsible for basic household duties and taking care of children. We assisted FALINTIL (the armed resistance of East Timor) in the preparation of food and other natural resources for combat rations, in the making of backpacks from palm-leaves for carrying munitions and for washing the clothes of FALINTIL as well as being fighters ourselves. Women functioned as a security watch in the free zones, taking combat rations in the free zones to be transported to the operational zones as well as taking munitions out of the operational zones into the free zones. Women also developed literacy campaigns and cultural interchanges in the free zones. In Clandestine Operations women acted as the link between the resistance inside and the Diaspora, we searched for means to obtain munitions from our husband or brothers to increase the munitions of FALINTIL; we wove *tais* and made sandals to sell them to Indonesian soldiers as a form of exchange for fatigues or shoes for FALINTIL, we prepared the combat rations to take to the armed resistance and during periods when there was no water, we looked for means to provide water to FALINTIL, and thus encountered dangerous

---

[42] CAVR, *"Timor-Leste Women and the Conflict: National Public Hearing, April 28–29, 2003,"* Dili, 2005, at http://www.cavr-timorleste.org/phbFiles/02_women_eng_WEB.pdf.

[43] Ospina, "Participation of Women in Politics," p. 21.

[44] Rede Feto, "The Role of Women in Maintaining International Peace and Security: Statement by Rede Feto," United Nations Security Council Special Session, Dili, 2000.

[45] Cristalis and Scott, *Independent Women*, p. 39.

situations. During the military sweeps under Indonesia, we hid members of the FALINTIL in our house and in difficult situations, took messages or urgent letters inside our clothing or hair to aid the leadership or FALINTIL. We contributed a monthly allowance and when captured by the Indonesian military, we resisted and thus suffered twice as much, either by being raped or by giving our life. [46]

Women were prominent in the political campaigning around the independence ballot, and we can assume (as no gender-disaggregated data was forthcoming) that women made up approximately half of the 78.5 percent of East Timorese who voted for independence in 1999. The early years of the FRETILIN-led struggle explicitly worked toward the emancipation of women, but the subsequent more pluralist leadership did not give a high priority to this element. Women are proud of their role in the resistance, but for twenty-four years, the struggle for women's rights was subsumed by the broader national struggle for independence.

WOMEN AND MEN'S CONTEMPORARY STATUS

While most Timorese live in rural poverty—a life devoted to subsistence farming—indicators for the health and well-being of women and children are worse than for men. There is substantial gender inequity in Timor-Leste, illustrated by the 2004 Human Development Index (HDI) (0.426) and Gender Development Index (GDI) (0.369), which show that women had a 13 percent lower standard of living than men.[47] Disparity between men and women exists across the domains of land ownership, political participation, access to education and economic activities, and domestic, including reproductive, decision making.

Women, overall, are less likely to participate in the salaried workforce, representing around 36 percent of non-agricultural-sector employees and, usually, occupy lower-level positions, which means they earn lower salaries, receive fewer benefits, and are less likely to be promoted.[48] In 2005, women represented around 25 percent of the civil service but held only 2 percent of the highest positions.[49] The gender wage-gap is great, with women earning one-eighth of what men earn.[50] In 2010, Timor-Leste received a rating of 55 in the Gender Equity Index (GEI) published by Social Watch (higher than Indonesia, at 52, and South Korea, at 54). This reflected an improved rating in education for females, but, overall, Timor's rating was pulled

---

[46] Rede Feto, "The Role of Women in Maintaining International Peace and Security: Statement by Rede Feto," United Nations Security Council Special Session, Dili, 2000, at http://etan.org/et2000c/october/22-31/24ther.htm

[47] Vanda Narciso and Pedro Henriques, "Women and Land in Timor-Leste: Issues in Gender and Development," *Indian Journal of Gender Studies* 17,1 (2010): 58.

[48] Monica Costa, Rhonda Sharp, and Diane Elson, "Gender-Responsive Budgeting in the Asia-Pacific Region: Democratic Republic of Timor-Leste Country Profile" (Adelaide University of South Australia, 2009), p. 5, http://w3.unisa.edu.au/hawkeinstitute/research/gender-budgets/documents/timor-leste.pdf, accessed July 3, 2012.

[49] Ospina, "Participation of Women in Politics."

[50] Asian Development Bank (ADB)/UNIFEM, "Gender and Nation Building in Timor-Leste: County Gender Assessment," 2005, p. 23, at http://www.adb.org/documents/gender-and-nation-building-timor-leste-country-gender-assessment, accessed June 2012.

down by low indicators for the economy and for women's empowerment due to the small percentage of women in technical, management, and government positions.

Women also face other problems: They have an average of eight children, with only 19 percent of those births being attended by a skilled health worker, meaning infant and maternal mortality is high, although this situation is improving.[51] Children and growing families are very welcome in a country that has been through such a brutal conflict, and many more traditionally minded rural parents believe children are their greatest wealth and a valuable asset in their subsistence farming lifestyle. Nevertheless, the high mortality figures speak for the negative impacts of this birthrate on mothers and their children. Equally, considerable child rearing and domestic duties limit women's educational and economic opportunities and political participation.

Anecdotally, many women express a desire for fewer children, yet they commonly are given few opportunities to make decisions about their fertility and sexual health, for those choices are often dictated by husband and family.[52] It is difficult for women to gain access to family planning services, and abortion is common, even though it now carries severe criminal penalties. The Catholic Church strongly opposes any changes to the abortion laws, even in cases of rape and incest, and the government is heavily influenced by church dogma. Women activists who speak out on these issues are fearful of being excommunicated.

Today the hierarchy of the Catholic Church in Timor-Leste remains conservative, stressing women's roles as wives and mothers, roles characterized by maternalism and sexual purity. While the Vatican has opposed and attacked rights perceived to challenge traditional family structures by increasing women's control over reproduction and sexuality, this does not necessarily reflect the position of all church personnel, some of whom have more pragmatic strategies to assist the poor people they serve. Giving women the right to choose how many children they have and when they have them are life-and-death choices in Timor. Understanding the cultural and religious influences on women and men in this regard is crucial.[53]

It is estimated that domestic violence accounts for 40 percent of all reported crime in Timor-Leste, yet a 2004 report found that formal justice systems dismally failed women attempting to pursue justice for such crimes.[54] Mild forms of domestic violence are viewed as normal and even as an educative tool in families. In response to these conditions, a concerted national campaign against domestic violence is well underway, which includes appearances by national leaders, suggesting a

---

[51] Some preliminary figures released in 2010 by the Ministry of Health indicate that the Total Fertility Rate (TFR) is decreasing and now may be as low as 5.7 children per woman (although an advisor to the Ministry of Health contends that this figure is based on statistics for a much wider survey group than used in previous surveys and includes unmarried women). Also reported are new figures for the maternal and infant mortality rates, and an increase in births assisted by health professionals. Presentation by Ministry of Health of the "*Strategua Nacional Saude Reproductiva Timor-Leste*," May 29, 2010, Baucau.

[52] D. J. Soares, "A Gender and Generational Perspective on Disunity," seminar paper, Crisis in Timor-Leste: Options for Future Stability Seminar, Development Studies Network, Australian National University, June 9, 2006.

[53] Esther Richards, "'Not with Fear': Understanding the Role of the Catholic Church in Reproductive Healthcare in Timor-Leste," paper delivered to "Understanding Timor-Leste," Timor-Leste Studies Association Conference, Dili, University of Timor-Leste, July 2–3, 2009.

[54] JSMP (Judicial System Monitoring Programme), "Women in the Formal Justice Sector: Report on the Dili District Court" (Dili: JSMP, 2004).

countrywide dialogue on this serious issue has begun. The campaign has been driven by strong pressure from the Timorese women's movement; many of the women involved are ex-resistance veterans. It is argued that these women strategically used the post-conflict moment and the international presence to legitimate and fund this campaign. This illustrates the crucial need to create "a locally grounded discourse of gender equality" that does not prompt political elites to respond by claiming that such reforms are simply "a western imposition."[55]

Every four years, beginning in 2000, the National Women's Congress in Timor-Leste has met to discuss priorities and concerns contained in a national platform of action. Out of the first congress emerged Rede Feto Timor-Leste, the national women's network. It has seventeen member organizations, including the oldest and largest groups—the OPMT, founded in 1975, and the Organização Mulher Timorense (Organization of Timorese Women, OMT), founded in 1998; both are nationally aligned to the two main political factions. Rede Feto's main programs are concerned with advocacy for gender equality and women's rights, and with strengthening members' organizational capacities. Rede Feto and its member organizations work together with the government and international agencies, such as the United Nations Development Fund for Women (UNIFEM) and United Nations Population Fund (UNFPA) to elevate and reinforce the status of women in Timor.[56] Much has been done, but considerable work remains.

The East Timorese women's movement has been particularly successful at advancing the more formal or "strategic" interests of women, while the more "practical," or grassroots, needs of women have not been dealt with so dynamically.[57] A tension between these priorities has been noted within the women's movement, indicated, in part, by a corresponding divide between middle-class, urban women, who are inclined to advocate a more feminist agenda, and less-educated, rural women.[58] Here we see, again, that class intersects with and has an impact upon gender. The elite women who, for the most part, form the leadership of the women's movement in the capitol of Dili have been responsible for advancing the "strategic" level initiatives (in partnership with international agencies) very successfully, while practical programs are less developed.

Political parties and campaign events are dominated by men due to women's low rate of public political participation. Women do turn out to vote in large numbers, however, which bodes well for the future. In the first National Parliament, an impressive 26 percent of members were women, yet this may not have much effect on decision making, as voting is broadly along party lines and parties continue to be dominated by men, although the UN-funded Women's Caucus and the Gender Resource Centre in the parliament are making inroads by supporting women parliamentarians. Women's inequality in Timor-Leste is also being addressed by programs of national government gender mainstreaming and budgeting. These programs have been held back by weak political will, poor technical skills, inadequate funding, and a generalized blindness, on the part of Timorese politicians,

---

[55] Hall, "East Timorese Women," p. 323.

[56] Cristalis and Scott, *Independent Women*; Ana Trembath and Damien Grenfell, "Mapping the Pursuit of Gender Equality in Timor-Leste," Globalism Institute, RMIT University, 2007.

[57] Helen Hill, paper delivered to the Australian Association for the Advancement of Pacific Studies Conference, Easter 2010, private correspondence with author.

[58] Hall, "East Timorese Women," p. 310.

to gender inequities. An essential resistance to change in the male-dominated hierarchies tend to marginalize gender equality concerns and reforms.[59]

How a post-war society treats its female veterans is a significant indicator of the status and future of women in that society.[60] In Timor-Leste, women who served either directly in the guerrilla army FALINTIL as combatants or by filling military-support roles have not been recognized and rewarded as male veterans have. Many of the women engaged in armed conflict acted as the partners of their guerrilla-fighter husbands in carrying out duties in the military camps, and they sometimes took up arms if their husbands were disabled or killed. Some of these women have been rewarded by programs for widows, but no female combatants have been included in any formal demobilization programs. This pattern is common in other post-conflict societies.[61] Sofi Ospina tracks the process:

> [Women] did not hold positions of power in the revolutionary structure or in the male dominated Falintil hierarchy. Falintil's registers, created by two independent commissions established by the President of the Republic [Xanana Gusmão] in April 2003 (for veterans and ex-combatants, respectively), did not include a single woman among the 37,472 people listed. Women, it was reasoned, were civilian cadres not combatants. Women interviewed for this study said they wanted to register but were advised by the President of the Republic to wait for the third commission, listing civilian participants. This commission, established in September 2004, registered 39,000 civil cadres *(quadros civis)*, political prisoners, and members of the clandestine front, 30 percent of whom were women.[62]

Female ex-combatants were sidelined more or less completely.[63] The current veterans' law covers Timorese citizens who engaged in warfare full time for at least three years between 1975 and 1999. There are different levels of qualified veterans—one's level is assigned according to the length of one's proven service—and benefits include ceremonial recognition, medical assistance, education, access to social programs, and housing. In 2010, there were 12,540 beneficiaries, of whom only 392 are women.[64] This program discriminates against women because a veteran's military service needs to have been continuous and full time, while most women provided part-time or intermittent support due to pregnancies, and to their responsibilities for raising families and caring for the sick, injured, and elderly. Cynthia Enloe has critiqued how postwar societies so often define "veteran" in a manner that privileges male combatants, saying, "Assignments of significance or triviality—that is, visibility or invisibility—are typically based on the gendered presumption that what men did must have been more important than what women

---

[59] Costa, "Gender Sensitive Budgeting," p. 6.

[60] Cf. Cynthia H. Enloe, *The Curious Feminist: Searching for Women in a New Age of Empire* (Berkeley, CA: University of California Press, 2004).

[61] Cahn and Ni Aolain, "Gender, Masculinities, and Transition," p. 115.

[62] Ospina, "Participation of Women in Politics."

[63] Myrttinen, "Poster Boys No More," p. 10.

[64] UNMIT (United Nations Mission in Timor-Leste), presentation on Women Veterans, July 2010.

did in determining how the war was fought."[65] As female combatants did not serve the armed struggle in ways that have been recognized by male leaders, or by international agencies involved in postwar reconstruction, women became invisible in the demobilization process and were not recognized or rewarded for their service.

In what can be described as a campaign for the recognition of women's actions during the struggle for independence, a series of documents has been published by Timorese women and their international supporters.[66] Like other issues of profound importance to women, this task has fallen to a few underresourced women who are "active in overworked local women's groups," allied with a "handful of feminists inside international agencies."[67] This work is being continued today by women concerned that their experiences are unrecognized, crimes against them have gone unpunished, and their current needs and rights are unmet. In August 2010, OPMT launched a history project. Women organizers were able to co-opt the support of elite, male political leaders—the president, prime minister, and leader of the opposition—to leverage donations from the local business community (while also taking credit for bringing these estranged leaders together on this issue and strengthening their relations with one another). Due to these laudable efforts, this issue—that women must be acknowledged for their significant contributions to the resistance—has been receiving more attention, and the recognition of women's roles is slowly progressing, though much more work is yet to be done.

In the contested world of modern Timorese history, the lack of acknowledgment of the crucial role of women in the resistance denies them a full and active role in the post-conflict society. This discrimination is being contested by women activists, but they need more assistance. Not only should female combatants be extended the same privileges as their male counterparts, but the categories of combatants need to be broadened to ensure that women who have provided unique support roles to military are included among those who have received acknowledgment and benefits.[68]

MILITARIZATION AND MASCULINITY

The dominance of men in contemporary Timorese society has been examined here. This contemporary situation is reinforced by a continuing and persistent militarization that has endured even after the Indonesian occupation ended. Cynthia Enloe, a feminist international political analyst, argues that militarization in post-war

---

[65] Enloe, *Curious Feminist*, p. 196.

[66] Rebecca Winters, *Voice of East Timorese Women* (Darwin: East Timor International Support Centre, 1999); Micato D. F. Alves, Laura. S. Abrantes, Filomena. B. Reis, *Hakarek no ran: Written in Blood* (Dili: Office for the Promotions of Equality, Prime Minister's Office, Democratic Republic of Timor-Leste, 2003); Cristalis and Scott, *Independent Women*; APSC-TL (Asia Pacific Support Collective-Timor Leste) with SEPI and MSS (published in Dili, 2008), *Segredu: Xáve ba Ukun Rasik-an* [Secrecy: The Key to Independence] (Dili: Rede Feto [with Fokupers and APSC-TL], 2012); Rede Feto (with Fokupers and APSC-TL), *Hau Fo Midar; Hau Simu Moruk* [I give sweet; I get sour] (Dili: Rede Feto [with Fokupers and APSC-TL], 2007); and Jude Conway, *Step by Step: Women of East Timor, Stories of Resistance and Survival* (Darwin: Charles Darwin University Press, 2010).

[67] Enloe, *Curious Feminist*, p. 225.

[68] Cahn and Ni Aolain, "Gender, Masculinities, and Transition," p. 120.

societies reentrenches the privileging of masculinity.[69] In East Timor, we can trace the militarization of society throughout the occupation by the Indonesian military and in the reactions of the armed and clandestine resistance organizations. Moreover, militarization did not stop at the end of the Indonesian occupation but continued with the arrival of around ten thousand UN peacekeeping forces. Vijaya Joshi describes this effect and also the "masculine nature" of the first UN administration.[70]

The predominantly male leadership of East Timor's armed struggle was engaged in a brutal and bloody war for most of their adult lives and suffered a variety of ill-effects, including displacement, imprisonment, torture, and loss of family and fellow soldiers, close friends, and colleagues. Just as disturbingly, their mothers, wives, and daughters have often been victims of sexual abuse at the hands of the Indonesian military or its militias, as Timorese women were often targeted because of their male associates, as noted. It is these male elites who now head up the government, military, and police, and the society they have shaped is heavily influenced by military thinking and behaviors and their own personal traumas. These influential men have become part of creating a dominant, or hegemonic, form of masculinity in Timor-Leste today that is not a positive one in terms of gender equity. Enloe reminds us that a militarized masculinity requires a "feminine complement" that excludes "women from full and assertive participation in post-war public life."[71] This analysis of gender relations applies accurately to Timor-Leste, as it does to many post-conflict societies.

An aggressive conflict within this male political leadership led to the 2006 national political crisis that shattered the process of reconstruction.[72] Graydon attributes some of the conflict to the "testosterone-charged question of 'Who is the biggest hero?'" and notes that local women commented that they wished male leaders could overlook their differences for the sake of the country.[73] While these events are common to post-conflict societies, such ongoing cycles of trauma, violence, and conflict are also attributable to persistent militarization in Timor-Leste. The fact that women played such a small part in the 2006 crisis—not only in causing it, but also in solving it—illustrates the reality that women lack an influential role in political and security affairs. Although it was largely members of the male political elite who caused this crisis, few analyses have held them responsible for it; security

---

[69] Enloe, *Curious Feminist*, pp. 217–18.

[70] Vijaya Joshi, "Building Opportunities: Women's Organizing, Militarism, and the United Nations Transitional Administration in East Timor" (doctoral dissertation, Clark University, Worcester, MA, 2005).

[71] Enloe, *Curious Feminist*, pp. 217–18.

[72] The national political violence of 2006 can be explained by complex internecine conflicts between male political elites and their agents, including divisions within the army, F-FDTL (between ex-guerrilla commander brigadier-general Taur Matan Ruak and rebels ultimately led by "Major" Alfredo Alves Reinado), and between the army and police force, PNTL, led until 2006 by Interior Minister Rogerio Lobato. The politicization of both forces was the result of the inept processes of selection and training of candidates under the auspices of the United Nations. These disputes opened old personal and political divisions between the then-prime minister, Marí Alkatiri, and his FRETILIN political party and then-president (now prime minister) Xanana Gusmão and his supporters. These dynamics played out a further, and some hope final, chapter in February 2008 with armed attacks on President Ramos-Horta and Prime Minister Gusmão by the rebel forces of Reinado, which led to Reinado being fatally shot during the coup.

[73] Graydon, *Women's Rights in Timor-Leste*, pp. 400–401.

and political analysts who are insensitive to gender issues rarely note the roles played by these leaders.

Another issue that is common across postwar societies with regard to demobilization is how it has failed to deal with the deep imprinting of violent masculinities in former combatants. We can see an illustration of this in Timor-Leste in the hypermasculine figure of deceased rebel leader Alfredo Reinado (see footnote 6), who was extraordinarily popular with young urban men, including some soldiers and police, many of whom aped his action-hero style. Connell highlights how this type of masculinity, shaped by and inclined to violence, is not just individualistic, "but is collectively defined or institutionally supported, whether in informal peer groups, formal armies, or militias or somewhere between the two."[74] To combat the creation of future Reinados, the Timorese should focus on addressing the causes and consequences of such negative masculinities within institutions, particularly the police and armed forces. The continuing expansion of military and police forces (whose members perpetuate fierce attitudes developed under the occupation) and the substantial purchase of military arms and hardware since 2007 appear excessive in such an underdeveloped economy. The ceremonies marking the ten-year anniversary of the police—with celebrations of weaponry—were distasteful to many observers. Even more distasteful is a new national insignia featuring crossed guns.

Today, military-style marching groups and martial arts groups throughout East Timorese society are pervasive. Since the early 1980s, Indonesian military strategy included the establishment of civilian militias, which by 1999 had developed into the national network of armed militias that fought the resistance in the bloody battle for independence. This plethora of groups, gangs, and militias gained strength again in 2006, and it remains strong in Timorese society. James Scambary notes, "While the Indonesian army and the militias may have retreated back across the border, they left behind the volatile, living legacy of a deeply militarized society with multiple, highly organized militant groups."[75] These gangs too must be engaged in programs that examine their own histories and related ideas, perspectives that underpin their actions today.

Yet the gender politics discussed here, particularly concerning perceptions of masculinity, are little monitored or addressed in contemporary gender programs. Most research on gender issues is instigated by donor agencies, while academics writing on Timor-Leste have shown less interest in gender than the NGOs have.[76] A national dialogue on masculinities and the legacy of the war is urgently needed, as is an affirmation of "a different and positive masculinity."[77] One model for this kind of campaign is the Men's Association Against Violence (AMKV), founded by twenty concerned Timorese men in 2002. They explain their work:

> Using a popular education approach, we focus on domestic violence and problems related to the tradition and customs that influence our perceptions of gender. We use common situations that would be familiar to the participants, and we talk about our own personal experiences of change. We

[74] Oxfam, *Gender Equality and Men*, p. 9.

[75] James Scambary, "Trapped in the Legacy of the Past," *Inside Indonesia* 96 (April–June 2009): 1, available at http://insideindonesia.org/content/view/1193/47/, accessed May 1, 2012.

[76] Costa, "Gender Sensitive Budgeting," p. 6.

[77] Cahn and Ni Aolain, "Gender, Masculinities, and Transition," pp. 120–21.

always promote examples of practical and realistic behaviour-change, so that on leaving the forums participants have the knowledge to make immediate change in their own lives. There are often heated debates during the discussions, but there is also a lot of humour and goodwill as participants reflect on the origins of their traditions, beliefs, and behaviour around gender differences. At the community level, there are men who are responsive and willing to be involved. However, at all levels of Timorese society, there is still a high level of disinterest and apathy around issues of gender and gender-based violence.[78]

This small group of men and other individual men have begun to challenge the widely accepted norms of male privilege, power, and use of violence, but such an important job should not be left up to underresourced NGOs and a few individuals.

CONCLUSION

Veteran and parliamentarian Maria Paixao clearly stated in 2009, "Patriarchal systems and male-biased traditional power structures within our society that impede women's leadership and equal participation in decision making still exist."[79] We know that women are profoundly important within indigenous Timorese society, that women can be powerful within their own domestic sphere, and that elite women too wield power and are very privileged. These powers and types of authority that have been granted to women traditionally, and earned by women more recently, must be built upon to improve the social situation, health, and political status of Timorese women generally.

Understanding the status and power women hold in indigenous systems is crucial, first because such an understanding can help and guide those who seek to resist contemporary pressure for women to take on a more subservient traditional role. In addition, any improvements in status for the majority of women must be made through an engagement with indigenous, or traditional, society, as this model remains culturally dominant in Timor and continues to engender a sense of identity and meaning to most people.[80] We must seek to understand how, in a strong and resilient indigenous culture like that in Timor, women's status, power, and income are maintained by traditional relations or customary practices, and how these relations can be strengthened. For instance, many rural women see *barlake* as protecting and valuing them within indigenous social systems, but the complexity and variability of the *barlake* system is little understood by scholars, international organizations, or Timorese politicians, and research about its everyday impact on women's life is sorely inadequate. Graydon outlines some promising strategies that could be used in this regard.

---

[78] Araujo, "Liberation for Everyone," pp. 143–44.

[79] Maria Paixao de Jesus da Costa, "Voices for Change: Women's Voices in Politics and Decision Making in Post-Conflict Societies," paper presented at the Second International Women for Peace Conference, Dili, March 5–6, 2009, sponsored by the Norwegian Ministry of Foreign Affairs and Fundasaun Alola.

[80] M. Anne Brown and Alex Freitas Gusmao, "Peacebuilding and Political Hybridity in East Timor," *Peace Review* 21,1 (2009): 61–69.

Issues of masculinity in Timor also remain unaddressed, and militarization as an ongoing social phenomenon is unmonitored. Enloe reminds us that "if we lack the tools to chart *postwar* militarization, we will almost certainly be ill equipped to monitor the subtle ways in which—democratic rhetoric notwithstanding—masculinity continues to be the currency for domination and exclusion."[81] Research on gender roles in Timor-Leste is sparse, and a locally grounded debate on gender roles and relations between men and women is still in its infancy. Most male academics and analysts have been gender-blind in their research on Timor, particularly in political and security analysis, and Enloe rates such analysis as not just incomplete but unreliable.[82]

There are, however, reasons to be optimistic about gender equity in Timor-Leste: The statistics show a difficult situation for women but not a hopeless one, and the crucial indicators relating to women's education and health have been improving over the last five years. The local women's movement is strong and stoic, women are well represented in parliament and the cabinet, and the current campaign against domestic violence shows the strategic strength of Timorese women leaders and their international alliances who seek to spark a cultural transformation using locally grounded debate. Moreover, the young population is not as closely bound by the conservatism of the past.

Women and men must live and work within the patriarchal systems that dominate human societies all over the world, and, acknowledging this situation, we grant the last word to a man, Mario Araujo from AMKV.

> AMKV recognizes that we have a long way to go both as an organization and as men working in the field of gender. We too are susceptible to the cultural norms of the society we live in, and it is a constant battle to be questioning long-held beliefs and customs against strong opposition. Even with the guidance and support of a Timor Leste women's movement, it will be a long and difficult journey to be accepted by both men and women alike. However the history of resistance in Timor is strong, and in a new era of nationhood we are optimistic, and determined that liberation will be for everyone, not just for men! [83]

In concert with every county and community around the world on the journey toward the ideal of gender equity, men and women in Timor have myriad perspectives that often jar and clash in a difficult post-conflict environment, making their journey a particularly difficult and bumpy one.

---

[81] Enloe, *Curious Feminist*, pp. 217–18.

[82] Ibid., p. 94.

[83] Araujo, "Liberation for Everyone," p. 145.

DECENTRALIZATION

Damien Kingsbury

In a country as linguistically complex, historically geographically divided, in which services are best delivered locally, and in which there have, more recently, been real tensions over linguistic and geographic origins, the idea of devolving key state functions to the local level has always made sense. It is also a requirement of Timor-Leste's constitution. However, the process of developing a clear idea of what such decentralization should look like, how it could work, and when and how to implement it has been far from straightforward. Importantly, too, while Dili is the source of political authority and government expenditure and is the site of most development, more than 80 percent of Timor-Leste's population live elsewhere, mostly in rural village settings. For Timor-Leste to function as a coherent state, it requires a mechanism to bring the state and its services to the people.

Although it is a tiny country, Timor-Leste's mountain ranges have historically divided its people. Situated between Southeast Asia, Melanesia, and Australia, its people have migrated from neighboring areas, bringing with them their languages and customs, the latter of which have over time found increasing commonality across the island. The traditional stories and rituals of Timor-Leste are remarkably similar, indicating a relatively high degree of nonlinguistic cultural fusion. Its languages, however, reflect the two principle sources of migration: Papua and Southeast Asia. These two chief language phyla are further divided into distinct languages and then subdivided on the basis of dialect, forming a complex linguistic patchwork of eighteen languages and sixteen distinct dialects. The preponderance of Papuan languages tends to be toward the east of the country, with Austronesian languages tending to be more located in the west, although there is a high level of mixing of these language groups across much of the country.

Geographic and linguistic groups were also traditionally divided by area among polities based on hierarchy, kinship, allegiance, and obligation. Reflecting the impact of European colonial reorganization, of Indonesian repression, political culture, and institutions, and, finally, of independence, the people of Timor-Leste have come together as a more or less politically bonded group. However, the older language divisions, kinship groups, and allegiances remain.

Also reflecting their origins, most of the people of Timor-Leste still live in rural and often quite remote areas. Despite being a relatively short physical distance from major centers, some rural communities are quite isolated from the still-limited levels of development found in the larger towns. Further reflecting the geography of the country, communication with the capital, Dili, is often difficult and inconsistent, while the people and government of Dili have limited access to the countryside. Especially given the limited resources and capacity available in Dili, there is potential for—and considerable evidence of—an urban-rural or a center-periphery divide. Given that linguistic distinctions also remain, there is also capacity for linguistic and, to some extent, geographic divisions, which came to be identified with the political violence of 2006. As a result of these factors, the government of Timor-Leste was, as this was written, in the process of establishing decentralized forms of government.

In light of the above circumstances, many political leaders have argued in favor of decentralizing the state's processes, to bring them closer to the people. There were also some strong arguments against decentralization, both in terms of practicality and vested interest. But despite these competing concerns and interests, at bottom was a commitment to this process that was articulated in the constitution of the state. Section 5.1 of the Constitution of Timor-Leste states that "the State shall respect the principle of decentralization of public administration."[1] In many respects, this constitutional requirement reflected what was already known about the linguistic and geographic make-up of Timor-Leste prior to its drafting, rather than try to impose a more common uniformity on its peoples; accepted their regional difference; and prefigured a potential contributing factor to the type of violence that characterized the events of 2006. Interestingly, the Ministry of State Administration, which was overseeing the decentralization process, had over its entrance the motto: *"Adeus Conflitu, Benvindu Dezenvolvimentu"* (Goodbye Conflict, Welcome Development), in recognition of the link between resolving conflict in order to allow development and development itself contributing to a lessening of conflict.

This chapter will consider the rationale for and strengths and weaknesses of decentralizing a developing state, and some of the specific issues that pertain to Timor-Leste. It will explain the rationale for decentralization as one principally concerned with creating greater responsiveness between the state and its citizens by devolving a degree of political and economic authority from the capital to the district level, as well as recognizing the diversity of Timor-Leste's society. The process of decentralization in Timor-Leste began in 2003 and, as this was being written, was scheduled to be implemented, at least in its initial stages, by 2014.[2] Section 5.2 of the constitution noted, however, that the laws intended to establish the characteristics of different territorial levels and administrative competencies were still to be determined.

In a normative sense, given their proximity to and often local familiarity with citizens, locally elected officials can be reasonably expected to be more directly representative of and accountable to electors. In a state in which there are structural blockages to the absorption of economic capacity, devolving greater fiscal responsibility to the districts also implies a greater flow of capital from the center to the districts, which, in turn, leads to greater capital liquidity in the districts and, hence, more equitable economic opportunity. The devolution of at least some authority to the districts also reduces pressure on what is sometimes still a poorly

---

[1] *Constitution of the Democratic Republic of Timor-Leste 2002.* See also Section 157h, www.constitution.org/cons/east_timor/constitution-eng.htm, accessed June 11, 2012.

[2] Susanne Kuehn, "Briefing Note on the Decentralization Process in Timor Leste," UNDP report, Dili, UNDP–UNCDF Local Governance Support Program, 2010.

understood or developing sense of state-based national identity, while reaffirming the legitimacy of a sense of the local in a still-evolving political framework.

In most prior development models, centralization, which paralleled modernization theory in development processes, was initially thought to be the most rational use of state resources, especially where those resources were limited. According to those who proposed this model, the center would be able to distribute appropriately and evenly the goods and services available, while at the same time helping ensure loyalty to a state, often recently constructed around a still-developing political identity, as opposed to devolving the available stock of allegiances to local, separate, and potentially antistate entities. For developing states that had developed a Soviet-bloc model of state administration, centralized control also ensured full state authority over political matters, notably through the omniscience of the party of government's central committee. In Western-bloc-aligned states, centralization was seen as a rational bureaucratic allocation of limited resources in areas of state responsibility. However, as with the "modernization" paradigm implied in both these models, centralization was often bureaucratically inefficient and insensitive to or unaware of local needs; it privileged centralized and sometimes ethnically specific elites; and it bred corruption and unproductive political competition over control and allocation of limited resources.

Following the failure of development of many centralized developing states (of both Western and Soviet camps), from the 1980s, there was turn toward decentralization, along with the diminution of high levels of government expenditure—often the main or only source of capital—and attendant moves toward the privatization of what were once government activities. There was also a parallel move on the part of many developing states to limit overall government expenditure, not least under International Monetary Fund "structural adjustment" programs. Under such programs, large central bureaucracies were often dramatically reduced, with responsibility for (often reduced) state services being allocated locally. These changes toward a more local model of state service delivery were increasingly promoted as a method for ensuring a more "authentic" path to development.[3] It should be acknowledged that some proponents of decentralization had been arguing in favor of this model since the early 1960s.[4] Like most ideas in development, the practice rarely matched the theory, and the experience of decentralization in the lives of people in developing countries was, therefore, mixed.

In Indonesia, the state decentralized in 2001, in response to regional tensions following the collapse of the Indonesian economy in 1997 and the fall of the highly centralized New Order administration in 1998. Indonesia's restructuring of its government was, at the time, regarded as the most radical decentralization program to have been undertaken in the Asia Pacific region.[5] No clear rationale was ever given for Indonesia's decentralization process, although it was widely understood to

---

[3] Philip Mawhood, "Decentralisation in the Third World in the 1980s," *Planning and Administration* 14,1 (1987): 10–22; Dennis Rondinelli, "Decentralisation in Comparative Perspective," *International Review of Administrative Science* 47,2 (1981): 133–45; Diane Conyers, "Decentralization: The Latest Fashion in Development Administration," *Public Administration and Development* 3,1 (1983): 97–109.

[4] For example, Henry Maddick, *Democracy, Decentralisation, and Development* (London: Asia Publishing House, 1963).

[5] Mark Turner and Owen Podger, *Decentralisation in Indonesia: Redesigning the State* (Canberra: Asia Pacific Press, Australian National University, 2003), p. xii.

be in response to an explosion of militant separatist claims, on one hand,[6] and a considerable sense of disenchantment with Jakarta's excessively centralized economic and political failure, on the other.[7] The Indonesian model of decentralization, then, gave renewed life to the idea of decentralization, not least as a means of quelling regional tensions.

Despite its relative popularity in recent years, decentralization does, however, have potential and actual weaknesses. These weaknesses include greater opportunities for patronage and nepotism, typically lower levels of organizational capacity among local (as opposed to central) government offices, the potential to weaken central planning, and reduced efficiencies of scale. In the short term, decentralization can also fragment national identity by reinforcing local ethnic identity relative to a state-oriented "national" identity. In the longer term, however, decentralization can strengthen national identity by appealing to and strengthening common democratic process through greater opportunities for participation, more direct representation, and greater accountability.

Through this shift toward greater representation and accountability, there is the potential for citizens to cohere around sets of values that reflect a reciprocal and equitable relationship between the citizenry and the state. From this development, a nation's citizens, initially understanding themselves as local and specific, further derive the potential to progress toward understanding themselves in common with others who share their civic values, which, in turn, creates stronger and more sustainable national bonds between citizens over diverse geographic and cultural spaces.

STRENGTHS OF DECENTRALIZATION

One of the biggest problems facing recently independent and other developing states, especially those with limited capacity,[8] is their tendency toward the centralization of what are often limited government services and resources.[9] This is a result of the need to concentrate the state capacity that is available close to the source of political authority so as to ensure the maximization of benefit from limited human and other resources. Timor-Leste was a good example of this centralization at work,

---

[6] In 2000 and 2001, when the decentralization policy was being planned and introduced, Timor-Leste had just separated from Indonesia; the separatist war in Aceh was at a peak of violence, and continuing at a lower level of violence in West Papua, Ambon, and other parts of Maluku; central and north Sulawesi were devoured by religious conflict, some of which religious violence had origins in separatist claims; there had been recent ethnic violence in Kalimantan; Riau was making noises about wanting separation; and even some Balinese were expressing discontent with what they saw as being shackled to a Java-dominated state, as represented by Jakarta.

[7] This observation is based on numerous discussions with Indonesians in Jakarta, as well as across much of the rest of the archipelago, in the period between 1997 and 2004.

[8] The limits upon or reduction of state capacity in post-colonial states is discussed in relation to sub-Saharan African states in Englebert Pierre, "Pre-Colonial Institutions, Post-Colonial States, and Economic Development in Topical Africa," *Political Research Quarterly* 53,1 (2000): 7–36; Richard Cornwall, "The End of the Post-Colonial State System in Africa?" *African Security Review* 8,2 (1999): 82–96; and David Hirschmann, "Early Post-Colonial Bureaucracy as History: The Case of the Lesotho Central Planning and Development Office, 1965–1975," *International Journal of African Historical Studies* 20,3 (1987): 455–70.

[9] Damien Kingsbury, *East Timor: The Price of Liberty* (New York, NY: Palgrave, 2009), p. 107.

especially under the newly independent state's first government, which through its central-committee-dominated political structure had a centralizing tendency in any case,[10] and which, under its prime minister, Marí Alkatiri, micromanaged much of government business. This micromanagement was intended to reduce waste within a limited budget and reduce the corruption that had been endemic under the Indonesian administration and that tended to decrease in the culture of the post-Indonesia administration.[11]

Despite the underlying good sense of the close control/micromanagement policy pursued by Alkatiri, it had two negative impacts. The first negative impact was that the degree of micromanagement meant that processing the numerous requests for expenditure created a financial bottleneck. This meant that desperately needed funds were often not made available in a timely manner for a range of projects, particularly those in the districts outside the capital of Dili, nor were basic government services always available.[12] The second negative impact was that Dili received a disproportionately higher degree of government revenue than the districts, creating increased competition for access to those resources within Dili and greater competition for political patronage beyond Dili. This then set up a situation in which underemployed people in the districts would come to Dili seeking work and services, creating an unsustainable growth in Dili's population and a large pool of unemployed persons, especially youths, in this urban area. According to former World Bank–appointed advisor to Timor-Leste's first government:

> Ramos-Horta [said] a 50 percent increase in housing investment last year marks a significant act of faith by the community in the country's future, despite its lack of secure land title. But these comments reflect the Dili economy, ignoring the one million or more people who live in rural areas, largely dependent on tilling small plots of land. The lack of public-sector investment outside Dili is blindingly obvious, forecasting a serious development trap. A booming Dili economy will draw more people from the districts, leading to more youth unemployment, more gangs and more crime.[13]

The disproportionate allocation of resources in Dili also meant that the restricted resources available in the districts outside Dili increased the numbers of needy potential clients and relatively more powerful patrons who controlled scarce government resources. This outcome both militated against democratic outcomes that were said to be desired by the government and which were enshrined in the constitution and facilitated corruption and nepotism on the part of local officials.

---

[10] Helen M. Hill, *Stirrings of Nationalism in East Timor—FRETILIN 1974–1978: The Origins, Ideologies, and Strategies of a Nationalist Movement* (Sydney: Otford Press, 2002), p. 3, regarding its earlier phase.

[11] Kingsbury, *Price of Liberty*, p. 108.

[12] Ministry of State Administration and Territorial Management, *MSATM Develops Joint National Programme to Support the Decentralization Process,* Democratic Republic of Timor-Leste, Dili, 2010.

[13] Paul Cleery, "Timor's Poor in Peril amid Plenty," *Australian,* June 26, 2010, p. 12.

The move towards decentralization, then, was intended to reduce or resolve funding bottlenecks, to provide a wider and more equitable allocation of access to government services in rural areas,[14] to increase the state's overall absorptive capacity, and to increase financial liquidity in areas that had little cash flow. Decentralization was also intended to soften the process of nation formation, in which alien concepts could be introduced too quickly or jarringly and thus lead to misunderstanding and sometimes rejection. The decentralization program was, importantly, also intended to recognize that while there is a sense of common identity in Timor-Leste, based primarily around a common struggle for independence, there was also a sense of specific difference between various language and geographic groups. The issue of absorptive capacity was particularly troubling, in that the state was often unable to spend the full allocation of the still relatively limited funds that it had available. That is, despite there being relatively little money to spend, ministries responsible for the spending of funds in order to implement state policy were not even able to allocate and spend the amount that was available. This meant that the limited economic stimulus that might have been available, especially for the majority of the population living outside Dili, was missing due to an inability of the state to "absorb" the finances that were available.

One of the key aims of decentralization was to promote transparency[15] through a more directly and locally accountable political process. However, there were some concerns that handing the allocation of funding projects to the district level would increase localized nepotism, corruption, and waste. There was already a tendency for officials to allocate spending on local projects to family members, sometimes through the districts in which the work, such as road building or maintenance, was to be undertaken. Given the relatively small size of local communities and the limited opportunities for advancement and, particularly, the small number and often interconnectedness of business and political elites, nepotism was not always overtly intentional, even if there was an awareness of the closeness of the contracting process. Similarly, notions of conflict of interest were not so much poorly understood as simply not understood at all. Corruption in its more formal sense was better understood, even if, in many respects, as an acculturated business practice. Many local citizens attributed corruption among local officials to the negative influences of the Indonesian occupation, during which corruption was indeed rife (and still is in much of Indonesia). However, this assumed that corruption did not exist in Timor prior to the Indonesian interregnum, an assumption challenged by the scanty evidence from before 1975, which tends to indicate that both Portuguese officials, as well as lower level indigenous employees, all engaged in varieties of corruption, contract rigging, favoritism in official employment, and skimming from the very few services that were provided by the Portuguese colonial administration. This is not, of course, to mention the numerous ways in which patron-client relations allow for nepotism, profit taking, and extortion in ways that did not even have the most distant relationship to notions of good governance. In that there was potential for waste, this possibility then raised the sometimes troubled issue of value judgments concerning the best use of money or the standards of goods or services acquired;

---

[14] Ministry of State Administration, *Decentralisation and Local Government in Timor-Leste: Policy Orientation Guideline for Decentralisation and Local Government in Timor-Leste*, Government of Timor-Leste, March 2008, Section 1.2.

[15] Ibid., p. 2.

what was "waste" to people with certain perspectives was "value" for money or appropriate disbursement to others. In short, the often poor standard of goods or services provided, the poor quality of workmanship, the (failure of) completion schedules, and very often the general disinterest in paid work (as opposed to support payments that require no work) were issues that could be found in developing countries all over the world. However, they were very evident in Timor-Leste, where common practices ranged from "fixing" something so that it always existed on the edge of again breaking down, to seeking a job in an office, particularly a government office, principally for its status and the opportunity to use computers to play games.[16] All too commonly, jobs were half done or done so poorly they were either abandoned or needed to be done again or recognized as having been unnecessary and badly planned in the first place.

In some senses, such concerns about the mismanagement of funds—important though this mismanagement undoubtedly remained—was less important than the fact that funds were being allocated into areas where the resident officials and citizens would, one way or the other, spend them on local goods and services. This was then intended to help produce fiscal liquidity and stimulate local economic activity in areas that had previously been economically stagnant and in which cash was a rare commodity, thus cutting off local people from all but bartered goods. In that funding would be allocated on a needs basis, it was hoped that the closer relationships between the funding body and the recipients and (externally applied) appropriate accountability mechanisms would help ensure the more nuanced and detailed allocation of funding to where it was most needed.

Finally, the state comprises peoples of diverse ethnic identities who in 2006 appeared to divide along broad geographic lines and also along language group lines. While there was a high degree of political manipulation in the conflict of 2006, based on political divisions that arose during the resistance, they did highlight the need for a devolution of politics and the economic decision-making authority intended to accompany national politics that might alleviate some of the strain from a still nascent sense of national identity. This reaffirmation of the local, as opposed the putatively "national," was expressed more positively as "the maintenance of ethno-linguistic homogeneity and local cultural identity."[17]

WEAKNESSES OF DECENTRALIZATION

The process of decentralization is not especially new as a means to allocate resources more effectively, to devolve administrative responsibility away from a sometimes remote center, and to place greater and more direct political control in the hands of local people. However, the experiences of decentralization have not always been successful, for a range of reasons. As Paul Smoke, Eduardo Gomez, and George Peterson have noted:

---

[16] The author had the experience, in Dili in 2008, of asking a young university graduate what he wanted to do. "Get a job with the government," was the answer. "Why?" the author asked. "So," came the reply, "I can have a computer and play games." To be fair, however, there are many conscientious government employees who work long and hard hours with few resources and limited reward.

[17] Ministry of State Administration, *Decentralisation and Local Government in Timor-Leste*, p. 3.

> During the 1990s it became clear that the normative expectations of decentralization had often exceeded its actual performance. Subnational deficits, debt, corruption, and inefficient resource allocation emerged in many countries, in a few cases threatening national fiscal stability ... In effect, normatively justified decentralization had met political and institutional reality.[18]

In this, Smoke, Gomez, and Peterson were primarily concerned with economic managerial capacity. Mark Turner and Owen Podger expressed similar concerns:

> In theory, decentralized systems of government are better able to address poverty because of their familiarity with the local situation, the greater accessibility of the poor to decision makers, and the more rapid response rates of local government. These assumptions begin to unravel if bureaucratic forms of organisation remain characteristic of regional government, if local elites monopolise the benefits of devolution, and if popular accountability is poorly articulated or implemented.[19]

However, at least as great a concern, and possibly a greater one, has been that by taking away financial accountability from a coherent center that is able to be scrutinized, decentralization can provide greater opportunities for patronage and nepotism. As noted by Turner and Podger, "Local democracy might tend to favor local elites, and the emergence of 'money politics.'"[20] In particular, the experience of decentralization in Indonesia often meant that a state that had experienced a high level of centralized corruption had, through the process of decentralization, in effect, decentralized the already high levels of corruption and arguably increased overall levels of corruption.[21]

While Timor-Leste is now independent, the administrative processes that most East Timorese have experienced and learned to use are those introduced by Indonesian bureaucrats during the period of the occupation. This administrative style has left a deep imprint on notions of how to administer both local and national government, along with notions of the privileges that can be claimed by those who wield administrative and bureaucratic authority. Parallel to this, as is true in Indonesia, has been the dilemma that faces government employees who receive low levels of income relative to their high costs of living and who, at the same time, enjoy greater access to sources of official funds. Recognition of corruption in Timor-Leste[22] has led to the establishment of an anti-corruption commission and a state-wide anti-corruption campaign. The question is whether this relatively new and, at the time of

---

[18] P. Smoke, E. Gomez, and G. Peterson, "Understanding Decentralization: The Need for a Broader Approach," in *Decentralization in Asia and Latin America,* ed. P. Smoke, E. Gomez, and G. Peterson (Cheltenham: Edward Elgar, 2006), p. 3. See also R. Sukma, "Conflict Management in Post-Authoritarian Indonesia," in *Autonomy and Disintegration in Indonesia,* ed. D. Kingsbury and H. Aveling (London: RoutledgeCurzon, 2003), p. 71.

[19] Turner and Podger, *Decentralisation in Indonesia,* p. 141–42.

[20] Ibid., p. xiv.

[21] T. Rinaldi, M. Purnomo, and D. Damayanti, *Fighting Corruption in Decentralized Indonesia* (Jakarta: World Bank, 2007).

[22] USAID, *Corruption Assessment: Timor-Leste* (Washington, DC: United States Agency for International Development, 2009), pp. 2–11.

writing, untested anti-corruption commission would be effective against significant vested interests and have the scope and capacity to reach beyond Dili and into the districts.

One of the further issues experienced when Indonesia underwent decentralization was that, in many cases, there was a dearth of administrative capacity at the local level. As Dennis Rondinelli noted, the lure of the metropolis, including national ministries, state corporations, and other agencies, also tended to attract away the most talented and best-educated officials from the regions, leaving a chronic shortage of talent at the local level.[23] Ismet Fanany also noted this phenomenon in Indonesia, whereby "the highly centralized system of administration in Indonesia has tended to draw capable administrators to the centre as they moved up through the administrative hierarchy, leaving what is perceived as a talent vacuum at the regional level."[24] According to Shabbir Cheema and Rondinelli, "Decentralization can only be effective when agencies and actors at the regional and local levels have developed the capacities to perform effectively the planning, decision-making and management functions that are formally granted to them."[25] Such studies demonstrate that the effectiveness of decentralization depends on the capacity of local institutions to identify problems, solutions, and opportunities to define and resolve development issues, decision making and conflict resolution, organization of resources, and management skills.

Although the government of Timor-Leste has significantly developed since the tabula rasa of 1999, there is still little administrative capacity within the state, and what capacity exists is often very shallowly rooted and—descending beyond the senior layers of bureaucratic management—quickly reveals low levels of understanding and performance in government administration. This is especially the situation at the district level.

DELAYED DECENTRALIZATION

While a lack of local capacity and localized corruption have been shown to be critical problems with at least some cases of decentralization, poor initial planning has also hampered the ability of a number of states to put in place an adequate, proper, functioning decentralized political system. The process in Timor-Leste was intended to be rolled out in two stages so as to test the process initially with just four districts—Dili, Bobonaro, Oecussi, and Baucau—before bringing the remaining nine districts into the program. However, even this plan was a modification of the original plan, according to which four districts were to be decentralized, followed by five, and then another four.[26] The plan to revert from a four-five-four rollout model to a four-nine model followed the extended delay in the process of drafting and approving the three pieces of requisite legislation, with the planned drafting and legislative process running over a year behind schedule and the initial date of

---

[23] Dennis Rondinelli, "Decentralization of Development Administration in East Africa," in *Decentralization and Development: Policy Implementation in Developing Countries*, ed. G. Shabbiir Cheema and D. Rondinelli (Beverly Hills, CA: Sage Publications, 1983), pp. 77–126.

[24] Ismet Fanany, "The First Year of Local Autonomy: The Case of West Sumatra," in *Autonomy and Disintegration in Indonesia*, p. 178.

[25] Cheema and Rondinelli, *Decentralization and Development*, p. 299.

[26] This is based on discussions with senior state administration officials in September 2008.

implementation pushed back from 2009 to 2014.[27] The three pieces of requisite legislation included legislation on defining the districts that would be granted greater political power (Law on Administrative and Territorial Division, approved June 2009), the composition of the new local legislatures (Local Government Law), and the competencies of the new local legislatures (Municipal Elections Law).[28]

Having passed through the council of ministers, the legislation in question was initially expected to be passed quickly, but is almost immediately ran into problems. Despite the fact that the government held a majority in parliament, it was clear from the outset that sifting through the eighty-four pages of Portuguese legal text that comprises the legislation would take time and require Timor-Leste's representatives to do more than simply rubber-stamp the document. There were problems from the outset, not least a statement in the draft legislation determining that the new district mayors would be both directly elected and elected by their councils and that a directly elected mayor could be removed by a vote of the council. Such glaring problems required a detailed reappraisal of the proposal. Beyond these problems there was some concern that the existing subdistrict administration, which appeared to serve communities relatively well, would disappear, to be replaced by municipal branch offices.

Delays in the drafting and legislative schedule, caused by efforts to address internal inconsistencies and weaknesses in the draft legislation, meant that the decentralization process was traveling well behind its original schedule. In particular, while there was little debate about the boundaries for the electoral districts given that they were based on existing districts, there was considerable debate about what powers should be devolved to district legislatures. In part, this reflected concern with local competencies, and in part, it reflected concern by some ministers over the devolution and, hence, loss of their own ministerial authority.

> The draft laws call for a strong central government with nominal powers for local government and give the central government control over everything the local government does, including the legislative assembly. And the central government proposes to retain the power to review all the legislative assembly's decisions.[29]

Finally, delays were caused by inadequacies in the national parliamentary system, in which the relevant parliamentary committee was unable to finalize its approval of the legislation to go to parliament. The deadlock in this committee was due, in part, to the constructed pedantry of some of the elected representatives who continued to disapprove of the formation of the government, which had carriage of the legislation. The deadlock also reflected a genuine weaknesses in the legislation as it was initially

---

[27] J. Coa, "Municipal Elections Postponed Until 2014," *Dili Weekly* 91, Year III, June 2010, p. 1.

[28] S. Kuehn, Briefing Note on the Decentralization Process in Timor Leste, UNDP—UNCDF Local Governance Support Program report, Dili, 2010, www.estatal.gov.tl/Documents/DNDLOT/LGSP/BriefingNoteDecen2011.pdf, accessed May 20, 2012.

[29] Silas Everett and Juan Mayo Ragragio, "Decentralisation in Timor-Leste: What's at Stake?" *East Timor Law and Justice Bulletin*, June 26, 2009, http://asiafoundation.org/in-asia/2009/06/24/decentralization-in-timor-leste-whats-at-stake/, accessed May 1, 2012.

proposed.[30] Delays were also caused by the committee often being unable to assemble a quorum. This was the result of two principal factors: (a) there were no party or parliamentary whips to ensure that members attended committee meetings and parliamentary sessions, and members of smaller parties sometimes had to attend different committee meetings at the same time, and (b) to help ensure that parliamentarians did not ignore areas outside Dili, there were financial incentives to spend time in the districts that exceeded financial incentives to remain in Dili.[31]

By way of comparison, in Indonesia the decentralization process was quickly conceived and implemented. The Indonesian decentralization process also showed that, despite a systematic and participatory regulatory process, the process of establishing regulation for decentralization was "disorderly," according to Turner and Podger, who further note that "Top level political support was lacking, central agencies were sometimes uncooperative, and regional stakeholders were rarely consulted."[32] While the Timor-Leste experience of decentralization was, in a number of senses, different from that of Indonesia, including the extent of the powers available to the local assembly, and the differences in scale, as Timor-Leste's government was so much smaller than Indonesia's, there were also clear parallels between the two. The main parallel was that both states regarded decentralization as a mechanism that would enable the state to better serve local communities, on one hand, while, on the other, reducing pressure arising from local groups that had political and cultural identities that were distinct from those of the political center. Indonesia came to this position more than five decades after independence; Timor-Leste had this requirement written into its constitution from the outset. Timor-Leste enjoyed another advantage over Indonesia with respect to decentralization; the extended delays that postponed the implementation of Timor-Leste's program meant that, although there was a degree of inadequate consultation with district-level stakeholders, lawmakers had more time to insure that requisite regulations would be in place before the program commenced.

In light of the slowness of implementation of decentralization, and following a national tour of Timor-Leste's districts, in May 2010, the prime minister, Xanana Gusmão, authorized direct payments of up to US$50,000 to each of the 442 *suco*-level (village-level) administrations.[33] This had the effect of injecting funds directly into local communities while the decentralization program issue was being resolved and of lessening the districts' reliance on central administration to disburse funds regionally. This move toward allocating funds directly to the *suco* level was resisted to some extent by ministers who saw a diminution of the funds thus available to them for disbursement. However, the total fund allocated was not great and did not have a meaningful impact upon ministers' departmental budgets. Rather, there was a feeling that this experience was a foretaste of the subsequent diminution of the ministers' political power, which they did not like. From the perspective of the prime

---

[30] According to a senior FRETILIN parliamentary source who said the original drafts contained numerous weaknesses that needed to be resolved (personal communication, July 2010, Dili).

[31] Based on discussions with Government of Timor-Leste advisors during 2009.

[32] Turner and Podger, *Decentralisation in Indonesia*, p. xiii.

[33] "Xanana Resist against Indonesia Used Strategic Guerilla Warfare and to Develop the Country with PEDN," *Tempo Semanal*, May 31, 2010, http://temposemanaltimor.blogspot.com /2010/05/xanana-resist-against-indonesia-used.html, accessed May 1, 2012.

minister, however, his tour of the districts, combined with the allocation of funds, helped shore up his personal popularity and, hence, that of his political party, the Council for Timorese National Reconstruction (Congresso Nacional Reconstrucção de Timor, CNRT), ahead of the 2012 elections. Indeed, such was the boost given to the prime minister's political standing by this gesture that it was widely thought that he could capitalize on it and call an early election. Such was the power of appealing directly to voters, and offering them even modest funding, where they lived.

One of the potential problems with decentralization, however, that was, to some extent, experienced also in Indonesia, was that the process had the potential to weaken national planning. Effective national planning can be disrupted if different districts embark on distinct and uncoordinated development programs, in particular regarding infrastructure and cross-boundary resource programs. This potential dilemma, in part, explained the limitations that lawmakers and analysts expected would be imposed upon districts, both in their initial start-up periods of decentralization as well as later in the process, when they would still be held accountable to the central government. In Indonesia, following decentralization, local economic disputes became commonplace and potentially destabilizing, in particular, in relation to access to local resources.[34] There was one case, in particular, in West Sumatra, in which one district administration halted the flow of a river that, downstream, supplied the water needs of another administration. This dispute did not last long but was indicative of the lack of planning that could go into such decision making, or the improper purposes to which these various, regional development plans could be put. The disputes that did arise concerning transport and water-basin management in Indonesia were finally resolved through interregional cooperation; it was in the interests of all parties to cooperate to achieve shared outcomes otherwise not individually available. Even where there was interregional cooperation, in Timor-Leste there remained potential for the central government to have to negotiate with each of the thirteen districts in order to achieve consensus on which development projects should be initiated across the state, and the coordination for that process.[35]

One of the advantages of centralization of resources is that a central government can achieve greater efficiencies of scale in planning, time, and expenditure by saving on replication and being able to purchase goods and services in larger quantities, hence, more cheaply. By way of contrast, smaller planning units would not be able to achieve such efficiencies, would tend to replicate a range of services that need implementation only once to be effective, and would buy goods and services in relatively small quantities, at less competitive prices. Fiscal management can also be weakened by economic decentralization in cases where regions have responsibility for raising, allocating, or forwarding taxes.[36] However, those who have shaped and implemented Timor-Leste's decentralization process do not envisage fiscal decentralization but, rather, expect that the central government will manage the economy and allocate resources to the districts on a per capita basis.

---

[34] Turner and Podger, *Decentralisation in Indonesia*, p. 142.

[35] See, for example, Sukma, "Conflict Management in Post-Authoritarian Indonesia," p. 70, on the Indonesian experience.

[36] V. Gandhi, "Intergovernmental Fiscal Relations and Economic Performance," in *Macroeconomic Management and Fiscal Decentralization*, ed. J. Roy (Washington, DC: World Bank, 1995).

Finally, in the short term, and noting that decentralization is at least in part intended to preserve and enhance local cultural identity, decentralization can have the potential to fragment national identity by reinforcing rather than resolving distinct and sometimes competing ethnicities. In a country in which a sense of state-based national identity had not yet been fully formed, that is weak or under challenge, strengthening the citizenry's local as opposed to the national allegiances may reinforce regional differences rather than commonalities. Given the regionally distinct character of political allegiances in Timor-Leste, this stood as a real problem, if in the planning stage it was still only a potential problem. In all, then, where decentralization has been attempted in developing countries, "in most cases, central governments initiated, introduced, and heavily publicized decentralization policies only to see them falter during implementation."[37] That is to say, decentralization has a number of theoretical advantages to offer a highly centralized state with limited capacity and resources, but it also presents a number of new challenges, many of which have not been adequately addressed in a number of decentralization projects that have been implemented elsewhere.

DOES DECENTRALIZATION STRENGTHEN DEMOCRACY?

There are two key normative features of decentralization, which are inter-related. The first normative feature of decentralization is the allocation of resources closer to the source of receipt to help ensure the more precise delivery of those resources to the citizens. The second normative feature of decentralization is that it brings accountability for such allocation closer to the people for whom it is intended. As Peter Aucoin and Ralph Heintzman noted, "Accountability is the cornerstone of public governance and management because it constitutes the principle that informs the processes whereby those who hold and exercise public authority are held to account."[38] Decentralization is intended to achieve its intended outcomes by strengthening the relationship between citizens and public authority, through the state's local manifestations.

The key element of Timor-Leste's decentralization process is the establishment of local municipal councils that were intended to have responsibility for overseeing local planning and the allocation of resources.[39] For many people in Timor-Leste, despite improvements in transport and communications, the center of the state in Dili remained physically and conceptually remote from their daily lives. Indicative surveys had shown that, short of the forced migration that characterized the Indonesian period, most Timorese never traveled more than forty kilometers from their place of birth. The localness of life—while not necessarily a factor in the success or failure of decentralization—was compounded by the often very poor infrastructure that made extensive travel difficult, if not impossible, and the prohibitive costs associated with travel. Further, Timor-Leste's use of a proportional

---

[37] Cheema and Rondinelli, *Decentralization and Development*, p. 297.

[38] Peter Aucoin and Ralph Heintznman, "The Dialectics of Accountability in an Era of Reform," *International Review of Administrative Sciences* 66,1 (2000): 45.

[39] The extent of the allocation of resources was, at the time of writing, not finalized, but appeared to have been reduced from extensive allocations to, at least initially, the allocations of health care, as per Section 57 of the Constitution, and water.

representation electoral system,[40] intended to ensure the greatest representation of disparate political views, meant that local citizens did not have locally elected representatives; politicians did travel to the districts, but there was a sense that, for most Timorese, these representatives were remote and not directly accountable or responsive. The establishment of local councils was, then, intended to establish a system of representation closer to where people actually lived and empower representatives who would be potentially better able to include local people in the political process, in terms of consulting and commenting on, and contributing to policy development. This then would help ensure accountability, as well as participation in the political process, for local citizens could potentially run for a seat on the municipal council.

The councils themselves were intended, potentially, to be better able to understand and reflect the concerns of local citizens in their policy prescriptions, and be directly accountable for the successes and failures of implementing such policies. As noted by Leena Avonius, in relation to Indonesia's process of decentralization, "The laws on regional autonomy were seen as an opportunity for establishing a new kind of local government which would be more democratic and transparent."[41] It may well be that there were a number of organizational difficulties in the implementation of decentralization in Indonesia, and there is little doubt that this particular process decentralized and thus dispersed previously highly centralized corruption along with political and economic capacities. But decentralization did give ordinary Indonesians greater and more direct access to government services and was a key component in helping to lessen regional tensions at a time when opposition to the political center, exemplified by the Jakarta bureaucracy, was at its highest point since the late 1950s. In terms of corruption, by way of comparison, in Timor-Leste some ministers who had already received kick-backs from promised contracts not yet awarded were frustrated by the reduction of their budgets for the 2010 *suco* funding program. However, even the *suco*-level direct funding was hamstrung by a number of Dili-based companies setting up district-level offices and applying for local contracts, with much of the money from the contracts that were won simply returning to Dili. This, then, explained at least some of the reluctance of Timor-Leste's central government representatives to embrace fully the decentralization program, even though decentralization in Timor-Leste took place in political terms and much less so in economic terms.

More positively, while decentralization is explicitly intended to enhance local cultural identity, general agreement that local identities can and should be supported in effect constitutes agreement on the principle of pluralism, or the acceptance of difference within a varied community. Further, while local communities might refocus their immediate attentions on local matters if encouraged to do so by decentralization, increased engagement with and participation in political processes, including direct representation and greater accountability, enhances the process of embedding democratic principles across the state. Accountability, in particular, further implies notions of social fairness, justice, and rule of law. Each of these

---

[40] The proportional representation electoral system is where candidates are elected from party lists across the state rather than on a seat-by-seat, direct representational basis.

[41] L. Avonius, "Indonesian *Adat* Communities: Promise and Challenges of Democracy and Globalisation," in *The Politics of the Periphery in Indonesia,* ed. M. Sakai, G. Banks, and J. Walker (Singapore: NUS Press, 2009), p. 232.

qualities is a key marker of civic political development, and general subscription to such values implies, not a replacement of local identity, but the addition of a consensus around civic values.

CONCLUSION

If we accept that the term "nation" refers to a state that has been founded upon, among other things, a common cultural or ethnic identity,[42] Timor-Leste faced serious challenges to national cohesion, as a consequence of the ethnic distinctions that characterized its peoples. These differences were widely claimed to have contributed to the breakdown of political order that wracked the state in 2006 and led to a situation perilously close to civil war. However, the citizenry's growing commitment to such civic values provided an alternative site of national unity that did not rely on primordial loyalties but to a growing sense of engagement in and identification with the state. This, then, was the glue that would, it was hoped, bond the nation as it continued to develop.

The benefits of decentralization in Timor-Leste, as elsewhere, were not at any point a given, and the process has continued to face significant challenges. The critical criterion in determining its success or otherwise appeared to be the extent of care in the design and application of the process. To that end, the plan to introduce decentralization first to four districts and later to others seemed sensible, as did the scrutiny being given to the legislative process (even if other factors also had an impact upon its progress). As noted by Smoke, Gomez, and Peterson: "Decentralization could be beneficial under appropriate political and institutional circumstances and if properly designed and applied."[43]

The success of decentralization also depended on whether it was linked to a genuine process of increased or enhanced democratization, in which citizens found a new and substantive outlet for their political voice. If this was not the case, as Rizal Sukma noted, "There has been a general consensus that regional autonomy would not work if it [were] not carried out within the context of democratisation."[44] The experiment of decentralization in Timor-Leste had gotten underway slowly; it was hoped that it would be a positive process, but it faced a number of challenges. As such, the outcome of this political experiment would not be known for some time to come.

---

[42] A. Smith, *The Ethnic Origins of Nations* (Oxford: Blackwell Publishers, 1986), pp. 13–18; and E. Gellner, *Nations and Nationalism* (Ithaca, NY: Cornell University Press, 1983), p. 44.

[43] Smoke et al., "Understanding Decentralization," p. 4.

[44] Sukma, "Conflict Management in Post-Authoritarian Indonesia," p. 72.

CONTRIBUTORS

Tim Anderson is a Senior Lecturer in Political Economy at the University of Sydney. He has published in a wide range of academic journals on trade, agriculture, and food security, health systems, and rights in development. His next book will be "Land and Livelihoods in Papua New Guinea."

Deborah Cummins is a consultant and a researcher on local governance issues in Timor-Leste. Her main research interests center on *suku*-level governance, including customary governance and *lisan*, democratization, community development, women's leadership, and domestic violence. She is an associate with the Peace and Conflict Studies Institute of Australia (PaCSIA) and a visiting lecturer at the Department of Community Development at the National University of Timor-Leste (UNTL).

Rui Graça Feijó graduated in History (Coimbra, 1978) and obtained his D. Phil from Oxford University (1984). He has closely followed the politics of Timor-Leste since 2004, was UN-sponsored advisor to the President of the Republic (2005–06), and an electoral observer in 2007 and 2012. He has written several articles on East Timorese politics and identity issues, and published *Timor-Leste: Paisagem Tropical com Gente Dentro* (Lisbon, 2006). Currently he is an Associate Researcher at the Centro de Estudos Sociais, University of Coimbra, and is developing a research project on the consolidation of democracy.

David Hicks is a Life Member of Clare College, University of Cambridge, and Professor of Anthropology at Stony Brook University. He has doctorates from the University of Oxford and the University of London. His publications include *Tetum Ghosts and Kin*; *Structural Analysis in Anthropology*; *A Maternal Religion*; *Kinship and Religion in Eastern Indonesia*; and articles in the *American Anthropologist, Journal of the Royal Anthropological Institute, Bijdragen tot de Taal-, Land- en Volkenkunde, Oceania*, and numerous anthologies.

Professor Damien Kingsbury is Director of the Centre for Citizenship, Development, and Human Rights at Deakin University. He was coordinator of Australian NGO observer missions to Timor-Leste's ballot for independence, and its 2007 and 2012 elections, and is a regular visitor to Timor-Leste. He is author of *East Timor: The Price of Liberty* (2009), and editor or co-editor of two other books on Timor-Leste's politics.

Michael Leach is an Associate Professor in Politics and Public Policy at Swinburne University of Technology. He has written extensively on East Timorese politics and history, and worked as an adviser to Timor-Leste's Ministry of Education and Secretariat of State for Youth and Sports. He is a founder of the Timor-Leste Studies Association, http://tlstudies.org/.

Andrew Marriott is a lawyer with a background in community advocacy and legislative development. He has worked extensively on justice sector projects in Cambodia, Timor-Leste and Sierra Leone. He is currently a peacebuilding adviser to AusAID in West Africa, and is completing a doctorate on the post-conflict role of legal professionals in Timor-Leste.

Sara Niner is a research fellow and teaching associate with the School of Social and Political Inquiry at Monash University. She spent many years working with East Timorese refugees in Australia, followed by many years consulting and researching in Timor-Leste, and is widely published in this field. Her works include *Xanana: Leader of the Struggle for Independent Timor-Leste* (2009). Her current research focus is gender in the post-conflict environment of Timor-Leste. She teaches in the fields of gender and development and anthropology.

James Scambary has been working in Timor-Leste since 2003 as an academic and research consultant. He has written a number of reports and publications on issues concerning youth groups, gangs, communal conflict, and peacebuilding for a range of agencies including AusAID, the World Bank, and the New York Social Science Research Council.

Pedro Seabra is a researcher at the Portuguese Institute of International Relations and Security (IPRIS). He holds a master's degree in political science and international relations from the New University of Lisbon and is currently working on a PhD in comparative politics at the Institute of Social Sciences in Lisbon. His research interests and publications have focused on Lusophone countries and Portuguese foreign policy.

Dennis Shoesmith researches in the comparative politics of state formation in Timor-Leste. Before retiring in 2011, he was an Associate Professor of Political Science at Charles Darwin University, where he remains an adjunct researcher. He has worked as a consultant for the United Nations in Timor-Leste and Cambodia, and for USAID and the Australian Political Parties for Democracy program.

Adérito Soares has worked for human rights NGOs in Indonesia and Timor-Leste. He was a member of the Constituent Assembly, which drafted Timor-Leste's constitution. He has taught at the National University of Timor-Leste and at the Australian National University (ANU). He has published in the *International Journal on Minority and Group Rights* and contributed chapters to several books. He was elected by the National Parliament as the first Commissioner of Timor-Leste's Anti-Corruption Commission in 2010. He holds an LLM (Master of Laws) from New York University (NYU) Law School and an LLB (Bachelor of Laws) from Indonesia.

Bu Wilson has worked on governance, law, justice, and security issues in indigenous Australia and Asia since 1990. She completed a PhD on the development of the East Timorese Police Force at the Australian National

University. Bu has published on police and security sector reform in Timor-Leste, regulation and policy implications of Indonesian fishing in Australia's territorial waters, and indigenous sea rights in Australia. She works as an independent consultant and is a Research Associate at the Australian Research Council's (ARC) Centre of Excellence in Policing and Security.

SOUTHEAST ASIA PROGRAM PUBLICATIONS
Cornell University

Studies on Southeast Asia

Number 59 *The Politics of Timor-Leste: Democratic Consolidation after Intervention*, ed. Michael Leach and Damien Kingsbury. 2013. ISBN 978-0-87727-759-0 (pb.)

Number 58 *The Spirit of Things: Materiality and Religious Diversity in Southeast Asia*, ed. Julius Bautista. 2012. ISBN 970-0-87727-758-3 (pb.)

Number 57 *Demographic Change in Southeast Asia: Recent Histories and Future Directions*, ed. Lindy Williams and Michael Philip Guest. 2012. ISBN 978-0-87727-757-6 (pb.)

Number 56 *Modern and Contemporary Southeast Asian Art: An Anthology*, ed. Nora A. Taylor and Boreth Ly. 2012. ISBN 978-0-87727-756-9 (pb.)

Number 55 *Glimpses of Freedom: Independent Cinema in Southeast Asia*, ed. May Adadol Ingawanij and Benjamin McKay. 2012. ISBN 978-0-87727-755-2 (pb.)

Number 54 *Student Activism in Malaysia: Crucible, Mirror, Sideshow*, Meredith L. Weiss. 2011. ISBN 978-0-87727-754-5 (pb.)

Number 53 *Political Authority and Provincial Identity in Thailand: The Making of Banharn-buri*, Yoshinori Nishizaki. 2011. ISBN 978-0-87727-753-8 (pb.)

Number 52 *Vietnam and the West: New Approaches*, ed. Wynn Wilcox. 2010. ISBN 978-0-87727-752-1 (pb.)

Number 51 *Cultures at War: The Cold War and Cultural Expression in Southeast Asia*, ed. Tony Day and Maya H. T. Liem. 2010. ISBN 978-0-87727-751-4 (pb.)

Number 50 *State of Authority: The State in Society in Indonesia*, ed. Gerry van Klinken and Joshua Barker. 2009. ISBN 978-0-87727-750-7 (pb.)

Number 49 *Phan Châu Trinh and His Political Writings*, Phan Châu Trinh, ed. and trans. Vinh Sinh. 2009. ISBN 978-0-87727-749-1 (pb.)

Number 48 *Dependent Communities: Aid and Politics in Cambodia and East Timor*, Caroline Hughes. 2009. ISBN 978-0-87727-748-4 (pb.)

Number 47 *A Man Like Him: Portrait of the Burmese Journalist, Journal Kyaw U Chit Maung*, Journal Kyaw Ma Ma Lay, trans. Ma Thanegi, 2008. ISBN 978-0-87727-747-7 (pb.)

Number 46 *At the Edge of the Forest: Essays on Cambodia, History, and Narrative in Honor of David Chandler*, ed. Anne Ruth Hansen and Judy Ledgerwood. 2008. ISBN 978-0-87727-746-0 (pb).

Number 45 *Conflict, Violence, and Displacement in Indonesia*, ed. Eva-Lotta E. Hedman. 2008. ISBN 978-0-87727-745-3 (pb).

Number 44 *Friends and Exiles: A Memoir of the Nutmeg Isles and the Indonesian Nationalist Movement*, Des Alwi, ed. Barbara S. Harvey. 2008. ISBN 978-0-877277-44-6 (pb).

Number 43 *Early Southeast Asia: Selected Essays*, O. W. Wolters, ed. Craig J. Reynolds. 2008. 255 pp. ISBN 978-0-877277-43-9 (pb).

Number 42 *Thailand: The Politics of Despotic Paternalism* (revised edition), Thak Chaloemtiarana. 2007. 284 pp. ISBN 0-8772-7742-7 (pb).

Number 41   *Views of Seventeenth-Century Vietnam: Christoforo Borri on Cochinchina and Samuel Baron on Tonkin*, ed. Olga Dror and K. W. Taylor. 2006. 290 pp. ISBN 0-8772-7741-9 (pb).

Number 40   *Laskar Jihad: Islam, Militancy, and the Quest for Identity in Post-New Order Indonesia*, Noorhaidi Hasan. 2006. 266 pp. ISBN 0-877277-40-0 (pb).

Number 39   *The Indonesian Supreme Court: A Study of Institutional Collapse*, Sebastiaan Pompe. 2005. 494 pp. ISBN 0-877277-38-9 (pb).

Number 38   *Spirited Politics: Religion and Public Life in Contemporary Southeast Asia*, ed. Andrew C. Willford and Kenneth M. George. 2005. 210 pp. ISBN 0-87727-737-0.

Number 37   *Sumatran Sultanate and Colonial State: Jambi and the Rise of Dutch Imperialism, 1830-1907*, Elsbeth Locher-Scholten, trans. Beverley Jackson. 2004. 332 pp. ISBN 0-87727-736-2.

Number 36   *Southeast Asia over Three Generations: Essays Presented to Benedict R. O'G. Anderson*, ed. James T. Siegel and Audrey R. Kahin. 2003. 398 pp. ISBN 0-87727-735-4.

Number 35   *Nationalism and Revolution in Indonesia*, George McTurnan Kahin, intro. Benedict R. O'G. Anderson (reprinted from 1952 edition, Cornell University Press, with permission). 2003. 530 pp. ISBN 0-87727-734-6.

Number 34   *Golddiggers, Farmers, and Traders in the "Chinese Districts" of West Kalimantan, Indonesia*, Mary Somers Heidhues. 2003. 316 pp. ISBN 0-87727-733-8.

Number 33   *Opusculum de Sectis apud Sinenses et Tunkinenses (A Small Treatise on the Sects among the Chinese and Tonkinese): A Study of Religion in China and North Vietnam in the Eighteenth Century*, Father Adriano de St. Thecla, trans. Olga Dror, with Mariya Berezovska. 2002. 363 pp. ISBN 0-87727-732-X.

Number 32   *Fear and Sanctuary: Burmese Refugees in Thailand*, Hazel J. Lang. 2002. 204 pp. ISBN 0-87727-731-1.

Number 31   *Modern Dreams: An Inquiry into Power, Cultural Production, and the Cityscape in Contemporary Urban Penang, Malaysia*, Beng-Lan Goh. 2002. 225 pp. ISBN 0-87727-730-3.

Number 30   *Violence and the State in Suharto's Indonesia*, ed. Benedict R. O'G. Anderson. 2001. Second printing, 2002. 247 pp. ISBN 0-87727-729-X.

Number 29   *Studies in Southeast Asian Art: Essays in Honor of Stanley J. O'Connor*, ed. Nora A. Taylor. 2000. 243 pp. Illustrations. ISBN 0-87727-728-1.

Number 28   *The Hadrami Awakening: Community and Identity in the Netherlands East Indies, 1900-1942*, Natalie Mobini-Kesheh. 1999. 174 pp. ISBN 0-87727-727-3.

Number 27   *Tales from Djakarta: Caricatures of Circumstances and their Human Beings*, Pramoedya Ananta Toer. 1999. 145 pp. ISBN 0-87727-726-5.

Number 26   *History, Culture, and Region in Southeast Asian Perspectives*, rev. ed., O. W. Wolters. 1999. Second printing, 2004. 275 pp. ISBN 0-87727-725-7.

Number 25   *Figures of Criminality in Indonesia, the Philippines, and Colonial Vietnam*, ed. Vicente L. Rafael. 1999. 259 pp. ISBN 0-87727-724-9.

Number 3   *Thai Radical Discourse: The Real Face of Thai Feudalism Today,* Craig J.
            Reynolds. 1987. 2nd printing 1994. 186 pp. ISBN 0-87727-702-8.

Number 1   *The Symbolism of the Stupa,* Adrian Snodgrass. 1985. Revised with
            index, 1988. 3rd printing 1998. 469 pp. ISBN 0-87727-700-1.

SEAP Series

Number 23   *Possessed by the Spirits: Mediumship in Contemporary Vietnamese
            Communities.* 2006. 186 pp. ISBN 0-877271-41-0 (pb).

Number 22   *The Industry of Marrying Europeans,* Vũ Trọng Phụng, trans. Thúy
            Tranviet. 2006. 66 pp. ISBN 0-877271-40-2 (pb).

Number 21   *Securing a Place: Small-Scale Artisans in Modern Indonesia,* Elizabeth
            Morrell. 2005. 220 pp. ISBN 0-877271-39-9.

Number 20   *Southern Vietnam under the Reign of Minh Mạng (1820-1841): Central
            Policies and Local Response,* Choi Byung Wook. 2004. 226pp. ISBN 0-0-
            877271-40-2.

Number 19   *Gender, Household, State: Đổi Mới in Việt Nam,* ed. Jayne Werner and
            Danièle Bélanger. 2002. 151 pp. ISBN 0-87727-137-2.

Number 18   *Culture and Power in Traditional Siamese Government,* Neil A. Englehart.
            2001. 130 pp. ISBN 0-87727-135-6.

Number 17   *Gangsters, Democracy, and the State,* ed. Carl A. Trocki. 1998. Second
            printing, 2002. 94 pp. ISBN 0-87727-134-8.

Number 16   *Cutting across the Lands: An Annotated Bibliography on Natural Resource
            Management and Community Development in Indonesia, the Philippines,
            and Malaysia,* ed. Eveline Ferretti. 1997. 329 pp. ISBN 0-87727-133-X.

Number 15   *The Revolution Falters: The Left in Philippine Politics after 1986,* ed.
            Patricio N. Abinales. 1996. Second printing, 2002. 182 pp. ISBN 0-
            87727-132-1.

Number 14   *Being Kammu: My Village, My Life,* Damrong Tayanin. 1994. 138 pp., 22
            tables, illus., maps. ISBN 0-87727-130-5.

Number 13   *The American War in Vietnam,* ed. Jayne Werner, David Hunt. 1993.
            132 pp. ISBN 0-87727-131-3.

Number 12   *The Voice of Young Burma,* Aye Kyaw. 1993. 92 pp. ISBN 0-87727-129-1.

Number 11   *The Political Legacy of Aung San,* ed. Josef Silverstein. Revised edition
            1993. 169 pp. ISBN 0-87727-128-3.

Number 10   *Studies on Vietnamese Language and Literature: A Preliminary
            Bibliography,* Nguyen Dinh Tham. 1992. 227 pp. ISBN 0-87727-127-5.

Number 8   *From PKI to the Comintern, 1924–1941: The Apprenticeship of the Malayan
            Communist Party,* Cheah Boon Kheng. 1992. 147 pp. ISBN 0-87727-125-9.

Number 7   *Intellectual Property and US Relations with Indonesia, Malaysia, Singapore,
            and Thailand,* Elisabeth Uphoff. 1991. 67 pp. ISBN 0-87727-124-0.

Number 6   *The Rise and Fall of the Communist Party of Burma (CPB),* Bertil Lintner.
            1990. 124 pp. 26 illus., 14 maps. ISBN 0-87727-123-2.

Number 5   *Japanese Relations with Vietnam: 1951–1987,* Masaya Shiraishi. 1990.
            174 pp. ISBN 0-87727-122-4.

Number 3   *Postwar Vietnam: Dilemmas in Socialist Development*, ed. Christine White, David Marr. 1988. 2nd printing 1993. 260 pp. ISBN 0-87727-120-8.

Number 2   *The Dobama Movement in Burma (1930–1938)*, Khin Yi. 1988. 160 pp. ISBN 0-87727-118-6.

Cornell Modern Indonesia Project Publications

All CMIP titles available at http://cmip.library.cornell.edu

Number 75   *A Tour of Duty: Changing Patterns of Military Politics in Indonesia in the 1990s.* Douglas Kammen and Siddharth Chandra. 1999. 99 pp. ISBN 0-87763-049-6.

Number 74   *The Roots of Acehnese Rebellion 1989–1992*, Tim Kell. 1995. 103 pp. ISBN 0-87763-040-2.

Number 72   *Popular Indonesian Literature of the Qur'an*, Howard M. Federspiel. 1994. 170 pp. ISBN 0-87763-038-0.

Number 71   *A Javanese Memoir of Sumatra, 1945–1946: Love and Hatred in the Liberation War*, Takao Fusayama. 1993. 150 pp. ISBN 0-87763-037-2.

Number 69   *The Road to Madiun: The Indonesian Communist Uprising of 1948*, Elizabeth Ann Swift. 1989. 120 pp. ISBN 0-87763-035-6.

Number 68   *Intellectuals and Nationalism in Indonesia: A Study of the Following Recruited by Sutan Sjahrir in Occupation Jakarta*, J. D. Legge. 1988. 159 pp. ISBN 0-87763-034-8.

Number 67   *Indonesia Free: A Biography of Mohammad Hatta*, Mavis Rose. 1987. 252 pp. ISBN 0-87763-033-X.

Number 66   *Prisoners at Kota Cane*, Leon Salim, trans. Audrey Kahin. 1986. 112 pp. ISBN 0-87763-032-1.

Number 64   *Suharto and His Generals: Indonesia's Military Politics, 1975–1983*, David Jenkins. 1984. 4th printing 1997. 300 pp. ISBN 0-87763-030-5.

Number 62   *Interpreting Indonesian Politics: Thirteen Contributions to the Debate, 1964–1981*, ed. Benedict Anderson, Audrey Kahin, intro. Daniel S. Lev. 1982. 3rd printing 1991. 172 pp. ISBN 0-87763-028-3.

Number 60   *The Minangkabau Response to Dutch Colonial Rule in the Nineteenth Century*, Elizabeth E. Graves. 1981. 157 pp. ISBN 0-87763-000-3.

Number 57   *Permesta: Half a Rebellion*, Barbara S. Harvey. 1977. 174 pp. ISBN 0-87763-003-8.

Number 52   *A Preliminary Analysis of the October 1 1965, Coup in Indonesia (Prepared in January 1966)*, Benedict R. Anderson, Ruth T. McVey, assist. Frederick P. Bunnell. 1971. 3rd printing 1990. 174 pp. ISBN 0-87763-008-9.

Number 48   *Nationalism, Islam and Marxism*, Soekarno, intro. Ruth T. McVey. 1970.

Number 37   *Mythology and the Tolerance of the Javanese*, Benedict R. O'G. Anderson. 2nd edition, 1996. Reprinted 2004. 104 pp., 65 illus. ISBN 0-87763-041-0.

Copublished Titles

The Ambiguous Allure of the West: Traces of the Colonial in Thailand, ed. Rachel V. Harrison and Peter A. Jackson. Copublished with Hong Kong University Press. 2010. ISBN 978-0-87727-608-1 (pb.)

The Many Ways of Being Muslim: Fiction by Muslim Filipinos, ed. Coeli Barry. Copublished with Anvil Publishing, Inc., the Philippines. 2008. ISBN 978-0-87727-605-0 (pb.)

Language Texts

INDONESIAN

Beginning Indonesian through Self-Instruction, John U. Wolff, Dédé Oetomo, Daniel Fietkiewicz. 3rd revised edition 1992. Vol. 1. 115 pp. ISBN 0-87727-529-7. Vol. 2. 434 pp. ISBN 0-87727-530-0. Vol. 3. 473 pp. ISBN 0-87727-531-9.

Indonesian Readings, John U. Wolff. 1978. 4th printing 1992. 480 pp. ISBN 0-87727-517-3

Indonesian Conversations, John U. Wolff. 1978. 3rd printing 1991. 297 pp. ISBN 0-87727-516-5

Formal Indonesian, John U. Wolff. 2nd revised edition 1986. 446 pp. ISBN 0-87727-515-7

TAGALOG

Pilipino through Self-Instruction, John U. Wolff, Maria Theresa C. Centeno, Der-Hwa V. Rau. 1991. Vol. 1. 342 pp. ISBN 0-87727—525-4. Vol. 2., revised 2005, 378 pp. ISBN 0-87727-526-2. Vol 3., revised 2005, 431 pp. ISBN 0-87727-527-0. Vol. 4. 306 pp. ISBN 0-87727-528-9.

THAI

A. U. A. Language Center Thai Course, J. Marvin Brown. Originally published by the American University Alumni Association Language Center, 1974. Reissued by Cornell Southeast Asia Program, 1991, 1992. Book 1. 267 pp. ISBN 0-87727-506-8. Book 2. 288 pp. ISBN 0-87727-507-6. Book 3. 247 pp. ISBN 0-87727-508-4.

A. U. A. Language Center Thai Course, Reading and Writing Text (mostly reading), 1979. Reissued 1997. 164 pp. ISBN 0-87727-511-4.

A. U. A. Language Center Thai Course, Reading and Writing Workbook (mostly writing), 1979. Reissued 1997. 99 pp. ISBN 0-87727-512-2.

KHMER

Cambodian System of Writing and Beginning Reader, Franklin E. Huffman. Originally published by Yale University Press, 1970. Reissued by Cornell Southeast Asia Program, 4th printing 2002. 365 pp. ISBN 0-300-01314-0.

Modern Spoken Cambodian, Franklin E. Huffman, assist. Charan Promchan, Chhom-Rak Thong Lambert. Originally published by Yale University Press, 1970. Reissued by Cornell Southeast Asia Program, 3rd printing 1991. 451 pp. ISBN 0-300-01316-7.

Intermediate Cambodian Reader, ed. Franklin E. Huffman, assist. Im Proum. Originally published by Yale University Press, 1972. Reissued by Cornell Southeast Asia Program, 1988. 499 pp. ISBN 0-300-01552-6.

Cambodian Literary Reader and Glossary, Franklin E. Huffman, Im Proum. Originally published by Yale University Press, 1977. Reissued by Cornell Southeast Asia Program, 1988. 494 pp. ISBN 0-300-02069-4.

HMONG

White Hmong-English Dictionary, Ernest E. Heimbach. 1969. 8th printing, 2002. 523 pp. ISBN 0-87727-075-9.

VIETNAMESE

Intermediate Spoken Vietnamese, Franklin E. Huffman, Tran Trong Hai. 1980. 3rd printing 1994. ISBN 0-87727-500-9.

Proto-Austronesian Phonology with Glossary, John U. Wolff, 2 volumes, 2011. ISBN vol. I, 978-0-87727-532-9. ISBN vol. II, 978-0-87727-533-6.

To order, please contact:
Mail:
Cornell University Press Services
750 Cascadilla Street
PO Box 6525
Ithaca, NY 14851 USA

E-mail: orderbook@cupserv.org

Phone/Fax, Monday–Friday, 8 am – 5 pm (Eastern US):
Phone: 607 277 2211 or 800 666 2211 (US, Canada)
Fax: 607 277 6292 or 800 688 2877 (US, Canada)

Order through our online bookstore at:
www.einaudi.cornell.edu / southeastasia / publications /